Satan's Playground

American Encounters / Global Interactions
A series edited by Gilbert M. Joseph and Emily S. Rosenberg

This series aims to stimulate critical perspectives and fresh interpretive frameworks for scholarship on the history of the imposing global presence of the United States. Its primary concerns include the deployment and contestation of power, the construction and deconstruction of cultural and political borders, the fluid meanings of intercultural encounters, and the complex interplay between the global and the local. American Encounters seeks to strengthen dialogue and collaboration between historians of U.S. international relations and area studies specialists.

The series encourages scholarship based on multiarchival historical research. At the same time, it supports a recognition of the representational character of all stories about the past and promotes critical inquiry into issues of subjectivity and narrative. In the process, American Encounters strives to understand the context in which meanings related to nations, cultures, and political economy are continually produced, challenged, and reshaped.

Satan's Playground

Mobsters and Movie Stars

at America's Greatest

Gaming Resort

PAUL J. VANDERWOOD

DUKE UNIVERSITY PRESS DURHAM AND LONDON 2010

© 2010
Duke University Press
All rights reserved
Printed in the United States
of America on acid-free paper ∞
Designed by Katy Clove
Typeset in Warnock Pro by Keystone Typesetting, Inc.
Library of Congress Cataloging-in-Publication
Data appear on the last printed
page of this book.

For GLS

Contents

Acknowledgments

This astounding story has never before been told. There are no biographies, memoirs, or diaries of the Border Barons. The mobsters appeared in newspaper headlines when they committed mayhem, but then they and their notoriety disappeared with yesterday's news. San Diego County Sheriff's Office records for the period have been destroyed. Agua Caliente is well-remembered as a ritzy, world-famous gambling resort, but not in print. Its records too are gone, probably crumbled to dust. So the tale of this remarkable gaming palace and the ambiance and circumstances which brought it into being has had to be stitched together from newspaper and magazine articles of those times, official and personal archives and collections in both Mexico and the United States, and memories of those who either experienced the period or later learned of it through others. Traditional historical sources yielded their bounties and are credited in endnotes and bibliography, but what brought this enterprise to fruition was the enormous enthusiasm with which so many people combed their memories, personal belongings, file cabinets, and attics for tidbits related to the whole. They made the venture possible and, better yet, thoroughly enjoyable.

Andre Williams is a California real estate broker who retired in Tijuana because he relishes the Mexican way of life. Attracted to local history, he collects memorabilia from Agua Caliente and proudly opened his valuable scrapbooks and cache of artifacts to me. He still telephones to tell of new finds. Beyond that, he introduced me to any number of Tijuanenses who had knowledge of the spa. His generosity is unbounded.

When researching in the labyrinth of Tijuana, both the town itself and its academic maze, gringos need a guide. For decades now, mine has been a friend and colleague, Raúl Rodríguez González, who teaches and directs the library at CETYS, Tijuana. For this project, he introduced me to sources, arranged appointments, recommended possibilities for information, and warned me away from blind alleys. I could not have navigated Tijuana without him.

Other Tijuanenses, of course, also went out of their way to assist me, among them Armando Estrada Lázaro, then Coordinador de Cultura Popular, Instituto Municipal de Arte y Cultura (IMAC), Tijuana; José Gabriel Rivera Delgado, Coordinador del Archivo Histórico, IMAC, Tijuana, and a freelance journalist; and Patricio Bayardo Gómez, Coordinador de la Revista Arquetipos, CETYS. Luis Tamés León, a chemist and avid local historian, allowed me to review important documents from his personal Agua Caliente collection.

Relatives of the Border Barons kindly fleshed out the personalities and multifarious activities of these assertive and often belligerent entrepreneurs: Georgia B. Allen of Sacramento for her father, Wirt Bowman; and Alvin Bronson "Bunker" Daniels of Hot Creek, California, and Barbara Gunning of Oceanside, California, for their uncle, James Crofton. Stories about the barons are assuredly legion. Axel Holm, president of the Nogales, Arizona, Historical Society, shared his scrapbooks on Bowman, while Joanne Ward, an artist, and Lorna Elliott, librarian, both of The Dalles, Oregon, systematically dug through myriad newspapers and public documents to piece together Crofton's early family history in and around their city. They also verified the employment of many young local townsmen at Agua Caliente.

A remarkable amateur historian in Bakersfield, California, Gilbert Gia, a retired school teacher who publishes professional history pieces in a local journal, rounded out Crofton's ranching years in central California, along with the early ventures of Carlie Withington, whorehouse king of that booming oil town before he headed for Mexico. Gilbert also dug Crofton's will out of the Kern County Hall of Records and put me in touch with ranchers around Tehachapi who had worked for Crofton. It is my pleasure to count Gilbert as a friend and fellow history sleuth.

Don McAllister, son of Wayne and Corine McAllister, the designers of Agua Caliente, graciously shared his parents' memorabilia and clipping file concerning the resort, plus a gem—an invaluable interview about the planning and construction of the spa that he videotaped with his father shortly before the famous architect's death. He also shared numerous colorful anecdotes that his parents relished about the elegant enterprise. Don's openness and hospitality are appreciated.

Archivists at many libraries and institutes extended themselves in my behalf: Bob Kingston, formerly of the Oregon Historical Society; Robert Ellis, U.S. Regional Archive in New York City; Dena McDuffie, Arizona Historical Society; Dylan McDonald, Sacramento Archives and Museum Collection Center; Morgan Yates of the Automobile Club of Southern California; Ellen Duval Hester, Folsom, California, Museum; Genevieve Troka, California State Archives; Marilyn Wurzburger, Arizona State University Library, special collections; Dace Taube, University of Southern California Doheny Memorial Library; Caroline Sisneros, American Film Institute in Los Angeles; Alva Moore Stevenson, University of California, Los Angeles, Center for Oral History Research; Susan Painter and Richard "Rick" Crawford, San Diego Public Library; David G. Schwartz, University of Nevada, Las Vegas, library special collections; and the staffs at the U.S. National Archives, Franklin Delano Roosevelt Library and Museum in Hyde Park, New York; as well as those at the Archivo General de la Nación, and Fideicomiso Archivos Plutarco Calles y Fernando Torreblanca, both in Mexico City. David Marshall, president of Heritage Architecture and Planning, San Diego, was especially helpful with architectural and design details.

A talented artist and friend, Sharon Crockett, skillfully prepared the creative maps and graphics for this book. Her husband, Glen Sparrow, assisted with details. Books need good maps to clarify complicated storylines, and my gratitude goes to Sharon and Glen for their graceful contributions.

Rosalie Schwartz and Eric Van Young have for years been my "mandatory friendly readers." Both are renowned, well-published historians, Rosalie as a freelancer and Eric as a distinguished member and former chair of the history department, as well as acting dean of Arts and Humanities at the University of California, San Diego. They bring different strengths to their readings. Rosalie stresses organization and identifies expendable sections. Eric is a wordsmith par excellence and roots out mixed metaphors, unclear passages, and erroneous word use. They each spent an enormous amount of time weeding through and shaping this manuscript, and the book is much better organized and more concise because of their criticisms. Every author needs good readers to massage his or her work into shape and to get rid of its embarrassments. Without question, I have the best.

Matthew Bokovoy, an acquisitions editor at the University of Nebraska Press, read the manuscript and rendered invaluable suggestions from a publisher's viewpoint. Duke University Press, with a special salute to its enthusiastic senior acquisition editor, Valerie Mullholland, is a genuine pleasure to work with. Ellen F. Smith is a meticulous freelance editor who is among the best at combing through a text for inconsistencies and errors that inevitably slip into any final draft. Her "final cleansing" is to be appreciated.

My right-hand man throughout this project was my good friend, Glenn Syktich. Glenn accompanied me on many of the research journeys necessitated by this book. Just as he has contributed to my other writing projects, he cared for logistics, assisted in research, kept me focused, and steered me away from falling into bottomless procrastination. He is not often a subtle critic and can raise one's hackles, but his observations mostly hit the mark. Glenn scrupulously retraced the route taken by the mobsters who held up the treasure-car on the Dike and drew a detailed map of their flight. He found individuals in Nogales who knew Wirt Bowman, and others in The Dalles who had familiarity with the Crofton clan. He knew the surroundings at Agua Caliente, because his father had taken him there to horse races as a kid. In short, Glenn Syktich, plain and simple, is an assistant to be valued.

So are you all, and I thank you.

Satan's Playground

The Mob Strikes the Border Barons

These Sons of Satan—vice lords or princes of pleasure, depending on one's inclinations—were on the run and headed for the border. California's ardent redeemers dogged their heels, playing out their role in a zealous reform movement sweeping early-twentieth-century America. The do-gooders hounded their prey across the international line into Mexico but hardly into perdition. Instead, these clever and experienced sportsmen, who became known as the Border Barons, soon turned tiny, dusty Tijuana from a mere tourist curiosity into their kind of town.

The Barons—Wirt Bowman, James Crofton, and Baron (his given name) Long—all of them risk-taking, well-heeled, charming sons-of-bitches, worked the vulnerable underbelly of the law to get rich. They did not manage all gaming and adult entertainment in Tijuana, but monopolized the most profitable ventures, including their crown jewel, a sprawling, luxurious gaming resort named Agua Caliente three miles south of the city center. For glamour and panache, Tijuana's Agua Caliente outdid even the celebrated Monte Carlo and France's aristocratic Deauville. Boosters dubbed it the "Playground of the Hemisphere," and it overflowed with celebrated habitués.

Diplomats, royalty, egoistic movie moguls and preening film stars, sports celebrities, moneyed bluebloods, and nouveau riche capitalists patronized the elegant spa, along with more ordinary folks out to mingle with the famous and daydream (quite hopelessly) of transcending their class. Mobsters like Al Capone also visited, as did Benjamin "Bugsy" Siegel, who borrowed his idea for a resort-style casino in Las Vegas from the Tijuana marvel.

Lesser gangsters attracted by the quick fortunes and flamboyant excesses of Prohibition also eyed the resort, but more for its riches than its cachet.

Some hoodlums reckoned, if the Barons could plunder patrons in their casino, they could, tit for tat, loot the vice lords. Other criminals reasoned it unfair that flush people had so much and they so little, and aimed to adjust the flow. Most crooks, however, were moved by pure greed, a sign of the times for many people, nearly everywhere.

One ambitious knot of Southern California bootleggers figured it would be a cinch to rob Agua Caliente's loaded money-car as it carried the weekend's receipts from Tijuana to a bank in San Diego. Typically for the Roaring Twenties, the caper was carefully arranged. The driver and guard of the transport were alleged to be part of the scheme, and local police had been paid off. Bribes assured political protection. Even several executives, including owners, of the famed gambling casino itself were later said to have been in on the robbery, which was alleged to be only the first facet of a much more grandiose and bizarre scheme to blow up the famed resort, collect insurance money on it, and set up shop elsewhere.

The two young hoodlums chosen to pull off the initial escapade knew when the money-car would leave the casino that Monday morning, May 20, 1929, carrying the weekend's receipts, anticipated at nearly $100,000 (over $1 million in today's money). They would briefly follow the vehicle in their own specially altered automobile and, at an appointed spot, would shoot out the rear tires of the money-car, bringing it to a halt, then pull alongside, shout "Stick 'em up!" and spray around a few shots from their automatic weapons to make the holdup look real. Then they'd toss some hot chili pepper in the eyes of the driver and guard to blind and confuse them temporarily, adding further authenticity to the venture, steal the money pouch, and head for their hide-out.[1] It would be a bold daylight escapade to be sure, but not out of keeping for the Jazz Age, which found Americans reveling in and reeling from a frothy exuberance of technological and cultural novelty marked by lawlessness.

The Barons were well aware that the mob had its eye on their money-car. Three weeks earlier they had received a tip that it would be robbed en route to San Diego, which sits eighteen miles north of the border. As precautions, they informed police of the threat, regularly switched vehicles and routes, and put on extra guards. When no assault occurred, however, they dropped the additional security, although they still regularly changed cars and altered directions to the bank.[2]

Thus the Barons anticipated no difficulties with this Monday's shipment. In his office, the resort's head cashier, Olallo Rubio, carefully counted out the proceeds to be transferred: a relatively modest $600 in cash, mostly in large bills ($50s and $100s) and $70,000 in personal, traveler's, and cashier's checks—certainly not the $100,000 in currency that the robbers expected.[3] The courier for Agua Caliente, José Pérez Borrego, a former Tijuana police chief now working for the casino company, put the cash and checks into a leather pouch, and drove to Bowman's nearby Foreign Club, a glamorous gambling cabaret on the town's main tourist street, where he collected an additional $10,000 in cash and checks. He then wedged the money bag behind the driver's seat in the tan 1929 Cadillac coupe and headed for the Bank of Italy (later the Bank of America) in San Diego. Beside him sat the guard, Nemisio Rudolfo Monroy; both carried .45 caliber automatic pistols. It looked like a routine delivery all the way around.

THE ATTACK

As they headed north, at the agricultural hamlet of Nestor a brand-new, black Model-A Ford touring car with its front windshield removed began to tail them. It was nearing noon on a sunny day along the busy main road between San Diego and the towns stretching south to the border. Traffic was steady but had slowed to pass through a four-lane bottleneck popularly known as The Old Dike (also spelled Dyke), a two-mile causeway that passed through wetlands before connecting to higher ground in San Diego proper.

Suddenly, rat-a-tat-tat, rat-a-tat-tat!

Automatic gunfire from the Ford punctured the rear tires of the Cadillac and brought it to a halt. The Ford swerved left and stopped beside the immobilized Cadillac. A man brandishing a weapon in each hand leaped from the Ford (he may have been riding the right running board) and shouted, "Stick 'em up!"

But the plan quickly went awry. Instead of surrendering, as expected, the guard, Monroy, fired a flurry of shots at the approaching gangster through the closed side window of the money-car, but he missed the assailant. Shattered glass sprayed the road. In return, the surprised bandit raked the Cadillac with automatic gunfire. Pérez Borrego slumped over toward his guard, mortally wounded or already dead.

By this time—only seconds had passed—the gunman's accomplice, the

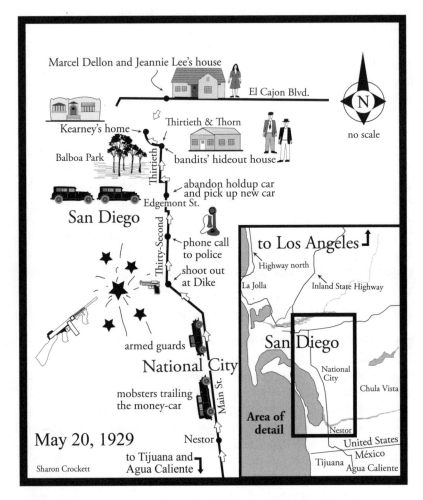

May 20, 1929: the robbery on the Dike. Sharon Crockett

driver, had raced to the right side of the money-car. When met there by more gunfire from the gravely wounded Monroy, he poured his own torrent of bullets into the occupants. During the melee, a slug burrowed into his left shoulder, but with the custodians of the financial deposit finally silenced, he plucked the money pouch from inside the Cadillac, scurried back to the touring car, hurled himself into the back seat, and ordered his buddy to get going. The "fix" had gone haywire.[4]

Many eyewitnesses and near victims—passing drivers and their passengers —saw the mayhem on The Old Dike. Bullets winged through several autos. Some drivers and passengers fled their vehicles and ducked for cover, but others were too stunned to move. All eventually told their stories to authorities. Several spectators surmised that police were shooting it out with bootleggers. Others thought that a hijacking had taken place with one gang of criminals bent on confiscating the illegal goods of another.

In an incredible act of bravado, Sally Stanley, who was driving her Buick sedan with a woman companion just a car or so behind the holdup vehicle, saw the shootout and, as the bandits sped away, decided to give chase. The race was on, but not for long. Northward, up the remaining stretch of The Old Dike they sped into San Diego proper, then right at the first possible turn, Thirty-Second Street, screaming through stop signs at busy intersections, with dust billowing up from the dry dirt road and nearly obscuring the getaway vehicle from its pursuers. A dozen blocks up Thirty-Second Street, approaching an open stretch of road, the women realized they had had enough. Fear overcame rash bravado. They found a telephone in a grocery store, called police, and reported the license plate number of the fleeing car. "I could have overhauled them, but I was afraid," Ms. Stanley subsequently explained.[5] It is a good thing that she did not try to do so. "Two women gave us chase as far as Thirty-Second and K Streets," one of the gangsters later recalled, "and it's a damn good thing they stopped, or we would have stopped them."[6]

Thirty-Second Street dead-ended at a deep canyon. After a short left, the Ford turned right on Edgemont Street and slammed to a halt. Frank D. Hartell, a retired railroad conductor who was mowing his front lawn across the street, wondered at the sudden hubbub in his quiet suburban neighborhood. He saw a young man jump out of the Ford, slip out of his dark blue overalls, and head for a car parked up the street. The second man, lugging one or two medium-sized pouches, closely followed. Then they sped off up Edgemont. Hartell could not identify the make of the getaway car, a light-colored touring vehicle, he thought—but he had gotten a good look at the two occupants who had deserted the Ford. One of them had noticed him staring at them, he said, and smiled.

POLICE RESPONSE

The San Diego Police Department clanked into gear. Sally Stanley, who had first given chase, had telephoned the alarm to headquarters, but it took twenty (unexplained) minutes for the message to reach either the new chief,

Arthur Hill, on the job for only three months, or Captain Paul Hayes, head of detectives. A swirl of uncoordinated activity ensued. All available detectives rushed to the crime scene, which left no one at headquarters to sift through the citizens' reports that began to filter in, and many tips furnished to the police went unanswered. Emergency lights on neighborhood police call boxes blinked on, motorcycle patrols answered, but operators ordered them to report to central headquarters rather than telling them what had occurred, describing the black Ford and its occupants, or ordering units to patrol getaway routes. More than an hour elapsed before headquarters informed the county sheriff's office of the attack and motorcycle police began to search and block off escape roads. Superiors told vice squad officers to hold off interrogation of their underworld contacts (crucial informants), fearing the snitches would only assist the fugitives. Police response was, in other words, slow and uneven.[7]

Because the police ambulance was in the shop for repairs, a slow-moving patrol wagon had to be dispatched to the crime scene. The department's emergency car was in use (detectives were investigating some bad check charges), so private cars and antiquated city vehicles had to be pressed into service. When authorities finally did converge on The Old Dike, they encountered a grisly scene.

The money-car from Agua Caliente had been punctured at least seventeen times; some bullets went in one side and out the other. The driver and the guard lay sprawled on top of one another, Borrego shot nine times, and Monroy, five. Borrego's .45 caliber pistol was out of its holster but had not been fired. Monroy's gun rested on his lap and had been fired five times. Although police questioned at least six eyewitnesses to the shootout, none could give more than a fleeting description of the robbers. Pieced together, however, they composed a tentative portrait. One killer was twenty-five years old, short, about 5'5" tall, and wearing a cap. The other felon was only a little older, maybe thirty, about 5'8" tall, wearing mechanic's overalls and a bandana over the lower part of his face. It was not much to go on.

When motorcycle police investigated Frank Hartell's report of the automobile hurriedly abandoned across the street from his home, they found it was the brand-new car used in the robbery. It had been amateurishly repainted black to camouflage its original color of "Bonnie [slate] grey," and the windshield had been removed. A quick check of the engine number showed that it had been stolen eleven days earlier from the showroom of a local Ford dealer and had been driven only twenty-eight miles, eleven of them before the vehicle had been stolen from the dealership. The license plates were registered to a San Francisco plumber who said they had been stolen from his shop in January that year. Inside the vehicle investigators found a pair of overalls, gloves, a cap that carried a red hair, two pairs of sunglasses, an unexploded .45 caliber bullet that a ballistics expert soon declared fit a machine gun, and a small bag of ground red pepper.

Tire tracks left by a car off to a hurried start had stirred the dirt just up Edgemont Street. Motorcycle cops followed the marks as far as they could, but within a short distance they faded into dusty nothingness.

MACHINE GUN FEVER

Double banner headlines in San Diego newspapers screamed: "Thugs Riddle Car with Machine Gun," "Machine Gunmen Shoot Down Two in Auto Holdup," "Machine Gun Bandits Kill Two in Hold Up of Tijuana Money Car." Always a city that lamented its second-class billing to Los Angeles and perennially felt marginalized from national affairs, San Diego abruptly emerged into a larger world via the rat-a-tat-tat of a machine gun. The *San Diego Union* began its coverage, "Employing tactics of Chicago's gangland . . . ," and breathlessly set the new city scene in an editorial headed "Professional Murder":

> THE BIG-TIME THUG as he is, and not as moviedom's lurid romances depict him, was exhibited yesterday by the machine-gunning on the National City Dyke. The killers murdered two men in cold blood for something like $6,000 in ready money [cash]. They gave their victims not the slightest chance in the world. They did the ugly job swiftly, coldly—and safely. They were as "daring" as a man who gets his fish by dynamiting a lake. The whole thing was as cruel and contemptible and sordid a crime as our criminal records reveal. Yet it was absolutely typical of modern gangster methods as practiced in our big cities. It was "big-time stuff."[8]

The handheld machine gun had become an object of both fascination and fear. The gun was invented by a Kentucky-born army general, John Taliaferro Thompson, toward the end of the First World War, as a portable weapon with high firepower literally meant to sweep the trenches clean of the enemy, yet short enough to run with and fire from the hip, even if it did require carrying a large supply of ammunition. After the war, however, the military labeled the gun "impractical," too big for a pistol, too small for a rifle, and therefore tactically useless. While civilian police liked its potency, they feared that spraying with it from curb-to-curb would mow down too many innocents along with criminals. This largely limited early sales to factory owners and their hired agents who aimed to intimidate striking workers. It was not until well into the 1920s that the "submachine" gun (also called the Tommy gun, after its inventor) gained its notoriety in the hands of rival big-city mobs anxious to protect and expand their bootlegging and other criminal activities.[9]

The gun was an ideal gangland murder weapon—light in weight, easily concealed, and possessed of enormous fire power. A pistol required an assassin to be near his (or her) target, and if the bullet missed, the target might fire back. If the intended victim had a bodyguard, the use of a pistol was out of the question. The Tommy gun could kill from a distance or from the safety and anonymity of a speeding car. So the gun made its first violent appearance in Chicago in 1925, where it was quickly nicknamed the "Chicago typewriter." Two years later, as the "piano," it took hold in Philadelphia, and a year after that in the Big Apple, New York City.

At first, law enforcement and the general public took a rather indifferent view of the Thompson submachine gun. If the mobs wanted to use them on one another, so much the better. Let them eliminate each other. But in Chicago, the bootlegging turf war between George (Bugs) Moran and Al Capone boiled over. Moran had been picking off members of Capone's gang one by one, so "Scarface" decided to retaliate and eliminate his tormentor's entire band all at once. His strategy set the stage for the infamous St. Valentine's Day Massacre on February 14, 1929.

The country's reaction to the slaughter was not what the mob expected. It was not one of good riddance to a fearful gang. Instead the press, radio, and public at large screamed "Foul!" The massacre was too blatant, too craven, and had gone much too far. As a result, the submachine gun became a symbol of excess. It should be banned, the public felt, taken from the hands of criminals. Memory of the St. Valentine's Day Massacre was certainly fresh in people's minds when, four months later, mobsters riddled the Agua Caliente money-car with automatic fire on the San Diego Dike.

Just listen to the shrill warnings and stern advice of editorials in San Diego newspapers. In his "Talks with Readers," the editor of the *San Diego Sun* advised, "Now that the machine-gun breed of bandits has arrived in San Diego, we would do well to recognize that we are in a state of war. . . . The police department should be provided with machine guns and armored cars. Every officer should be taught to shoot quickly and straight. A 'war college' should be established at police headquarters, with carefully studied plans formulated for immediate action in case of an outbreak of banditry in any designated section of the city."[10]

The rival *San Diego Union* carried a similarly vehement admonition against trafficking in machine guns. "THE MACHINE GUN used in the National City [San Diego] Dike murder last Monday," it wrote, "was sold to the killers by someone who, for all that law has to say about it, can perhaps claim to be a legitimate business man." The editorial called the vendor "no better than an accessory to the crime of murder. . . . When such a weapon is sold to any but official representatives of military or law-enforcement departments, the transaction is a deal in murder. . . . A traffic in machine guns can never be any more legitimate than a traffic in blackjacks or brass knuckles."[11]

An odd comparison, to be sure, but there it was. In any case, neither plea was heeded. Gun trafficking was not regulated, and the city developed no "war plans" to combat machine gun–wielding mobsters.

POLICE THEORIES

In the immediate aftermath of the carnage on the Dike, eyewitnesses recounted for police more of what they had seen. One spoke of a red roadster which seemed to be part of the assault. It was behind the Ford when the attack took place, and as the robbers fled, it followed, screening the getaway car from possible pursuit. Then it too disappeared. No one claimed to have seen the driver of this vehicle, but police began to visualize a team at work in the holdup.

Another witness thought that he had seen a third person in the attack car. Based on additional accounts, police calculated that as many as four or five individuals may have committed the crime, two in the Ford as it approached its target, another in the red diversionary vehicle, and two others who may have been standing on the roadside at the scene of the holdup and jumped into the killers' car at the last moment.

None of this inspires much confidence in eyewitness accounts. Because of their varied life experiences, people see the same event differently. The creative mind, excited by a spontaneous, untoward, chaotic happening with lives at stake, further conflates reality and imagination. Yet eyewitness reports carry extraordinary weight in judicial proceedings.

Frank Hartell is a case in point. He was the only "eyewitness" to get a good look at the armed felons and later became the state's star witness for positive identifications. Hartell first told authorities and news reporters that a second car had pulled up in front of the robbery vehicle, and that the killers then hurried into it before it quickly drove off. Hartell was sure he saw this pickup car arrive on the scene, even if he could not identify its make. But later one of the confessed killers told police that as part of their escape plan, he and his partner had planted their getaway car on Edgemont before the hijacking took place. All criminal procedures seem to have their unresolved inconsistencies, contradictions, and loopholes, some due to sloppy and incomplete official investigations, but many of them rooted in those personal, blurry, reconstituted eyewitness accounts.

Pressed by both public expectations and their image of themselves, police grasped at theories about the Dike murders. Although no eyewitness reported seeing it, they surmised that the pouch of money had been lifted from the locked trunk of the Cadillac. They did not think it possible that the trunk had been closed but left unlocked. Yet neither the lock nor the trunk had been forced; the trunk, therefore, must have been opened with a key. Detectives found the key to the trunk hooked to the car keys still in the ignition switch inside the car. Accordingly, the robbers must have had their own key to the trunk.

Cadillac dealers assured investigators that their cars did not have interchangeable keys and that only one key could open the trunk of that particular car. The police then concluded that another key must have been fashioned from a wax impression of the lock. That supposition focused attention on employees at Agua Caliente—or anyone who had had access to that Cadillac who could have cast the impression. Just as important, someone must have known that particular vehicle would be used to transfer cash on May 20. In other words, the holdup was an inside job.

Pursuing that trail, however, would not be easy for investigators. Agua Caliente was a private company immersed in gambling in a foreign country. Ownership and operation of the resort involved politically and economically influential individuals on both sides of the border. Launching any probe there would require cooperation not readily forged. Despite a veneer of *amistad* (friendship), border relations always have been marked by opportunism, corruption, blustering nationalism, and a stubborn, even defiant, determination to defend one's own turf.

As soon as he learned of the money-car robbery and the deaths of the courier and guard, Border Baron Wirt Bowman announced a $5,000 reward for information leading to the capture or death of the culprits. The next day he added $1,000 for tips that steered police toward arrests of the robbers.[12] Bowman and one of his fellow Barons, James Crofton, posed for newspaper photographers beside the riddled Cadillac, and on Tuesday afternoon, May 21, rushed off to deliver "special information" to the Los Angeles Police Department. The exact nature of that "special information" remains a mystery, as does the reluctance of the Barons to share it first with San Diego police.

In fact, as the crime investigation moved into its second day, authorities were stymied. Escape routes, especially those heading north, were supposed to be sealed off with police roadblocks, although San Diego lawmen admitted their inability to patrol all such roads. Still, there were at the time relatively few ways to get from San Diego to Los Angeles on paved roadways. Deputies had the battered money-car and the robber's Ford towed to Harley's Garage near downtown police headquarters and dusted for fingerprints, but markings found on the Cadillac turned out to be those of the slain driver, Borrego, as did the palm smudge found on the trunk of the car. Police surmised the robbers must have been glove-wearing professionals. Machine guns, gloves, insider assistance, meticulous planning, and defiant execution all mirrored the workings of organized mobs in places like Chicago and New York.

Truth was that mobsters who had received their training and experience in Midwestern gang wars and then filtered West at this moment had their sights trained on the Border Barons themselves, said to be fabulously rich from their earnings at Agua Caliente, fast becoming famous as the world's greatest gambling resort. And as the astonishing story of the renowned spa unfolds in these pages, mobsters continue to hover about.

Mobs

National Prohibition, which went into effect nearly a decade before the robbery at the Dike, had spawned an enormous web of criminal opportunists throughout the country. Bootlegging became both profession and pastime. Actually, most people (probably all of them drinkers) hardly considered bootlegging to be criminal, and local lawmakers and police largely winked at and profited from the law. It was generally accepted, if not always true, that when liquor deals were being made, officers took payoffs to glance the other way, though the authorities did make occasional headline-grabbing raids on minor offenders to satisfy moralists, ministers, and politicians. Most Americans shrugged their shoulders and called it a sign of the times.

Gangsters wallowed in the bonanza, and bootlegging operations, big and small, sprouted up everywhere. By the mid-1920s, however, for most people, "mobs" meant loosely organized criminal syndicates headed by the likes of Al Capone, Charles "Lucky" Luciano, Guiseppe "Joe the Boss" Masseria, and Morris "Moe" Dalitz, gangsters who matched wits for large stakes in big cities such as Chicago, New York, and Cleveland. Eastern mobsters considered the West Coast only a crime colony, albeit sunny, dry (in terms of humidity anyway), and occasionally entertaining (especially glamorous Hollywood), but lacking the tradition of Irish and Italian gangs thumping one another and only potentially, but not yet sufficiently, lucrative. Therefore, while young Eastern hoods such as Johnny Rosselli (and soon Bugsy Siegel) started making inroads Out West, the syndicates made little concerted effort to organize crime along the Pacific Coast. Besides, they had their hands full defending their enclaves against competitors and federal investigators on their home turf.

WEST COAST GANGSTERS

Southern California's home-grown mobs had many gears, all in motion, few in synch. They bred and mutated like no others around the country, came together, often by happenstance—the place, the moment, the opportunity —and dissipated just as erratically. Few of the loyalties, such as family, ethnicity, or trade, which gave shape and stability to many Eastern gangs, existed on the West Coast.

In cities like Los Angeles, protection racketeering gained a toehold through its musclemen, but rarely sustained itself, for lack of savvy and sufficiently ruthless leadership willing to maintain pressure until it got what it wanted. No top-level headman arose to organize mob activities and map out terri-tories. Some five or six "big shots" handled the wholesale liquor business in Los Angeles's North End, two others worked the San Fernando Valley, and Hollywood had its own well-known coterie of dealers, who paid police and politicians a fee to serve movie land's czars and minions.[1] Aside from these few established "regulars," however, mob activity was pick-up and piecemeal.

Nonetheless, a menagerie of nondescript, personally colorful, daring, and dangerously volatile bootleggers disdainful of the law emerged on the Pacific Coast to traffic in liquor smuggled into the United States by land and sea. Bootlegging proved risky, but the profits immense. Before Prohibition, individuals who captained water taxis around Los Angeles harbor earned $10 or $15 a day, but smuggling booze to shore from big, outlying rum runners bagged them $100 to $200 daily. Such windfalls enabled them to buy and outfit cars and stock up on weapons, other equipment, and special clothing in order to engage in even more profitable onshore hijacking, netting thousands of dollars per load.[2] These crimes *did* pay, and West Coast lawmen acknowledged that the region's gangs might eventually be organized by an outside czar such as Al Capone. "A golden throne is ready for the taking," a columnist wrote in 1931, "and with money reeking in alco-hol, the stairway could be built."[3] In fact, such a pretender, Ralph Sheldon, was already in town.

Sheldon, a seemingly heartless hoodlum, was said to have been Capone's personal body guard, and Chicago authorities suspected him of half a dozen murders and gang killings. Arrested for three of them, each time he escaped conviction. His name also surfaced in the spectacular machine gun slaying of an assistant district attorney investigating crime in Cook County, but nothing came of it. His rumored connections on both sides of the law were legendary. Every time there was a Chicago gangland killing in the 1920s, police and public thought of Ralph Sheldon. The Windy City's rough play between mobs, however, finally caught up with him, and "Bugs" Moran vowed to take him for a "ride" for killing two of Moran's friends. Sheldon fled to Los Angeles in early 1929. There he assembled a new gang of mainly ex-Chicago thugs to pick up where they had left off in the Midwest. They wanted quick and easy money, and kidnap ransoms seemed promising. Moreover, newspaper headlines following the heist of the money-car from the opulent Agua Caliente gaming spa suggested a target.

A covey of ex-Chicago thugs later gathered in December 1930 at the Phoenix, Arizona, home of "Dutch" Reese to identify wealthy Southern Californians as potential kidnap and ransom targets. Sheldon himself may or may not have been at the brainstorming, but one of his gang members was, James Gatewood, alias Jimmy Doolen, who then informed Sheldon of the prospects. They put the Border Barons, along with other Agua Caliente officials, at the top of the hit list.[4]

SCURRYING HIJACKERS

But that was more than a year after the Dike killings—and that plot had gone terribly wrong. And, as it turned out, one of them had accidentally shot his partner in the frenzy. From where they had parked their getaway car on Edgemont, the two robbers sped to the house they had rented as their hideaway, only five minutes away. There they changed clothes and telephoned the nearby residence of Marcel "The Greek" Dellon, a crude, boastful, middle-aged California racketeer, who seemed to be orchestrating this entire affair and who already had a bulging police file. Nicknamed "The Greek" because of his ancestry and heavily accented English, this boot-legger was an accomplished sea captain who owned a frequently used high-powered speed boat that could outrun Coast Guard cutters.

Dellon was not home to take the emergency call, but his cohort, Jeanne Lee Ktesticher, an attractive, vibrant, twenty-year-old redhead widely known as "The Rumrunning Queen," responded and drove the wounded gunman to the Spanish-Mediterranean-style home of Captain Jerry Kearney, less than ten minutes away, just off the edge of fashionable Balboa Park, San Diego's civic centerpiece.

Kearney, who was twenty-seven, had run a boat rental and water-taxi business (intertwined with bootlegging) at the Los Angeles harbor for nearly a decade, but for the last two years had, by his own admission, devoted himself to full-time liquor smuggling and hijacking. Known around town as the "big wise guy of Southern California bootlegging," he had made his "arrangements" with law enforcement.

Kearney had an explanation for everything. He blamed his bootlegging on Prohibition (perhaps not far off the mark) and later told authorities and the press that "I never took the liquor law seriously when I saw the very people who made the law breaking it." Money gained from bootlegging propelled him into hijacking, but "I never hijacked anybody," he claimed, "until they started to hijack me. Then I got even. I don't think that's against the law either. Just a case of protecting yourself."[5] Some state prosecutors thought differently.

Captain Kearney was off on "business" when Jeanne showed up at his home with the hurt gunman. Kearney's wife, Agnes Grace, opened the front door. "We need a bed. Don't ask any questions," Jeanne blurted out.[6] They put the robber in the front bedroom, and Jeanne left.

Grace, as she was called, tried to phone her husband, who was delivering bootleg liquor to a customer on Coronado Island, a plush residential district across the bay from the City of San Diego. She could not contact him, but an hour later, about 2 P.M., he phoned to ask if they had received any new whiskey orders (Kearney manned two liquor depots, one in Coronado and the other at his house). His wife told him to hurry home. When he arrived, Captain Jerry found the wounded gunman, whom he had known for several years and called a friend, in agonizing pain. As he later reconstructed their immediate conversation for police, Kearney asked his buddy, "What happened?"

"We got double-crossed on a heisting job [north of San Diego]," the bedridden fugitive supposedly replied. "The coppers were there."[7] In other words, the hijackers thought their caper had been "fixed," so that no police would be around, but officers arrived, and a shootout commenced. Now a bullet needed to be removed from the victim's shoulder.

Kearney attempted to dig the bullet out with a penknife, but blood spurted from the wound, and he feared that he had cut an artery. The emergency required a doctor, and Grace, who had lived in San Diego with her family for several years before marrying, phoned her physician, Dr. R. O. Taylor, who agreed to come to the house and inspect the shoulder. Once there, he advised hospital attention, but Kearney said that would be impossible, "No hospitals. He was in a rum job and caught a slug." So Dr. Taylor agreed to see the patient later that evening in his clinic.

The wounded man's accomplice, accompanied by Jeanne Lee, arrived about 3 P.M. at Kearney's house, carrying a worn suitcase into which he had stuffed the coveralls and other clothing the murderers had worn in the robbery along with the money sack, the checks, and cash. He had phoned his wife at their Long Beach home (just south of Los Angeles) and urged that she hurry down with their three-year-old daughter to be with him in the crisis. Jeanne agreed to drive the two hours or so to Long Beach and bring them back.

Later that afternoon Dellon arrived at the Kearney home and held a hushed, private conversation with the wounded man, in which he was heard to say, "How you feeling, kid?"

"Rotten," came the reply.

"Don't worry, kid. I take care you."

Dellon then asked Kearney if this Dr. Taylor was "regular"—in other words, conversant with the needs of the mob. Kearney insisted that he was. "He'd better be," said Dellon, "or I kill him. I go to jail for no one, and if he squeals on me in this case, I get him."[8]

Dellon then left, taking with him the nearly $6,000 in cash seized in the robbery and leaving the worthless checks behind.

Jerry Kearney drove the injured man to Dr. Taylor's clinic at about 7 P.M. The robber resisted any sedative, because, he said, he did not know what he might say when under ether. "I know about psychology," he said before trailing off into unconsciousness.[9] The doctor removed the .38 slug, and as he held it, wondered if it had any connection to the money-car robbery he had read about in the evening newspaper. Kearney reassured him that it did not and handed the doctor $200 in cash for his services—at that time a substantial payment for a relatively simple procedure, but not too much to pay for loyalty. About 1 A.M. that night Jeanne returned to the Kearney residence with her passengers.

CLUES

Next day, Tuesday, May 21, Kearney and the injured criminal had several hushed conversations (which Kearney later repeated in court) about what had occurred on the Dike. The robber admitted that it was he and his partner who had "pulled the job." He said the holdup wasn't worth it, that they had expected to get $100,000 in cash, but all they got was about $6,000 and a bunch of useless checks. "We tried to blow the tires off the money car," he continued, "and as we drew alongside the machine from the border, the men inside started shooting. We returned their fire and dropped 'em. We then stopped beside the car. I ran around to the right side and Cochran stood between the two machines."[10]

Now we know the name of one of the killers: Cochran. His full name was Robert Lee Cochran, a normally good-natured, rather callow, and easily led young man of twenty-four, generally known as Lee. Like Kearney, he captained water taxis and bootlegged liquor off Long Beach, where they had met. Cochran, in partnership with the wounded man, had become an inveterate hijacker, adept at switching and camouflaging cars as well as an accomplished gunman. Less than two weeks earlier, the pair had sold Kearney twenty cases of hijacked scotch at $50 a case. "When they [first] told me they had been in a hijacking job [north of San Diego]," Kearney later said, "I believed them, for I knew they had been in the hijacking business. I've been a hijacker too. . . . It's all fair in the liquor racket."[11] As it would turn out, however, Kearney had invented the whole North County angle to distance himself from the Dike killings. He knew the truth from the start, firsthand.

The wounded killer continued telling Kearney his dark tale. "As I reached into the Cadillac [for the money bag], the men inside fired again, one bullet clipping the button off the top of my cap and another passing under my left arm. Cochran then shoved his gun into the car and fired. We then got the money into our car and beat it. Cochran did not know one of the bullets from his gun had hit me."[12]

The mobsters decided that the automatic weapons (possibly including a submachine gun) used in the killings were too "hot" to keep around the house, and that night Kearney and Cochran dumped them in the ocean. Before dawn the next morning, Wednesday, May 22, Kearney and his young brother-in-law, Virgil Maddox, poured gasoline into a liquor crate, ignited a small bonfire in the captain's backyard, and burned the robbers' clothing along with some two hundred personal and travelers' checks and money orders taken from the Agua Caliente moneybag. Kearney recalled in court that, as the checks flared and curled into cinders, he had noted one partially burned check worth $100 or $1,000 that had been signed by "Bow" preceded by an "ara." He presumed it that of Clara Bow, Hollywood's silent film star, the famous "It Girl," flapper queen of the fabulous Twenties, and frequent visitor to Agua Caliente.

Midmorning that day, Kearney and his sister-in-law, Helen Maddox, loaded the robbers' remaining collection of weaponry and the empty money bag into Kearney's car and headed north toward the San Pedro docks at the Port of Los Angeles. The port and its adjoining counterpart at Long Beach had boomed since the nearby discovery of oil and the opening of the Panama Canal. During Prohibition, the waterfront became a melting pot of bootleggers, rumrunners, and their clients, including those who rode the water taxis to the gambling ships that flourished at anchor in international waters just outside the country's three-mile limit. Kearney, who had plied these waters for years, had a good many friends and contacts there, as well as competitors and outright enemies.

Lee Cochran, his wife, Marian, and their child left the Kearney residence shortly thereafter. "My neck's in danger," he realized. "Listen, Baby," Lee confessed to Marian, "Colson and I did do that job." In tears, she blurted out, "I warned you to stop running around with Marty."[13] She was referring to Martin Colson, the wounded robber, who was nicknamed "Frenchy," because he recently had adopted the alias Pierre Le Beaux (Peter the Handsome, no less). Cochran and Colson had met a year or so earlier while hobnobbing with other bootleggers and hijackers around San Pedro. Imagining bigger jobs with more return, the two had joined the Dellon conspirators planning the Agua Caliente caper and had been chosen (authorities speculated that lots were drawn) to pull off the brazen holdup on the Dike. Now all were in desperate trouble.[14]

The nation's fascination—and that of neighboring Mexico—with the sensational crime and the frustrated chase stemmed not only from the murders on the Dike, the presence of machine guns and East Coast mobsters Out West, police complicity, and the frantic search for the perpetrators, but also from the aura of fabled wealth and storybook glamour associated with Agua Caliente itself, the thriving resort complex nestled at the end of the rainbow in romantic Old Mexico. The robbery focused attention on the "good life" to be had just below the border in raucous and fun-filled Tijuana, and while the Border Barons certainly lamented the killings, they also welcomed the notoriety. In the public mind, casinos and crime blended into one giddy mood of mounting and limitless prosperity cresting toward the end of the Roaring Twenties. Most figured the effervescence would spill right over into the next decade. Some, ignoring prosperity's jeopardies, sensed it would never end. Agua Caliente and the holdup were, in effect, emblazoned side-by-side on the badge of the times.

The holdup car, a brand-new (1929) black Model-A Ford touring car with its front windshield removed for shooting action. University of Southern California Special Collections

Border Baron James Crofton inspects Agua Caliente's robbed money-car, a tan 1929 Cadillac coupe punctured by at least seventeen bullet holes. University of Southern California Special Collections

"Silent" Marty Colson, the brooding and calculating twenty-five-year-old
prime suspect, wounded in the wild shootout on the Dike. Colson was labeled
"silent" because he refused to speak to anyone, even his own lawyers.
University of Southern California Special Collections

The normally genial Robert Lee Cochran, a twenty-four-year-old water
taxi skipper, another major suspect in the killings. Los Angeles Public Library

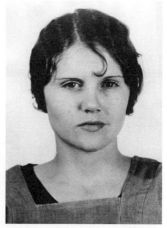

Marcel "The Greek" Dellon, a well-known bootlegger and hijacker,
the brains of the mob that attacked the Agua Caliente money transport.
Los Angeles Public Library

Jeanne Lee, the feisty, elusive raven-haired "Rum Running Queen" who
taunted authorities trying to capture her. Los Angeles Public Library

Capt. Jerry Kearney, a boastful bootlegger with political contacts and a
vaunted machine gun he openly vowed to use, who was at the center of the investigation
of the killings. Los Angeles Public Library.

Grace Agnes Kearney, the captain's wife, whose tearful deposition
helped police crack the case. Los Angeles Public Library

The Kearneys' California Mission Revival–style "casita," where
the mobsters hid out after the spectacular crime. University of Southern
California Special Collections

San Diego Police Chief Arthur Hill, an experienced lawman
but a recent political appointee to department head, who directed
the frantic manhunt for the killers. San Diego Historical Society

The elaborate chime tower with its mixed architectural and decorative
styles—Orientalist, Mission Revival, and Art Deco—welcomed visitors to Agua
Caliente and became the internationally known symbol of the gambling resort.
California State Library Special Collections

23

The Mission Revival–style Agua Caliente hotel
with its graceful arches, long corridors, and red tile roofs with viga supports,
here framed by oaks, the only original trees remaining from the arid high-desert
landscape that was transformed into lush, exotic gardens for the spa.
California State Library Special Collections

An advertisement for the resort, featuring the chime tower, a luggage
sticker, and a Spanish dancer in Jazz Age dress. Andre Williams Collection

The patio of the elegant spa with its remarkable façade of hand-painted tiles featuring a combination of Art Deco themes, facing The Plunge, the resort's Olympic-sized swimming pool. California State Library Special Collections

The magnificent entrance to The Plunge, mixing Arabesque and Mission Revival architecture with Art Deco touches. The Moorish-style minaret in the background housed the chimney of the steam power plant. California State Library Special Collections

The barbershop accented luxury with its Arabesque arches, Art Deco ceiling, and interior decorations common to the period. California State Library Special Collections

ENTRANCE TO HOTEL

Hotel Agua Caliente
Tijuana, Mexico

Table d' Hote Dinner

$2.50

Japanese Crab Flake Cocktail or
Supreme of Grape Fruit au Dubonnet

Celery Hearts   Crissinis   Colossal Olives

Lamb Veloute Leishman   or   Essence of Clams en tasse

Choice of:
Stuffed Fresh Lobster Cardinal
Live soft Shell Crabs fried in brown butter
Sirloin or Tenderloin Steak broiled with fresh Mushrooms
Milkfed Chicken saute garnie Helder
Noisette of Milk lamb, Ballandar

Potatoes Demi French
Braised Swiss Chard with Marrow

Salad Caprice

Biscuit glacee Tortoni - Fancy Wafers

Cafe Noir.

Friday, August 23, 1929.

Miss VERNA GORDON in Dance Divertissements

Handsome printed menus offering gourmet meals
changed daily. California State Library Special Collections

28

The wishing well outside the casino where patrons tossed coins to Lady Luck before seeking fortune in the gaming hall. California State Library Special Collections

The ornate interior of the casino's salon with its lushly carpeted floor, imported European chandeliers, Roman-style columns, and a geometrically proportioned Art Deco ceiling, highlighted by primitive motifs painted on panels. California State Library Special Collections

The grandstand at the racetrack was said to be among the most stately in the world. At the left stands the deluxe Jockey Club, luxurious inside and out—and for carefully screened members only. California State Library Special Collections

Movie stars, statesmen, sultans, business tycoons, and sports celebrities from around the world frequented the resort. Andre Williams Collection

"Agua Caliente, where all nations meet and speak the tongue of happiness,"
according to the spa's advertisements. Andre Williams Collection

Rita Hayworth, then an attractive teen-ager known as Rita Cansino, danced at the complex, where a movie mogul "discovered" her and launched her screen career. Andre Williams Collection

Images of Rita Cansino (soon to be Hayworth) appeared on small picture cards like these, featuring popular film idols, which were stuffed behind the cellophane on cigarette packages. Andre Williams Collection

For prestige, travelers put Agua Caliente suitcase stickers
on their luggage, whether or not they had patronized the resort.
Andre Williams Collection

The proud Border Barons at the 1930 dedication of their $2 million racetrack,
which they proclaimed the finest in the world: James Crofton (left), Baron Long (right),
and Wirt Bowman (second from right). John P. Mills, a millionaire land developer
(second from left), was general manager of the track. Los Angeles Public Library

Playground of the Hemisphere

When the mob struck in May 1929, the Agua Caliente resort had been operating less than a year and was prospering beyond even the dreamy expectations of its flamboyant and greedy proprietors, the Border Barons. One of them, the chronically overconfident James Crofton, boyishly buoyant at thirty-four, bragged that he was one of California's six millionaires and intended to stay that way.[1]

None of the Border Barons enjoyed inherited wealth or social privilege. Instead, Bowman, Crofton, and Long had found a (tawdry) niche in a society testing its traditional ties and ways of thinking in a pivotal epoch of historical change. They wormed their way in, and then up. As teenagers, each had left home to try his fortune farther west and took catch-as-catch-can jobs en route—Crofton as a flamboyant circus barker and Long as a traveling flimflam medicine man, while Bowman bummed around as a lumberjack and railroad section hand before heading for northern Mexico. As they moved around by their wits, they learned to suck sustenance from both sides of the law and eagerly dared to do it. Once well into the Roaring Twenties, their paths crossed along the border. Aggressive, unscrupulous enterprisers and full-blown participants in gaming entertainment (then labeled *vice* and now called *leisure*) along the border, they formed an uneasy but lucrative partnership at Agua Caliente.

The Barons did not like or trust one another. They treated their mammoth, glorious resort as an achievement to be honored, but only one trophy garnered on their individual roads of personal ambition. Bowman had high national political aspirations focused on his home state of Arizona. Long craved to be the maitre d' of movieland, the social organizer of glitzy, name-dropping, pretentious Los Angeles. Crofton, a devil-may-care playboy at heart, yearned for fancy cars, good-looking, classy ladies, blueblood status, and heaps of money. Bowman seems to have taken the younger Crofton under his wing in "sporting" ventures before Agua Caliente, but they never stayed good friends. Neither of them much tolerated Baron Long, and vice versa. Less than four years into the Agua Caliente enterprise, they were at each other's throats and looking to dissolve the relationship. But in terms of whirlwind excitement, despite endless frustration and draining disappointments, it was a wildly exuberant four years that spanned the zenith of the decade and extended well into the Great Depression. And despite some uninvited interruptions, when the success of Agua Caliente first faded and then evaporated in the late 1930s, all three men landed firmly on their feet, caught gainful (if unsteady) trade winds, and moved on to their next undertakings, and then the next. Capital amassed at the resort, laundered and otherwise invested, propelled them along the way for the rest of their lives. All three of the millionaires died in bed of natural causes, well into their seventies.

Earnings of gambling enterprises can only be estimated, because owners skim so much revenue and design elaborate schemes to hide and launder their earnings to avoid taxes. Governments showcase their occasionally successful prosecutions of these evasions but all too often prefer to take their own cut through contracts, licenses, taxes, and payoffs. Agua Caliente was no exception to these practices, and at the time of the robbery its casino was said to be grossing at least $2 million a month, ten times that in today's dollars.[2]

The gaming resort was indeed a beacon, not only to social elites with their autocratic mannerisms, superior airs, and preening sense of entitlement, but also less pretentious folks, mainly from conservative, more down-to-earth Midwestern backgrounds, who worked hard at an alternative form of grace and manner found in Southern Californian informality, garish spontaneity, and candidness that could be considered crass, even rude. These people, mistakenly thought to be homebound, had pulled up stakes, often with no regrets, and headed west; some referred to them as "tumbleweeds."[3] They just tumbled into town and lodged up against the sunny coast, with some worries to be sure, but also a sigh of relief for leaving past entanglements. The mood was palpable at Agua Caliente, which displayed more than a dollop of aristocratic snootiness, but was also a place where many saw blueblood as a curiosity though hardly a badge of honor.

THE LUXURY LIFE AT AGUA CALIENTE

Where else in the world might one mingle so openly with neither fanfare nor modesty among royalty, movie stars, ambassadors, ministers of government, Hollywood moguls, and pure-blooded thoroughbreds (horses as well as their owners)? Whether you paid the notables much special attention was your choice—and many did not. It may have been titillating to consort with the well known, but you had come with friends and family to have lunch (at $1 a plate during the week and $1.50 on weekends) under the arches of the hotel's lavishly tiled patio, bordered with privet, rose geraniums, and petunias in lavender, red, and white—and with the charming Fuente de la Estrellita, the Fountain of the Little Star, as its centerpiece. Overhead, colorful tropical birds squawked and screeched (and periodically relieved themselves) from royal palm trees, perches, and cages ringing the patio, set in the *au courant* Spanish Mission Revival architecture, often with eclectic decorative touches, so popular throughout the region.

Mexican musicians with colorful serapes draped over their shoulders played background music on xylophones and guitars. Mariachis in bolero vests and legging trousers, familiar *ranchero* dress highlighted by wide-brimmed sombreros, enlivened the setting with their lusty, popular *corridos* of unrequited love and national passion. Show times featured Flamenco dancers along with troupes of *Mexicanos* performing folkloric dances.[4]

Among the most popular performers was the comely teenager, Margarita Carmen Cansino, nicknamed Rita, who was born into show business in New York City, her father a Spanish-born dancer and her mother a Ziegfeld Follies showgirl. Rita began dancing professionally at twelve. When her father's career carried the Cansino family west, she went to school through ninth grade and then joined his dancing act in various Tijuana clubs and the heralded Agua Caliente. She was only sixteen when spotted at the resort by a Los Angeles film producer who hired her to dance in Hollywood movies. Three years later she married (the first of her four marriages) a man twenty-two years her senior who promptly declared himself her manager and altered Rita's image from a black-haired Latin beauty to an auburn-haired, glamorous metropolitan. He also drew upon her mother's maiden name of Haworth to change Rita's surname to Hayworth. Now "The Great American Love Goddess" was ready to dance in motion pictures with Fred Astaire and Gene Kelly and to garner lasting fame and notoriety with her relatively modest striptease in *Gilda* (1946). All the while gossip columnists ardently reported her parade of marriages to and divorces from picturesque personalities such as the brilliant renegade filmmaker Orson Welles and Prince

Aly Khan, later Pakistan's ambassador to the United Nations. Tales of Rita Hayworth's metamorphosis from child dancer to one of her country's most beloved movie stars recalled glamorous and freewheeling Agua Caliente long after the place had shut down.[5]

The resort endeavored to immerse customers in romantic escapism with exotic overlays. Pseudo-sophisticated Southern Californians dabbled in *haute culture* but generally gave it limited priority. Still, they could appreciate—that is, make an ostentatious fuss over—the resort's daily printed menus that offered creamed chicken and sweetbreads, *pattie jolie* fillet or potted venison *en cassolette* with wild rice; St-Hubert *poulet* or *sautéed* fillets of rockbass covered with sauce *au vin blanc Silensienne* or scrambled eggs with scalloped calf's brain.

The chef (hired from an exclusive New York City restaurant in 1930) also prepared specialties with Mexican sauces such as *pipián sabroso de pato salsa con ajonjolí* (potted Long Island duckling in Mexican sesame seed sauce) and more common national dishes including turkey enchiladas, chiles rellenos filled with white cheese and hot peppers, and *machaca con huevos revueltos* (scrambled eggs mixed with dried, shredded beef). Plain, unvarnished fresh (and healthy) garden vegetables were out of the question at Agua Caliente. The eatery offered, instead, new parsnips in *velouté* sauce or sliced new potatoes *sauté persilles*. Desserts included fresh peach *religieuse*, *gâteau mille feuille*, Polish *babas au rhum*, or pudding *marquisette* with brandy sauce or, perhaps, another alleged Mexican delicacy: cactus ice cream.

Meals routinely carried a beverage special, for example, a $1.00 pint (how déclassé; had they not heard of carafes?) of Santo Tomás claret (grapes from nearby vineyards) or a $5.00 glass of French House of Veive Clicquot champagne. One can imagine recent migrants from mid-America trying to fathom these plates, or the ladies club from San Diego pretending to understand them. Or the naval officer just off a duty tour trying not to embarrass himself. Just what could one pick up with one's fingers? And where do the elbows belong? Thank goodness the place also offered old-fashioned lentil soup, a broiled top sirloin steak with mushroom sauce, tutti-frutti ice cream, and coffee.[6]

But then haute cuisine was not the only flavor on people's palate. Many savored a leisurely drink of liquor in a public place, a pleasure which had been abruptly interrupted by Prohibition on the other side of the international line. It was delightful to drink one's alcoholic preference in open air, blessed by the region's temperate climate, on an enchanting patio, rather than resorting to an illegal speakeasy that required patrons to identify in a low voice the individual who had sent them (low voice: "speak easy," which is how the hangouts got their nickname) or clandestinely purchasing booze of uncertain makeup and quality from a bootlegger.

The Border Barons understood the "dilemma" of their patrons and ensured that they could choose from a wide variety of imported liquors, some of them highly distinguished brands, such as Hiram Walker six-year-old bourbon, 100 proof Four Aces rye, Johnny Walker Black Label, anis from Mallorca, or Bols Gold liquor, Piper London Dry Gin, and Cordon Bien cognac.

The proprietors stocked the wine cellar for royalty, with many imports directly from the French chateaux that produced them. The delicious "Green Fairy," absinthe, banned in the United States because it contained the chemical thujone (then considered an addictive, psychoactive drug, but now known to be no better or worse than ordinary alcohol), could be purchased at Agua Caliente, thanks to the acquisition of a prewar stock from an Antwerp, Belgium, warehouse, where it had been safely stored during the First World War.[7]

Fine drink was also sold to customers by the bottle or case. Of course, those purchases, if unconsumed in Mexico (as most were), had to be smuggled into the United States, but inventive minds created ingenious schemes for getting booty back home, and there was always the probability that customs authorities could for a fee be encouraged to turn their heads at the point of passage.

When Prohibition ended in the United States, the resort feared losing its liquor drinkers to their old haunts and issued booklets reminding them about "Agua Caliente in Old Mexico where drinking never ceased." One booklet, titled *Bottoms Up*, listed exotic cocktails served at the complex, plus a short history of their main ingredients. Agua Caliente's chef suggested in print what wines went best with specific meals, and advised that Napoleon loved Courvoisier brandy; George Washington, Canary sherry; and Julius Caesar, Chianti ("We have it"). The publication also had practical advice for tipplers. If one wished a drink, order a "dram, tiddly, nip, or snort," and after one too many, feel free to admit, "I feel a bit oiled, shicker, socko, or stinko." Finally, it recommended for the "day after" a "tequila sunrise," old pilsner, gin fizz, or tomato juice, the latter, however, only if the others were not available.[8]

The most formally served and varied fare, at $2.50 a plate, awaited in the casino's elegant dining room: fresh lobster tails or olives and celery hearts, then Maryland-style soft-shelled crab sautéed in butter or broiled sirloin steak covered with fresh mushrooms, followed by a vegetable salad, dessert, and coffee. A magnum of champagne cost from $10 to $15. In this classy setting, a noted orchestra from Los Angeles or New York played popular dance music (couples danced more closely than in previous times and even dared to touch), including still memorable tunes such as "Singing in the Rain," "St. Louis Blues," "Broadway Melody," and "Little White Lies." One of the country's most popular composers, Walter Donaldson, wrote "There's a Wah Wah Gal in Agua (A-Wah) Caliente," and the original Wah Wah gal, screen star and songwriter Grace Poggi, sang it. Listen closely; you can hear the rhythm:

> There's a wah-wah gal in Ag-ua Cal-i-en-te
> What a wah-wah, wah-wah-, wah-wah, what a gal!
> You can have each Hula, hot bam-boo-la ba-by,
> You can have each jol-ly hot to-ma-le Sal!
> But that wah-wah gal in Ag-ua Cal-i-en-te . . .
> There's a gal![9]

Entertainment also featured world-class acts. Van and Shenck, the famous New York City vaudeville team, billed as the subway motorman and conductor who got their singing start on the same Brooklyn line (even if they did not), sang their hit songs, "Ain't We Got Fun?" and "Carolina in the Morning." No wonder captivated guests did not notice that Punjabi maharajah, Washington politician, or university president at the adjoining table. But they probably did eye the loveable "tramp," Charlie Chaplin, or the glorious queen of cinema, Gloria Swanson, or the sleek Olympic swimming champion, Johnny Weissmuller (later cinema's Tarzan), seated nearby.

There was always something special "going on" at Agua Caliente. Patrons simply strolled from one activity to another even if gambling remained their priority. "Never at anytime is the visitor in want of diversion," reported the *Los Angeles Times*. "Something for everyone" is the rule that keeps people at such resorts (and environs), and a special, easily recognizable "touch of class" adds a shade of respectability to the overall experience (much as the fine art galleries at several contemporary Las Vegas casinos).

A "bevy of bewitching manikins [meaning starlets] from Hollywood" in September 1929 presented "Fall and Winter Fashions of Hollywood," a pageant of specially designed fashions—furs, wraps, and evening gowns, all costing "a fabulous amount"—from "the style center of the West." And as if to ensure the quality of the event, this "will be the first attempt in this country [Mexico] to follow in the footsteps of the Paris salons, whose manikins present such a furor as they parade the startling modes of the fashion center of the world."[10] Agua Caliente might borrow from abroad but never be outdone.

The same was true of shopping on premises. Agua Caliente's two lavish shops, leased to internationally renowned import houses at one end of the casino, saved customers one-third to one-half the normal price of luxury goods sold in the United States. Honold's offered British Dunhill pipes, French perfumes, exquisite Mexican glass and lacework, along with more common Mexican curios and souvenirs. Milnor's featured finery from around the world: Japanese kimonos; French jewelry, silks, and purses; Irish linens; Dutch woolens; pottery and embroideries from Yugoslavia; and silverware from Denmark. Sweden contributed its glassware, dolls came from Hungary, and leather goods from London and Italy. There were full lines of high fashion in men's and women's clothing, camel's hair and hand-woven tweed coats, along with golf and riding shirts for males, and Scottish knitwear, silk blouses, and neckwear from Paris, and Charles Perrin gloves for ladies. These stores made extravagance seem affordable.[11]

Tourists could carry $100 worth of duty-free merchandise into the United States, but as with liquor, they smuggled the great majority of deluxe goods purchased back home, often in the guise of personal property. Confiscations by customs officers remained minimal. What agent would dare question the origins of a classy fur coat worn by a movie star or diplomat's wife? Or ask how it came to be that this gentleman was wearing three fine, imported silk shirts, one over the other, under his jacket? A kind of understood impunity existed at the crossing.

A niece of one of the Border Barons remembers her parents' ruse. She was six or seven years old at the time, living in San Diego, and when her parents wished to make a "run" into Mexico, they took her along, because she was cute and distracted official attention. Officers practically never quizzed parents accompanied by children. Today the lady laughs at the scam and still wonders how many cases of booze and other smuggled items she sat on as a youngster crossing the international line.[12]

SELLING THE PRODUCT

Ballyhoo blanketed the complex. Hyperbole thrived.

"America's Deauville, where the door to romance opens," aimed at wealthy Easterners who had been spending too many vacations (and too much money) at France's renowned spa for the privileged, but also at more common people who could now pamper themselves with regal treatment in their own backyard. Pretentious, perhaps, but also sublime. Admonitions and assurances came from the *Los Angeles Times*; it was no longer necessary to "think Europe" when pondering a ritzy vacation destination. "All the elegance of the most famous gathering places on the other side of the Atlantic is reflected in Agua Caliente, that palatial play spot just across the border in Old Mexico. . . ." The new resort on *this* continent "offers the jaded spirits of resident and tourist alike the entire ensemble of sport [gambling was called a sport] such as is linked inseparably with the renowned French watering place."

"The Playground of the Stars" catered to hordes of movie fans who had just begun to experience talkies. Al Jolson, whose singing initiated sound movies in 1927, was a frequent visitor at Agua Caliente. And the czars and stars themselves craved to flaunt their egoism, so much a part of their crafted mystique.

"Breathtaking . . . Agua Caliente will excite your wildest enthusiasm . . . yet manifest a cordial elegance reminiscent of the languid days of the Dons . . . embrace you with the friendly warmth of Old Mexico."[13]

Strange and alien Old Mexico was (and is) a steady draw on the American imagination. How exhilarating that ancient pyramids of uncertain source also soared skyward in *our* hemisphere, and that inscrutable descendants of great civilizations dwelled close to home. Mexican culture, stereotyped as The Spanish Alhambra, bullfights, and romantic guitar serenades, lay at our doorstep. Crossing the border to savor bawdy Tijuana, the Ace of Dives, had for some time tempted tourists yearning (or daring) to touch a toe on foreign soil. Now travelers could have the best (or worst) of both worlds. Tourists and their awed listeners considered it adventure travel.

Besides, everyone needs a change of pace; it is crucial for good health: "People who vary their existence get a great deal of enjoyment out of life. Many are finding this change of pace in a few hours or days spent occasionally at Agua Caliente. Whether you come to rest or play; for the relaxation of flower-filled patios or the excitement of the Casino, the 'change of pace' will refresh you in mind and body. The complete sports ensemble will satisfy your every whim. Bring your visitors to Agua Caliente, for to come to California without seeing Agua Caliente is like dinner at the Ritz, minus the *hors d'oeuvres—They miss the thrill.*"[14] Indeed they did miss the tingle and titillation.

Finally, a touch of history, that sense of a meaningful past which coats unadorned, pleasurable, restful tourism with a veneer of worthwhileness, a thin film of culture, and a satisfying feeling of money well spent. The Border Barons knew how to pluck that chord. Just listen to the temptress. The indefatigable Barons deliberately situated their resort in a land which was . . . the "home of beautiful Amazons" (the fabled Brazilian beauties far from their habitat?), that had been "rich and prosperous when George Washington was a baby." (Bad arithmetic. Washington was three in 1735; the first missionaries came to Tijuana in the 1760s; the first land grant in the valley was issued in 1829.)[15] The Border Barons themselves must have chuckled at this sort of marketing hype, but any lure that hooks is a good lure in the tourist business. Manufactured history excites and attracts patrons.

Tijuana had a reputation, alright, but no romantic history. It was pretty much the same for the entire Baja California peninsula. Scholars, of course, had discovered the gigantic cave paintings in the center part of the thousand-mile long land mass, noted the various American filibustering expeditions which sought to rip Baja California from Mexican rule, and written about the radical Leftist incursion from the United States into Tijuana in 1911, but the place lacked wonderment about the past. As a remedy, the Barons invented a majestic history for their surroundings and placed it in a spiffy handbook called *Bottoms Up*, to which they added a dash of their own philosophy, "There is a pathos in ruins of the past splendor which brings a sobering sense of the transitory works of man."

There were no such ruins to appreciate around Agua Caliente, but inside the complex, ornamentations such as imported Milan chandeliers, frescoed ceilings, marble columns, eighteenth-century furniture, Renaissance artwork, and handsomely tiled public spaces reminded clients of past, mainly

European, splendors. "HERE INDEED IS INSPIRATION FOR DREAMS IN THE MELLOW LIGHT OF THE DYING DAY," assured the Barons in capital letters.

Then the propagandists hallucinated: "On the summit of yon mountain a Spanish fort once frowned. A thousand Indians vainly assaulted its walls. Now a squirrel crouches low in play on the sunken bastions, but soldiers and flag are gone."[16] One wonders if any guest ever investigated, or even inquired about, the location of these fabled ruins. If so, they'd have found nary a remnant, but quite possibly squirrels quarreling over a twig or leaf in arid surroundings.

Visiting writers expressed awe at the gaming resort, so much so that one suspects that their exuberance was fueled and rewarded by the hospitality of the publicity-conscious Border Barons. Reporting for *Vogue*, the nation's premier ladies' fashion magazine, Eleanor Minturn James seemed positively mesmerized. In her hands, Agua Caliente became the "Gambling heaven [note: "heaven" not "haven"] of the West. . . . A place where blossom and brilliance have been coaxed from sterile desert as though by super-human witchery. . . . Suddenly you come on a dazzling, dream-like city in miniature," where one finds "an embarrassment of diversions."

No doubt about it, Agua Caliente suited *Vogues*'s high-fashion-conscious readers:

"There is a holiday air about the gambling at Caliente," James wrote. "Nothing is taken very seriously, not even losses. If losses are heavy, it is because heavy losses can be sustained. . . . Throughout the room is a carefree light-heartedness, quite unlike anything sensed in French gaming houses."[17]

European casinos, especially the French ones, fared badly in the hands of these New World writers. Ms. James seemed pleased to conclude that "The Frenchman is no longer the croupier of the world's gaming."[18] So while French cuisine, French perfumes, and French fashions were still in *Vogue* (and all of them featured at Agua Caliente), American gamblers and their joy palaces now surpassed their famous French and other European counterparts.

A somewhat cynical and occasionally acerbic writer and poet from Oregon, H. L. Davis, who in 1935 won a Pulitzer Prize for his novel *Honey in the*

Horn, toured Tijuana and Agua Caliente for *The American Mercury* in mid-1930, when conventioneering evangelists and other church people visited the town. "Their expeditions are worth watching. They march through the crowd of drunks, sailors, oil-riggers and their sweeties like an embassy bringing a declaration of war." But the crusaders had not (dared not?) approached the bastion of Agua Caliente, where Davis surmised that patrons appreciated that "there aren't any processions of church-tourists to stare sin out of countenance. . . . The place is too pretty, maybe, to justify a moral conclusion." Like *Vogue*'s James, Davis also found the casino gamblers a happy-go-lucky lot. "They take their gambling, not religiously, not as if it were a devilish lure that had hold of them," he wrote, "but with a sort of whole-souled curiosity, as if they were out to find out what there was about the darned racket."[19] For him, then, in the casino, habitual American inquisitiveness trumped even Satan.

Church preachers and other righteous do-gooders, to be sure, hurled fiery condemnations at the resort from their pulpits and lecture stands on the other side of the international line. They positioned patrons of Agua Caliente on the road to Hell. Maybe so, but if so, these miscreants certainly enjoyed the journey, and Prohibition had only thickened their flow and quickened their pace.

REAPING PROFITS

Starting with its opening day, Saturday, June 23, 1928, crowds came in droves to revel in Agua Caliente's entertainments—but mainly to gamble. In the casino, patrons eagerly fed slot machines labeled with come-on-you-can-trust-me names like the Little Dream, Ben Franklin, the Liberty Bell, and the Umpire. They played as though the slots were not rigged and they had a fair chance to win. Although some rationalized their betting as an investment in their family's future, or at least a chance to fulfill the day's needs, most reflected the "Oh, what the hell, might as well" temper reported by correspondents James and Davis.

The inflated, unwarranted, almost giddy optimism of the 1920s (a virulent mutation of that American trait said to be spawned by thrift and hard work) encouraged customers at Agua Caliente to risk substantial stakes on a spin of the roulette wheel or toss of the dice (often while rubbing a talisman or performing a quaint, quixotic ritual for luck), and engage in card games of chance with unfamiliar (to all but regulars and professionals), foreign-sounding names such as baccarat, chemín de fer, ecarté, and faro. They also bet on and rooted for long shots at greyhound races, and when satiated with gaming, might "roam the unfrequented paths of Old Mexico on five-gait horses," play tennis, or pitch and putt on a miniature golf course. Many visitors, however, did none of these things. They came to people-watch, just to see and, of course, be seen. And throughout all, the Border Barons raked in the profits. One weekend in late February 1930 the casino grossed $460,000. Remember that the bandits who held up the money-car on the Dike expected to reap at least $100,000 in cash, a normal weekend's receipts.

Enormous initial returns by 1929 allowed the owners to speed up expansion. The Barons poured $2 million into tripling the number of hotel rooms, all air-cooled and with bath, added forty-eight bungalows with four to six rooms in each, and built an eighteen-hole championship golf course to showcase a tournament of the world's best golfers. They extended the kitchens for both the hotel and casino, enlarged the casino itself, and spent another quarter of a million dollars in additional landscaping. In one of his typical embellishments, Crofton matter-of-factly bragged that the new palm trees were European imports, but in reality Southern California produced them.

The Barons ordered the three miles of road between the town of Tijuana itself and the resort proper paved and had built an architecturally unique parking garage with an arched ceiling unsupported by stanchions or trusses; it held 150 vehicles. Construction crews erected a new steam powered heating plant with its 150-foot-high chimney disguised as a Moorish minaret, the pinnacle covered with hand-painted tiles. A $110,000 refrigeration plant cooled all structures in the complex, and an airstrip served customers flying in from Los Angeles, San Francisco, and San Diego. A lavish $650,000 spa with an Olympic-size pool, or "plunge," steam caves, and vapor baths utilized the therapeutic sulfur waters flowing at a steady 124 degrees Fahrenheit from the underground river that gave the entire locale its name, Agua Caliente, or Hot Springs.[20]

At the insistence of Wirt Bowman, the Baron most conscious of the resort's precarious dependence on the goodwill of Mexican officialdom, the entrepreneurs also built (just off premises) a large swimming pool for their Mexican employees and other Tijuana residents. Entrance was free. Some said then (and still maintain) that the Barons did so to avoid the racial tension (politely termed "possible embarrassment") of having brown-skinned locals swimming with Douglas Fairbanks Jr. or next to Jean Harlow. Bowman, however, who had worked in Mexico, married a Mexican woman, and enjoyed amiable personal and business relationships with elite as well as more ordinary Mexicans all his adult life, seemed genuinely determined to retain those strong, friendly ties. No doubt, a noxious layer of racism hovered over all Tijuana including the resort in those days; de facto racial segregation existed.[21] But Bowman never countenanced it and did small things to counter it, while at the same time protecting his income and status.

OFF TO THE RACES

The gemstone capping this cluster of opulence called Agua Caliente was the new $2-million thoroughbred racetrack, which opened in December 1929. Tijuana had featured horse racing since 1916, when the famed boxing promoter from San Francisco, James "Sunny Jim" Coffroth ("Sunny" because he so frequently beamed a smile), turned his promotional talents and political acumen to horse racing and built a track nestled up against the international line, just a few hundred yards from the main crossing at San Ysidro. His track was aged and patched but still thriving when the Border Barons determined to eliminate Coffroth's presence and build a track of their own. They offered Coffroth a share in the new venture, and Sunny Jim had no choice but to join. The Mexican government then transferred Coffroth's racetrack concession to the Barons, after which it took the new, unscrupulous owners only little over a year to ease an irate but resigned Coffroth out of racing altogether and into retirement.[22]

To attract the world's top thoroughbreds to far-off, unpredictable, and disreputable Tijuana for the winter racing season—to draw them away from well-loved, familiar, and established tracks in Florida, New Orleans, and Cuba—the Barons needed to offer huge purses and an imposing track which would become the talk of the racing world. They did both with their brash, fiercely ambitious, duplicitous, and charming youngest member at the helm: Jim Crofton, the former Eastern Oregon country bumpkin, now a multimillionaire and yearning for more.

To learn the latest about racetracks, Crofton and Wayne McAllister, the young architect hired by Baron Long to design the entire Agua Caliente conglomerate, toured some of the country's most celebrated tracks in New York, Baltimore, and Miami and then traveled to Havana. John P. Mills, a

Southern California oil magnate and real estate developer, himself heavily invested in the new resort, joined them, along with Marshall Cassidy, a nationally respected horse racing official hired to be the starter at the new Agua Caliente oval. The foursome returned with visions, innovations, and efficiencies that soon brought their track the international renown it had coveted.[23] The members-only clubhouse at the track mirrored the Mission Revival style of the nearby hotel and casino—a white stucco structure covered with baroque embellishments and topped with a traditional red tiled roof. The grandstand, less dazzling but still distinctive, seated 4,500 spectators (most fans stood in front and nearby). Workers moved an amazing four million cubic yards of dirt to level the site for structures and the track itself. What McAllister never told the Barons was that the finished racecourse was actually tilted, seven feet higher on one end than the other, "but we were up against a deadline, and it would have taken another million yards of dirt to level it off, so we left a slight slant."[24] The architect admitted that the tilt affected running times and track records, but no one seemed to notice. Noel Richardson later rode the famous Seabiscuit at Agua Caliente to a two-length victory on the tilted track.[25]

Seven stakes races marked the inaugural season, which lasted eighty-one days and climaxed on March 3, 1930, with the $140,000 Agua Caliente handicap, at that point the richest purse in the racing world; everywhere horse owners and fans took notice.

Agua Caliente blossomed overnight into a sports, entertainment, recreational, and gambling capital basking in worldwide acclaim. Sophisticates and plainer people alike declared it the place to go, while both big-time and small-time mobsters envied its riches. Gangsters had struck their first blow against the Border Barons on the Dike. Now, more than forty-eight hours after the brazen holdup, police harbored some clues, but had made no arrests and knew little or nothing of the gang itself, its size, makeup, or ties to the underworld and the resort. Investigators throughout the region needed a break, serendipitous or not, to crack this case.

Fortuitous Breaks

A frustrated Police Chief Arthur Hill sat at his big desk in downtown headquarters the morning of Wednesday, May 22, awaiting reports from his deputies scouring the field for clues to the Dike murders. Lawmen checked out the Ford and looked for a light-colored second car. Who owned the cap with the red hair, gloves, sunglasses, and clothes found in the abandoned attack-car? Hill needed a tip, a break. Plenty of possibilities had crossed his desk, a few looked promising, but none checked out. Communications with law enforcement up and down the California coast as well as eastward into neighboring states produced no results, although all assured Chief Hill that they were diligently searching for suspects.

Then, a former fellow–San Diego police officer, C. L. Cline, now a real estate broker in Los Angeles, sent Chief Hill a note saying that it might be worthwhile checking out a cocky young water-taxi captain named Jerry Kearney, known for bootlegging around Southern California. Cline had read in newspapers that a machine gun had been used in the Dike heist and remembered that after serving jail time for bootlegging the preceding year, "Captain" Kearney had openly boasted of purchasing a machine gun and had vowed to make it hot for any lawmen who tried to interrupt his future business.[1]

Hill had no expectation that the tip would lead to much, but dispatched three detectives, headed by Lieutenant J. T. Peterson, to the Kearney home on Villa Terrace, along with the state narcotics inspector, William B. Luckenbach, and his son, William Jr. About one o'clock that afternoon Detective W. H. "Chuck" O'Connor came up to the rear of the residence, and someone inside slammed the back door in his face. Moments later, Grace Kearney opened the front door and admitted Detective Peterson, one of his partners, and the Luckenbachs into her home. Young Luckenbach, who was unarmed, rushed into the front bedroom, saw a man in bed reaching for a .38 caliber pistol lying in the open drawer of a nearby stand, and shouted for help. Before the laid-up man could grab the firearm, detectives overpowered him and took him into custody. The suspect squirmed in miserable pain from a bandaged bullet wound in his left shoulder and put up no resistance.[2]

The officers also arrested Grace Kearney, who told them friends had brought the injured man to her home two days earlier, asked her to care for him, and admonished her to reveal the person's presence to no one. Grace then clammed up and refused to answer further questions.

A search of the premises turned up a blood-stained leather coat and a pair of overalls; several cans that had contained black varnish, one still half full; gun oil and cleaning rods, and three ammunition belts filled with .30-30 caliber bullet clips in the garage. Neighbors verified that Dr. Taylor (they seem to have known him) had recently visited the Kearney home on several occasions but insisted they knew nothing of his purpose.[3]

"SILENT" MARTY

The wounded man refused to talk to authorities. He moaned from pain but said nothing. Who was this stricken man who refused to talk? Was he connected to the Dike massacre? The department's superintendent of identification lifted fingerprints from the sides of the stretcher that the wounded man gripped en route to the county hospital in the police ambulance. Checked against the criminal card file at police headquarters, the prints matched those of a convicted felon, Martin B. Colson, alias Pierre Le Beaux, age twenty-five, of medium build (5′10″ tall, 160 pounds), and on parole from San Quentin prison. Police noted he had two small identifying moles on his left cheek and a small scar over his right eye.[4] He had been arrested on suspicion of grand larceny in Los Angeles in January 1925, then fourteen months later for suspected robbery, again in Los Angeles, and a month after that had been convicted of arson in the same city and sent to San Quentin for a little over a year. Police showed witnesses to the Dike shootout Colson's photo, and they identified him as one of the killers.

Judicial proceedings during the next few months filled in Colson's background and illuminated his personality. Mainly the details came from his mother, Mrs. Josephine McDonald of Los Angeles, who declared her son "one of the most tender-hearted boys I ever knew."

As proof of his sweet disposition, she volunteered, "People knew how tender-hearted he was and would take advantage of him. He wouldn't kill a chicken or a rabbit [for dinner; they were a poor family], and if they were killed, you couldn't force him to eat them. Once his little sister struck [pulled] the trigger of a gun and hurt her fingers, and she came in [the kitchen], and when he saw it [the pistol], he turned as pale as death and he couldn't eat another mouthful." Mother did not explain why the family had a gun in the house.

"Neighbors would say what a wonderful boy he was," she continued. "He would put himself out of the way to do anything for them and carry them [in his car] anywhere they wanted to go. He had an automobile ready at all times."

Martin did not smoke.

He did not drink

He was "very studious" and claimed to be a writer. He told people he had published a magazine article, but the piece was never identified, and authorities did not press the point, as interesting and revealing that article may have been.[5]

Born in South Dakota in 1904, Martin Colson was living with his mother (neither his father nor presumed stepfather are mentioned in any documentation) in Los Angeles when at the age of fifteen (he told his employer that he was seventeen to get the job) he went to work at San Pedro Harbor for the government in an unknown position, probably manual labor, as he was a self-taught auto mechanic. Colson would have been working there when Prohibition set in and smuggling became commonplace. In his mother's recollection, "He used to work there all day and work extra time at night, and he would lie down in the kitchen [at home] and sleep until morning, and he did that about three times a week. He used to say that he didn't want to hoard gold and pile up millions, that he just wanted enough [money] to have a wife and a couple of children and [so that] whenever he would meet deserving people who were down and out, [he would have sufficient funds] to help them out and straighten them up."[6] How one's ambitions change or can be changed.

There was indeed an unpredictable and ingenious strain in Martin Colson. He romanticized, fantasized, created tales, and lied. He could be brutally frank (especially about himself) and demonstrably sentimental toward those he loved. When his mother asked him to be her "pal," he put his arm around her and began to weep, "Mama, I would give half my life to be able to pal with you, but I can't pal that way." He could not live with her, so he said, because he wanted to write and needed a quiet room away from home. She did not question his work or whereabouts. "I always thought that whatever he was doing was all right."[7]

A YOUNG MAN IN LOVE

At twenty Colson was a plumber, a trade learned at United Plumbing Company in Los Angeles and then declared himself an independent building contractor. His mother remembered seeing a sign on an office at his business: "Martin Colson, Contractor," a fabrication, to be sure, but in keeping with his personality. He was scraping through life, pretending to be more than he was, aiming to do better and be someone else. A newlywed couple, Edna and Clarence "Pep" Walden, hired him in June 1924 to install bathtub fixtures in their "honeymoon" bungalow recently constructed in Harbor Boulevard Gardens, a new housing development between Los Angeles and the sea.

Martin was installing a bathtub when the remarkably pretty, twenty-four-year-old Edna Walden strolled in, one presumes to see how work was progressing. Colson became smitten with her; it was love at first sight. But she had just married, and Colson's position was untenable, except to himself. He was lovesick. He tried to earn her affection, probably with sweet words and small gifts, but she rejected him. Martin brooded. Then his wildly inventive mind devised a strategy. If he could somehow render the newlyweds so forlornly destitute that the new wife would be deprived of the "little things which women so dearly love," she would accept Martin's presents, his affection, and fall in love with him.[8]

The Waldens returned from a short vacation to find their new bungalow virtually destroyed by fire. Fire marshals and insurance adjusters suspected arson, and the Waldens fingered Colson. Authorities arrested him, and Colson confessed to entering the home with a pass key, piling up newspapers, clothing, and magazines on the kitchen floor, pouring gasoline from a five-gallon can on the heap, placing two lighted candles on top, then perhaps turning on some of the stove's gas burners (he could not remember whether he had done so or not), leaving by the backdoor and locking it. He covered up windows from the outside with newspapers to obscure public view and drove away in his automobile. Within an hour, neighbors spotted flames belching from the bungalow and summoned firemen, but by the time the blaze was extinguished, the house had been reduced nearly to cinders. Marty told investigators he had done it "to secure the love of a girl," Edna Frances Walden. "I thought that she might leave Clarence Walden, and especially so if he did not have anything at all. . . . They were not always, I thought, on very good terms, and I thought that if I did this, they might separate and I might get the girl."

Marty also said he had seen Edna since the fire.

The interrogator perked up: "What conversation did you have with her?"

"The conversation which we had was rather on the topics of life—how some people got all they wanted and others did not. She cried for her husband."[9]

The response renders more than a hint about Marty Colson's state-of-mind. Colson and Edna had mused about topics of *life*. How some people had it good and others not so, how some got all the breaks and others none, how luck showered some but not all, how any number lived at ease and many more had it tough. (Recall Colson's comments to his mother that all he wanted out of life was a wife and children and to help the unfortunate.) Then, seemingly, he indicated how much he loved Edna, but she did not reciprocate that affection. The young lady had cried for her husband, "Pep," but not for Marty. Significantly, Colson was not casually airing these feelings with buddies over a beer; he was giving a statement to police authorities who aimed to punish him.

When he chose to speak, "Silent" Marty, even if prone to fantasy, could be quite introspective about himself. Yet, his contemplations lacked clarity. Shadows engulfed his soul.

How could newspapers—and the city—not revel in the arson tale?

"FIRE SET TO WIN ANOTHER'S WIFE"
"Plumber Confesses Plot to Burn Home, Gain Love"
"Hoped Destitution Might be Chance to Press Suit"
"Held on Suspicion of Arson; Young Pair Separated"[10]

Fire Warden Flintham, however, had his doubts about Colson's confession. He called Colson a victim of "misguided chivalry," and said investigation had unearthed evidence that proved Colson's confession a hoax. The plumber could not have entered the house as he claimed he had done, and the fire had been started by means other than gasoline. A gas jet had been left open in the kitchen, and when the gas ignited (by whom or by what means was not explained), the house exploded, and neighbors rushed over to quell the blaze. The house did not burn all the way down, although it had been badly damaged.

Warden Flintham suggested that Mrs. McDonald talk to her son in his jail cell and urge him to tell the truth. She went and asked her son, "Why don't you tell them what you know about this and come home? If you don't, they will send you to prison. It is a serious offense."

"My word is given on it," Marty replied. "I couldn't say anything else if I am sent [to prison] for fifty years and then fifty years longer."[11] Such silences later became his trademark, perhaps accompanied by promises to keep his word.

Colson, nonetheless, did talk to the district attorney's office, recanting his confession, recasting his version of events, and implicating the Waldens in a scheme to burn the bungalow in order to collect $2,500 in fire insurance. It took authorities three months to sort out the intricacies of the case and to catch up with Clarence Walden, who had fled to Tijuana. When he returned, they nabbed him along with his wife. All three were charged with arson.

Josephine McDonald once again visited her son in custody and said she had learned that Edna had set the fire; she was to blame for all. "Why don't you tell the truth about this heartless, wicked woman and come home?" she asked.

Martin bowed his head and began to weep. "Mama, you don't know anything about that girl," he replied and then changed the subject.[12]

The court sentenced the two men to one to twenty-five years in San Quentin, while the complaint against Edna was dismissed. Boatmen on the docks where Colson had worked before the money-car robbery said of the arson charge, "He took it for the girl who started the fire. He did it to protect her."[13]

After fourteen months in San Quentin Colson was paroled in June 1927 and joined a promoter of small chain-store operations, first in Denver, then Chicago, and finally Los Angeles. Colson's boss had attempted to establish some 150 such stores in various cities without success. They were all underfunded, profits were slim, and they soon went broke, like the one in Denver. Employees earned little income; they hoped that the string of stores would catch on and flourish as a public convenience, but it never did.

The Los Angeles chain, called Roly Poly, was a grocery store on wheels, and as second-in-charge Colson handled considerable sums of money, reportedly honestly and without mishap. His customers, coworkers, and business contacts considered him to be of high character, a painstaking worker, honest, and gentle—even meek.

These petty businesses called themselves "corporations," and Colson prided himself as being on the board of directors of one such venture and then secretary-treasurer of another. He sent his mother a picture of the Driver Oil Building in Chicago, where he professed to have an office, but apparently failed to inform his parole officer that he had relocated to Illinois, a violation but one not pursued by authorities.[14]

We shall never know what moved Martin Colson from Roly Poly to the Dike. A dispute with his superior, perhaps, or failing business, higher ambitions, or an invitation from the mob, but in the summer of 1927, he took the alias Pierre Le Beaux and cast his lot with bootleggers and hijackers. Grace Kearney said she had known Colson eight or nine months. Cochran's wife, Marian, had urged her husband to "stop running with Marty." Exactly why he joined the mob was the sort of thing that "Silent" Marty might have talked about with confidants (like his dear Edna), but not with others.

Persistent interrogation of Colson by detectives and representatives of the district attorney's office certainly proved fruitless. He would not talk, not even give his name, to authorities, who promptly nicknamed him "Silent"—"Silent" Marty Colson. Eyewitnesses to the murders peered at the suspect on his hospital bed and identified him as one of the culprits. Police were sure they had apprehended one of the killers, but he would not talk and his accomplices—who and how many?—ran free. Jerry Kearney was a suspect, and his wife, Grace, under arrest. Interrogators worked to break her down.

ACCOMPLICES

Dr. Taylor, who had removed the bullet from Colson's shoulder, also had some explaining to do. He surrendered the bullet he had extracted from the wound, and police sent it to the Los Angeles crime laboratory to determine whether it had been fired by one of the guards (who had .45 caliber pistols) or from a machine gun wielded by an assailant. Suspicions arose that the wounded prisoner had been shot accidentally by his partner during the confusion of the robbery.

The doctor himself was twisting in the wind. He first insisted Marty's wound was an old one, or at least had occurred prior to the assault on the Dike, telling the press that the wound was "probably two or three days old." He later adjusted that to eight hours, which would place it about the time of the attack. Dr. Taylor asserted that the earliest news reports (hurried and incomplete) he had read of the holdup had stressed that neither of the Mexican guards had fired their guns, so there was no reason to believe that the bullet removed from Colson's body had anything to do with the deadly events on the Dike. Besides, Kearney and the others had assured him that the wound had been acquired in a "rum job" (hijacking) distant from the Dike.[15] Under questioning, Taylor remained feisty and confident in his explanations, and interrogators could not seem to shake him.

As long as Martin Colson refused to talk, investigators trained their spotlight on Grace Kearney. She also refused to say much, although her few confused and conflicting utterings revealed her anxiety. Grace frequented Agua Caliente (Wirt Bowman confirmed her recurrent presence there), and police remained deeply interested in how the mobsters had timed the robbery. Perhaps she could be coaxed or driven into admissions.

Grace bobbed and weaved before the law. "Jerry and I didn't have anything to do with the robbery," she said. "All those fellows come to Jerry when they get into trouble, and we didn't know how Colson got shot when he came to the house."[16] But she knew soon enough, and she knew how her husband and those visitors meant to destroy incriminating evidence before and after they fled town. She, along with Dr. Taylor. would be asked some hard questions at the official coroner's hearing scheduled the following day, May 25, at the funeral home where the bodies of the slain guards lay ready to be transferred to Tijuana for burial.

On behalf of Agua Caliente's management, Wirt Bowman expressed his thanks to San Diego's police and sheriff's departments for their diligent work in pursuing those who had assaulted the company's money-car.[17] Still, the Barons were concerned. The Dike job could not have been attempted had the gangsters not gathered inside information about the money exchange between the resort and San Diego banks. The bandits knew when and where to expect the money-car. The Barons employed their own detectives to work the case, but the results of such inquiries seldom become public knowledge. Any cleanup at Agua Caliente was done quietly and avoided outside scrutiny and scandal. Newsmen seemed not to have pressed the Barons for explanations or may have been compensated to protect the resort. The Barons guarded their findings in-house, and there they remain.

CATS AND MICE

The hoodlums who robbed Agua Caliente's money-car seem to have had no specific exit strategy. Just divvy up the loot and scatter, with perhaps a future rendezvous in mind. When the holdup plan went awry, however, even that simple formula disintegrated. Criminals, however, have a way of devising on-the-spot escapes from jams, and the ineptness of local authorities gave these fugitives breathing space. The mob's brain, Marcel Dellon, quietly assured his compatriots that everything would "work out," and then two days after the crime literally took the money and ran, destination unknown. That left Kearney and Cochran to get rid of the evidence—the money pouch and any remaining automatic weapons used in the robbery, and on Thursday, May 23, the two headed north in separate cars.[18]

Cochran and his wife, Marian, had known happier times. The *Los Angeles Times* in a touching human-interest story had charmingly reported their wedding on Cochran's boat four years earlier.

> Because she wants to be a real sailor's wife, Marian Thomas of 330 Liberty Boulevard, this city, yesterday married her sailor, Robert Lee Cochran, skipper of the water-taxi *Sea Hawk*, on the bow of that craft out beyond Breakwater Light at the harbor. It was the tenth wedding on shipboard . . . performed in two years. Friends of the newlyweds aboard six other units of the water-taxi fleet . . . attempted to catch the couple for the usual shower of rice but the *Sea Hawk* slipped away to Catalina [Island] where Cochran and his bride will spend their honeymoon. Cochran, one of the most widely known power-boat pilots at the harbor, is 21 years of age. His bride is 18.[19]

The blithe ceremony occurred less than a year after Lee Cochran had been dishonorably discharged from the U.S. Navy, which he joined at fifteen

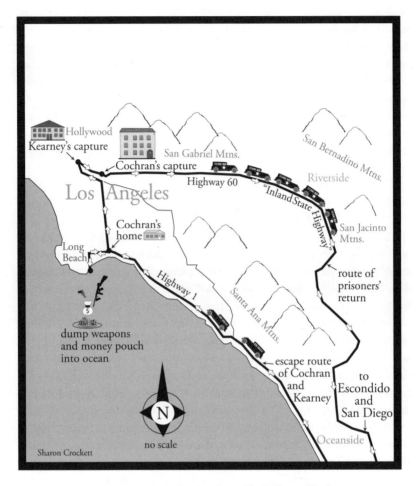

May 20–25, 1929: to Los Angeles and back. Sharon Crockett

in his home state of Georgia. He had overstayed leave and been released. The naval experience, however, had honed his nautical mechanical skills, and he became a small craft captain at the busy port of Los Angeles, which swarmed with bootleggers. Kearney plied the same waters, and soon enough Cochran, with fast money on his mind (some thought him blinded by greed), was running with a mob. Now Lee and Marian found themselves in a treacherous maze.

Kearney and his sister-in-law, Helen Maddox, drove north in a tan coupe carrying the money bag and weapons in a secret compartment behind the front seat. The Cochrans closely followed. On arrival in Long Beach, Lee told his wife to move their three-year-old daughter, along with their house furnishings and personal belongings to the home of her parents in South-gate, a suburb of Los Angeles. He abruptly kissed her goodbye, saying he would phone her from San Francisco. Leaving both women and the child behind, Kearney and Cochran drove the coupe to Long Beach harbor, where they planned to dump the incriminating evidence off the wharf. They found too many workers and visitors milling about the site, however, so they hired a water taxi with a friend at the helm and headed for more open water a mile off the San Pedro lighthouse, right about where Lee and Marian had married on the *Sea Hawk*.

Kerplunk!—into the bay went the stolen money pouch, which they first perforated with bullet holes and weighted with ammunition clips, through 120 feet of ocean to the silty bottom. Cochran's pistols followed. Back on shore, Kearney and Cochran parted company. They planned to meet in San Francisco, but until then each was on his own.

Authorities in San Diego meanwhile grilled the one bird they had in hand, Agnes Grace Kearney, a brunette whose large brown eyes were described as being warm, sympathetic, and appealing. Newsmen thought her appearance "charming," even if she had become an emotional wreck.

Police, however, were less interested in her looks and teary demeanor. They found her explanation of events surrounding the crime full of gaps and threatened to charge her with complicity if she refused to come clean. The harried woman burst into tears the evening of May 22 and sobbed out a confession, first to detectives and then William G. Cayce, a reporter with the *San Diego Union* who enjoyed special access to police matters in exchange for defending and whitewashing departmental affairs in his columns.

Cayce, patting himself on the back for the scoop, wrote for page one of the *Union* the next day, "From the city jail where she is held as an accessory to the holdup and murder of two guards of the Agua Caliente money-car last Monday, Agnes Grace Kearney, who held the key to the solution of the crime, last night gave out the first newspaper interview since her arrest late Wednesday afternoon."[20]

Grace did not exactly turn the key which solved the crime—many loose and intriguing ends remain untied to this day—but her anguished admissions gave the police inquiry some needed direction. She said that in her house she had heard Colson and Cochran tell her husband that they had pulled the treasure-car job. In naming names, she strengthened the case against "Silent" Marty, and for the first time authorities had the name of an accomplice. An immediate check turned up no arrest record for Cochran. Grace identified her family doctor, R. O. Taylor, as the physician who had tended Colson's wound and said her husband and Cochran had left for Los Angeles shortly before the police raid on her home. A crime trail was developing.

"All I know about Colson and Cochran and the others who have been mentioned in connection with this thing," Grace said, "is that they were in all kinds of rackets, including bootlegging, hijacking, and rum-running, but the only racket my Jerry had was bootlegging."

She burst into tears and then composed herself. "What worries me is where is Jerry? I can't understand why he has deserted me in this hour of need. He knows [from newspaper accounts or contacts made with confidants] I have been arrested: he knows I am innocent." More tears streaked the light rouge on her cheeks.

She thought Cochran had convinced her husband to go into hiding. And in a quivering voice, she hoped that Jerry had not been "taken for a ride" (executed by the mob) for what he knew of the Agua Caliente caper. Then Grace smiled. "But I'll get out of this thing in the end. I'm innocent and so is Jerry. We were just a couple of fall guys for trying to be good fellows [helping out acquaintances in trouble]."[21]

Pressed for information about the scope and organization of bootlegging in the state, Agnes Grace raised the eyebrows of her inquisitors. Yes, she said, a large and powerful bootlegging mob was operating in California. As reported by the *Los Angeles Examiner*, "a new ruler who sits on a throne of robbery and murder" headed the syndicate from San Francisco. His "paraphernalia" included ten or fifteen powerful automobiles, machine guns, fast water taxis, and speed boats. "The gang's bankroll is heavy and more than sufficient to provide attorney's fees, bail money and all of the other overhead of organized pillage." And there was a pension plan for the wives or sweethearts of henchmen who "get sneezed [caught]."[22]

A Mrs. Kirby Castle had come to the Kearney home only a few weeks earlier, looking for the "big boss," Grace revealed. Mrs. Castle explained that her spouse was in a federal prison for liquor law violations, and that the mob had fallen behind in the $150 monthly support payments promised her while her husband was in jail. The "big boss" was supposed to be in San Diego. It was not Kearney, but Jerry would know who he was and where he could be found.[23] This unnamed czar (the San Franciscan?) was behind the holdup on the Dike and provided the weaponry. "It was he who planned the robbery," said the *Los Angeles Examiner*, "and it was he who set the stage for the entrance of the machine gun and the methods of Chicago's gunland in the state which has been a stranger to both."[24]

Police, however, seem not to have followed up on this tantalizing lead. Authorities urgently wanted to solve the Agua Caliente crime, all right, but hesitated (or feared) to probe further, as if they dreaded (or knew) the path might lead deeply into officialdom. They focused, instead, on principals in the Dike murder case announcing, "We are closing in on them. We may get them at any time."[25]

Once the Los Angeles police learned the names Cochran and Dellon, snitches provided their local addresses. At Cochran's home the police found Marian tending the couple's baby and packing up household goods for a move to her relatives. They took her into custody. Across town, Mrs. Dellon told lawmen that she knew nothing of her husband's whereabouts. Police took her to headquarters for questioning, and when it became obvious she knew nothing of the Dike crime, they released her to go home.

Marian Cochran was a different story. Amidst tears and sobs, the frail young mother told investigators that when Jeanne Lee had brought her to her husband in San Diego, he freely admitted that he and Colson had pulled the Dike caper and spelled out details. Her story coincided with that outlined in Grace Kearney's confession. Marian said that on their drive back to Long Beach she had urged Lee to turn himself in—to face the law and its penalties —but that once at their house, he kissed her goodbye and rushed off to his destiny. When she finished her pained testimony to detectives, Marian fainted.

Late Thursday afternoon, May 24, Los Angeles police received inside information from an underworld woman who claimed to hold a grudge against

Cochran. The wanted man was still in the city, she said, and indicated where he could be found.

Deputies, guns drawn, smashed through the door of the plain but tasteful apartment at 630 Lucas about seven o'clock that evening and found Cochran, fully dressed, asleep on a davenport. A pistol and a pair of brass knuckles lay under an outstretched hand. The noise of the break-in startled him awake, and he groggily groped for his gun. A detective kicked his hand away from the weapon. Cochran realized the hopelessness of his plight and surrendered to his captors. A red-haired woman in the apartment identified herself as Cochran's half sister, Lucille Brophy. Both were handcuffed and taken to police headquarters for questioning.[26]

NOW KEARNEY

Jerry Kearney checked into the Los Angeles Cinema Hotel under the name George MacDonald that same Thursday afternoon. He walked to a nearby barbershop for a shave, and a few hours later detectives went straight to his hotel room and took him into custody without resistance. As Kearney later explained:

> Had I gone ahead and shaved myself that day, I might never have been caught. When I got into the chair and laid back for a shave, I saw a newspaper on the shelf beside the barber. My picture, covering about three columns, was printed smack on the front page. Quickly the barber looked at me. Then he looked back at the paper. From the expression in his eyes, I knew that he had recognized me. There was nothing I could do about it. After the shave, I checked back into my hotel room. But the game was up, and I knew it.
>
> The barber watched where I went and I knew he would tip off police. It was a case of waiting for the officers to come for me.
>
> They did—that night.
>
> In the meantime, I amused myself by taking a bath every hour. I was even in the tub when the police came. Had the police not arrested me that night, I fully intended surrendering myself the next day. It is not an easy game to play hide-and-seek with the law. I *know*![27]

Parts of the story of his arrest ring of familiar Kearney malarkey, but he always enjoyed making good news copy.

At the Hollywood precinct house Kearney admitted meeting Colson and Cochran at his San Diego home after the robbery and trying unsuccessfully to remove the bullet from Colson's shoulder. Dodging responsibility for getting rid of any weaponry with Cochran, he said that he overheard the pair admit throwing machine guns used in the robbery into the surf off Coronado. Jerry then confessed to burning the checks obtained in the holdup and said he then "beat it for Los Angeles."

"I don't believe in the 'heavy' crime," Kearney told investigators. "That is, I don't believe in holdups and killings. That's why I have told the truth about what Colson and Cochran did. Had they been injured in a hijacking job as they told me they had, I would have stood pat for them. But then I learned they had pulled that murder, although I realized I had become an accessory after the crime for helping them to hide and destroy the evidence."

Then he continued, "Personally, I've never violated any law but the liquor laws, and that doesn't count."

Jerry insisted that if he beat "this rap," he planned to go straight and "cut away from companions like Colson and Cochran."[28] Police seemed skeptical.

In the ensuing weeks, both informally and on the witness stand, Kearney changed details of his story many times, but throughout all steadfastly maintained that he had nothing to do with the planning and execution of the robbery itself and the ensuing murders.

"Sure I took care of Colson and my wife did all she could for him," he told the police. "It wasn't anymore than I would do for any other fellow I had known like I knew Colson. . . . But I didn't have anything to do with the framing of this job and only got into it because I tried to help a friend."

Jerry had a question for the officer holding him in custody: "What do you think I'll get out of this?"

"You'll probably make the penitentiary," came an unhesitant reply.[29]

Lee Cochran also spoke about his role in the crime. He confessed that he and Colson had planned and pulled it off, but despite the obvious, claimed they had done so with no outside assistance or advice. He and Colson in many ways were opposites: Cochran good-natured, carefree, open, smiling even in difficult times; Colson brooding, introverted, contemplative, threatening, "silent." Others easily led Lee Cochran; Marty Colson remained steadfastly his own man. One gets the impression that if Cochran were not bootlegging, he would be out sailing kites with kids; he seemed immune to gloom, while Colson carried the world on one shoulder and a croaking raven of death on the other.

Detectives questioned Cochran closely about weapons employed in the holdup. The prisoner said that .38 caliber German Luger semi-automatic pistols had been used, not dreaded Thompson submachine guns like those employed by Eastern mobsters.[30] Lee claimed to have tossed the pistols into the ocean off Coronado Island the day after the crime, and police vowed to dredge for them, but never did so.

Kearney admitted being with Cochran when the hoodlum hurled the assault weapons into the ocean. Interrogators handed Kearney a firearms catalogue and told him to identify the type of guns thrown into the surf. In the machine gun section, he pointed to a .45 caliber Thompson submachine gun and declared it a likeness to the ones discarded by Cochran. Usually when authorities caught up with a Thompson submachine gun, they couldn't wait to get their hands on it and treated it like a trophy, but in the Dike case they never recovered any weapons used by the assailants.

The fascination with machine guns was not limited to the police. A newspaper report on May 30, 1929, described how officers of the U.S. Navy, which had much of its Pacific Fleet anchored in San Diego Bay, went to the First City Bank to collect a payroll, traveling in a naval ambulance instead of a more customary car or truck. In the rear of the ambulance squatted two uniformed Marines, one armed with a submachine gun, the other with a sawed-off shotgun. Two officers up front entered the bank, one carrying a large black bag. In a few minutes they returned with payroll in hand. As the ambulance drove off, a bystander noted, "Guess the Navy isn't taking any chances of losing its payroll in a holdup like the one on the National City Dike last week."[31]

The Dike affair became the biggest event to enthrall San Diegans since 1912 when the Wobblies (the radical International Workers of the World) staged a Free Speech rally in the city center. Vigilantes, among them some of the town's leading citizens, had violently expelled the rowdy orators from town. With that sort of history in mind, police not only had to protect their prisoners from mobsters but from an aroused public.

JUDICIAL MOVES

Evidence in the Dike affair began to pile up. Public and political pressure urged expedient and unceremonious judicial action, and not a few city and county officials in this drama scrambled for the spotlight. The city coro-

ner, Schuyler Kelley, took center stage on Friday morning, May 24, at the
Bradley-Woolman Mortuary, where the bodies of the slain guards, Nemisio
Monroy and José Perez Borrego, had been examined and lay embalmed and
iced down in closed metal containers, pending their funerals and burials in
Tijuana the following Monday. Coroner's hearings are routinely called simply to establish cause of death, but Kelley, assisted by two deputy district
attorneys, Oran N. Muir and J. H. McKenney, ensured that witnesses related all they knew of the crime and its perpetrators. The lawyers wanted
top billing in the drama.

The witnesses had been carefully rehearsed as the state looked forward to
prosecutions. Eyewitnesses to the holdup positively identified Martin Colson as the bandit they had seen firing his weapon at the two occupants of
the treasure-car, grabbing the money sack, and then fleeing in an automobile driven by his accomplice. Some details in their testimony differed
from accounts originally reported in the press, but overall were more cohe-
sive and assertive, their officially schooled memories more certain and
confident.

A more composed Grace Kearney essentially reiterated her original confession to police, expanding on some particulars, and stoutly denying any
association with the murders and robberies themselves. "Jerry and I were a
couple of fall guys, and we listened to them," she said. "That is why I am in
jail and why every officer in California is looking for Jerry. Maybe they will
find him; I don't know. But when this thing is cleared up it will be plain that
neither Jerry nor I had anything to do with it."[32] The state, which would
catch up with Jerry that afternoon, thought differently.

The only starchy exchange at the hearing occurred between Coroner
Kelley and Dr. Taylor. Possible indictment for obstructing justice hung over
the physician's head.

"Why did you not report the wound?" Kelley asked at the hearing.

"It is not customary to report the business of patients," Taylor replied. "If
that is done there would probably be war [over patient/doctor confiden-
tiality] in this room right now."

"You think it is ethical to withhold knowledge of this sort?"

Dr. Taylor said that he had no reason to doubt Kearney's explanation that
the wound resulted from a hijacking gone bad.

"Is it ethical to treat a man who has been shot and keep it from authorities?"

"Yes, there is no law to affect this. When I read in the newspaper that
no shots were fired from the [guards in the money-]car, it reassured me on
the point."[33]

The coroner could not rattle the doctor's testimony and allowed him to step down, but district attorneys, listening closely, kept him in their sights.

The San Diego district attorney's office felt that by Friday it had sufficient evidence to file robbery and murder charges against Colson and Cochran plus a John Doe, presumed to be Kearney. Two Los Angeles attorneys engaged by Colson's mother had arrived the previous day and had attempted to consult with their dour client at the county hospital, but he simply shrugged them off.

The district attorney had no intention of playing delaying games with Colson. Bail had to be set. Police drove Colson to the San Diego city jail lying on a gurney in an ambulance surrounded by police on motorcycles and in patrol cars. They carried him into an adjoining courtroom on a stretcher accompanied by a dozen officers. Township court justice Eugene Daney read out loud the complaint against Colson: robbery and murder. Then a translator repeated the charges in Spanish. As Colson had maintained silence, prosecutors feared legal repercussions leading to mistrial should the prisoner never indicate—never confirm—that he had heard the charges against him. Colson did not budge, but the allegations stood anyway. Lying on his stretcher, Marty simply was "out"—or was he?

As Judge Daney rendered the complaint, a photojournalist snapped a blinding flash picture of the prostrate prisoner with his Speed Graphic camera. At the flash and the loud, distinctive "pop" of the exploding bulb, Colson jerked and his eyes fluttered, confirming for onlookers that the prisoner was only pretending to be senseless. A medical doctor surveying the scene declared that an unconscious person would not react to the flash as had Colson. That, however, would have depended upon the prisoner's level of mindfulness. Colson had been sedated for his shoulder wound. A sedated person with reflexes intact would likely blink or twitch (involuntarily?) if a flash bulb were fired off in his face.

Marty, in fact, was talking, if only to whom he pleased. Soon after the preliminary hearing a guard overheard him joshing with fellow inmates. He also began to draw childlike pictures of specific foods he wanted, an orange if he desired the fruit, or a cone next to an ice box if he wanted ice cream. Whether or not he received the diagramed requests is not known, but it was one more way in which the prisoner disdained authority and maintained personal control of himself. Undersheriff Oliver Sexson, who did much of the interrogation in this case, conjectured that "The picture writing he affects may be a game or it may be a stall. If a game, Colson is just amusing himself, perhaps, because of a mental condition of shock which is placing him in the position of a spanked child." Sexson thought the sketches might be "nature's only defensive mechanism against the serious fix that Colson has got himself into." On the other hand, he continued, "If the picture writing is a stall, Colson may be trying to simulate insanity. That might be the 'defense' he is working up."[34]

A TENSE TRANSFER

Moving the Cochrans and Jerry Kearney from capture in Los Angeles to prosecution in San Diego invited mob retaliation—a challenge to protect or snuff out its own as deemed necessary. This journey would be especially precarious because the press had hyped the confessions of the prisoners. True, their testimony, or that released to reporters, seemed limited to the Dike affair, but the hoodlums, if pressed by interrogators, undoubtedly had much more to reveal. A caravan of five automobiles left Los Angeles Police Headquarters an hour or so after daylight the morning of Saturday, May 25, headed for San Diego. Cochran joked and laughed a lot during the trip. Jerry lamented that he had been caught before he quit the bootlegging business. "I've saved a little money and was going to buy this fire extinguisher business June 1 and quit all rackets," he told detectives. "I was going to take my 19-year-old kid brother-in-law [Virgil Maddox] in as a salesman."

"The payment always comes just before you're going to quit, doesn't it?" remarked a deputy sheriff.

"Every time," Jerry smiled.[35]

Police kept the details of the journey secret. The coastal highway was the most direct route but full of traffic and heavily populated. The caravan, therefore, took the long way around, east on Highway 60 to Riverside, then through mountainous canyon backlands, past agricultural Escondido, and into northeast San Diego. If they were ambushed, officers wanted a clear shot at their foe.

The heavily armed cavalcade arrived without incident at police headquarters in downtown San Diego about one-thirty in the afternoon, where a large crowd had assembled to see the prisoners. Police lines kept things orderly. Lawmen escorted the prisoners in front of news reporters and photographers; the officers reveled in their catch. In the exhilaration of the moment, authorities did not mention that two known members of the mob, Dellon and Jeannie Lee, still ran loose or that the mob probably encompassed many more members and widespread connections. Deputies still had not found weapons used in the crime, and a principal suspect refused to talk. Many details of the killings remained unanswered, among the most important, the probable complicity of Agua Caliente personnel.

The Border Barons, meanwhile, received periodic written reminders from mobsters that the hoods had not finished with them. Truth was, at the moment, the untamed and resolute Ralph Sheldon was polishing his plan to kidnap and ransom the owners. Yet for the public and press, the Barons feigned nonchalance. They blanketed their dazzling spa with announcements of new feature attractions and hubbub about the imminent opening of the world's finest winter racetrack. Their radio broadcasts heralded the increasing patronage of royalty, Hollywood stars, politicians, and diplomats. For most, a whiff of gangsterism added an air of excitement and expectation to the mélange.

Border Babylon

Patrons of Agua Caliente were not wed only to the grand resort. Many of them desired to experience Tijuana's downtown tourist row, where a few casinos, cabarets, and restaurants offered enjoyments comparable to those at the spa, but also where innumerable hangouts featured more earthy entertainment which had long been part of the border town's reputation and charm. Visitors to the resort bragged about spending a few hours "slumming" downtown. It became a ritual. Word was out: by all means call on Agua Caliente, but be sure to sample the spicy enticements at Tijuana's city center.

Well before the arrival of the Border Barons, Tijuana possessed international repute for gratifying libertines and angering preachers. Amusement and recreation to one observer became vice and sin to another, but then, as now, few bothered to draw much distinction between the two choices. Tijuanenses occasionally complained foreigners had unjustifiably given their town a black eye, and locals periodically vowed to "clean up" the community. They still do, but such cleansings have never been more than cosmetic, and the indecorous image remains, mainly because it brings in money. Tijuana, despite widespread poverty and concentrated wealth, does not boast one of its country's highest per capita incomes for nothing.

For visitors anxious to sample something "naughty," Tijuana blended into a colorful concoction of expectations sprinkled with tickling surprises. So what that the Devil lurks there? The popular *Liberty* magazine in 1926 captured the spirit of the place in an article headlined: "Aunt Jane [literally

Tia Juana]: The Old Lady from Hell. The Story of Tia Juana, 'Where There Aren't No Ten Commandments and a Man Can Raise a Thirst.' "[1]

Such assertions, of course, deserve a sense of balance and a mark of rightness. Tijuana judged as raunchy, then and now, refers only to the one main tourist street in town, Avenida Revolución. It is barely six or seven blocks long but laced with narrow, jumbled *callejones* (alleyways with modest stores and stalls) jutting off on each side. Beyond the contrived tourist ambiance lies Tijuana proper, where locals live, shop, go to school and the movies, and enjoy cultural events and fiestas. They pursue ways of life that do not much interest tourists and that residents mean to protect for themselves. In this way it is like defining the wondrous metropolis of New York City as just Broadway or the Theater District or Times Square. As with "The Big Apple," however, mention of "Tijuana" conjures up all sorts of images (stereotypes) largely irresistible to outsiders. Moths to the flames, some might say, but sheer delight for most.

The persistent lure of Tijuana seems to nudge, even challenge, something quite profound in the American psyche. Crossing the border evokes a feeling of "freedom," not just raising hell and having a good time, but as *Liberty* put it, a sense of "playing hooky from the world's greatest supervisor of morals—Uncle Sam."[2] Well said, then and now.

EARLY DAYS

Government-hired surveyors drew the international line to separate the Californias in the mid-nineteenth century after the U.S.-Mexico War. Approaching its Pacific Ocean terminus, the new demarcation cut through the extensive rural lands of a well-to-do prominent politician and military man, Santiago Argüello, who enjoyed residing in San Diego and cattle ranching around the Tijuana River valley. An astute and practical businessman, Señor Argüello would become the first of many individuals to work both sides of the line to his benefit.

By the 1880s the main eastbound wagon road between San Diego and Yuma was not much more than a rutted, meandering trail, looping through a sliver of northern Baja California's high desert country. The Mexican government established a customs post on its side of the crossing, San Ysidro, as it was a place to show the flag and collect meager duties (and larger bribes), even if most proceeds went into pockets of the collectors and their superiors.

Hotels and restaurants began to spring up around the port of entry, a general merchandise store and post office on the U.S. side, while across the line tourist curiosity created a patchwork of flimsy stalls and shops selling simple handicrafts like seashells strung into jewelry and little horses fashioned from the long arms of a tule cactus. Manufactured goods included rough woolen blankets, brightly colorful manufactured serapes, and picture postcards. For refreshment one could taste a beer, crude tequila, or fiery mescal, and sample enchiladas, tacos, *carne asada tortas*, and shrimp ceviche. Vendors aimed their fare at callers who yearned to inch onto foreign soil but dared not go much farther.

A writer for the *Nation* surveyed the scene in 1889, and the first thing he saw "was a young burro with silky hair not longer than a Newfoundland dog. . . . The dividing line is occupied by a restaurant which bears the modest name of Delmonico's"—after one of New York's finest. Opposite he found "a cigar store which has the suggestive title of Last Chance. There are more saloons in Tijuana than buildings. . . . Some are in tents, open in the front, with a counter in the center and empty beer barrels for seats." The correspondent encountered "only so many Mexicans with their ponchos and serapes seated on their haunches. I told myself, 'My God, this is a desolate place.' "[3]

Desolate, perhaps, but oh, so exotic. Seedy and strange, perhaps, but intriguing and positively entertaining. These observations and emotions paved the earliest paths to Tijuana. Mexicans staged bloody cockfights and amateurish bullfights for visitors. They broke broncos and raced scrawny horses around nearby open fields, which recalled a not-so-distant Wild West.

"Across the border" also became a haven for sporting banned in the United States. With bare-fisted boxing outlawed in California, for instance, promoters scheduled such matches for a shabby bullring constructed just a few hundred yards from the international line in Tijuana territory. At the start of a fight in 1886, Mexican soldiers halted the proceedings for lack of licenses. The organizers understood that sort of shakedown, handed the soldiers six dollars for permits, actually *mordidas* (bribes), and the fight went on, refereed by none other than Wyatt Earp, visiting San Diego in search of a land deal.[4]

So this affair outlined the way Mexicans did business. A proprietor could not tell when officialdom would step in to rewrite, cancel, or befuddle an agreement. Some two thousand boxing fans showed up about two years later to witness a double bill, but with the pugilists already in the ring, the district governor declared that American spectators could not watch fights on Mexican territory. Speculation had it that the governor had not received his fee. He did not, however, ban the matches, so the promoters moved them into an open space abutting the international line, where from home soil, Americans still had a clear view of the bare-knuckle fights.

In the preliminary bout two San Diegans, a 145-pound blacksmith named McLaughlin and a 158-pound longshoreman, O'Neal, who courted a grudge against one another, slugged it out. In round four,

> O'Neal came to the scratch breathing heavily and looking as if a dozen cats had been scratching his face. McLaughlin, with the aid of his second, staggered to the center of the ring, but when the second let go of him he fell back into a half kneeling position. He put up his hands and looked to see where his adversary was, when the latter struck him a blow full in the mouth, sending several teeth down his throat, and he keeled over again. Immediately he arose to the same half-kneeling position, and while streams of blood poured from his mouth, he fought wildly in the air, trying to reach O'Neal. The latter walked around him, and to end the fight struck McLaughlin a heavy blow on the side of the head, laying him out insensible.
>
> This ended the fight. Both men will be laid up for weeks.[5]

As Tijuaneses have long contended, for a price they gave Americans what they really wanted and could not experience at home.

Not everyone, of course, went to Tijuana to witness blood sports, drink themselves senseless, challenge Lady Luck, or steep themselves in licentiousness or carnality. Most crossed the line for a short look-see, to sample foreign soil (for many, an exciting first-time experience), and buy a cheap souvenir. The great majority who visited resembled those two thousand conventioneering schoolmarms who visited in 1899 to have a "high old time on Mexican soil." There "they reveled in the delightful pastimes of the land of sun and cactus, sipped daintily at unknown Mexican beverages, burned the lining out of their stomachs with chile con carne," and returned home "with a warm taste in their mouths and a pleasant recollection of a grand time."[6]

The territorial governor himself welcomed the teachers with the district's military band, folkloric music, and dances that utterly stupefied and scandalized a journalist with the group. "The gorgeous uniforms of the dusky musicians from the peninsula and their lively Spanish airs," he wrote, "stirred the blood of the native Indians, and some of them entertained the ladies with as uncouth and outlandish dances as ever human eye witnessed. Their scant and tattered attire, hanging in streamers around their angular forms, wafted hither and yon by the writhing motion of their sinuous bodies; their glittering eyes, set in bushy brows as black as night, flashed with scintillations of light and seemed to illuminate faces as hideous as any pictured in Dante's inferno."[7]

"Dante's inferno" expresses a sentiment that some have felt toward Tijuana over the years. They call the town "Hell," but most think of it as "Hell-Raising."

The wide-eyed teachers certainly loved the spectacular, climaxed with a great fandango, or *bal masque*, where the mescal flowed freely, "good fellowship prevailed, and merriment was unhampered by those rules of social etiquette which in America preclude the possibility of a gentleman dancing with his inamorata with his spurs on." The joyful school group returned to San Diego "satisfied, but not surfeited with the glimpse it had had of high life in the land of the Montezumas."[8]

With San Diego undergoing a land boom in the late 1880s, the Argüello family made the major decision to subdivide and sell their most valuable property, a mesa lying on the west bank of the Tijuana River. An engineer drew maps to block out streets, parks, and properties for a new city, and sales began in 1889. The first buyers were merchants from Ensenada, but American entrepreneurs soon followed with multimillion-dollar plans for a new Monte Carlo. Reformers in the United States picked up the signals, and the *Los Angeles Times* warned, "If their plans are carried out, San Diego will be converted into one of the wickedest cities in the world, and the whole of Southern California will be affected, more or less."[9] The promoters dropped the scheme for lack of funding, but Lady Luck proved to be an impatient and persistent mistress.

DAME FORTUNE ARRIVES

Only 242 people lived in Tijuana proper by 1900, and another 108 farmed on the outskirts. Two curio shop owners, Alejandro Savín and Jorge Ibs, lived well, selling wide-brimmed sombreros with swirling embroidered decorations, Mexican flags (the Tricolor), and inexpensive silver jewelry, along with Tijuana pennants, picture postal cards (as they were called), garish and often puzzling plaster-of-Paris figurines, and other ordinary tourist buys. A few small restaurants offered the typical tacos and burritos, beans and rice to be washed down with beer, tequila, or *muy fuerte* mescal. For variety, two Chinese eateries heavily spiced their chop suey with hot salsa to suit Mexican taste buds.

The pace quickened in 1908, when the national government approved certain types of licensed gambling for the district. It legalized dice, card games, and horse racing, while banning roulette and slot machines. The lawmakers reasoned that when bettors possessed some personal control over their fate, they could gamble, but when the game involved pure luck, it should be outlawed. The law, in other words, approved games of "skill," but prohibited those of chance. It sanctioned chess, billiards, dominos, stud poker (cash only, no chips), and various card games such as *panguingui*, but outlawed roulette, monte, "twenty-one"(blackjack), and other games of sheer fortune.[10]

To many the division seemed artificial and arbitrary, but lawmakers meant to authorize gambling for those with talent and know-how, while banning it for players beholden to Lady Luck. They noted that games dependent on the spin of a wheel or the drop of a coin could easily be rigged, while in games of skill, experienced players could defend themselves against cheaters.

The specter of class distinction is clear in such legislation. Protect the poor and untutored against themselves and swindlers. Better that they till the soil and man the manufacturing assembly lines. Leave gambling to elites.

Mexico's gaming particularities remained all during the heyday of Agua Caliente and the multitude of other gambling establishments in Tijuana. The Border Barons and other operators paid them little attention. Roulette wheels spun and slot machines clanged everywhere, protected by law enforcers paid to look the other way.

Such arrangements, nonetheless, had their drawbacks. An operator could fall out of favor with officialdom or become the victim of the complaint of a competitor. He could suffer the repercussions of political change or be threatened by enforcement unless he upped the ante. If a proprietor refused to employ the relative of someone with clout, his place could be shut down temporarily, for a long time, or for good. It happened often, and even the Border Barons felt the sting. The price of doing business in Tijuana remained high and uncertain, which created a get-rich-quick mentality among gaming owners.

CROSS-BORDER PARTNERSHIPS

In the United States, Progressives demanded an end to political boss-ism and business monopolies and thundered against "vice." They equated sporting with mental, moral, and physical debauchery and called it a national disgrace. Boxing, horse racing, gambling, prostitution, and liquor all caught their wrath, and state legislators driven by shrill, self-righteous minorities steadily imposed bans on such pursuits. Pressures forced proprietors of such activities underground or into a search for new outlets, which took them south of the border where deals could be made.

But deals with whom? Mexico exploded in Revolution in late 1910 and the country soon collapsed into ferocious civil war, with no one faction in charge for very long. With the country's leadership in doubt, official appointments in the far northern federal district of Baja California became a revolving door. There was no opportunity for municipal plans and programs. Certainly, there were no elections. Powerbrokers simply took for themselves what they could garner during their few months in authority.

Vice establishments represented their main benefactor. For a steep stipend, which they pocketed, they issued a raft of permits for casinos, prostitution, cantinas, liquor stores, and horse tracks. Mexicans and Americans, many with prior experience in gaming and sporting operations, gobbled them up. Taxes on these concessions funded civic improvements and also went into the pockets of politicians and their henchmen. Once turned out of office, these short-termers disappeared into the United States or obscurity elsewhere.

Tijuana's tourist district emerged as a circus and boomtown when small-time vice entrepreneurs settled in with the customary retinue of professional gamblers, card sharps, bunko men, prostitutes and their pimps, who thrived and proliferated in such a roiling atmosphere. Damon Runyon (who later came to know Tijuana) would have called it a colorful cast of characters. Others were not so impressed. "Fleeced Bare at Tia Juana" became a common theme for press accounts about tourists victimized by hustlers: "The average American citizen is easy for them," the *Los Angeles Times* wrote, "and when Stephen Emerson, a young Kansas farmer, wealthy in his own right and supposedly 'city broken' to the wiles of the 'bunco' game, fell into the gambler's clutch, the result was one well-plucked young man with much less self-esteem."[11]

The *Times* headlined another account,

> Fleece Lambs at Tia Juana: Nearly $10,000 was lost today in a Tijuana gambling joint by tourists. . . . The place was filled with spectators watching the players who proved to be capers [participants in the scam]. One of the capers finally shouted to shut the doors, that everyone was in on this round, as he had won the royal prize. As he put down his money, everyone in the room rushed to place their money, and when all the money of the crowd was on the counter, a man, purporting to be a police officer, ordered the people to get out, and the crowd left without its coin.[12]

"Pluggers" rode sightseeing buses from San Diego to Tijuana and inveigled "suckers" to lose their money. The stories of their schemes are wondrous, as are those of victims who took revenge. Most of these tales are funny and harmless, but, then, some are tragic.

ENTER CANTÚ

This free-for-all prevailed for a few years, but as the balance of power and military victories shifted toward one contender on the national front, northern Baja California began to stabilize. A semblance of order descended on the territory, even if tourist diversions remained unruly and rousing. An ambitious, devious, colorful, personally engaging army cavalry colonel, Esteban Cantú, distinguished by his handlebar mustache, orchestrated the modulation. He had been sent to the border in 1911 to stem the intermittent incursions of anarchists from the United States and came to command the federal garrison at Mexicali. But which side to support in his country's raging civil war? Cantú maintained an independence from the central government that allowed him to hold onto his rule of the territory. He posed here and double-talked there, feigning allegiance to one side and then another. Only in mid-1915, when it became more certain that the Constitutionalists under Venustiano Carranza (also Alvaro Obregón and Plutarco Elías Calles) would eventually triumph, did he declare for their cause. Despite understandable reservations concerning his loyalty, Carranza rewarded Cantú with the governorship of Northern Baja California. He only meant "for the time being," but Cantú schemed to make it more lasting.

Everything and nothing changed in the district under Cantú. Concessions for casinos and other "entertainments" went to the highest bidders. The interim governor reaped notable personal profit from the exchange but also directed millions into public improvements which helped to build a satisfied constituency. Dirt roads got paved, schools built, electric lighting installed, and architecturally attractive municipal buildings constructed. His military and para-military forces maintained order; his fine military band provided pomp. The United States, anxious about the First World War raging in Europe and suspecting that German spies were working the border, welcomed a cordial Mexican neighbor. In Cantú, diplomats and sportsmen alike finally had someone with whom to deal. The governor immediately had a waiting line of prospects.[13]

Cantú is a reminder that Americans did not impose big-time "sporting" (commonly called organized vice) on the other side of the boundary, but worked toward that goal in tandem with Mexicans in gainful but testy formal and informal business partnerships, if seldom as trustworthy and predictable friends. Cantú and a seasoned American sportsman named Carlie Withington became just such partners, not hand in glove, not peas in a pod, but as profiteering comrades of convenience.[14]

Carlie became known as the "Border Pleasure Prince," meaning the King of Border Vice.

King of Border Vice

Carl H. Withington, known as Carlie, avoided publicity and did his dealing quietly under the table and behind the scenes. He was smart and tough-minded, and came to the international line at the age of forty with gaming experience. He had run a string of fancy, highly remunerative bordellos around oil-rich Bakersfield, California, before being pressured by moral reformers to try Baja California, about the time that Cantú became governor and deals, while still competitive, became more certain.

Carlie seems to have inherited his fortune-hunter, strike-it-rich aggressiveness from his father, Robert, who around 1850 caught gold fever at fifteen and abandoned his comfortable Pittsburgh home for northern California's rowdy gold fields. He mixed his panning (no luck there) with more lucrative freighting and boomtown amusements and later moved his profitable wagon transport business to the Bakersfield area, where he bought large properties in what later became the center of town. Then, quite unexpectedly, Lady Luck spit out Black Gold near his holdings.[1]

Spectacular oil strikes in the early 1900s (best remembered for photos of their astounding, spewing geysers) attracted swarms of young workers and soaked the city of Bakersfield in hotels, dance halls, saloons, bordellos, casinos, and bundles of loose cash. Mostly single men in their vigorous twenties, the drillers, roughnecks, riggers, and roustabouts craved more and more macho diversions. Carlie provided them with the largest, most raucous, pleasure palace in Bakersfield, called The Owl, and laundered his mounting earnings through similar ventures around town, as well as movie theaters and apartment houses in San Francisco and Los Angeles.[2]

There was a lot of con-artist in Carlie Withington. In 1910 he wooed Maybelle Thoene, a pretty, young San Francisco girl, with promises of great wealth and marriage. He represented himself as the owner of the flourishing dance hall in the city's downtown at Sutter and Pierce and vowed to sell it and other properties in exchange for her hand in matrimony. When Maybelle checked his story, she discovered that no one in the neighborhood had ever heard of Carl Withington. She sued him for $100,000, alleging breach of promise, but the case does not seem to have gone further, and Carlie fled town.[3]

BAKERSFIELD AND BEYOND

By no means did Withington hold a monopoly on Bakersfield's bordellos. Many of the town's most prominent citizens competed to own such flourishing businesses—from which local taxes funded a bounty of civic growth and redevelopment. The good citizens of Bakersfield frowned on vice but for the most part basked in the rake-off. As always, however, there was a segment of the community, the moralists and allegedly more ethical individuals, who not only decried sex and sin but also the corruption that such licentiousness can bring (and in this case, brought) to city hall. Reform was in the air; it was sweeping the nation, and Bakersfield could not escape it.

Betterment and righteousness seeped into town along predictable lines. Ban women from public places where liquor is served. Fence off the "Tenderloin" (red-light) district; make it a bullpen, stockade, or "concentration camp." Keep prostitutes off the streets and out of sight. Reverend B. Dudley Snudden, the hard-shelled pastor of the town's First Methodist Episcopal Church, told his congregation in ringing fundamentalist fashion what Christ would find if He came to Bakersfield. "The multitudinous saloons," the minister wailed, "the bleary-eyed, whisky-soaked men, the jumble of shacks and cribs [small whorehouse rooms with a mattress on the floor and sink in the corner], the women of shame and their lecherous paramours, and the advocates of the white slave traffic [the importation of white women from other states for prostitution] as a necessary evil, [these] are advertisements of the city's immoralities."[4]

Under the pressures, proprietors of prostitution houses began to squabble with one another over slumping business. One hotel owner complained to the sheriff that she was losing guests because of the proximity of Carlie Withington's famous brothel. In response, Carlie hired two detectives from San Francisco who proved that her hotel also provided prostitutes for *its* house guests, but because her business had fallen off, she blamed Carlie. Authorities dismissed her complaint.

Such exchanges, however, soon became moot. In December 1911 a local judge ordered that the state's ban on prostitution be enforced. It was illegal to place a woman in a whorehouse or to make a livelihood off her earnings.[5] Close down the red-light district. Of course, such laws did not stop prostitution; the ladies simply dispersed to other venues, but the edict knocked Carlie Withington out of business. So he went south.

By the summer of 1914 Withington was in Mexicali, already the owner of a small casino. Certainly Withington knew of the wide-open, rip-roaring, Wild West atmosphere saturating the territory just below the boundary, but did he have contacts there? Did he know Cantú, for example, or did he speak Spanish? (He did have a Spanish-speaking mistress.) Or did he just wander in and take his chances? Unfortunately, the historical record is mute in response, even if his obituaries pictured him as a rags-to-riches sportsman. Answers to the questions may be of interest but of minor importance. What mattered is that Carlie and Cantú did speak the same "language."

Whatever his finances, Carlie dressed in one of the $150 suits that he bought four at a time and headed straight for the district's seat of government in Mexicali, a thriving community of seven thousand, awash in gambling, prostitution, dope (opium largely for the town's large Chinese farming population), barrooms, cantinas, and hotels. Call it entertainment for all types (blacks and Asians had their own clubs) against a musical backdrop provided by some of the best jazz and ragtime musicians of the epoch. Carlie knew from experience how to maneuver in this heady, if risky, cutthroat ambiance with something to lose but much more to gain. It was a gambler's paradise. He had opened his bustling casino in town, but the competition from fellow Americans in the same business chafed and hemmed him in. The "King" craved to expand his domain.

Racketeers like Carlie Withington strive to monopolize their business interests. Few succeed, however, and most are forced into a détente or partnership with competitors, even as outside challenges continue. Such rivalries are especially virulent and incessant in Mexico, where personalities govern rather than law, and those who have the power to grant monopolies (concessions and permits) are invariably hounded by family, friends, and ever more wealthy petitioners for *entrada* into a fruitful enterprise already granted to others. Contracts are regularly undermined and broken. Both the Border Barons and the King battled the same monster.

Carlie Withington paid Governor Cantú $8,000 a month for exclusive rights to gambling and prostitution in the sporting section of Mexicali, where he opened a larger and more opulent replica of his infamous Owl club in Bakersfield; for old times sake, he named it El Tecolote (The Owl). Famed for its spectacular floor shows, gambling salons, cafeteria, and whores, 220 of them—Anglos, Mexicans, blacks, Orientals, Indian peoples (of uncertain nationality), and mixed-bloods—its notoriety spread throughout the hemisphere.[6] Jack Tenney, the composer and lyricist best remembered for his "Mexicali Rose," played piano in a seven-piece band there, and recalled the place as "rough and unattractive," but distinctive for its "profuse display of large, potted, imitation palms," still a staple in so many of Southern California's garish taverns with their replica brass rails and laminated oak floors.[7]

With its capacity of three thousand, The Owl featured thirty-five poker tables, others for keno, twenty-one, and monte, and six roulette and faro wheels, where odds were said to be eighteen-to-one in favor of the house. Cribs for the prostitutes and their customers were located toward the back of the building. Outside, a separate, smaller building called The Little Owl, was for "coloreds," or blacks, who had their own diversions. The Owl was said to earn its owner a million dollars a month, a blatant exaggeration but good propaganda.[8]

F. C. Spayde, a *Los Angeles Times* reporter, took a tour of the place in 1919. Leaving Los Angeles at 10:30 at night, he arrived at the border town of Calexico (opposite Mexicali) at 10 o'clock the next morning. He could see The Owl in the distance across the border. It was one of the largest buildings in town and the only one with an electric sign that blinked away even in daylight. The club proudly advertised:

Both night and day
Across the Way
You will never find closed
The Owl café.

Across the line Spayde found plenty of English spoken and dollars the currency of choice. He sauntered into The Owl expectantly and later wrote, "If old Bill Hart ["Westerns" movie star, William S. Hart], stern, dusty, had walked into The Owl with his two huge revolvers, and had held the crowd at bay while Dorothy Dalton [top-billed silent film actress] jumped from the stage in her spangles of a queen of the Yukon and been taken away by Doug Fairbanks Sr., the tenderfoot from the East, who was swinging from one of the chandeliers, the picture would have been complete." Spayde described the main hall as "a barn of a place, 200 feet long, a rough wooden bar along one side, twenty or more rough wooden tables at which crap, keno, twenty-one, and roulette [are] being played by Mexicans, American ranchmen, Hindu [actually Chinese] farmers and Japs, and off in a corner, discreet women drinking with men, an orchestra of eight men playing modern jazz at the upper end of the room, while couples dance and others watch from pens, or boxes, in a balcony above—such is The Owl."[9]

A free cabaret offered vaudeville and other acts backed by a $2,000 piano, and an employee projected motion pictures on the wall of a side room. The club's manager asserted that the place was secure, no gun slinging, no fights like in the Gold Rush days of California. Daily proceeds at The Owl topped $5,000 (some $60,000 in today's currency).

Spayde called the clientele "the new frontiersmen of the new West."[10] For him, at least, America's frontier had hardly closed, as some claimed, or changed much in character. It had only shifted southwest and straddled the border with Mexico.

ENTER THE A.B.W.

The Owl was only one jewel in the King's crown, and Carlie coveted additional sparklers. In 1915 he took in two partners well seasoned in gaming and kindred activities: the reserved Tennessean Marvin Allen, who shunned the spotlight, and the more colorful, outgoing Frank "Booze" Beyer, card sharp and philanthropist. Together the trio molded the A.B.W. syndicate—Allen, Beyer, and Withington. Carlie knew Allen from oil boom days around Bakersfield, where they both operated in the entertainment business; Allen specialized in liquor and Carlie in prostitution. It is likely that they came to the border together, bent on revitalizing fortunes truncated by reform. Allen helped run Mexicali's Owl and before long, at thirty-three, found himself in charge of supplying spirits to the syndicate's expanded holdings which ran along the international line from Algodones, below Yuma, Arizona, west to Tijuana near the sea. Like many such compatriots seeking social status and a more salutary reputation, Allen spent much of his cash breeding and racing thoroughbreds. His ranch outside of San Ysidro produced horses that earned him high stakes, but casino gambling was in his blood. When The Owl slowed down at the end of another busy, lucrative day, Marvin would gather his card dealers together and try to beat them at draw or stud poker, and he usually did.[11]

"Booze" Beyer was a picturesque show-off. Once he had earned his nickname by downing prodigious draughts of liquor, he acted like his honor was at stake if he did not sustain the pace. He traveled a familiar road through mining boomtowns en route to the border. Born in Norristown, Pennsylvania, he graduated from two colleges distinguished for mining engineering, the University of Pennsylvania and then the Missouri School of Mines. "Booze" worked for the Guggenheim mining interests during flourishing times in Alaska and then Colorado and followed the chaotic silver strikes in Nevada during the first decade of the twentieth century. Along the way he gave up engineering for professional gambling; he was known as a card sharp "from the old school," in other words, akin to the legendary Mississippi riverboat breed, reported to have known every trick of their trade.

As the mines played out, the border beckoned, and in 1915 Beyer, a millionaire approaching forty, arrived in Mexicali set for new ventures.[12] Withington appreciated his gambling income and expertise, and along with Allen they incorporated the A.B.W. With Cantú's protection (for a high price), the A.B.W. came to dominate border "entertainment." The King of the Border now had his princes. Their tentacles reached everywhere, including the little wooden hotel by the hot sulfur springs of Agua Caliente, outside Tijuana proper, which they thought someday could be developed into a unique, elegant resort, the most splendid ornament of all in the crown.

A.B.W. was not the only game in that town, however. Tijuana's Jockey Club, reinforced by several well-to-do American sportsmen, thirsted to build a horse racetrack (*hipódromo*) with adjoining casino, and in 1915 the project hurtled forward. It was the right time to do so. Private money was available and the outcome of Mexico's revolution more predictable, as the Constitutionalists gained control and neared formal diplomatic recognition by the United States. Tourism was rising, and San Diego had announced a magnificent hemispheric exposition for mid-year to celebrate the opening of the Panama Canal. Thousands and thousands of visitors with money to squander would be coming to Southern California, with any number of them relishing a peek at naughty Tijuana.[13] Cantú made ready to welcome them.

First the governor had to "sanitize" Tijuana, not scrub the place clean of what do-gooders called "vice," but rid tourist areas of riff-raff that pestered and sometimes frightened visitors rambling there for a sample of border life but nothing more. Critical comments from across the border, such as those leveled by May Bliss, the sister of Michigan's former governor, rankled Cantú. The *San Diego* Union printed the letter she wrote to the city's mayor in which she blasted Tijuana. "I have been all over Europe and America," she said, "in the slums of Paris and London and every large city of this country, but I have never seen anything so openly insolent, corrupt and defiant of law or decency as Tijuana."[14]

Many who read that letter undoubtedly said to themselves, "That's my kind of town," but Cantú thought it best to announce a "clean up," and in the spring of 1915 ordered his police and henchmen to round up the town's more obvious hustlers, smugglers, con artists, drifters, hop-heads, pimps, and other such streetwise "nuisances"—many of them refugees from America's raucous mining camps and roughneck urban tenderloins—and toss them back from whence they came. Mass detentions followed.

After twenty-five dapperly attired bunko artists signed affidavits that they would never come back to Tijuana, Mexican military officers escorted them to the border and turned them over to San Diego police who took them to jail in big sight-seeing cars so the public could appreciate its lawmen at work. Once there, the chief of police, Kino Wilson told the conglomeration how unwelcome they were in one of America's finest cities and ordered them out of town. At this point, the con men disappear from the historical record, but chances are they were soon capping new "suckers" in some other border town.[15]

Tijuana made ready for a typical Mexican fair, timed to coincide with the California-Panama Exposition in San Diego. To assure that tourists tasted the varied and piquant spices of Latin life, the Jockey Club induced a politically prominent mining magnate, Antonio Elosúa (brother-in-law of Francisco Madero, a martyred leader of the Revolution) to establish a *feria típica*, a traditional Mexican fair, in Tijuana. "*Típica*" meant cockfights and bullfights, a gambling hall, colorful folk dancing, *carnitas* (pork fried in bubbling cauldrons of fat), tasty tamales, margaritas served in gigantic glasses, and endless stalls vending a mélange of cheap curios and picture postcards which showcased sexy women and advertised a boozy time for all. Visitors mailed thousands of those cards back home with a handwritten message—"Having a good time," "I dared Tijuana," or "Wish you were here" —and many of the recipients assuredly wished that they were . . . or were glad that they were not.

Elosúa also advertised acts to make Americans feel more at home while abroad. Walker's Ragtime Demons played jazz, and nearby a Hawaiian troupe danced the hula, both slow and fast versions. He announced booking a circus from San Francisco, vowed to stage a twenty-round boxing match between Jack Clark and Mexican Kid Carter, and claimed to be fetching variety shows from Europe's famed Monte Carlo. Much of his bombast proved to be dishonest; the promised acts never appeared, but conventioneers like the Aetna Life Insurance group still arrived at San Diego's Santa Fe train depot shouting, "Where's Tijuana?"[16]

The *feria* opened on the July 4th weekend, 1915, under the banner "Where Everything Goes and Where Everyone Goes."[17] That seemed appropriate, and twenty-five thousand visitors, including high-rollers from Coronado's plush resorts, piled through the border gates that weekend. The main, or at least most lucrative, attraction took place in a gaming casino erected just outside the premises of the hipódromo with its medley of gaming tables (cards and dice), slot machines, and roulette wheels, most of them illegal but running full blast to assuage the appetites of patrons and owners alike. A bar, a dining area, and an immense dance floor featuring a notable ragtime orchestra offered respites from gambling. As described in the *Los Angeles Times*:

> Patriotic Citizens in their frantic efforts to celebrate the fourth at the gaming tables at Tia Juana . . . were so zealous they exhausted the supply of silver dollars. But that did not delay the game, as the men behind the tables quickly supplied them halves. . . .
>
> More than $12,000 [ten times that in today's dollars] was won yesterday [July 4] over the tables in the Casino and just how much changed hands is hard to say. The crowd, many of whom were women, good-naturedly fought to bet their money at the tables, and unable to find a place at the table solaced themselves by dancing. [San Diego had banned cabaret dancing earlier that year.]
>
> Society from Coronado and San Diego deserted the '49 [gaming] camp at the

[San Diego] exposition, where gambling has been the favorite attraction, to go to Tijuana where one could gamble without bothering about scrip. All day today and yesterday big cars of the millionaires of Coronado and guests at the hotel [del Coronado] could be seen traveling on the auto roads between the peninsula city and Tia Juana. Debutantes and matrons usually seen dancing at the dansants at Coronado rubbed elbows with the Mexicans celebrating the Fourth in the dance hall of the Casino.[18]

The spectacle must have made Cantú cackle, while an ever-opportunistic Carlie Withington schemed to muscle in on the mounting profits.

THE PONIES, AT LAST

Finally, la crème de la crème: thoroughbred horse racing. Its time had come. Since many U.S. states had banned betting on horses, owners, breeders, trainers, bookies, jockeys, shills, and fans yearned for an unencumbered out-let for their favorite sport. California's famous tracks, Santa Anita (Los Angeles) and Tanforan (San Francisco) had closed down; even better-known tracks back East had been forced to empty their paddocks. Who knew how long such bans might last? Strident "Hallelujahs" (Christian reformers) paraded triumphant in 1915, and while there had always been considerable outspoken and underground resistance to the reform wave, there was no hint of any impending change in the dominant national mood. If one wanted to bet on a horse race (and what's the fun, if one cannot), you'd best look south of the border. Tijuana was ready.

Or was it? The question of who held the official concession to build and run any such racetrack remained in contention. The problem stemmed from Mexico's political upheaval. A governor would grant the permit for a track and then be deposed. Alberto Madero, brother of the slain revolu-tionary president, Francisco Madero, headed a syndicate including several Americans well known to racing in their country, and claimed to hold a concession from Pancho Villa to construct a million-dollar track in Ti-juana. But in the spring of 1915 the Constitutionalists drove Villa from power, Cantú became acting governor in northern Baja California, and he promptly awarded a new contract for racing to the Tijuana Jockey Club, managed by H. J. Moore of San Diego and backed by several Dallas mil-lionaires, as well as Adolph B. Spreckels (shortened from von Spreckelsen), son of the late San Francisco sugar magnate who was currently amassing a new fortune in California petroleum. The Constitutionalists expressed dis-may at Cantú's independence, promising to deal with him later, and the plan for a racing oval advanced when the Madero group agreed to partner with the Jockey Club in constructing a track.[19]

With deep money pockets, the Club then contracted with two of the West Coast's best known sportsmen—"Sunny" Jim Coffroth and Baron Long—to bring the project to fruition. Coffroth, a San Franciscan, earned a hefty income as one of the country's top two or three boxing promoters. People called him "Sunny" because of his contagious smile and unbounded vigor. It was also said that he deserved the name because it had never rained on any of the hundreds of outdoor boxing matches he had promoted over the previous decade or so.[20] Long courted and hobnobbed with Los Angeles elites, politicians, movie moguls, and stars in his string of prominent hotels, gaudy nightclubs, and epicurean restaurants. People considered the easygoing, rotund glad-hander a connoisseur of fine food and the good life; like many in his social group, Long was also enamored of thoroughbred horses.[21]

Both men were talented, obstinate, personable, and experienced practitioners in a tempestuous, hazardous world. They also had a history of flimflamming and strong-arming rivals.

The Jockey Club tendered Coffroth and Long 5,025 shares of stock to build a $175,000 hippodrome. The block of stock assured them control of the board, and the first thing they did was to eliminate Moore from any say-so in the enterprise. Then they went after Madero, demanding that he give additional money to the project. When Madero refused, they also removed him from the board. Finally, the pair declared that they need not spend so much money on the complex. They could build for less now and make improvements later, when the enterprise began to profit. Board members disagreed, but Coffroth proudly announced that construction was under way, with racing to begin on January 1, 1916. Indeed, the inaugural was a highly anticipated event with celebrities, politicians, touts, and racing fans of every stamp making plans to attend. "Sunny Jim" declared it the recrudescence of thoroughbred horse racing for Californians and followers everywhere.

"They're Off"

James Wood "Sunny Jim" Coffroth was the son of James Wood Coffroth, one of California's most distinguished early lawyers and legislators. The elder Coffroth had been a Pennsylvania printer who joined the Gold Rush in 1850, became wealthy, socially prominent, and stayed on. Home-schooled by his astute mother in San Francisco, young Jim was expected to follow in his notable father's footsteps. Indeed, he took a few halting steps in that direction, both as an office boy for several well-known law firms and then as clerk of the San Francisco courts and secretary to several State Superior Court justices, positions considered to be "juicy plums" around city hall as well as solid steppingstones to political good fortune. But Jim loved the clamor and glamour, the excitement and wheeling-and-dealing of the boxing world (and "sporting" in general). He would hang around the Baldwin Hotel just to see the great John L. Sullivan stroll into the bar, and he sneaked into his first fight disguised as a Western Union messenger boy rushing inside to deliver a telegram. Then, while in his early twenties, passing through New York City on a pleasure trip to Europe (Coffroth was an avid reader about and aficionado of ancient Greece and Rome), he called on "Big Jim" Kennedy, an Eastern premier boxing promoter, who was in a funk because boxing had just been outlawed in his state. Coffroth did not miss a beat: "Why not try the Golden State?" Why not work California—together? There was nothing shy about this visionary, young, red-headed, blue-eyed Irish-American, a gambler at heart.[1]

THE PROMOTER

In 1903, the new partners staged in San Francisco the historic rematch between "Gentleman Jim" Corbett and Jim Jeffries, the heavyweight champion. Three years earlier Jeffries had taken the crown from the "stylist" Corbett after twenty-three bruising rounds. This time around, Jeffries hurt Corbett early and "Gentleman Jim's" trainer threw in the towel in the tenth round. The following year, Coffroth and Kennedy toured the west with a stable of fighters, including Jeffries. In a preliminary bout, Coffroth spotted the potential of a Polish-American named Stanley Ketchel, whom he groomed into one of the most entertaining middleweights in boxing history.[2]

"Sunny" Jim earned a reputation for taking such chances with young boxers, as well as for a number of sparkling innovations he brought to the entire game: the highest purses ever offered at the time ($20,000, toward a quarter million in today's dollars), referees dressed in tuxedos, and fighters in flashy silken robes embroidered with their names. He lowered ringside seat prices to $20 and insisted that legitimate ticket-buyers got their chairs. (Counterfeit tickets and other seating scams ran rampant at the time.) And he sharply curtailed complimentary tickets—"freebees." As generous as he came to be for genuine charities, Coffroth the promoter abhorred giving out "comps," a personal quirk that he cultivated and advertised.

In fact, Coffroth made his money not so much on ticket sales for an event but on exclusive rights he negotiated with boxers to make motion pictures of their fights. Theater owners, many of them small store-front operators, sopped up these grainy, jumpy films. Blue-collar Americans loved them; most any moving picture fit the fad of those days, but nothing aroused a spectator's passion more than blow-by-blow slug fests. For all his promotional contributions to the fight game, Cofforth, a marvelous raconteur with an encyclopedic knowledge of the sport, was named to Boxing's Hall of Fame.[3]

There were, of course, stumbles along the way. In 1906 political reformers spotted Coffroth and his sidekicks (who controlled most of the city's boxing events) trying to bribe San Francisco's Board of Supervisors for prizefight permits. As a result, he was banned from promoting fights in the city. In reply, he simply moved his business outside city limits to neighboring Colma. Police then cited him for circling the law by selling tickets to Colma fights from the poolroom of his saloon on San Francisco's notorious Barbary Coast. Such stunts left Coffroth in "bad odor" with municipal officials. The press spoke of his "continuous performance game of befooling the public."[4] He also ran on a short fuse, and newspapers gloried in reporting that he had tossed a jar of pickles at a rival or tweaked the nose of an antagonist. He got in a Tenderloin bar brawl in 1909 and stabbed a notorious gambler, "Butch" Geggus. Next day, "Butch" played down the incident: "It was just like a fight that friends would have when they were drinking, see? And no damage was done me. See my face? There ain't no marks there, is there?"

Newsmen found the gambler's cheeks "undented." They also reported Coffroth "out of town for a few days."[5]

TIJUANA'S NEW TRACK

It took only sixteen days to build the hipódromo in Tijuana, a clue to the quality of construction. (Remember, Jim was out to save money.) Materials came from the San Diego area; labor, except supervisors, from Mexico. The one-mile oval track lay just below the border at the present San Ysidro entry. A long, covered wooden walkway connected the crossing to the grandstand, which seated three thousand spectators. An immense cafe, slot machines, and other gaming opportunities lay beneath the stand itself, while a low dirt levee protected against any rise in the nearby river, on the other side of which lay Old Town Tijuana. Fervent expectation surrounded the first races on New Year's Day, January 1, 1916. The racing world and beyond was watching, its field glasses trained on the little border town standing big on this special day.[6]

"Sunny" Jim's disposition and reputation guaranteed clear skies and a fast track for the start of the racing season. Both aristocratic society and the hoi polloi made their plans and reservations for grandstand boxes at the gala event. General admission cost a dollar. There was, however, a buzz concerning the possibility of rain, not that the threat impeded anyone's preparations. Still, there was a conundrum at play: San Diego, indeed much of California, had suffered drought throughout 1915, and although sprinkles fell toward the end of the year, the city council worried about its overall water supply, and in mid-December it hired a pluviculturist, a rainmaker, named Charlie Hatfield, to fill the large Morena reservoir in the mountains sixty miles northeast of downtown. A thin man of forty with a strong reputation for rainmaking, Hatfield was given a year to work his skills at the reservoir, built to hold 15 billion gallons but at the time only a third full. Success would reward Charlie with $10,000 (nearly $200,000 today), and the towers from which the moisture accelerator worked his magic produced intermittent sprinkles by the end of the year. His accomplishments, however, caused worries: "Fill the reservoir, Charlie, but don't ruin opening day at the races," was the cry.[7]

Los Angeles had faced a similar predicament in 1904 before its beloved annual New Year's Rose Bowl Parade. The city had hired Hatfield to produce rain, and the rainman had done the job and then some, but the citizenry feared that it might shower on its famed parade, scheduled for Monday, January 2, 1905. An anonymous individual wrote a delightful poem about the quandary:

> Oh mister Hatfield, you've been good to us:
> You've made it rain in ways promiscuous!
> From Saugus [a Los Angeles County railroad hub now merged into the City of
>   Claritas] down to San Diego's Bay
> They bless you for the rains of yesterday.
>   But Mister Hatfield, listen now;
>   Make us this vow:
> Oh, please, kind sir, don't let it rain on Monday!
>
> And other doings full of fun and glee
> For New Year's Day are planned abundantly
> From Saugus down to San Diego's Bay
> And they will bless you on tomorrow's day,
>   Great moistener, if you will listen now
>   And make this vow:
> Oh, please kind sir, don't let it rain on Monday!"[8]

Hatfield (or nature) complied. Although it rained earlier in the day and drops fell where Hatfield had sown seeds five miles off the parade route, no rain fell on marchers themselves. (Since its inception, rain has dampened only 10 of 119 Rose Bowl Parades.) But a decade later Hatfield could not entirely turn off the spigot for the Tijuana races. Although opening day fared relatively dry, it had rained on and off for several days before the big event, turning the track and surroundings to glutinous muck. Nonetheless, that hardly diminished the ardor and joviality of ten thousand spectators relishing the scene that momentous day. Jim Coffroth, now well into his forties, put on his best smile, saying, "It's a heavy track but that won't matter. Frequently races of this sort are the most entertaining."[9]

Crowds approached the oval in automobiles ranging from light roadsters and Model-T Ford flivvers to more elegant Cadillacs and Pierce-Arrows, which their owners craved to show-off—as well as in lumbering thirty-passenger touring cars. The roads were in terrible shape, and slow going, barely over the six-miles-an-hour speed limit. Still, passengers waved merrily as they bypassed horse-drawn buggies headed in the same direction. Most fans, however, rode from city to border in electric trolley cars or took the thirty-minute trip in special carriages on the steam-powered San Diego–Arizona Railroad, both owned by the San Diego magnate, John D. Spreckels, himself a rabid racing fan.

Governor Cantú showed up carrying a cane in one hand and a poinsettia in the other. Surrounded by Mexican officialdom, he entered between files of school children waving Mexican flags with his regimental band signaling his grand *entrada*. Hollywood celebrities abounded, among them the comedian Eddie Foy and the director Mack Sennett. Coffroth's boxing buddy Jim Jeffries was also there, along with baseball's Frank Chance, of "Tinker to Evers, to Chance" double-play fame. Los Angeles Sheriff J. C. Cline added a touch of officialdom, and the ubiquitous Baron Long, stockholder and hospitality professional, catered food, drink, and other refreshments, while acting as official greeter for the occasion.

Multimillionaires attended this memorable extravaganza along with day laborers, prompting a newsman to quote (supposedly) King George: "All men are equal on the turf and under it." That, of course, was only half true. Still, Tijuana had a democratizing effect on the Sport of Kings. It was more a West Coast than an East Coast crowd: "Mexican *soldados*, slouching in their uniforms and puffing cigarettes, added their usual touch of color. . . . Flashy looking sporting gentry with 'headlight' [big diamond] necktie pins, flaring topcoats and an air of prosperity . . . Milady Fashion (in) gorgeous furs, silver foxes and brown foxes predominating . . . sables, ermines and seal skins . . . fur-trimmed coats, fur-trimmed skirts and fur-trimmed boots."[10]

In such resplendent attire, they were fortunate that it did not rain.

Fans thronged the cafe beneath the stands. Customers—many of them women—packed the adjoining saloon four deep. Some quipped that the ladies seemed not only to represent the gentler but also the thirstier sex.[11] The betting ring lay just to the east, with the paddock and jockey's quarters nearby. One hundred yards past them stood stables for four hundred horses. A few Easterners representing renowned stables had sent mounts to the meet, but luring the best to Tijuana proved difficult. Snooty owners of the greatest horses tended to look down their noses at racing their equines on an untested track in a disreputable town. The gatherings at Coffroth's oval, nevertheless, reminded regulars of celebrated days at Santa Anita, Ingleside, and Tanforan, all great California racetracks now shuttered by reform. If one looked at the pulsating stands though a gauze-covered lens, one could see the outlines of the illustrious Sheepshead track off New York's Coney Island or mingle with French peerage at the famed La Piste des Aigles (The Race-Course of the Eagles) at charming Chantilly.

THE DELUGE

In the next few days of this incredibly muddy racing season, crowds came despite the intermittent drizzle. Charlie Hatfield (or Mother Nature), meanwhile, was hard at work. People never quite knew what Hatfield was up to; he kept the details secret. They suspected he mixed certain chemicals and dispatched vapors upward into the clouds from his thirty-foot tower at the end of the reservoir. Booms were heard, smoke rose from the site, and rain, then more rain, fell on ever-buoyant "Sunny Jim's" racing domain.

Drizzle, rainfall, and then a deluge accompanied Hatfield's labors. It poured for ten straight days, and on January 18 the Tijuana River overflowed its banks and berms and swirled through the racing grounds. The grandstand itself stayed put, but fast currents swept most of the other structures toward the sea. The torrent separated Tijuana from San Diego, and ministers throughout the region gloated that the Devil had got his due.

A week later a new storm created even worse flooding in and around San Diego. Torrents washed out railroad lines and halted transportation north and south. That left only ocean transport and the Marconi wireless for communication. The dam on the Otay reservoir in southeast San Diego crumbled and sent a wall of water through settlements to the ocean. Some estimated the wave at forty feet, perhaps exaggerated but still formidable. Twenty to fifty people, mostly Japanese fishermen living in modest dwellings on the shoreline, died in the onslaught. The topography, the face, of all

San Diego changed dramatically; new wrinkles, crevices and scars appeared —yet within a decade or so nature mercifully restored the surface, and the new, deeper contours became familiar. In all, almost thirty inches of rain fell in the high-desert Morena district that January, and the reservoir filled up. (Average annual rainfall for the area was about twenty inches.) It looked like Charlie had done his job despite the destruction so much precipitation had unleashed.[12]

Hatfield felt due his $10,000, but the town demurred. Newspapers discredited him and called the flood a natural disaster. "All I have to say is that Morena has had 17½ inches of rain in the last five days and that beats any similar record for the place that I have been able to find," Charlie calmly replied.[13] Human moisture accelerator versus natural phenomenon; there was much at stake here.

In the wake of the tragedy that engulfed their town, San Diego residents filed lawsuits worth $3.5 million, claiming the city council had negligently hired a rainmaker without pondering the damage he might cause the community. If Hatfield had produced that much rain, then the city was culpable. "I entered into a contract with the city and it was up to the city to take the necessary precautions," Hatfield stated.[14]

The council waffled—who could prove the source of rains? In a sarcastic gesture, the city offered to pay Hatfield his $10,000, but only if the rainmaker agreed to pay off the legal actions brought by aggrieved citizens against the city. Charlie responded with his own lawsuit. Sparring between the two sides went on for years. In two flood-damage cases brought against the council, judges ruled the catastrophe an unfortunate natural happening. Yet the city paid off several claimants willing to settle out of court. Hatfield wilted, then gave up, and his case was finally dismissed in 1938 for lack of prosecution. Without doubt, however, San Diego welshed on its pact with the rainmaker.[15]

REBUILDING

Jim Coffroth was neither cowed nor dismayed by his misfortune, and by disposition he could not admit defeat. Throughout life, at least outwardly, he gave and took heavy punches like the pugilists he promoted. Reviewing the near total devastation of the hipódromo complex, he optimistically told a friend, "This isn't so bad, George. All we have to do is turn the river, dam it up and build a new track."[16] As the flood waters receded around the ruined track, he promised publicly that the track would be quickly rebuilt and the hundred-day racing season resumed. For financing he turned to his friend, Adolph Spreckels, fellow stockholder and member of the board.

Precisely when the Spreckels clan first met Jim Coffroth is not known, but they frequented the same lofty social circles in San Francisco, where liaisons between well-off and prominent families and entertainment and gaming celebrities were frequent and cozy. Yacht and jockey clubs, charity balls and community banquets, high-roller gambling, and more often than realized, business deals brought them together.

Coffroth visited Aldolph Spreckels lamenting his loss but determined to rebuild. How much did he need, Dolf asked.

"I think I can get the job done with a little credit for about $30,000," Jim replied.

Spreckels handed him $40,000 (not quite a million today) but declined to accept any note. "If I didn't know you were good for it," he said, "I wouldn't lend it to you."[17]

The track reopened on April 15 with the Spreckels Handicap its featured race, and when the enormously successful season ended on schedule in June, Coffroth exuberantly proclaimed Tijuana "one of the great cities of the world for its horse racing."[18] He then headed east, resolved to attract the nation's best-known owners to send their thoroughbreds to his track for the next winter racing season. As always, Jim stretched for the top. His success with the track, however, created strident new challenges from aggressive competitors, one of them, Carlie Withington, with his sense of entitlement to all gaming proceeds in Tijuana. Carlie believed he had paid Cantú for the monopoly. Now Withington aimed his gaze at Coffroth's track, and Antonio Elosúa's decision to sell his feria presented an inroad.

Elosúa had grown disenchanted with his feria. Crowds, tired of advertisements for events that never materialized, dwindled along with profits. Besides, the politically active Elosúa much preferred his country's capital to the provincial little border town catering to gringos, and so sold (with Governor Cantú's blessing) the entire enterprise to Carlie Withington.

Carlie noticed that many who patronized the hippodrome visited neither the feria nor other attractions in Old Town Tijuana. After the races, for the most part, the track crowd just turned around and went home or to lodging in San Diego. Therefore, rather than expanding the feria's Monte Carlo, Withington opted to build an exquisite, new $100,000 (now $2 million) casino right on the border, with an inviting, manicured garden balcony overlooking the track. Its location gave Withington first crack at tourist trade. To lure and keep gamblers on the premises, the new Monte Carlo served decent enough 75-cent meals, and the dance hall stayed open all night. Carlie also incorporated many of the feria's most tourist-beguiling spectacles (such as bullfighting) into the casino's bloated schedule of ancillary attractions. Coffroth and associates fumed at the intrusion into their neighborhood, but with Cantú as his protector, Withington seemed untouchable.[19] The First World War and the U.S. government, however, intervened. They stanched the flow of some of Carlie's best customers—free-spending Navy personnel stationed in nearby San Diego—and temporarily banked the King's ambitions.

NAVY TOWN

Despite second thoughts about the location and serviceability of its great bay, the U.S. Navy decided (after strenuous lobbying by the city) to make San Diego a major West Coast defense base. President Theodore Roosevelt himself settled the debate by sending his Great White Fleet to the port in 1908, and the town rapturously received the sailors. Still, it took the single-minded work of the district's congressman, William Kettner, to do the necessary schmoozing and cajoling in Washington to convince Admiral of the Navy George Dewey of San Diego's unique position to serve the country's needs. Once Dewey came aboard, the House of Representatives appropriated money to dredge (widen and deepen) the shipping channel in the bay. Call it pork barrel legislation, if you wish, but William Kettner proved himself to be a tough and persistent lobbyist who earned his title as "San Diego's Million-Dollar Congressman."

When Assistant Secretary of the Navy Franklin Roosevelt visited the 1915 California-Panama Exposition in Balboa Park, the future president hinted that the naval training base in San Francisco Bay might best be shifted to San Diego. The city expeditiously donated the land required, and Congress budgeted money to "construct the most beautiful and picturesque military post in the United States." Almost overnight, San Diego had become a fledgling "Navy town."[20]

"Navy town!" San Diego had plenty of raucous joints in which sailors could entertain themselves while off duty or on leave. The city council periodically debated in exceedingly graphic (including purple) phrases just how much vice should be allowed to flourish in town. Moralists, of course, wanted to crack down on all of it. Others, claiming practicality, thought the growth of any port city with a burgeoning naval presence demanded a peppering of licentiousness. The sailors themselves decided the issue at the close of the First World War. They warned that if the city closed down their favorite haunts, they would take their paychecks to San Francisco to have some fun, a threat that tempered any reform movement.[21]

Nearby Tijuana with its wide open gambling, whorehouses, and cantinas was, however, another matter. Preachers, ranking naval officers, and others saw that peppery community as corrupting the morals and endangering the health of young people. (Is it only the young who get corrupted and diseased south of the border?) A watchdog group, the United Veterans of the Republic, wrote Washington that the A.B.W. "was responsible for drawing diseased prostitutes and 'dope' peddlers and as a result increased the sicknesses and diseases to an alarming extent to say nothing of the narcotics addicts" among young servicemen at San Diego's Naval Training Center.[22] The Navy lectured its sailors about the perils of venereal disease. (Vets still cringe when reminded of those training movies that featured raw, festering sores on private parts.) It imposed regulations and curfews. The YMCA provided writing paper and stamped envelopes encouraging the young men to spend their free time writing home to mother or a sweetheart, but boys would be boys.

Only when the United States sent an expeditionary force to France in April 1917 did the government act with authority and close the border for the duration. American entry into the First World War demanded increased surveillance at all crossings, and officials proclaimed: "Tijuana, as a tourist town for Americans, will cease to exist during the war."[23] And the gates swung shut.

Official explanation for the drastic action, one with some justification, concerned suspected German and Japanese activity below the line, deeper down in Baja California. Bits and pieces filtered to U.S. military intelligence that the Japanese planned to establish (with barely disguised Mexican consent) a naval base midway down the peninsula. German spies and sympathizers were thought to be operating closer to the border. Rumor, or perhaps more than rumor, had it that Germany had orchestrated the infamous raid by Pancho Villa's ragged forces on Columbus, New Mexico, in the spring of 1916 and triggered the failed Black Jack Pershing retaliation. Pershing's expedition had, in fact, created a war scare with Mexican Constitutionalists.

The Germans and Japanese would have been happy to see a war between the United States and Mexico, forcing Americans to concentrate more on their southern boundary than European intervention. And the aggressive Japanese looked to establish whatever presence they could in the Western Hemisphere. At the same time, Mexicans had daydreamed of retaking territory lost in the U.S.-Mexico War—or the War of U.S. Intervention, as they put it. None of these scenarios seemed too far-fetched for the intrigue at play.

In June 1917 a respected journalist, Clare Kenamore, asked in *The Bookman*, "What is Germany doing in Mexico?" He reported that a "highly intelligent, pleasant, companionable" German civil engineer working out of Baja California had produced "the best maps I have seen" of California's (southeastern) Imperial Valley, and "has as clear and comprehensive knowledge of the region as any man in the valley."

Then the warning: "Knowing this man to be a trained soldier, one can easily see what an immense opportunity he now has to serve his country. This Lower California engineer is but one of many—men of his type are strung along the border coast to coast."[24]

Such intelligence naturally concerned Washington, and the boundary remained sealed (if porous) for the duration of the war. There was also the need to impede "slackers," men who refused military duty and sought safe haven in Tijuana and beyond. Their full story has yet to be told, as is that of soldiers who deserted to receive better pay working as military specialists for Mexican rebels.

WARTIME

Now there was no tourism in Tijuana. The town suffered but survived. While Governor Cantú provided essential social services, the entire pueblo was placed on hold. James Coffroth closed down the track—temporarily, he emphasized—and signed on with the United War Work campaign, promoting boxing matches that raised more than $1 million to buy gymnasium and athletic equipment for military camps around the country. Ranking politicians, military officers, and the public at large lauded his achievement. A popular sports columnist writing for the *San Francisco Chronicle* suggested that Jim had earned a break from niggling laws that restricted his personal boxing promotions.

> If there was ever a time when Federal and State officials could afford to wink the other eye and overlook infractions of the law, it is with reference to Jimmy

Coffroth's proposed handling of the Willard-Fulton match either in New York or Chicago. Both New York State and Illinois have laws that prohibit long distance [many rounds] bouts—or any bouts for that matter.

Also the United States bans the transfer of fight films from one state to another. And if Coffroth puts over what he wants to put over that our soldiers may be provided with gymnasium and athletic equipment and upkeep for the same, there will have to be a general disposition on the part of officials to look the other way.[25]

Whether or not Coffroth received special dispensations in these matters is not known; winks leave no paper trails.

The war ended six months after the United States joined it. Soon after, the border gates lifted, and gaming vigorously regenerated south of the border, but with new puzzlements. In the wake of the conflict, two new surges bore down from opposite directions upon little Tijuana and border life. To the south, the Constitutionalists had taken control of the government. They still needed to mop up remnants of opposition and otherwise consolidate their control, but with a new constitution in hand, they proposed widespread reform to be directed and enforced from federal headquarters in Mexico City. Their insistence made Cantú's position dubious and challenged the survival of his outlander regime. With the sympathetic governor gone, what might happen to the likes of Carlie Withington?

To the north, the national mood of the United States was in transition. Deviations from traditional nineteenth-century habits and fashions, values and morals, had been observed earlier in the new century, but now much of postwar America seemed disillusioned with notable portions of its past and more determined than ever to break loose from accustomed restrictions and entanglements. This new openness certainly unveiled its downside in virulent racism, ideological xenophobia, and authoritarian repression of civil liberties, but it also heightened curiosities, enlivened experimentation, and freed expression, all of which encouraged people to sample titillating places like Tijuana.

Prohibition sealed the compact. It gave folks an excuse (or even a reason) to go south of the border. Law does not slake thirst, just the opposite. A billboard posted by preachers at the crossing warned visitors that they were on "The Road to Hell," but a writer for *American Mercury* found in Tijuana "no sins more gorgeous than those enjoyed by every Massachusetts Lodge of Elks at its annual fish-fries prior to 1920 [Prohibition]." Noting that most tourists he saw seemed to be "middle-income people—babbits—from the Mid-West," he concluded:

> They either have sorrows to drown or pleasures to accelerate in a way that is relatively difficult and expensive and sometimes socially inexpedient at home. . . . The more one frequents the Mexican border resorts, the more one is brought to realize that the great American gift for depravity is for playing devilish rather than being it. . . . The real thing, obviously and always sought in a border debauch, is to carry the memory of from two to nine drinks back to some town like Coon Rapids or Memphis, and be able to say at the next gathering of cronies or lodge brothers: "Lemme tell you. Li'l ole Juarez [or Tijuana] is some town to raise hell (feminine equivalent: raise the roof) in, and boy, we sure raised it."[26]

"Road to Hell." "Town to raise hell." No doubt about it, as it roared into the 1920s, Tijuana (at least its main tourist district) was one hell of a town.

Prohibition's Bounty

The Eighteenth Amendment laid John Barleycorn to rest at midnight on January 16, 1920. The King was dead; long live the King. At a funeral staged in Norfolk, Virginia, the once merry ole gent reposed in a twenty-foot coffin, which had been borne to the church by a team of horses, followed by a down-hearted, definitely deflated, if not totally defeated Satan. None other than the fire-and-brimstone evangelist Billy Sunday thundered at the wake, "Goodbye, John. I hate you with a perfect hatred."[1]

No turning the other cheek for Billy Sunday at this merry (as opposed to solemn) funeral; liquor had its place, and that place was Hell.

State and local dry laws had been creeping into American communities bit by bit for many years, but few celebrated the event like Billy Sunday. When bars closed down in Los Angeles, the mourning was sentimental and real. On Main Street,

> two bands, and a jazz band, moved from studio to studio, and a confusion of pretty women, gaily colored lanterns, and artists of all sorts and descriptions held sway.
> Exactly at midnight, a pageant, "The Rise and Fall of John Barleycorn" was staged in the spacious hall of the building. . . . Beautiful cabaret girls, dancing, poetry, song, everything that old John ever claimed for his own were represented.[2]

At The Eagle cafe, a short distance away, "a large audience gathered around the coffin surrounded by candles stuck into the mouths of empty bottles, and some of the mourners reinforced themselves with long, bitter draughts of the things that were about to pass out." A speaker delivered a "sad, sad, oration" claiming that John had come to the end of his career "from a solar plexus blow delivered by a bunch of longhairs while the boys were away in the trenches." (Many historians believe that the country's participation in the First World War contributed to a national mood which hastened ratification of the Constitutional amendment that sealed Prohibition.) "But," he sobbed, "costly flowers and empty beer bottles bring no condolences to the dead."[3]

Most Americans carried away arm-, car-, and truckloads of liquor from outlets at the stroke of imposition of the dry laws and treated the advent of Prohibition as casually as a New Year's Resolution: here today in a moment of reflection, or a harmless, perfunctory ritual (quite often to assuage guilt); forgotten tomorrow. The citizenry enjoyed flouting the new law, twisting the tiger's tail. At least they considered the statute nonbinding—for themselves. Besides, enforcement was underfinanced and minimal; police and other authorities readily took bribes to keep the liquor flowing. Plain and simple, Prohibition corrupted officialdom.

Bootlegging encouraged petty criminals to organize in mobs and then syndicates. Uneducated tough guys became millionaires; brutal killers morphed into Robin Hoods and heroes. Frank Sinatra had it right when he crooned, "Chicago, Chicago, the town that Billy Sunday couldn't shut down." The Windy City, with its proximity to Canada, may have been the most wide-open city in the country during Prohibition (with New York, Cleveland, and Detroit close seconds), but even much smaller towns, and those like San Diego with reputations of being sunny and safe (and dull), rippled with their share of subversions and crookedness, debaucheries and derelictions, opportunism and profiteering.[4]

Of course, Americans could still get liquor in their own country. Stills, which formerly had steamed and smoked to avoid taxes, now produced illegal, and often lethal, alcohol for profit. Home brewing was popular, but the quality of product was poor and could be dangerous to one's health. San Diego's coroner reported that adulterated liquor killed nine people in 1926: two from wood alcohol, three others from canned heat (Sterno, or jellied alcohol), and four due to acute alcoholism caused by bad booze.[5] Industrial alcohol could be turned into drinkable liquor—maybe. With a doctor's prescription, one could still purchase alcohol. Legal near-beer might be strengthened. More than two hundred thousand speakeasies sprang up around the nation. Bootlegging became the underworld's primary occupation—an industry, at that. Smuggling (the best way to get decent liquor) flourished. And, finally, only thirteen of the forty-eight states declared themselves bone-dry. Twenty states permitted the manufacture of alcohol but with restrictions. People designed ingenious schemes to slake their thirst for liquor, and there was the additional thrill of breaking the law. Still, in most such cases, there was risk. But for those in reach of international borders, why change one's habits and take unnecessary chances?

TIJUANA'S REVELRY

Southern Californians and visitors to the region flocked to Tijuana. Banner headlines read:

GAIETY, PONIES, GAMING, RUM AND DANCE HALLS BOOM BELOW THE LINE.
TIJUANA HOME OF HAPPY HYSTERIA

"The thing is rather psychological," one article explained. "Americans—that is, the pleasure-loving, free-spending, hip-hip-hurrah sort—are feeling exactly as the boy does who plays hooky from school. The Eighteenth Amendment is with us and the tendency in certain quarters is to commit transgression against this latest addition to the Constitution. Mexico, or that bit of sand and sun, sage brush and hills that comprises Tijuana, offers a playground, and every day thousands of perfectly upright, law-abiding Americans are going out to play."[6]

No wonder people went to Tijuana for diversion, "to cast off restraint, and kick up their heels." Social reformers in the United States had dug deeply, not only into drinking habits, but into other social customs, such as dancing, or at least, touching while dancing. A Los Angeles ordinance warned: "Dancing with the cheek or head touching one's partner is forbidden. The male can place his hand only on his partner's back, between the shoulder and waist. The female can place her hand only in her partner's left hand. No music 'suggestive of bodily contortions' can be played. Moreover, women are forbidden to smoke in any room or place adjacent to a ballroom or dance academy."[7]

The law, it seems, permitted waltzing with probity and decorum, but how about trying the Charleston (swirling beads, knocking knees, and crossing hands), camel walk, tango, and fox trot or the hootchy-kootchy:

"Hey, mama, you better talk to Sue. She's doing the hoochi coochi coo. They're swirling in the kitchen . . . ," according to the popular tune of the day. No holding back this kind of energy, and Tijuana beckoned.

Despite continuing challenges to his ownership, capacity crowds filled Jim Coffroth's racetrack on the weekend of July 4, 1920. The matinee cowboy favorite Tom Mix and the outrageous Fatty Arbuckle mingled with spectators. (Before his legal difficulties, Fatty frequently rented two railway cars for private parties to and from the track.) More than 65,000 visitors crossed the border that weekend, 12,654 of them in cars. San Diego literally ran out of gasoline trying to fuel all the vehicles, forcing out-of-towners to spend the night in a hotel, to the delight of proprietors.[8]

A.B.W. had rebuilt the Monte Carlo (critics called it "The Devil's University"). The sumptuous casino featured fourteen card games, eleven roulette wheels, ten craps and two poker tables, four chuck-a-luck outfits, and two wheels of fortune in a gigantic hall that held up to a thousand gaming patrons. Carlie Withington wanted a first-class restaurant on the premises and interested (it did not take much convincing) Baron Long in building a chic dining and dance hall next to the casino where showtime featured jazz bands and flamenco dancing. Long called it the Sunset Inn after a similar establishment by the same name he owned on the Santa Monica Pier.

Gloria Swanson, the acerbic, humorous social critic Will Rogers, and the comedians Harold Lloyd, Charlie Chaplin, Buster Keaton, and Lew Cody could be seen among faces in the crowd at the gaming complex, along with Mary Astor, Norma Shearer, Mary Philbin, and Clara Bow. Chaplin was a steady newsmaker. Once, when returning home after a soirée south of the border, Chaplin was stopped by a San Diego policeman for speeding in his Locomobile. The comedian was unfazed. Overhead he saw a plane carrying his friend, Jack Pickford, back to Los Angeles, flagged the pilot down onto a nearby field, scampered aboard and waved to the cop as he flew off.[9]

The Universal Studio mogul Carl Laemmle and Joseph Schenck, chairman of United Artists, were among the specially treated highest-of-the-high rollers at the next-door track. Schenck, known to have dropped $100,000 on a single race, would arrive next to his chauffer in the front seat of his limousine, while his beautiful wife, Norma Talmadge, studied in back with her French teacher.[10]

In 1923 the millionaire cosmetician Helena Rubenstein hosted an exclusive outing for twenty-one guests at the Sunset Inn, among them David P.

Barrows, president of the University of California, and Cornelius Vanderbilt Jr. This tony casino-with-eatery was *the* place to play and be seen.[11] It was, moreover, a social phenomenon. In these early years of the movies, traditional bluebloods normally stood apart from Hollywood's studio owners and stars, most of whom had worked their way up from modest beginnings, but clubs like the Sunset brought them into proximity, and mutual interests quickly developed into comfortable friendships, marriages, business associations, and showy pretentiousness. Moviemakers gained the social status they craved, and elites nourished their insatiable egos.

BARS, BORDELLOS, AND OTHER HAUNTS

Along the main tourist street in downtown Tijuana, saloons with inviting names like El Caballito, the Klondike, and the Black Cat doubled in number from thirty to sixty in four years. As a drawing card, the Alhambra Occidental advertised a ladies restroom with "maid in attendance." (Ladies restrooms were not lavatories. They had no toilets. They were plush parlors with comfortable chairs and lounges where women, attended by maids, could read and rest, or freshen their perfume from imported stock, or escape unwanted male attention.) In its Climax Bar and Grill, the Lower California Commercial Company sold for 60 cents "unexcelled dinners daily," with 75-cent chicken specials on Sundays. Sweet jazz flowed from "Nibs" Miles on piano, Cal Callard on trombone and saxophone, and Frankie Moriett on sax and banjo. Dick Eastman played drums and was the vocalist. Just down the street, the Imperial Café featured Al Gardner on piano, Jack Edwards on saxophone, Worth Thomas on cornet and sax, and Al Derick on drums and xylophone. No wonder that Tijuana was the place to go. There was nothing quite like it—anywhere:

"The drinkers slowly making the rounds . . . ," *The Saturday Evening Post* wrote for its more than two million subscribers:

> starting at the Last Chance Saloon at one end of Main Street Avenida La Revolución, and proceeding through the Cantina Vernon, the Savoy Café, the Long Cabin Bar, the Nuevo Palacio, the Tivoli Bar, the Anchor Bar, Booze's Place, the Red Mill, and so on.
>
> . . . From every saloon on Main Street come the hectic strains of a jazz orchestra or a jazz piano. In the doorways of the dingier and smaller saloons on the side streets stand little clumps of somewhat underdressed ladies who lure the passerby with honeyed words.
>
> The local beer is what is technically known as green beer, and frequent indul-

gence in it is apt to result in an internal upset similar to that which might be caused by swallowing a lighted pinwheel. . . . The science of blending alcohol with creosote, concentrated beet juice, and faucet water has reached such a high stage of development on the North American continent that the drinks of Tijuana seldom cause death, if taken in moderation.[12]

The most chic cabaret of all was said to be the San Francisco, with its oversized crystal windows, copper doors, and mahogany floors, a posh palace where Lon Chaney and John Barrymore dined on dove. The Frisco's owner, Eddie Baker, met guests wearing a chocolate brown suit with wide white stripes, an orange tie, and felt homburg hat. At the nearby Aloha bar, it was said, for effect, that the Devil himself once appeared there.[13]

The black ex-heavyweight boxing champion Jack Johnson fought in town and ran two nightclubs; one, The Newport, catered to blacks only. He called the other The Main Event. The Newport "was right off the main street and it was all colored: colored girls in there, colored bartenders, colored entertainers." Johnson had been charged with a Mann Act violation, taking a (white) girl across a state line for immoral purposes and had come to Mexico to avoid arrest in the United States. In 1920 he crossed back over the line and gave himself up. A man who saw the bulky, slightly balding Johnson surrender surmised, somewhat wistfully, "I guess he wanted to get back into the United States and spend the rest of his life there, because he was getting old."[14] The champ served a year in jail.

Many clubs had their own small boxing rings where lesser-knowns slugged it out before rambunctious, vociferous betting fans. One spacious saloon, the Ballena, better known as The Long Bar, claimed to feature the longest bar in the world, 215 feet in all. It took ten bartenders and thirty waitresses to serve customers, who drank 30-cent beers, much of it brewed locally, out of glass jars. All of these places had walls lined with slot machines and illegal bigger betting opportunities in backrooms.

So did the most famous brothel in town, the Moulin Rouge, easily recognizable by the red windmill on its roof; it was owned and operated by a Japanese immigrant, Soo Yasuhara. It billed itself as "Tijuana's leading place of entertainment" and as "the "headquarters for real recreation." Indeed, it was. The bordello's employees—Mexicans, and whites, Asians, and blacks of various nationalities—worked their clientele for a negotiable price. Red Pollard, Seabiscuit's famous jockey, was said to frequent the plush club.

Good restaurants abounded. Among the best was the Fior de Italia, opened by a former Italian military pilot named Alex Cardini, who served patrons while singing operatic arias. Rudolph Valentino ate fine food there as did Clark Gable, W. C. Fields, and everyman's tough guy James Cagney, just about to emerge from vaudeville to movie stardom. Besides entertaining guests, Alex experimented with salads, and one day he mixed grated Parmesan cheese, barely coddled egg, garlic, olive oil, a bit of lemon juice, anchovy paste, and seasonings, poured it over lettuce with fried croutons, and christened it his "Aviator's Salad." It proved immensely popular, so he renamed it in honor of his brother, Caesar.[15]

SPREADING THE WORD

A perceptive and sympathetic *New York Times* reporter, Stephen Chambers, surveyed the panorama for his paper's Arts and Entertainment section in June 1920, writing that, "South from San Diego, Cal., there runs a road. It is not a straight road, nor is it narrow. Broad and crooked, it winds a more or less serpentine way to Tia Juana, across the international line in Old Mexico. . . . Against the paving of that road, against smoothing out the ruts in the way of the transgressor, the clergy of Sunshine City [San Diego's nickname] have thundered protest, and to that road to Tia Juana the pulpit has given a name which, to the joy of the irreverent, has stuck—'The Road to Hell.'" Chambers understood, however, that

> wickedness has a charm of its own and human nature was not changed by the Volstead Act [Prohibition], the auto-stage companies and livery stables of San Diego and Los Angeles are sowing a whirlwind and reaping a harvest. They do not have to advertise that particular route—all who visit San Diego must "do" Tia Juana.
>
> For at Tia Juana, just sixteen miles from the arid lands [liquor-dry San Diego], "there ain't no ten commandments." There the weary and law-oppressed may find an oasis in the desert, a place where he may rest his tired foot on a brass rail and drink to the health of Pancho Villa, or whoever it was who invented Mexico.[16]

Chambers may have understood human nature, but he knew nothing of Mexico, past or present.

The correspondent then cruised in a car through customs, across the Tijuana River on a rickety wooden bridge labeled La Marimba because cars rolling over the crossties played a clacking tune, and down the town's gaudy main street, which he depicted as a cross between a Bret Harte mining camp and Coney Island. Like so many other tourists, he saw Tijuana as the extension of an envisioned American Wild West.

> Imagine a wide main street after the old Western style, or the Spanish plaza of colonial pueblos [he obviously had no inkling of Spanish colonial pueblos]. On either side is a succession of saloons, dance halls, movie picture barns, and gambling dens. In other places, not so largely advertised, one may cook a pill [smoke opium] or otherwise dally through the lotus hours. The air reeks of dust, warm humanity, toilet perfume, stale tobacco and that curious congenial aroma which makes the camel twitch his nostrils afar. And also the welkin rings and vibrates with laughter and chatter of abnormal good spirits, the noise of an occasional fracas, the whirl of the roulette wheel, the clatter of the little white ball seeking its owner's salvation, the musically liquid swickety-swish-swish of the American cocktail, the tap-tap-tap of hammers where joy palaces are being shot up overnight to accommodate the business of this prohibition boomtown.

He then turned to the conglomeration of people he met in this freewheeling ambiance. "And the people—ah, the people!—they that dwell in Tia Juana," he said. "All nations! But the American, the Mexican, the Chinese and the 'colored gem'man from the Souf' predominate. . . . But there are others not in keeping with the general kaleidoscopic picture—wide-eyed damsels, who clinging to escorts, have come across the line 'to do' Tia Juana." Chambers spotted a lady at a roulette table, where she collected a quick win but then settled into a string of losses; two hours later, her escort tried to get her to leave, "and Dearie pleas, 'Oh, just once more. I just know I'm going to win next time.'"

And he expounded on the prevalence and types of gaming in town and those who gambled knowing they would lose.

> The gambling? Every form of it ever invented in vain but persisting efforts to beat Chance at her own game. Even the humble shell game, playing openly on sidewalks—that is, any old place where there's parking room finds "comers" still. For excepting always the professional gamblers, touts, &c, who make permanent camp at Tia Juana, most people visit the place in the spirit that Mr. Barnum discovered and patented. They know they are being humbugged, and like it. They are wise enough sometimes to come with a limit in mind, and prolong the agony of being "trimmed" of that fixed amount for as long as possible.
>
> To the serious minded newcomer it is staggering, however, and intoxicating, this passing recrudescence of wild and wooly [18]69. It is no place for a St.

Anthony, for the wheel and stacks of bright new-minted dollars make one dizzy, and the brass rail [in cantinas] fascinates by its very shininess.

But it was time for Chambers to return to San Diego:

If you have a liking for the sort of life that once made the Bowery [in New York] famous, you may linger in Tia Juana until 10 p.m. until repassing the gates of respectability on the north side of the river. You may, if your taste runs that way, explore other and more devious channels of Tijuana life. But along about five in the evening there is usually a rush for the line before dark, as that crazy bridge must be negotiated, and one by one the cars are halted at United States Customs for search. As frequently from 500 to 1,000—oh, sometimes more—automobiles from the United States are parked like a mass of black beetles at Tia Juana, your chances of getting back to San Diego are slim.

And he detailed the irritating ritual of passing through U. S. Customs at the border.

You are halted in that narrow alley, which is the only official entry and exit point. You are requested to step out of the car—ladies too—sometimes ladies in particular. An urbane official, while perhaps smiling at the possible faint exhalation of ambrosia [alcohol], deftly runs his hands over your clothing, perhaps lighting [lifting] your hat for you, if it happens to have a high crown [in which people smuggled goods], while another officer opens up the hood of the car, sounds the radiator, studies the tires, peeps into the horn, removes cushions, investigates the tool box and even examines the spark plugs, or peers under the rubber matting in search of opium. . . . [Regulations permitted each traveler only one package of goods and that in the form of a personal belonging.] Hence, the "package" is frequently as much as a single-bodied man can carry unassisted.

Then, if your bill is clean, you can go ahead, free to enter a respectable republic, where the demon [John Barleycorn], buried alive still turns in his coffin and makes strange noises.

Once there, the traveler is met by the billboard "Road to Hell" . . . , which points at the sinner with a kind of goading insolence and cries: "Do Not Attempt to Bring Liquor into the United States."

Chambers spoke like a drinker and wrote as if he did not countenance anyone calling him a sinner. He obviously liked spicy Tijuana as a getaway for fellow-countrymen seeking escape from onerous reform laws which had crimped their harmless enjoyments, dampened their legitimate passions, and tamped their free spirits. Simply put, overbearing reform was sapping the nation's *joie de vivre* and right at a time when many folks were thinking about and experimenting with new ways to live their lives, as evidenced by rollicking Tijuana. "Good times" from one perspective, perhaps, but what of morality? What of dignity, decorum, and rectitude? What of flimflam, inebriation, and extortion? A new regime in Mexico City scrutinized and weighed alternatives that threatened to dim the lights and dry up the fizz.

PERILS OF FRIVOLITY

The Constitutionalists who won their nation's barbarous civil war had long meant to rid themselves of Esteban Cantú's independence, arrogance, self-importance, and control of his district's stuffed money bags. All over the country they aimed to bring these sorts of regional bosses under central control. With this in mind, in late 1919 they had sent General Abelardo Rodríguez to a small rancho outside of Mexicali, purportedly to study the topography but actually to spy on Cantú. His reports must have confirmed the governor's entrenchment and firm intention to stay. So the following year, the national government ordered an army detachment from the neighboring state of Sonora to depose him.

Cantú wavered. Should he fight or flee? Those like Carlie Withington, who had prospered from the governor's largesse and certainly did not welcome an unpredictable turnover, offered to bankroll a defense, but too many others felt differently and foresaw an advantageous future with the new administration in the country's capital. Cantú weighed his alternatives. Why risk annihilation by an army battalion? His cause hopeless, Cantú fled into the United States with a coterie of close followers. Over the next two years, with Withington's financial aid, they made bold but futile armed forays from U.S. soil into the district. At one point, the harried governor's agent asked Carlie for more support.

"This makes $7,000 I have paid for Cantú experiments," Withington testily replied, "and that is all he is going to get unless I get something in return."

"You will see that you will not only have gambling in Tijuana and Mexicali," the agent assured him, "but you will not have to wait for the [fixed] Supreme Court in Mexico to give you the racetrack [in Tijuana]."

"Well, that's all you will get from me until I see that you fellows can do me some good," said Withington, driving a hard bargain.[17]

The harried governor had most of Tijuana's leading merchants in his camp, but he could not garner sufficient public support to restore himself to power. The King of the Border's support system had been dismantled.

But did it matter? From 1920 to 1923 the federal government, now headed by Wirt Bowman's close personal friend, Alvaro Obregón, assigned three different cohorts to govern northern Baja California in Cantú's stead. None proved up to the task, politically, emotionally, or administratively. Corruption abounded; vice (for a price) thrived. At the same time, Obregón proclaimed a moralization campaign from Mexico City: gambling, drinking, vice in general (prostitution would still be permitted in *La Zona*, meaning red-light districts) was to be eliminated as deleterious to the national good and places that fostered it shut down. (Moralization may also be seen as social control. Governments use such devices to systematize everyday life, to shackle the masses to stultifying daily routine under central authority.)

Regardless of the purpose, Baja California's governors paid only lip service to the edict; they turned off the spigot when pressured from the capital, and turned it back on when demands from superiors diminished. All along they claimed that only through taxes on gaming could they finance the district.[18] The state government of Nevada faced the same dilemma a decade later—tax money needed for development—but Nevada caved in, or faced reality, and President Obregón did not. Still, the president's bureaucracy, including some of his highest-ranking ministers, continued to wiggle and worm their way into noncompliance.

Not only did northern Baja California's governors dillydally with the reform measures and brazenly lie to Mexico City about compliance with them (and line their own pockets in the process), but the office of the Interior Secretary (*Gobernación*), now with official power to grant gaming concessions, did the same despite the president's campaign. The Interior Secretary in charge, Plutarco Elías Calles, was a compadre of Obregón, both Sonorenses, both triumphant military generals (Obregón lost an arm in the fighting), and both in agreement that Calles would succeed Obregón as president, and then four years later, it would again be Obregón's turn. The documentation, however, is clear; Calles's office granted gaming concessions during Obregón's drive for reform, and when Calles became president, his office was open to similar deals.[19]

No wonder that the King of the Border, Carlie Withington, did not skip a beat, did not suffer a smidgen, when his old patron Cantú disappeared in exile. Carlie's only concern was that he no longer held the near-monopoly he enjoyed under Cantú, that other players would quickly and aggressively crash his game, among them Wirt Bowman, who, thanks to his earlier machinations on the Sonoran border, now had powerful connections at the pinnacle of power. Carlie sought to alleviate his concerns. When Calles went to San Francisco for one of his periodic health cures in 1924, Withington met him at his hotel. Nothing is known of the words or money they may have exchanged, but Carlie retained his hegemony in Tijuana.[20]

HELLFIRE AND BRIMSTONE

U.S. reformers had long portrayed Tijuana as Sodom and Gomorrah and urged government controls to contain the scourge south of the border. Authorities responded to the outcry by closing, then reopening the gates, or limiting the hours of passage, not so much to prevent contamination by vice but to pressure the neighboring nation for political position or economic advantage. Vice was only a pretext, but a potent and emotional one. When Coffroth's track opened in 1916, the *Los Angeles Evening Express*, disgruntled because San Diego had grabbed the spotlight and was profiting from its hemispheric exposition, launched a monthlong tirade against its rival, including San Diego's embrace of horse racing below the border. The publisher characterized Tijuana as a place where, among other depravities and tragedies, "young women have gone astray, young boys are treading in the pathways of evil, mothers are on the verge of insanity, and Tijuana's shame is San Diego's shame." He then unloaded on San Diego itself: "The San Diego newspapers have been muzzled, the city is overrun with thieves, grafters, and gambling is flourishing on an extensive scale."

After such accusatory finger-pointing by the publisher himself, the first piece in the long series began, "If you were searching for the filthiest cesspool that ever defiled the face of the earth, you would [travel to Tijuana]. The miasma of the cesspool arises like a withering blight and assails your nostrils with its deadly stench." And worse, "Tijuana, with its cutthroat Mexicans, its smug American gamblers, and its thieves and prostitutes of all nations, snuggles complacently . . . [near San Diego]."[21]

Sharply etched racism branded the reportage: "Here are three white women and a negro man. They are giving him silver to bet on the horse they fancy will win," the *Express* contended. "Here is a negro woman talking to a white man. Yonder is a slender negro, as black as Jack Johnson, wheedling money from two Castillian girls who are badly over-dressed. The negro is clad in white flannels and his eyes gleam like coals of fire." Example after example saturated the newspaper's columns.

Reformers must have gasped, even sobbed, and been angered by the vignettes disclosed: a child holding a racing form; "a white woman of fifty dividing the winnings from a $10 note with two ferret-eyed negro men"; "the father gave his children a quarter in nickels. They dropped the money into a slot machine and lost"; bankers, city authorities, and other public officials gambled, drank, and swore.[22] Visiting Tijuana was like meandering with rather more clothing in the damnation panel of Hieronymus Bosch's *Garden of Earthly Delights.*

Rebuttals to and commendations for the inflammatory series poured in, even if the *Evening Express* printed only the latter. It provided fodder for social reformers, their bulletins and organizations, while other publishers printed denials, alleging falsehoods and exaggerations. Overall public impact of the series is difficult to assess, but one can safely say that because or in spite of it, tourism in Tijuana soared.

"ONE FIGHT MORE"

The election of Alvaro Obregón heartened reformers everywhere, especially Californians who foresaw an end to Tijuana's evils, and a flurry of letters and telegrams to Mexico City praised the president for his morality campaign. But in 1922 the Devil reappeared. Carlie Withington announced reconstruction of his infamous The Owl cabaret in Mexicali, which two years earlier had been nearly destroyed by a spectacular fire.

Flames had consumed four wooden buildings on the site. Only the cribs were spared, along with the "dug out" (which guarded liquor worth $70,000, the bulk of which had been rushed over from the U.S. side when Prohibition began) and the nearby blacks-only "Little Owl" gaming quarters. When the fire erupted, customers (some one thousand people were in the complex) scrambled for cash on the gaming tables, but local police fired pistols to scare them off. Shots in the skirmish wounded three patrons. The orchestra strived to maintain calm by playing soothing dance music (reminiscent of the *Titanic* disaster), but it proved futile; panic reigned.

Money (total unknown) in the count room was saved. "A truck load of silver coin, containing 700 pounds of silver dollars, and requiring eight men to lift, made its way, heavily guarded, into Calexico [the U.S. side of the line], where the money was placed in safe keeping."[23] Still, losses were staggering, an estimated quarter of a million dollars (nearly ten times that today), and nothing was covered by insurance. Insurance companies, fearing spontaneous upheaval by irate gamblers or arson by owners squeezed for cash, hesitated to write policies on such vulnerable structures.

The cause of The Owl fire remained undetermined. Some speculated that competitors of the A.B.W. had started the conflagration, others blamed enemies of Cantú, moralists saw the Hand of God at work, but most likely a lit cigarette dropped in an upstairs dressing room frequented by orchestra members sparked the fire, quickly fueled by the explosion of gasoline containers stored there. Hundreds of Jack Tenney's song scripts went up in the blaze, but he simply moved up the street to the Chinese-owned Imperial Café, where in 1923 he noticed a woman named Rose, maybe sixty years old and more than somewhat overweight, at an estimated two hundred pounds. Rose frequented the club after midnight and was said to run a boarding house for railway workers in the Imperial Valley town of Brawley across the border. Rose was usually intoxicated, a tearfully sentimental, aging woman, whom the boys in the band dubbed "Mexicali Rose." Tenney had written a tune a month earlier that still awaited its lyrics, and so began to compose them.

In the second line, he advised Rose to "stop crying." And because the night outside was wet and windy, he then wrote, "I'll come back to you some sunny day."[24] Of such romantic, but lovely pap, classic songs are spawned.

Following the fire, "Booze" Beyer confidently announced that gambling would continue in The Little Owl, but for the time being, for whites only. Meanwhile, a "bigger and better" main club would be constructed. When rebuilding began in 1922, reformers vigorously reminded Obregón of his heralded crusade (a solemn pledge to them) to moralize his countrymen by clamping down on their debauchery, carnality, and degradation.

A thirty-nine-year-old Methodist firebrand named John Wood, at the peak of his evangelical enthusiasm, heralded the new campaign against Tijuana's wickedness, and specifically cited plans to reopen The Owl. In his denomination's *California Christian Association* newsletter, the Southern California preacher offered a long list of news headlines extracted from the *San Diego Sun* which dramatized lurid conditions below the border:

"Racing secretary of the jockey club shot to death." "Fire caused to cover up double murder in crib." "Mayor's son held in jail for murder at Tia Juana." "Body of man found in Tia Juana river, body mutilated, man brutally murdered." "San Diego man takes life following loss at [Tijuana] race track." "Tia Juana trip ends fatally, beautiful girl found dead." "Tia Juana orgy kills youth." "[American] Legion man slugged at Tia Juana. Man found unconscious."

The above list is but partial [nor is it the newsletter's entire printed list] and does not cover loss of morality, arrests for defaulting [on gaming losses], young girls missing from their homes, and thousands of other things which are the direct product of vice conditions across the border.[25]

Reverend Wood promoted a relentless letter-writing campaign to President Obregón, demanding permanent closure of the infamous Owl and a zealous assault on all border iniquities. Every letter (and he called for at least a thousand to be sent) counted: "one man shall chase a thousand and two men put an army to flight" he urged, in a loose reminder of the David and Goliath story. Then the stentorian battle cry:

One fight more,
"The last is the best."[26]

Paradise would follow Armageddon as promised by Holy Word.

The president's secretary patiently replied to the numerous petitions pouring into his office. (They now are lodged in Mexico's National Archive.)[27] Some petitioners were thanked and assured that the government was doing everything possible to rectify "indecorous exploitation" along the border. Others were to be "studied," which meant hurled into the bottomless pit of Mexican bureaucracy. A few went to the district governor of Northern Baja California, José Inocente Lugo, who promised reform but at the same time granted gaming concessions and pocketed remunerations for favors granted. Poor Reverend Wood. He was being humbled and demeaned, and soon would be lost.

Will Rogers, relishing these sorts of quarrels, weighed in with oozing sarcasm:

Americans don't want to drink and gamble. They just go over there to see the mountains, and these scheming Mexicans grab 'em and make 'em drink, and make 'em make bets, and make 'em watch those horses run for money. It seems that Americans don't know these places are over there at all, and when they get there these Mexicans spring on 'em and they have to drink or the Mexicans will

kill 'em. . . . We come nearer to running Mexico than we do New York State. . . .
For the love of Mike, why don't we let Mexico alone and let them run their
country the way they want to!

Then Will had a suggestion. "If we have to admit to the world, that we are
raising people that don't know enough to take proper care of themselves,
we will have to do it by another Amendment [to the Constitution], as
follows: 'Americans are not allowed anywhere they will be subject to evil
influences.' "[28]

The New Wave

The programmed lockstep from Obregón to Calles as Mexico's president did not proceed precisely as planned. One of the government's strongest supporters, Adolfo de la Huerta, thought he deserved the top-ranking job, and when he did not get it, surged into rebellion, urging his countrymen to resist the budding dictatorship. To fight the insurgency, the government solicited donations from any quarter, and Wirt Bowman generously responded with what was reportedly $250,000, a favor later reciprocated. So did A.B.W., with similar results. The man who ensured they received their due was the new governor of Baja California's northern district, Abelardo Rodríguez.[1]

Rodríguez ruled the federal territory for the next seven years, from 1923 to 1930. Although his political position precluded much openness about his connection to large, well-financed, powerful gambling conglomerates, he rightly deserves to be counted among the Border Barons, standing tall next to and intimately in league with Bowman, James Crofton, and Baron Long. The four of them, working in tandem, blended prominent political associations with dog-eat-dog sporting expertise to found and operate for much of its existence the fabulous, highly remunerative gaming resort at Agua Caliente.

THE FOURTH BARON

Of the four, Abelardo Rodríguez started lowest on the social ladder. While his family was not mired in dreadful poverty, it certainly was poor. His father, who could not seem to hold steady work as a teamster in northwestern Mexico, gravitated to the steamy port of Guaymas on the Gulf of

California, where he married. The union bore eleven children, among them Abelardo, born in 1889, and soon after the family sought better fortune in the Mexican portion of Nogales on the border. Young Abelardo preferred boxing and baseball to books, yet during school vacations, his prescient mother insisted that he cross over the line to learn English at an American institute, and fluent bilingualism stood him in special stead for the rest of his life.

As a teenager, Rodríguez worked in a brother's metal shop, hobnobbed with older people of authority, concentrated on body-building for his possible boxing career, and then in a fit of adolescent exuberance announced that his sonorous voice pointed toward success as a professional singer. He traveled to Los Angeles, where after only a few weeks of instruction, his voice teacher encouraged him to forget singing and go back home. There, his robust physique and popularity as a local boxer and ball player helped him, at twenty-three, to become his hometown's police chief. Rodríguez fortuitously joined the military faction that eventually won Mexico's bitter civil war, proved his loyalty to superiors, and received his reward as governor of Baja California Norte. He certainly was not the only triumphant military general to turn good fortune into fabulous wealth, but he was *sans parallèle* at investing, saving, laundering, and spending the mammoth profits extracted from his privileged position.[2]

As governor, Rodríguez sanctioned (for a substantial tax, plus mordida) the district's bustling, dominant casinos and racetrack, along with a lively assortment of cantinas, bordellos, dance halls, strip joints, alley retreats, opium dens, and a patchwork of other noisy, unsavory dives with their varied offerings. He reminded his superiors in the national capital that casino owners like Bowman and Withington had financially supported the federal government in its armed struggles against dangerous adversaries and advised that such loyalty be rewarded by not interfering with ambitions of the sportsmen. "These people have demonstrated their friendship and good faith toward the government in its critical moments," he wrote President Calles. "I ask your help in bringing this contract [for another casino] to conclusion."[3] Rodríguez sent $100,000 from his district's tax receipts to Mexico City to reinforce his point. He was by 1924 calling Wirt and Carlie "good friends." In turn, Withington bragged that he had the governor in his pocket.

Governor Rodríguez steadfastly defended gaming in Tijuana against his critics, noting that in "civilized countries" people gambled and went to the races. Casinos exist in France, he said, and the French do not complain. "In Florida, one of the U.S.'s most prosperous states, an infinite number of these clubs like the Foreign Club exist, but in Florida one plays roulette and all classes of gambling [not allowed in Tijuana], and no one protests." All of which, he noted, contributes mightily to tourism. "France lives from tourism. Tijuana lives from tourism. Without it, the town would not exist, nor would workers' organizations, nor an *ayuntamiento* [city hall]."[4]

A high union official from the capital visited the border town in 1925 and complained about the proliferation of gambling establishments. The governor responded sharply, calling the administrator's visit short and confined to the "tourist street," where he dropped into the Foreign Club, which "is carefully regulated and inspected." No violations there. Nor in any others on the strip, where "none are in worse condition than the best in the capital." Had the union representative gone two blocks farther, he "would have seen the schools, potable water, drainage systems and roadways as good as or better than others in the republic," all financed by gaming taxation.

Tourism, moreover, produced jobs with decent pay. If the union boss would return, Rodríguez promised to show him *colonias* (sections of town) where hundreds of families who had lived as indigents in the neighboring United States had been repatriated and were doing well. "Workers do better here than in any other part of the republic," the governor asserted. "Stone masons earn twenty-four pesos a day [$12 U.S.] and carpenters, eighteen. Peons earn at least four and one-half and up to six or eight pesos a day," at least four times more than wages paid common laborers in other parts of the country.[5]

Governor Rodríguez was, in fact, keenly aware of his district's workers and their political clout, confirmed in the country's new constitution and by a federal government determined to broaden its popular base. Mexican proletarians now had the legal right to much improved wages, working conditions, and employment practices, and could challenge shortfalls in court, or in the streets. Militant trade unionism flourished and was especially virulent along the border, where combustible complaints of foreign exploitation were most common. Mexico for Mexicans!

All foreign business felt the pressure. "Booze" Beyer, for example, had seen to it that his acquaintances, the Rottman family from Chula Vista, received the parking, checkroom, cigar, and cigarette concession at the racetrack. As Tijuana officials had to sign off on such agreements, the deal involved mordidas. "We found out that if you will donate to the schools . . . , you could do almost anything you wanted to in Mexico," remembered Leonard Rottman, barely twenty years old at the time. "So we were giving $100 a month to the schools. In 1924, all of a sudden, here come some Mexicans who were going to run us out of their country. . . . The labor unions got strong and they wanted that concession. We had to put on fifty percent Mexican help. There were three of us, so we had to put on three Mexicans." Two years later "they took over. We had to get out, and then it was all Mexicans. They wouldn't stand for any Americans having any concessions down there."[6] No concessions, that is, unless one had the right connections and paid the fee.

Tijuana merchants complained in February 1923 that the Sunset cabaret and casino on the border was ruining downtown business. Tourists gorged themselves on entertainment and purchases there and went home without even sampling offerings on the town's main street. The businesspeople demanded that the casino be shut down in accordance with the latest moralization edict from Mexico City, but local officials, prospering from its presence, guaranteed that it remained open.[7]

Infuriated workers took matters into their own hands six months later. Some 100 to 150 unionists stormed the Tivoli casino on September 11, claiming that the military protected illegal gaming interests against closure. They turned over card tables, ripped down roulette wheels, generally tossed the place upside down, and sent customers scurrying into the streets. Dice, chips, money, and croupier rakes flew everywhere (the aggressors later claimed they kept nothing for themselves). By the time police and soldiers arrived, the workers had dispersed. A few arrests followed, but no prosecutions.[8] Within a year or so, Rodríguez raised the district's minimum daily wage and mandated that the workforce in all businesses be at least 50 percent Mexican, soon expanded to 60 percent and then 80 percent.

The governor, meanwhile, worked on broadening and deepening his own investment portfolio, which over time revealed widespread, eclectic interests in real estate (including Agua Caliente), construction companies, hotels, golf courses, cinema productions, oil, aircraft and construction companies, telecommunications, mining, carbonated soft drinks, vineyards, shrimp and shellfish packing plants, several banks, and undoubtedly much more either hidden or registered in the names of others. Almost a third of his properties lay in the federal district, and his political ascendancy culminated in the interim presidency of the republic from 1932 to 1934. From then until his death in 1962, he enjoyed a prosperous political, business, and personal life. No question, however, that Agua Caliente and other gaming interests in burgeoning Tijuana during the rousing Twenties framed the foundation of his good fortune. He was a true Border Baron both in heart and performance.[9]

CARLIE PASSES THE TORCH

The Prince of Pleasure, Carlie Withington, died in a San Diego hospital on October 23, 1925, after a yearlong bout with stomach cancer. As might be expected of the man, it was not a peaceful passing. For the previous ten months or so he had been consorting with a new lover, Lucille Moore, and in his final days favored her with lavish gifts of money, jewelry, and clothing from his $3-million estate. The affair outraged Carlie's estranged wife, Georgia May. In her divorce suit filed only a week before Withington's death, she claimed that he was under the influence of pain opiates and unable to resist maneuvers of the woman "who has usurped the wife's position in the home." Georgia May demanded her half of their community property which included large blocks of shares in casinos, saloons, a racetrack, brewery, and other such enterprises in Baja California, as well as a movie theater in San Francisco, interest in the Reno racetrack, stores in Los Angeles, real estate in Bakersfield and San Diego County, and thirty thoroughbred racehorses on a ranch near the border. She estimated that Carlie's activities earned him $1 million a year, which he stashed in banks scattered from Southern California into Canada. She also hinted at hidden assets.

Georgia May was one scorned and vengeful woman. She charged Carlie with fraud, misconduct, and desertion. It seems that he had a liking for prostitutes. When they married in 1919, she said he promised to give up his whorehouses, but never did so. She charged that Carlie "compelled her to sit with women of ill repute in Tijuana, and if she did not drink, called her a poor sport, and if she did, upbraided her for drinking. He forced her to associate with criminals in his offices [at] The Owl resort in Mexicali, and in the presence of gambling employees in Tijuana, declared he preferred to live with a prostitute [rather] than with her, and to her declared that he had lived with her longer than with any other woman and had not been married to them."

Withington fought back in his style. He accused his wife of misconduct with an Italian in early 1924, beat her savagely and dragged her across a gravel driveway near their San Ysidro home, causing cuts and bruises that required hospital treatment. Under the frightful circumstances, she went to live with her brother in neighboring Chula Vista. When the brother asked Withington why he had deserted Georgia May, the sportsman replied that he had "lived with eighteen women. What, more or less, was another one?"

When Carlie died, she went to court claiming her husband was insane when he made out his last will eight days before his death. Five years later, an appellate judge ruled that Carlie had an "undoubted right to dispose of his $868,000 estate as he saw fit." Trying to mollify Georgia, he had offered her a $250,000 settlement. She wanted another $100,000 and turned him down. In the end, she got nothing; Lucille Moore, $40,000; and Withington's brother and three sisters the remainder.[10]

Carlie's gaming legacy, however, lived on. On his deathbed he had admonished his longtime sporting associates, Marvin Allen and "Booze" Beyer, to "Get Bowman!" and they did. For $25,000 a year he would be their "contact man" with Mexico City and run their gaming concessions in Tijuana. Once Bowman had a foot in the door, however, he moved quickly to control the syndicate and its assets. Concessions that A.B.W. held in Tijuana (the Foreign Club, for example) suddenly expired and were then reissued by the Mexican government to Bowman. In other words, the crown was refit for a new king. The press caught wind that Bowman had succeeded Withington as ruler of border vice. Wirt, of course, denied it.

"LUCKY" WIRT

Wirt "Lucky" Bowman was the eldest Baron, twenty-six years Crofton's senior, and seven years older than Long. But age difference mattered little to the Barons, among whom there was no pecking order. Bowman was born in the eastern Mississippi cotton plantation town of West Point, where his father, John, worked as station agent on the Mobile and Ohio Railroad. John Bowman descended from hardy German immigrants named Bauman (meaning "builder"), who in the mid-eighteenth century received British land grants to farm around Edinburg (near the famously historic Belle Grove Plantation) in Virginia's bucolic Shenandoah Valley. When the Civil War surged through the valley, Bowman joined the Confederacy as a telegraph operator, but Federals promptly caught him tapping their telegraph lines for information about troop movements and sent him to prison. Bowman escaped, and nothing more is known of his wartime activities.

Two years after the conflict, John took a railroad job in West Point and married Lucy Young Cochran; over the next two decades the couple had six children. Wirt (the word means the owner of a building in German) was the third-born and thirteen years old when his father's health, probably a pulmonary illness, forced the entire family to move west. They settled in the northern Panhandle of Texas, hot and less humid but hardly a health resort, where they bought prairie land at $2 an acre and began cattle ranching near the isolated hamlet of Kirkland, pressing against the Oklahoma border.

Wirt and the other Bowmans knew little of farming and ranching, but in his own words, "it didn't take us long to do everything we had seen the Negroes do in Mississippi, plow and drive teams, and in a very short time we were apt farmers and ranchers."[11] Drought, however, created hard times on the Bowman ranch, and in the late 1880s the sons scattered to make their livings elsewhere. For five years, from the ages of fourteen to nineteen, Wirt buckarooed on ranches throughout northwest Texas. He did not much like the hard, dirty work, but what he learned from it later paved his way to fortune.

John offered to set up his son in ranching closer to home, but Wirt told him that he was "through with Texas and everything in it." So on May 23, 1893, Wirt "rode the rails" on a passing train headed west, where he waited tables and washed dishes in a northern New Mexican lumber camp, tamped ties for a railroad that ran through the district, and decided that low-paying manual labor was not going to be his lot. His father, the former railroad station master, had taught him Morse code as a child, and now Wirt yearned to be a telegrapher, preferably a railroad agent like his dad. When a railroad friend wired him of a station master opening in the desolate Sonoran pueblo of Pozo ("the well," in Spanish), Wirt jumped to northern Mexico. The place was only a cluster of typical adobe dwellings, plus a general store and a cantina, between Nogales and Hermosillo, but it was an important desert oasis where the Southern Pacific's steam engine trains stopped for water. There, in such forlorn surroundings, Bowman erected the central pillar in his rise to prominence and prosperity.

With experience as a stationmaster and telegraph operator, Bowman was just what the Southern Pacific needed in this region, and during the next decade the railroad promoted him from trainmaster to terminal superintendent at Nogales, Arizona, and finally superintendent of the entire northern division of the line. The railroad venture—not the low-paying job per se but the contacts it provided with affluent, influential, and investment-minded Sonorans—was a perfect backdrop for the young man's aspirations. Bowman treated these notables well and earned their gratitude doing so.

Wirt made Nogales (pop. 8,000) his home, and in 1896, at twenty-one, cemented his stature below the border by marrying the sixteen-year-old Magdalena J. Bernaldo, whose distinguished family enjoyed powerful business and political connections in Guaymas. Soon the Bowmans were rearing two daughters (the first two of their three daughters) in Nogales, where administering the railroad's business taught Wirt how customs policies, procedures, and evasions worked in an isolated border town (actually split by the international line) and led him to ponder establishing his own import-export business. When Arizona became the country's forty-eighth state on February 14, 1912, he also plunged into politics. Bowman became a big fish in a little pond.

REVOLUTION IN MEXICO

Raging rebellion in Mexico forced Bowman out of the railroad business. Better said, it gave him the chance to get rich quick. The revolt to depose the country's longtime dictator erupted in November 1910, and seven months later Porfirio Díaz sailed off to exile in Europe. As he predicted, however, the revolt's success unleashed a tiger. Uprisings occurred almost everywhere, as myriad groups jockeyed for quick spoils and political position. Sonora threatened to fall apart; mayhem erupted with railroads a major target. As a result, Bowman resigned from the railroad and established an import-export business less than a block from the border crossing in his hometown. Fees he garnered brokering the sale of cattle for Sonoran revolutionaries in the United States made Wirt Bowman a wealthy man. Moreover, as he worked the exchange for the eventual winners in the bloody fratricide below the border, he reinforced his acquaintanceship with them and deepened their appreciation of him. In this regard, his nickname "Lucky" fit to a T.

A boastful and demanding man of enormous energy who appreciated political power and knew how to make deals on and under the table, a boldly ruthless person who could also be warmly tender and overtly sympathetic, Bowman was the right man, at the right place, at the right time. Now in his late thirties, he seemed comfortably established with family and place by other people's standards—but not his own. He caught a powerful scent of war profit and had the experience, confidence, gall, and connections to take advantage.

Mexico writhed in agony during 1913. Irate and self-seeking Sonorans grouped under Alvaro Obregón, an amiable but demanding commercial farmer nearing his mid-thirties, who had openly opposed the old dictator's politics. Now he began to sweep away remnants of the *ancien régime* along with those who had usurped its power following its demise. Obregon's men, largely hastily formed militia outfits, needed arms, ammunition, and supplies as well as money to purchase them from the nearby United States. This meant securing reliable ports of entry, Nogales among the most obvious. Wirt Bowman was there waiting and willing to cooperate through his newly established mercantile business.

Obregón's forces took Nogales on March 13, 1913, and the commander-in-chief placed one of his most trusted officers, none other than Plutárco Elías Calles, a sullen hypochondriac subject to volatile mood changes, in charge of supply operations there. Calles was labeled a "Border Broker," and one of his jobs was to curry favor with American officialdom to ease the flow of goods into Mexico.[12] How fortuitous for Wirt. He and Calles had known each other for nearly twenty years; Bowman called him "my close personal friend." Obregón was also Bowman's family friend.[13] As fortune had it for "Lucky" Wirt, when the revolution ended both Calles and Obregón became presidents of Mexico in the 1920s (with Calles retaining power well into the 1930s), and they did not forget those who helped them in wartime.

About the only asset the rebels could trade for war supplies was cattle, hardly any of it their own, but animals they unabashedly confiscated from friends and foes for sale abroad. Cattle drives north to the international line were nothing new to Sonorans. On immense Mexican ranches the cows grazed their way substantial distances for their daily fill of various grasses, shrubs, and tree pods, a long wander over harsh, sun-baked expanses that made their meat sinewy and tough to foreign taste. (Still, when it comes to beef steak, there is little as tasty as marinated *carne asada* grilled over red-hot mesquite coals.) For the highly profitable export market, Sonorans, therefore, sold their cattle by the head, not the pound, to ranchers on the U.S. side, shipped by train to pasture mainly in Montana, Wyoming, and the Dakotas, later to be fattened up to suit the American palate.

At Nogales, Bowman was the perfect choice to suit the rebels' needs. He had worked on a ranch as a teenager, knew something of the business, had strong marketing and banking contacts in Arizona, and was an experienced former railroad administrator whose line had shipped cargoes from Sonora through Nogales far into the United States for a decade. Now himself a flourishing exporter-importer, he was thoroughly familiar with customs intricacies. Whether the cattle he shipped were stolen or not did not much concern him, and government neutrality regulations regarding the shipment of weapons to a friendly neighbor were easily and regularly breached. In fact, the rules were officially relaxed by a Woodrow Wilson administration anxious to support the "right" (meaning not radically inclined) faction in Mexico's fratricide and to spread democracy south. Wirt joined the president's crusade and became affluent doing it. The U.S. Justice Department investigated reports, but found no proof, that Bowman actually sold arms and ammunition to the revolutionaries, but he certainly facilitated their purchase in the United States and their movement to border supply depots. A Justice Department inspector put it mildly when he wrote that he "would not be surprised if Bowman cut corners a bit in some transactions."[14]

The revolution fractured further into civil war: Francisco "Pancho" Villa and Emiliano Zapata versus Venustiano Carranza's Constitutionalists commanded by Obregón and supported by Calles. Bowman supplied his friends, Obregón and Calles, with food and war materiel and set up an account for them in the Nogales bank he owned. When cattle exportation became less profitable and the Sonorans ran short of cash, he provided credit. They owed him $87,000 by the spring of 1916, a debt which if not repaid in cash, was later settled at least ten times over in commercial concessions.[15]

"The Carransistas [Carranza's followers] naturally felt grateful for this assistance," wrote the Justice Department inspector, "made him their purchasing agent [exports and imports] at this point, allowing him a fair commission, and allowing him to charge *the market price on the day of delivery*, a good thing in face of constantly rising markets. [For example,] one load of flour he purchased for the Carrancistas raised in price between the date he purchased it and the date it arrived here [Nogales] at $6 a barrel, and he collected the higher price plus a commission."[16] How much money Bowman accumulated in this period cannot be calculated with any precision, but the government estimated that, "Bowman bought $1,100,000 [nearly $20 million now] worth of goods in the last six years and cleaned up $250,000 [over $2.5 million today] in profits."[17]

PROTEST

Wirt Bowman's spectacular profiteering invited relentless protest from his competitors who felt cut out of the bonanza. Because they called for federal government inquires, we have official, confidential reports that tell us much of what is known of Bowman's business dealings.

Animosities between warring parties in Nogales increased after Villa's daring raid on Columbus, New Mexico, in the spring of 1916. The U.S. military quickly followed with a retaliatory strike into northern Mexico under the rambunctious West Pointer, General John Joseph "Black Jack" Pershing. Clamorous war threats rang out from both sides of the border before American soldiers were called to France to assist the Allies in their deadlocked struggle with the German Kaiser. Throughout all, Bowman continued his highly profitable shipments of goods to Mexico. His detractors predictably accused him and his cohorts of illegally trading with the enemy, of being un-American and unpatriotic. As one critic wrote:

> People talk about Mexico across the line, what they do there and so on, in the customs house, the officials [engaged] in [a personal] business line, smuggling, grafting, dirty work, etc., let me say right now, the bunch on this side are not far behind the Mexicans on the other side; there is very little [difference] between them, and to a certain extent they work [together] in lots of things such as crossing merchandise, cattle, and at a time that everyone thought that this country was on the verge of war with Mexico . . . , [Bowman] was busy rushing everything across the line to Mexico that he had here, such as flour, groceries, etc., and in these shipments he was shoving over lots of ammunition and for no other purpose than enriching his pockets.[18]

To an extent, the Justice Department agent concurred, reporting, "There was a good deal of feeling against Bowman in the summer of 1916, because it looked like [full] American intervention in Mexico was imminent and he [Bowman] was selling large quantities of food supplies and forage to the Sonora State government. They thought he was unpatriotic when we were likely to go to war against Mexico."[19]

PATRIOTISM AND PROFITS

Bowman bristled under the charges, especially those that challenged his patriotism. He organized and was proclaimed president of a "One Hundred Percent American Club" dedicated to "enlisting the enthusiastic loyalty of all citizens," and in 1918 went to Washington to volunteer for active military service, probably as a Spanish-speaking interpreter. (Why Washington? There were recruiting stations much closer to home, but Wirt was a showman and a politician. He was well into his forties by then, and was, of course, thanked but turned down by the army.) He donated office space without charge in his hotel to army intelligence and Justice Department personnel monitoring the border. He also loaned them two cars and a typewriter and prided himself on riding sidekick (by automobile or truck, but not in his own splendid Cadillac 8) with the local sheriff to run down arms smugglers and German spies said to be prowling the border. He claimed "several important arrests," including that of a German spy tried in San Antonio, sentenced to execution, but instead deported. "That's what Wirt Bowman likes," the sheriff said. "Just let him get on the trail of anybody the government is after, [and] he's as happy as a little boy with a red wagon."[20]

Fearful that his enemies (Wirt called them "small town gossips envious of my properties") might try to frame him by unobtrusively slipping weapons and ammunition into his food shipments south, Bowman offered to pay the salary of a special customs inspector specifically to survey his shipments and to certify their legality, but customs thought that unnecessary. There was a brief flare-up when customs informed Bowman that he had violated the Trading with the Enemy Act by sending supplies to a Sonoran military garrison that was commanded by a German officer, but Wirt pleaded ignorance, suspended such shipments, and faced no official charges. "He naturally feels grateful to the Mexican government," wrote the Justice inspector, "[but] with him it's America first." Then the inspector concluded, "He [Bowman] is sharp, and lots of people here look on him as somewhat of a Shylock, but I do not think it fair to attack his loyalty."[21]

Bowman still felt picked upon. He claimed that customs agents said to favor his interests actually impeded them. "Obstacles put in my way to prevent me from exporting burlap sacks to handle the garbanzo bean crop [Obregón farmed garbanzos] out of Sonora cost me $100,000." Others, he said, received permits to sell such sacks south, but by the time he received his clearance, the crop had been bagged and sold. And when in July 1918 the War Trade Board delayed his shipment of thirteen freight car loads of merchandise into Mexico, Bowman hurried again to Washington to set the matter straight.

There he met his match. At the War Trade Board, Bowman marched into the office of the man in charge, Herman Oliphant, a Columbia University professor, who in Wirt's words, "treated me in a manner which clearly showed that he had heard ill reports of me." Indeed, Oliphant had. Bowman had been ordered by the War Trade Board not to ship the cube-sugar stored in his warehouse into Mexico, but the government had learned that he used a fictitious name to avoid the prohibition. The professor received Bowman like a criminal and refused to speak to him: "Get out!"

Bowman left, but knew the political game and had an ace up his sleeve. An old family friend from West Point, Mississippi, the Honorable Thomas Watt Gregory, had been appointed U.S. Attorney General by President Wilson. Gregory's mother had been Wirt's elementary school teacher (Bowman only went through fifth grade). Bowman visited Gregory, and the attorney general wrote a letter to the professor testifying to his friend's good character and asked that Professor Oliphant assist in resolving Wirt's shipping problem. Bowman triumphantly hand-carried the testimonial to Oliphant. We can hear him whistling and humming. "Within thirty minutes after presenting this letter," he crowed, "an arrangement was made to release the thirteen carloads of merchandise and they were thereupon lawfully delivered to their consignees in Mexico."[22] Bowman reveled in his coup, and undoubtedly considered it justice due, justice done.

Without question, Wirt Bowman was "a big man around town" on both sides of the border. He lived with his family and five German shepherd police dogs in a magisterial $40,000 (now nearly half a million) home he had built on Calvary Hill overlooking the town that was run by a tight clique he dominated. But he did not lead a totally charmed life. Family tragedy struck in 1918, when his four-year-old daughter, Georgia, burned to death in a backyard accident.

The people of Nogales twice elected Bowman alderman to the town council, and he overcame strong opposition within his own party to become mayor for a one-year term, followed by a stint in the state legislature. A favorite son of Arizona's Democratic Party in state and national politics, he followed a path of economic and political ascendancy. Yet his past had woven him a frightful legacy.[23]

When, a decade later, he was reveling in the riches of Agua Caliente along with other gambling houses and business investments, with no end to his soaring trajectory in sight, Wirt Bowman received an ominous note. A friend, the Los Angeles customs collector, wrote that he had seen, or at least knew about, Wirt's confidential personal file in the hands of federal authorities. In the bleakest terms possible, he said that it "STUNK." The report was replete with serious allegations of illegalities, even traitorous activities, by Bowman.

Wirt was stunned. It had never occurred to him to examine the profile that the government had drawn of him. He learned furthermore, that he was under investigation for tax evasion. Bowman spent the rest of his highly influential and celebrated life attempting to eradicate the odor of illegality. Despite the assistance of political allies at the highest echelons of the Democratic Party and a sound endorsement from FBI chief J. Edgar Hoover, who personally reviewed the matter, he never succeeded in removing the stench, and it cost him.

In the immediate aftermath of the First World War, Bowman owned flourishing export-import border businesses with warehouses on both sides of the boundary in Nogales and at the crossing between Douglas, Arizona, and Agua Prieta, Sonora. He also had invested with New York capitalists in silver, copper, and lead mining in northern Sonora and with Obregón's brother-in-law in one of Mexico City's largest brokerage houses. He unsuccessfully prospected for oil in Texas. Wirt, at the same time, reinforced his high profile in Nogales through his hotel; his bank, the First National; and numerous real estate properties and businesses—as well as membership in local civic organizations, such as the Shriners. As wealthy residents often do, he also contributed to the community, in his case, a coliseum, which attracted spectaculars, vaudeville, and roadshows (*Othello* played there in 1915). Wirt's Southern drawl oozed graciousness when he spoke of bringing "culture" to "the little ole border town" of Nogales.[24]

Bowman also engaged in bootlegging. His competitors forwarded accusations to the Justice Department, but Bowman replied that while he regularly took late afternoon cocktails with friends and government officials in his office, he broke no laws. Perhaps it cannot be proved that Bowman violated liquor regulations, but strong signs are there.

Arizona had gone dry on December 31, 1914, preceding national Prohibition by six years. With the permission of the provisional governor of Sonora, Bowman a year or so later rented a warehouse in Guaymas and stocked it with 331 barrels of imported whiskey. Profits from sales were to be divided with local Sonoran schools. It seems unlikely that Bowman meant to sell all that hard liquor to Mexicans who ordinarily prefer beer, tequila, mescal, or in rural cantinas, homemade pulque. That whiskey more likely quenched American thirst in a dry state.

With U.S. Prohibition in effect, Bowman wrote a pitiful letter to Obregón on August 17, 1920, saying he felt like he was drowning and needed the president to save him. Competition was killing his liquor business. "At the time [of the original permit] we could make about $20 a gallon. Then I was taxed $5.00 a gallon. Times have changed. [Prohibition had commenced.] Competition is fierce. [I] can't profit because of high taxes and with them whisky costs $22 a gallon, and we have to compete with numerous venders of whisky and tequila who can undersell me."[25] Mexican customs officers, moreover, had shut down his Guaymas warehouse, held the keys, and would not reopen it until Bowman paid duty due on the merchandise. Wirt told Obregón, with whom he had recently vacationed, that he was willing to pay the duty but that he wanted relief from warehouse costs.

The Mexican federal government may have softened Bowman's tax responsibilities, but the new Sonoran governor admonished, "Don't forget to charge $10 for each gallon of whiskey that Wirt Bowman has been permitted to warehouse."[26] Bowman, the multimillionaire, had a peculiar habit of histrionic poor-mouthing when profits dipped a bit or when he ran into obstinate adversaries, but he did not always get his way, even with friends in high places on both sides of the international boundary. Despite his protestations, he was still in the liquor transfer business in 1924, then in the Mexican border town of Agua Prieta, where authorities fined him for an unknown violation of a state alcohol law.[27] Bootlegging, however, never did satisfy Bowman's pecuniary appetite. He craved the legendary assets of gambling casinos and envisioned a luxurious joy palace in a plush resort setting. A gem called Agua Caliente was on his mind, if not yet in his grasp.

Agua Caliente in Gestation

All along, the glamour and earnings of "sporting" establishments south of the border had attracted Wirt Bowman. His personal success with them would depend on his strong personal friendship with Alvaro Obregón, who became the country's president in 1920. The president invited Bowman and friends to his inauguration, and they arrived on the cheerfully decorated Nogales–Obregón–Home-Folks train chartered by Wirt. Before the sham elections, Bowman had issued a statement to the U.S. press asserting that, "General Obregón is the popular idol of the people and is assured of election as president of the republic. The general is one of the ablest men I have ever met. His election will be a distinct advantage to his country, as through his rule Mexico is bound to take on a wonderful commercial impetus. This is conceded on all sides."[1]

Not quite on all sides. Many American capitalists took a wait-and-see attitude toward the new regime. Mexico had promulgated a new constitution only three years earlier which challenged foreign investments and promised radical land and labor reforms that threatened business, and there were no assurances about which clauses the Obregón administration might enforce. Uncertainty counseled caution for most but not Bowman, who counted on the financial and material assistance he had rendered the government to yield its pay back.

FIRST THOUGHTS

Bowman and associates had first eyed the isolated and desolate Coronado Islands off the coast of Northern Baja California, only fifteen miles from San Diego, for a luxurious recreation and gaming site. (The Mafia also favored islands for gambling locations, its catchword being, get the patrons to places they cannot easily depart, where they are not distracted and easily watched, and take their money.) In February 1921 Wirt's syndicate offered Obregón's government $25,000 a year for a twenty-five-year lease of the Coronados. Then all developed property—docks, roads, housing, hotels, recreation centers, a lighthouse, military barracks, "everything necessary to beautify the islands"—would revert to Mexico. Taxes on liquor, tobacco, and other goods would be paid; all parties would greatly profit. But Obregón, who had announced a national moralization program, rejected the deal, saying that he did not believe it opportune to sell liquor and tobacco on the islands. More likely, he considered the islands of strategic military importance and did not favor American encroachment. Mexico's periodic moralization campaigns frequently had political, financial, and personal underpinnings.[2]

At the time of the Coronado petition, Bowman also requested exclusive rights to thoroughbred horse racing in Tijuana, which would have meant the delicate ousting and resultant legal wrangling with other interests already involved in racing there, A.B.W. included. Obregón held that request in abeyance, but Bowman's time would come.

He wrote to the personal secretary of Interior Secretary Plutarco Elías Calles on August 30, 1923, that he wished to be informed if and when the government decided to hand out concessions for new casinos in the territory, or elsewhere. As a reliable financial contributor to the Sonorans (in 1921 he loaned them $5,000 for school materials, and two years later dunned them for repayment with interest), Bowman hungered for special consideration.[3]

Following Withington's death in 1925, Bowman staked out his claim. He formed the Mexican Development Company in 1926 with the old A.B.W. partners "Booze" Beyer and Marvin Allen, along with the hotelier Baron Long and Joseph Zamansky, a Los Angeles gambler with Hollywood connections. Within two years Bowman had ousted Allen, Beyer, and Zamansky and brought in his young, cocksure, rambunctiously ambitious friend, James Crofton.

BECOMING A BARON

Wirt had become acquainted with Crofton a few years earlier through sporting establishments in Nogales. Jim was a happy-go-lucky, handsome, and daring young fellow in his early thirties, who was energetically working his way up through the region's gaming circles. His life story is a wondrous tale of spunk and luck. It is the American Dream, perfectly developed, even if not along the route of honesty, patience, hard work, self-denial, and strong determination traveled by Horatio Alger. (Who wants to be like Horatio Alger, anyway, burdened with such high morals and satisfied with small achievements?)

Born in 1895 on the south-central plains of Washington State in the tiny farming hamlet of Centerville, James Nugent Crofton displayed much of his father's restlessness, tenacious will power, and willingness to give most anything a try. The elder Crofton, of Irish immigrant descent, farmed 240 acres in the district, but shortly after James's birth moved into Centerville proper to run an attractive, three-story hotel named The Klondike, along with a livery stable and general store. Fired up by news of spectacular gold strikes in the Yukon, the father left his wife, Nannie, in charge of the Centerville businesses in 1898 and traveled to the boomtown of Dawson City to experience the bonanza and rake in a share. There he ran a casino, lost out to Lady Luck, and with winter approaching, returned home. In 1906 he moved his family some fifteen miles south to The Dalles (from the French *dalle*, meaning flagstone), a decaying stage, boat, and rail regional hub of forty-five hundred residents and at least thirty-seven saloons set along the narrows of the Columbia River. Crofton bought the historic Umatilla House, built in 1857, a three-story hotel with 120 guest rooms that was once a cherished meeting house for a picturesque and beguiling bevy of guests—river boatmen, railroad workers, ladies for hire, prospectors, real estate sharks, and bums—rivulets of humanity headed east-west and north-south in search of succor and prey. Remnants of the flotsam still patronized the hotel, where young Jim was assigned daily chores. A curious and experimental teenager, Jim indifferently attended public school in The Dalles but learned lessons-in-life at Umatilla House.[4]

Jim strove to be best, whether womanizing, riding a bucking bronc at the county fair, motorcycling flamboyantly about town (he later he gave up motorcycles for big, flashy, extremely expensive cars), or building an airplane and flying it (not far, but without mishap) off the roof of a barn. By the age of fifteen, he found The Dalles pinching his style. Maybe it was the do-gooder reforms taking root in town that impelled him to run from home: no more liquor sold (Oregon officially went fully dry on January 1, 1916), along with the ban on boys under twenty-one in pool rooms, which meant no more billiards, cards, pool, bagatelle, tossing dice, or any other games of chance. Convictions for violations carried two-to-thirty days in jail, or a $4-to-$60 fine. Or perhaps a cramped family life (parents and seven children) fueled the romantic wanderlust of adventurous youth. Possibly for no good reason at all, beyond the impulsive self-assuredness that charged his personality (he kowtowed to no one and tossed a stinging punch), Jim jumped a freight train headed west. Now he was on his own, though he kept in occasional touch with his kin. His father seemed to understand; gambling was in the family genes.[5]

Crofton learned to scrape by. First he shoveled coal at a boiler factory in Portland; hard work, move on. He then tamped railroad ties outside San Francisco; too hard, go to Los Angeles. Answering an advertisement for busboys at a local hotel, Jim assured the manager, "I know all about buses. I've been driving a bus for my dad's hotel. I've much experience as a bus boy."[6] He did not get *that* job, but learned they were hiring in San Diego for the 1915 Panama Exposition. He signed on as a spieler for a fairway show, where he learned that the real excitement around town centered on the opening of "Sunny Jim" Coffroth's Tijuana racetrack. Soon after, mornings found him riding bareback around the city shouting through a megaphone about the stirring thoroughbred horse racing just below the border. Afternoons, he donned a Mexican mariachi suit and walked downtown San Diego urging all to visit Old Mexico (Tijuana).

Barnum & Bailey Circus was in town for the exposition, and as he was meandering around the circus grounds looking for work in the off-season, Jim met a dainty, teen-aged bareback horse rider named Vera Emrie. He briefly courted her around the port city and they wed in a Reno, Nevada, marriage mill. They both worked for a year at the circus. She rode horses in spectaculars; he played trombone in the clown's band. As a rank beginner, his repertoire of sour notes brought transfer to ticket seller.

When the United States entered the First World War, Crofton briefly considered joining the Navy but settled for a machinist job at Mare Island Naval Shipyard north of San Francisco. The pay was decent, but Jim never favored a proletarian's routine or pay. After the war, he returned to San Diego just as Prohibition set in, and he flowed with the crowds to the liberation and exhilaration of roguish Tijuana, where he felt at home and where fast-money beckoned.[7]

Crofton was hanging out at Tijuana's racetrack in 1921 when "Booze" Beyer hired him to deal blackjack at the Sunset Inn. Beyer filled his young acolyte's head with stories of how he had struck it rich at Tonopah, Nevada—not digging for ore but dealing cards. "If you are going to gamble," Beyer advised young fellows, "get on my side—in other words, run the game, because you cannot lose; it is impossible to lose; the percentages are with you. Oh, yes, once in awhile a person gets lucky, but you can't beat luck. Don't ever gamble again, because you can't ever win. You've been around here [the Tijuana racetrack] long enough to see that."[8]

Youth listened hard to the experienced hand's advice, and when a new (the last) gold strike in the Nevada hills came in the early 1920s, Crofton moved to garner his fortune. He took Beyer's advice and bought a share in a gambling den, within a month or two pocketed $12,000 or $13,000 (approaching $150,000 today), sold out, reinvested in another gaming outlet in Mexicali, made a good deal more money, sold out, and bought into other gambling joints just across the border, first in tiny Naco (the international line splits the settlement into two Nacos), and then in Nogales, where he owned The Southern Club, a fancy cabaret fashioned from a natural cave on a steep hill rising above the main commercial street in town. Jimmy and Vera Crofton enjoyed a spectacular and meteoric ascension into high society. "The Southern Club in Nogales, Sonora, continues to be the leading attraction in Los Ambos Nogales," said *The Border Vignette*. "Manager Crofton and his charming wife are past masters in the art of entertaining and all who attend the Southern Club are assured of a royal welcome and fair treatment [unadulterated liquor at decent prices], as always."[9]

And the same newspaper wrote on December 8, 1923, "Manager Crofton of the Nogales Southern Club has made a number of needed improvements for the comfort and convenience of club members and their friends, including a reading room for gentlemen and a restroom [resting room] for ladies. A special music [vaudeville] program has been arranged for tonight."[10] Crofton was fast catching on to big-time.

TEAMMATES

Wirt Bowman met James Crofton at the Southern Club. They recognized their mutual engagement in gaming and became friends and business partners. When Withington died, they took over Tijuana's Foreign Club, which Jimmy managed and ran the counting room. They also joined Baron Long and "Sunny Jim" Coffroth on the Jockey Club's board of directors. Together Wirt and Jim raised and raced thoroughbred horses, and socialized at all-night soirées at Bowman's Spanish-style hilltop mansion in Palm City, only a few miles north of the Tijuana border crossing, and at the private gambling club on Marvin Allen's nearby 137-acre San Ysidro ranch. Crofton was running Allen's club one early Sunday morning in April 1927, when sheriff's deputies raided and flabbergasted fifteen well-dressed men and women who were mixing haute cuisine, illegal liquor, and sweet live-orchestral music with betting at three roulette and two twenty-one tables, as well as dice and cards. To escape jail, Crofton posted a $500 bond, which he probably forfeited; nothing more seems to have come of the unwelcome incident.[11]

What would come next for these Border Barons? Had they been on the East Coast, they would have been seen at Gatsby-like parties. But the Barons intended to outdo even those infamous soirées; they already had an image of Agua Caliente in their sights. James Crofton later reminisced, "Even in those days [when he owned clubs in Naco and Nogales] I visualized a place which would be exclusive and beautiful. A place to which people would come from all over the country to see. This was my visualization of Agua Caliente."[12] Baron Long imagined an idyllic traditional Spanish design for the complex. Governor Rodríguez understood how to navigate treacherous legal swells surrounding the purchase and legalization of Mexican property, and Wirt Bowman possessed the overall acumen, experience, and political connections to stitch together the segments. The ebullient Barons could already see a brimming pot of riches at the end of the rainbow.

Building Camelot

Fabled Agua Caliente emerged quite magically at a barren desert oasis. First there was nothing to speak of at the site, then all of a sudden, magnificence. First, hardly a sprinkling of people, and then a deluge of the internationally renowned and enthusiastic hangers-on. The transformation occurred in an incredibly short period of time, three years overall, 1927 to 1930. Like all such castles, it was built in stages, in this case with profits of early operation and investor capital funding expansion. Even as the hub of the project, the hotel and casino, were under construction, greyhound racing on a makeshift track lured bettors to the site and produced building funds. Constructing the horse-racing track came last, after investors had witnessed the immediate, meteoric success of the enterprise. The Barons, relying on the sale of public shares, spent as little of their own personal millions as possible on the project, but they held tight reigns over its operation.

There was, moreover, some urgency in the atmosphere; a sense of bonanza permeated the enterprise. The Barons seemed not to consider Agua Caliente a long-term investment, but more as a get-rich-quick-and-then-move-on endeavor, a mind-set that marked their other forays into gaming ventures. And reality nudged them along. Patronage at Tijuana's joy palaces and the town's booming tourism in general depended to a great extent on U.S. Prohibition, and no one knew how long that might last. Pressures were mounting to repeal the Constitutional amendment that had enacted it. Gambling restrictions and the ban on racetrack betting were also under attack and seemed destined to fall. The Progressive movement appeared to have seen its day, and the Barons knew from experience in their line of work how quickly bonanza could go bust. Better get started on Agua Caliente.

FIRST MEASURES

First, the site for the spa, the land itself, had to be procured—legally, if possible. The Barons eyed an open tract of high desert that gently sloped down toward the Tijuana River on the southern outskirts of town. Its main attraction was a natural hot water spa called Agua Caliente, a 20-by-40-foot pool that had been crudely gouged out and lined with wooden planks. There visitors dipped in sulfuric waters, lay in hot mud baths at the edges, and picnicked under a few surrounding trees. Back in the 1880s the president of San Diego's Medical Society, Dr. David B. Hoffman, a surgeon, had nurtured "one lungers" (tuberculars), arthritics, and rheumatics there. In 1921 a Turkish-American joined with a Japanese merchant to take advantage of the carousing ambiance of tourist-Tijuana to build a two-story wooden hotel, cabaret, and casino at the springs. The lodge was an unsavory place where patrons reveled in vaudeville shows, gambled, got drunk, fell into fierce fist fights, and lounged with ladies of the night. Gamblers gathered there late evenings with their female friends to sober up in the hot waters, settle into the hotel bar, and drink themselves into their next stupor. Lawmen from both sides of the border had ribald outings at the springs, at times leading to an international scuffle. Mothers might have told their young sons to avoid the site, but the boys took the mandate more as a challenge to be tested than an order.[1]

A scion of the Argüello family owned the land itself, inherited from his grandfather, Santiago, whose heirs had been selling off their parcels piece by piece, although litigation over who owned and therefore had the right to sell what continued far into the twentieth century. As Mexico's constitution prohibited foreign ownership of property near the country's borders, the tract meant for the Agua Caliente resort had to be purchased by a Mexican. Governor Rodriguez ensured that it was. He bought 491 acres from Alejandro Argüello for $10,000, fought off legal challenges by other Argüellos through the nation's highly politicized Supreme Court, and then leased the tract (all but seventy-five acres he retained for himself) at $25 annually for seventy-five years to the U.S. Barons, after which the real estate, including improvements, would revert to the governor's estate. Now the Barons were ready to design and build.[2]

LONG'S VISION

Baron Long, the wealthy hotelier with long-time experience in horse track, nightclub, and casino operations, handled the architectural design and planning of the main complex. Baron was his given name. When he learned of his son's birth, Long's father had just witnessed a play in which the good-looking, husky, heroic leading male was called Baron. He named his new-born after the actor. Europeans considered the name a royal title and accorded Long the special attention he coveted.[3]

Baron himself had a remarkable upbringing. His father was a gambler and drunkard when he received The Word and converted into a raging "born again" preacher. Born in 1883 in Fort Wayne, Indiana, Baron went to Franklin College where he excelled in baseball but not much else, dabbled in newspaper reporting, and then fled the Midwest for San Francisco, where he became the pitchman for a traveling patent medicine company. Ogling sightseers remembered the hefty, 6'4" "Chinese coolie" who sold "tiger fat," good for whatever ailed one. His father's preaching style came in handy, but sporting was his bloodline.[4]

With gaming competition in the Bay Area established and fierce, Baron headed for Los Angeles, where he partnered in an athletic club with the ex-heavyweight champion Jim Jeffries, tabbed "The Great White Hope." Together they bought and sold several hotels and cabarets that catered to Hollywood and sports superstars, politicians, and police. Soon Long was schmoozing with the brightest of L.A.'s luminaries and playing the City of Angels' lovable devil.[5]

When Los Angeles reformers banned liquor and curtailed sporting, Long opened California's first all-night club in 1912 (others closed at 1 A.M.) just outside city limits in the wide-open, wet, boss-run, corrupt little town of Vernon. For *the* place to be, Long's Vernon Country Club hardly looked fashionable from the outside. It was not much more than a roadhouse set in a beet field with parking in front. Long, however, gained a reputation for giving entertainment's newcomers their initial public appearances. He might find youthful aspirants on the beach picking a guitar or singing for coins outside an amusement center and bring them to Vernon where they gratefully performed for coffee, cakes, and tips. Others came recommended by The Baron's friends. (He insisted on "The" before his given name, and most complied.) The budding artists rightly considered it a big break to perform at the club.

The orchestra leader Abe Lyman started at the cabaret and went on to star at London's Kit Kat Club. His brother, Mike, did vaudeville there and in the 1930s, after hiring the chef from Maxim's in Paris, opened his famous Mike Lyman's Grill in Los Angeles. Paul Whiteman fiddled and Buddy de Silva strummed his ukulele at the Vernon Club. The last of the red hot mamas, Sophie Tucker, sang and danced there (and played Santa Claus at Christmas parties) and the famous songwriter Cliff Friend played piano for Harry Richman's vaudeville act. Customers first heard Rudy Wiedoeft, the world's foremost jazz saxophone player, at the club. In fact, the Vernon may well have introduced jazz to Southern California.

Other notables also got their first break at the Vernon, which featured Gus Arnheim at the piano, Vincent Rose of Casey Jones fame, and the beloved vaudeville singer Blossom Seeley. Even as starters, they were an impressive lot, especially appreciated because they were among the first such entertainers to play audience requests. The club's mix of orchestra, floor show, dancing, and chorus girls became a standard in future nightclubs.[6]

Revelers dubbed the Vernon the entire region's "one bright spot," and The Baron soaked in the accolades. Long personally met most of his guests at the door with a glad hand and chatty word, and Hollywood's finest streamed in: Wallace Reid, Mary Pickford, and D. W. Griffith among them. Another regular, Fatty Arbuckle, one night put a hot steak between two pieces of bread and ate the huge sandwich. Soon after, a new item appeared on the club's menu: "steak sandwich." About that time, Tom Mix drove his automobile through the building's wide front entrance right into the club itself, announced his presence, and bought everyone a drink. Hollywood's legends are forever growing and mutating.[7]

Despite his outward charm, Long could be intimidating, bossy, or rude. In other words, a bully. He liked to brag that he fired Rudolf Valentino, then a skinny, tango-dancing kid earning $35 weekly at the Vernon. Late one night, after the show, the boy got hungry, went to the club's kitchen, and against house rules made a sandwich for himself. Long caught him and fired the delinquent. Valentino later claimed he left the club for better-paying work elsewhere. Who knows? Both parties were prone to exaggerations and distortions.[8]

Then, late one night, a cute, coy teenaged girl sought to charm her way into the famous nightclub. Baron asked her age, she replied sixteen, and Long declared her too young and unsophisticated to enter the club. So Gloria Swanson, then already a Mack Sennett bathing beauty, left.[9]

At some point she returned and became a regular at the Vernon, along with her fellow movie stars Clark Gable and the Marx Brothers. Jackie Coogan, a child-star sensation, showed up with his father at the club's picnics and other outdoor events. The budding billionaire Howard Hughes drank regularly at the Vernon, while sports headliners such as the racecar driver Barney Oldfield, with his inevitable cigar, enjoyed jazz there. Of course, the Baron's close friend Jim Jeffries joined the revelries.[10]

The risqué reputation and star quality of the Vernon was bound to attract legal problems. Sheriff's deputies raided the Vernon Club early the morning of January 28, 1915, and arrested Baron Long for sponsoring illegal lotteries. The *Los Angeles Times*, a strong supporter of reform, concluded its flavorful report:

> The raid is the latest move of authorities against the notorious resort, the name of which is freighted with a long list of deaths and injuries and with charges of debauchery. The casualty list has become fat with names of those who imbibed unwisely at the Baron's tables and who were crushed when [their] speeding automobiles returning to Los Angeles smashed [together] in the gray morning hours, [and left their] torn bodies among the debris. There youths have taken "the highball road to pleasure" and there ruined men, criminals, have told the police they gained the lust to spend that drove them to steal.[11]

In other words, to the *Times*, gaming, the hootchy-kootchy, and wetting one's tonsils sharpened one's appetite for riches and induced the money-hungry to steal.

Because of a defective search warrant and political uncertainties (Los Angeles was awash in political machinations, intrigue, and corruption), the district attorney dismissed the case against Long and returned all gaming tools and liquor confiscated from his place. Anti-liquor forces charged the prosecuting attorney with dereliction of duty, and the accusation played itself out in future elections, but Baron Long emerged unscathed.[12]

Long frequently knew legal trouble, some of it serious, like the challenge to his (and Coffroth's) ownership of the Tijuana racetrack in the 1920s, and on other occasions, frivolous nonsense. A movie actress named Dorothy Cardinal sued him in 1919 for $30,000 when a tipsy man trying to dance the shimmy on a stage intended for the Vernon's genuine performers, tumbled off, fell on her leg, and broke it. She blamed Long for allowing the drunk to dance on the platform. The judge dismissed the case, noting that the actress went to "the club with [her] eyes open" and had done considerable drinking herself. "By the way," the judge asked the defense attorney, "what's this dance called the shimmy?" In response, the lawyer offered only a guttural noise which "may or may not have satisfied the court."[13]

Baron Long and his well-paid attorneys treated lawsuits as hurdles to be jumped in the steeplechase of sporting life. Jump, steady oneself, and race on to other ventures.

Besides the Vernon, before Prohibition The Baron owned the famous Ship Inn at Venice, California's fantasy-by-the-sea, a sparkling and cluttered collage of canals, roller coasters, theaters, opium dens, lunch rooms, "noodle houses" (Chinese restaurants), and ballyhoo. He also bought the glamorous Sunset Inn just a few miles north in Santa Monica. Filmland's preening notables danced and reveled their nights away in both all-night pleasure lands. It is no wonder that Long also lured Hollywood's best to his haunts below the border.

In 1919 the irrepressible Baron bought San Diego's landmark hotel, The Grant, built eight years earlier by Ulysses S. Grant Jr., the late ex-president's son, and in the Roaring Twenties, the city's central meeting place for sports and businessmen, as well as the socially prominent. At the same time, Long zealously protected his interests in the Tijuana racetrack and its adjoining Sunset Inn. As a serious sidelight, The Baron bred thoroughbred horses on his scenic 2,500-acre ranch in Las Viejas, in the Cuyamaca Mountains thirty miles east of San Diego. When several of California's leading breeders died in the mid-1920s, Long bought their entire stock and developed one of the premier stud farms in the country.[14] Not bad for a thirty-five-year-old Midwesterner who got his start as a teenager pitching "tiger fat."

CONSTRUCTING THE RESORT

But now Agua Caliente was his paramount passion. Long asked five well-known Southern California architects to submit designs for the new spa. Tied to the trends of their times—the Bauhaus School or Soviet Constructivism—they drew renderings of steel and cement, behemoth high-rise structures considered "modern" for the day. Long, however, envisioned

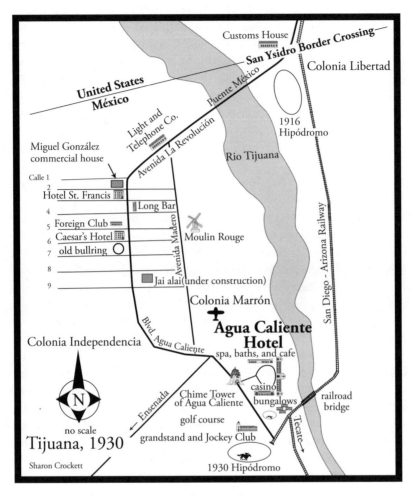

Tijuana, 1930. Sharon Crockett

something more romantic, peaceful, and restful for Agua Caliente, a place where moneyed patrons would be comfortable while dispensing heaps of cash.[15]

Through friends, Long met a nineteen-year-old, largely self-taught draftsman named Wayne McAllister, a likeable, enthusiastic lad, who had quit San Diego's Hoover High School the previous year to work at a small architectural firm. Long, with nothing to lose, decided to give the youngster a chance at designing his dreamland, drove him to the dry, largely desolate site of the proposed resort, then covered with scrub brush and a couple of beautiful sycamore trees, which later framed the entrance to the hotel. The Baron mused that he wanted the resort designed "so a weary traveler coming across [the border] turns down this little ravine and sees a beautiful old mission, and I want you to create this mission."[16] McAllister and his fiancée, Corine, also an aspiring architect whom he soon married, worked day and night for most of the next year, sketching Long's dream into reality.

There was nothing original about the over-all design. Mission Revival style had spread like an epidemic from the San Diego Exposition of 1915 to encompass residences, store buildings, apartments, gas stations, roadside cafes, and post offices and other public buildings—as well as mortuaries. It was commonplace in Southern California by the 1920s, and in many other parts of the United States as well: whitewashed stucco buildings with over-hanging red-tile roofs, often supported by open beams. Baroque ornamentation frequently highlighted arched entranceways and windows. A bell tower might grace the main entrance, and fancy iron grillwork covered windows, at times fronted with balconies. A hallmark of the design was the interior courtyard, elaborately tiled patios with decorative landscaping. It was estimated that by 1937 90 percent of San Diego residences erected since the Exposition were Revival style, as were an indefinite, but large, percentage of commercial buildings.[17]

Wayne and Corine did not deviate from the theme. Baron Long would have his mission. Specialists, of course, later added Louis XV style furnishings, Mudéjar tile work, Art Deco styling, and Mediterranean-type landscaping, and what these touches lacked in symmetry and cohesion was compensated by lavishness. The McAllisters somehow pulled the components together into a celebrated, world-class jewel that architectural digests singled out as unique and praised as a marvel.[18]

At the roadway entranceway to the complex stood the resort's trademark, a massive 80-foot tower of Moorish inspiration resting on an arched base through which motor vehicles passed to and from the hotel and casino. On top, a revolving light warned and welcomed approaching airplanes. At Baron Long's insistence, chimes adjusted to sound like a tolling mission bell, sounded on the hour. But when hotel guests sleeping in after a long night at the gaming tables complained that the clanging bells kept them awake, Long had the chimes moved to the steam plant's chimney tower, disguised as an Arabic minaret, where to his delight their bonging continued to remind patrons of the enchanting ambiance that enveloped them. The chimes amounted to Long's oblations to Aphrodite, goddess of pleasure, and to Prialaga and Chant, god and goddess of hedonism—and to Tykhe (Fortuna to Romans), goddess of chance. The divinities had their critics who excoriated excess and imbalance, but by and large these deities ruled the times.

Construction on the $1.5 million project began in mid-1927 with the governor's brother, Fernando Rodríguez, in charge and took only ten months to complete the core of the enterprise, including the hotel and casino. With few exceptions, the hundreds of laborers were hard-working Mexicans earning good wages. All building materials came from San Diego, except the hand-painted decorative tiles imported from Spain. Equipment and goods entered Mexico duty-free, courtesy of the federal government, which declared the project crucial to local employment (Agua Caliente was by far the largest employer in town) and for the permanent public improvements that it spawned: paved roads, water mains, an electric power plant, up-graded telecommunications, new bridges, and an airstrip.

Governor Rodríguez made a number of underhanded contributions to the resort at federal government expense. Mexico City previously had authorized construction of a huge, expensive dam on the Tijuana River, ten miles east of town. It was a badly needed civic improvement, both to control flooding and to create a reservoir for the water-starved community. Now Rodríguez ordered construction materials for the dam, to be imported duty-free—the expected cement, wire, and steel—but also one hundred tons of tiles and bricks, a thousand gallons of paint and varnish, twenty tons of lead attachments, fifteen tons of electric wire, and another fifteen of roofing tar paper. Certainly laborers utilized a portion of these latter materials for their quarters at the dam, but the bulk must have ended up at Agua Caliente.

The long list of items requisitioned, purportedly for the dam, further included five hundred doors and one thousand windows, five hundred beds with the same number of pillows and double that number of sheets and pillow covers. Five tons of kitchen utensils and tableware capped the inventory.[19] So Agua Caliente was being outfitted with government money. No one seemed to mind. No investigation followed. No exposé. No sensational headlines.

The fashionable hotel accommodated five hundred guests; all rooms featured distinctive embellishments and outside exposures. A famous New York chef prepared international cuisine for up to four hundred guests in the casino's ultra-modern kitchen. Agua Caliente, however, was still very much a work in progress when it opened to a thrilled, dressed-to-the-nines crowd on June 16, 1928. The resort's moneymaking machine—its casino—performed like a veteran, gnawing away at purses and wallets. Patrons feigned disappointment at losses and remarked they would soon return to whatever new enjoyments the Barons concocted. Their mood and resolutions fit the mood of the period.

By the time of the First Anniversary Celebration, the Barons had invested another million dollars (the earnings of stockholders, not their own) in 116 additional hotel rooms, all deluxe doubles with distinct color schemes, most with private baths painted pink and featuring a tortoise shell toilet seat. Signed photos of visitors—Mary Pickford, Douglas Fairbanks, and an Italian countess—hung on room walls, and New York's Mayor Jimmy Walker was among the honored guests who raved about the premises.

Nearby stood a colony of fifty bungalows, arranged and decorated to resemble a small, picturesque Old World town with winding streets, manicured gardens, quaint rustic bridges, and imported vegetation identified with labels. Extensive landscaping had transformed arid high desert to semi-tropical luxuriousness through which bridle paths wandered. Hundreds of mature palm trees were transplanted to the site. "We did not bother to grow our gardens," Crofton crowed. "We bought them already made."[20] Turf for the grounds was imported from Europe, he said with typical hyperbole, and then rolled out like carpets where appropriate.

A top golf professional designed and seeded a world championship eighteen-hole golf course at the site. Its inaugural open tournament scheduled for January 1929 offered the sport's largest purse to that date, $25,000. "The Squire," Gene Sarazen (the first golfer to win a career grand slam), triumphed, and with great fanfare Wirt Bowman delivered his prize money on the course—in a wheelbarrow full of silver dollars, later converted into a more manageable $10,000 check.[21]

The new half-million-dollar Olympic-size swimming pool called The Plunge, bathhouses, mud bath, and massage parlors utilizing the hot springs were soon in service. A gem of a $2-million thoroughbred horse racetrack, billed as unparalleled, the finest in the world, opened its first season just after Christmas Day, 1929. Agua Caliente's reputation as the hemisphere's finest gaming resort, one which challenged Europe's best, fast became confirmed.

Today's Las Vegas palaces may exhibit their frenetic ostentations, but they lack the warmth and hospitality of an Agua Caliente. Las Vegas feels fake; Agua Caliente seemed genuine, perhaps because it was the first in the long line of such pleasure palaces Out West or because people today are more jaded. Hal Rottman, who patronized both venues, compared them for the San Diego Historical Society in 1972. "In Caliente you could not go into the casino without a coat and tie," he said. "You could not go into the Gold Room unless you were in a tuxedo and evening dress. Now, in Vegas they don't care if you go in there in the nude, if you have someone to carry your money. Down there [in Agua Caliente] it was class, strictly class."[22]

Merriment was at its height at the first anniversary celebration advertised as the "Carnival at Caliente." The eminent interior decorator Louis Sherman, whose tastes had styled the resort's interiors, bedecked the premises for the occasion. Lou Anger, chief assistant and producer at United Artists, himself a stockholder in the resort, supplied showy Hollywood entertainment. Fresh from New York's Club Richmond, The Commanders played the day's dance music, and more than a thousand bluebloods (some genuine, most nouveau riche), ranking politicians, royalty, business moguls, sports greats, movie stars, and media people poured into the gala.

The preceding day's preliminary festivities included "a fashion show featuring the greatest collection of beauty prize winners ever assembled at one time on the Pacific Coast. . . . Ten of these dazzling specimens of pulchritude. The pageant they put on is the last word in fashion shows and both the first and last word in beauty and style, featuring especially sport and beach costumes and lingerie."[23]

None of the socialites at the resort's mirthful anniversary party appeared to be fazed by the robbery of the resort's assets and the wanton slaughter of its custodians that had taken place only a few weeks earlier on the Dike. The press covering the celebration did not mention the crime. It was as if the Barons and the delights they offered had blotted the bullet holes and blood stains from memory and swept the probable collusion of Agua Caliente people under the expensive imported carpets of the establishment. Such silence among the Barons themselves is perhaps understandable. After all, they knew they were targets of mobsters who periodically sent them fearsome reminders. The Barons kept their surveillance crews and body guards standing by awaiting another thunderbolt from their tormentors.

The public-at-large throughout the region and beyond, however, had hardly lost sight of the horror and sensationalism that the atrocity had tattooed on their minds. They remembered the frightful headlines:

FIRST TIME A MACHINE GUN USED IN WEST COAST ROBBERY!

EAST COAST GANGSTERS MOVING WEST!

THE MOB IS HERE!

Concerned and curious citizens overflowed hearing rooms at every step of the prosecution's legal proceedings against the defendants in the money-car murders, who remained under heavy guard for fear of the mob's intervention. So many questions remained unanswered. The state readied its star witnesses to testify, among them Jerry Kearney, who had turned state's evidence in hopes that complicity charges against him would be ameliorated. Excited but wary observers anticipated an extended, suspenseful trial revealing the unanticipated and unwelcome prevalence of mobsters in their midst.

Looking dapper and largely unconcerned, Capt. Jerry Kearney, left, and Lee Cochran, captured in Los Angeles, are returned to San Diego in police custody for criminal proceedings involving their complicity in the murders on the Dike. University of Southern California Special Collections

Bitter and seemingly unconcerned, "Silent" Marty Colson read books and dozed during the legal hearings against him. University of Southern California Special Collections

Lee Cochran in happier times with his three-year-old daughter, Gloria, and wife, Marian, who helped the state's case against her husband. University of Southern California Special Collections

During the first decades of the twentieth century, Tijuana, along its main tourist street, presented a rousing free-for-all of cantinas, gambling joints, bordellos, con men, and suckers. Sophisticates patronizing Agua Caliente went "slumming" there. University of Southern California Special Collections

Governor Esteban Cantú, an opportunistic showman,
ruled the federal Territory of Baja California (including Tijuana,
Mexicali, and Ensenada) from 1915 to 1920 as a potentate,
financed by rake-offs from the vice halls he licensed.
San Diego Historical Society

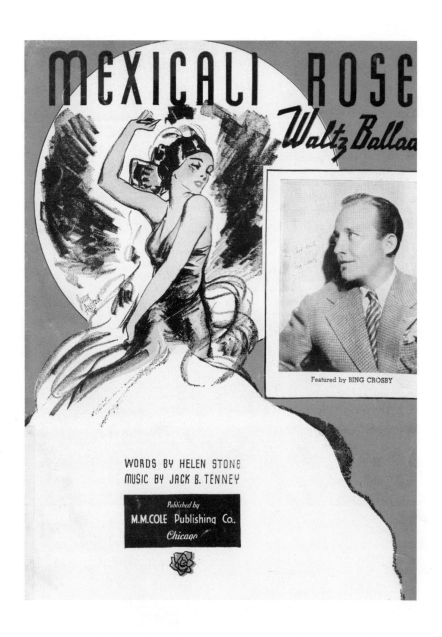

Jack Tenney played piano and wrote his immortal "Mexicali Rose"
in 1923 at Mexicali's The Owl, an internationally famous gambling and
prostitution club owned by the earliest group of Border Barons. Bing Crosby
recorded his famous rendition of the waltz ballad fifteen years later.
Andre Williams Collection

Jack Johnson, the first African American heavyweight
boxing champion, fled the United States when charged with a Mann Act violation.
He ran a popular nightclub with boxing and gambling mainly for blacks
just off Tijuana's main tourist strip. Andre Williams Collection.

Parched by drought in 1916, San Diego hired a famous rainmaker,
Charles M. Hatfield, to mix his secret chemicals, stimulate precipitation,
and fill the local reservoir. A deadly deluge followed, inundating and
isolating the city and surroundings, causing deaths, and washing out Tijuana's
brand-new horse-racing track. San Diego Historical Society

Mexico's central government appointed a trusted military commander,
Abelardo Rodríguez, as governor of Baja California Norte in 1923.
He linked up with the U.S. Border Barons to pave the way for their highly
lucrative Agua Caliente venture. San Diego Historical Society

The hot springs called Agua Caliente became a medicinal
spa for rheumatics run by a San Diego doctor in the late 1800s.
Picnickers and carousers later frequented the site, and a hotel with a rowdy
reputation emerged there before the Barons transformed the fetid springs
into an exquisite gaming resort. Andre Williams Collection

The Border Barons issued stock certificates to finance their extravagant enterprise, investing a minimum of their own capital into the construction stages of the project, which cost more than $10 million. Financiers, land developers, politicians, and sports and film stars eagerly bought shares in the enterprise. Andre Williams Collection

Wayne McAllister (right), barely twenty years old, won international renown as general architect of Agua Caliente, praised more for its stylistic cohesiveness and decorative touches than overall originality. The boldly ambitious Border Baron, James Crofton (left), who aimed to become California's richest citizen, managed the casino and racetrack. Andre Williams Collection

The ornate entrance to the Jockey Club reflects some of the
baroque tendencies that Art Deco borrowed from the earlier Art Nouveau,
with flora and fauna and curvilinear and frequently playful designs, all in vibrant color.
The surfaces above the archway and to its right are full of wonderful surprises.
California State Library Special Collections

Well-to-do and influential patrons rented (or were complimented)
lovely bungalows, set in gardens planted with rare specimens
from around the world. A few of these structures remain
on the premises, currently leased as private homes.
California State Library Special Collections

The Plunge—for patrons only. (Employees had their own pool off premises.)
The adjoining spa with an eclectically styled Art Deco tile façade
at the entranceway, offered massages, hair parlors, mud baths,
and medicinal hot springs, all in opulent settings.
California State Library Special Collections

Art Deco motifs abounded in the hotel lobby detail designed
by Wayne McAllister. Richly decorated primitive-style corbels supported
the beamed ceiling. The sinuous wall-light fixtures and iron
grillwork banister were typical of Art Deco design.
California State Library Special Collections

Orientalism blended with Art Deco motifs on hand-painted tiles
imported from Spain in the lobby of the bathhouse at the spa.
The ceiling displayed the energized cosmic imagery common to such
decorative schemes in the Twenties.
California State Library Special Collections.

Lighting sunbursts illuminated domed ceilings above a parquet
dance floor with various veneers of hardwood in the casino's dining room.
Geometrical designs, chevrons, and Mesoamerican motifs adorn borders,
while murals above depicted the sensuous frivolity of flapper society: a man at
the piano (left), playing with one hand, cocktail in the other and a flapper leaning
in; a nude woman (center) chasing two hunting dogs; a man seated in
modernistic chair (right), cocktail in one hand and cigarette in the other,
a cigar-smoking man leaning on a table, cocktail in hand,
and a flapper with cocktail raised.
California State Library Special Collections

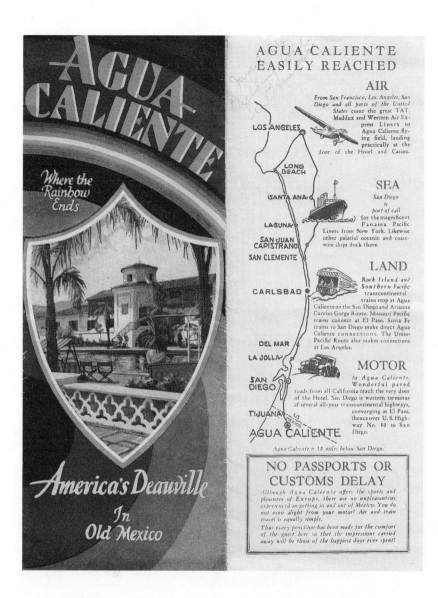

Promotions placed the resort at the end of the rainbow—in other words, where one would find the pot of gold promised in childhood fantasies, undoubtedly by slinging dice or playing roulette in the casino. The come-on assured patrons that America's Deauville in Old Mexico could easily be reached by air, sea, train, motor car. No passports or customs delay. Just come, stay, and open your wallets and pocketbooks. California State Library Special Collections.

165

Where to go at Agua Caliente

Key to Diagram
1. Agua Caliente Hotel
2. Casino, Patio and Cafe
3. The Spa, Baths and Plunge
4. Aviation Field
5. Pitch and Putt Golf Course
6. Garage
7. Championship Tennis Court
8. Campanile (Chimes Tower)
9. Golf Course (18-Hole Championship) and Club House
10. Power Plant
11. Bungalows
12. San Diego & Arizona R. R.
13. Train Depot No. 1, Hotel
14. Dog Track
15. Train Depot No. 2, Race Track
16. Race Track Grandstand
17. Agua Caliente Race Course
18. Race Track Club House

Overview of structures, recreational and entertainment complexes, and transport connections at spacious Agua Caliente, known as the Western Hemisphere's greatest gaming center and favorably equated with traditional world-famous gathering spots for royalty and bluebloods at Monte Carlo and France's Deauville. Andre Williams Collection

Super tri-motors, such as this Fokker F-X, a Western Air Express airplane with a wooden frame wing, carried a maximum of twelve passengers from San Francisco, Los Angeles, and San Diego to and from Agua Caliente's private airstrip. Andre Williams Collection.

Nicknamed "Hollywood's Playground," Agua Caliente catered
to the wealthy and prominent and employed a full-time publicist to hype
the notables and furnish a torrent of publicity to the press and radio.
More ordinary people also visited the premises in droves to look and see,
to bet, and later to brag to others that they had been there.
Andre Williams Collection

Agua Caliente became the setting for many motion pictures,
mostly potboilers that had horse racing in the plot. Film studios, however,
did make one memorable feature there: *In Caliente* (1935), starring the sultry
Dolores del Rio with Pat O'Brien, Leo Carrillo, and dance extravaganzas designed
and directed by Busby Berkeley, one of them to the memorable
hit song, "The Lady in Red." Andre Williams Collection

Relishing notoriety, two of the millionaire Border Barons,
Wirt Bowman (left) and his protégé, James Crofton,
basked in photo opportunities of themselves as owners
of the extolled resort. University of Southern
California Special Collections

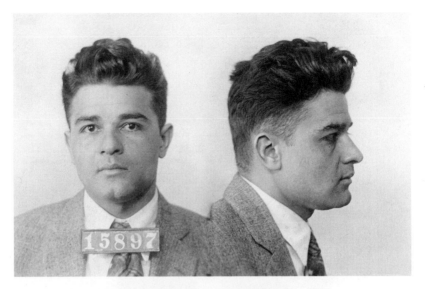

Prison mug shot of "Silent" Marty Colson,
sentenced to life in Folsom Prison for his deadly attack
on the spa's money-car. California State Archives.

Lee Cochran, accomplice in the murderous holdup on
the Dike, was sentenced to life in San Quentin, but earned parole
for good behavior. California State Archives

8/6

Lloyd E. Sampsell, a meek-looking, soft-spoken, brilliant
jailhouse lawyer, and deadly as a rattlesnake. Sampsell joined Colson
in a failed attempt to break out of Folsom Prison in 1933.
University of Southern California Special Archives

CAPTAIN JERRY'S DAY

With the public demanding swift justice, prosecution of suspects-in-hand rushed ahead, even if pieces of the puzzle were still missing. Marty Colson and Lee Cochran, the suspected murderers, were in custody but not talking. The state possessed the fevered statement of Jerry Kearney, self-admitted bootlegger and complicit in the cover-up, along with that of his wife, who overheard only fragments from the defendants when they were harbored in the Kearney home. The district attorney also possessed remarks by Lee's teary, unstable wife about her husband's admissions. The state was holding the two women and Jerry as material witnesses, but it could be much worse for them should the government decide that they had in someway participated in the crime or conspired to do so.

The coroner's hearing on May 24, 1929, had produced particulars concerning time and manner of death, forensic details, eyewitness identification of Colson, vehicles involved, money stolen, and a rough timeline from Tijuana to the site of the robbery, all mandatory for trial but hardly the sort of substantial evidence needed for conviction. At this juncture the district attorney's case seemed brittle and certainly challengeable by a rigorous defense. Yet the prosecution publicly exuded confidence and predicted that Colson and Cochran would admit their guilt in expectation of life sentences instead of the death penalty. The pair, however, displayed no such inclination. Cochran had become less cheerful and more guarded, while "Silent" Marty, his wounded shoulder somewhat improved, continued to draw childlike pictures for snack food.

At one point in this cat-and-mouse spectacle, deputies escorted Kearney, at his request, to Colson's cell to plead that Marty come clean and absolve

Jerry and his wife of involvement in the crime. "We took you in when you came to us wounded," he said. "You owe it to Grace and me to help us out now." In response, Colson nonchalantly stared away. "Tell the truth, even if you swing for it," Jerry begged. "Don't be a rat. And keep your word to me and my wife."[1] Marty remained distant and silent.

Township Judge Eugene Daney Jr. scheduled a preliminary hearing for Thursday, June 20, to consider whether or not the prosecution held sufficient evidence to forward the case to superior court. Two days before the scheduled hearing authorities thought it best to rearraign Colson and Cochran. Cochran presented no problem; he had clearly pleaded "not guilty" at the earlier procedure and did so again. Colson's silence created the dilemma. He had said nothing when carried into the original session on a litter, and investigators now admitted he might not have been fully conscious. Even if he were faking, better not take a chance and face an appeal. Or Marty might not have understood the judge's English. Because of his muteness and dark complexion, many still presumed him to be a Spanish-speaking Latino. Furthermore, he had no attorney at the proceeding, the sort of flaw that could generate legal recourse.

Although there was sufficient time and opportunity for a customary courtroom hearing, Judge Daney conducted the rearraignment in Colson's jail lockup. The afternoon of June 18 four unannounced visitors stood at the prisoner's cell: Judge Daney; the prisoner's Los Angeles lawyer, George W. Wicke; the jailer, Harry Hubbell; and a newspaperman to record the episode (another example of the incredible entrée and rapport that certain newspaper reporters had with San Diego police and judicial authorities).

"When the quartet entered the cell, Colson was eating. Wicke explained to him that the rearraignment was a necessary procedure, but Colson continued to eat his jail fare," the *San Diego Union* reported. "He presently laid down his fork, gazing fixedly at the floor. Justice Daney asked him if he could understand English. Colson merely waved his hand slightly to signify that he was ready to have the court proceed."[2]

That little hand wave apparently was enough to convince the judge that Colson could understand him, meant to confirm the "not guilty" plea already entered for him, and wished to get on with further judicial proceedings. Seems like a good deal of certainty drawn from the slight wave of a hand, but that is what happened.

"POSITIVE" IDENTIFICATION

So many spectators wanted a glimpse of the accused that the preliminary hearing on June 20 had to be moved up the hall to a much larger courtroom. The judge allowed people to stand around the edges. Even then, deputies had to turn people away. The court decided first to hear the case against Colson and Cochran, and then turn to Kearney, his wife, and Marian Cochran, "clad in a blue ensemble with a blue thimble hat pulled rakishly over one eye."[3]

The state opened before Judge Daney with perfunctory police and coroner reports, those of the surgeon's autopsy and the first officer to arrive on the scene, all previously detailed in the press and along legal steps already trod. Then it turned to eyewitnesses, who had now become less certain and more reserved about what they had seen and experienced on the Dike. Defense attorneys—two for Cochran, Ed Johnson and Edgar Hervey, and Wicke for Colson—pointedly challenged and piercingly picked apart their inconsistent and conflicting remembrances. Wicke had been hired by Marty's mother. The professional backgrounds and affiliation of the other two lawyers were a mystery. They refused to confirm or deny in court that they were in the pay of the Southern California Protective Bootleggers' Association to which the defendants supposedly belonged. (The association may well have been an invention of the press, public, or police. It was not mentioned again, but the mob assuredly protected its own.)

The defense shook all eyewitnesses but Frank D. Hartell, the retired railroad engineer who was trimming grass outside his home on Edgemont Street when, he swore, the Ford crime-car slammed to a halt across the street, two men got out and stood chatting on the sidewalk for a moment before a second car swung by and picked them up. Quite likely Hartell was mistaken. No second car ever arrived to rendezvous with the killers, who had parked a getaway vehicle on Edgemont before heading off to sack the ill-fated treasure-car. The exchange happened in a blur, Hartell got confused, but still claimed to recognize the individuals involved. He pointed to Colson and Cochran, seated side by side in the courtroom, and declared, *"They are the ones!"*

Cochran's attorney wanted to be sure and told his client to march before Hartell. "A sheepish, boyish smile spread over Cochran's face as he stood erect before Hartell, who also smiled."

"Yes," Hartell suddenly remembered, "that's the man who drove the second car away. He's not as sunburned now though, as he was then."[4]

Those implicated in the crime—except for Colson—listened intently to the first day's testimony. "Several times when his name was mentioned, Cochran showed [special] interest. . . . while Mrs. Cochran appeared on the verge of collapse, but soon regained control of herself without interrupting the hearing." At the same time, "Colson sat slumped in his chair, appearing half asleep, and took no interest in what was going on. The fact that his life is at stake seemed far removed from his mind."[5] The first day of the hearing provided scant drama and no fireworks, but the next day promised more emotion and possibly some histrionics, when the prosecution's star witness, the theatrical Jerry Kearney was to take the stand.

CAPTAIN JERRY TALKS (OR SQUEALS)

Buoyed by the district attorney's promise that his testimony would never be used against him, when the rotund Captain Jerry entered the courtroom, "he embraced and kissed his wife. He smiled and joked continually, often turning around to nod at an acquaintance in the court room." He took the witness stand determined to clear himself of any connections to the mayhem on the Dike. Nothing, he doggedly maintained; he knew nothing of that job until getting entangled in its aftermath.

> Kearney never faltered in giving his testimony, and spoke as if he were a small boy telling his mother about something wrong he had done.
>
> Openly and frankly, Kearney recited details of the crime as he said were told to him by Colson and Cochran. When he had finished, court attachés [court employees, among them lawyers] agreed he had not only told all, but had welded the chain with which the state expects to send Colson and Cochran to the gallows.[6]

According to the newspaper report, Colson reacted to the damning remarks in his accustomed manner. He "sat slumped in his chair, paying little or no attention to what was going on." Indeed, occasionally, he catnapped. "But Cochran, his wife, and Mrs. Kearney sat forward on the edges of their chairs and like the rest of the men and women in the crowded courtroom, drank in every word." In fact, Cochran, nattily dressed, smiled and joked with his guards throughout the hearing. Maybe he was nervous; his life was at stake. Or perhaps he felt that fellow mobsters would somehow bail him out of his predicament.

Although there was little new in Kearney's testimony, it was devastating, and it was now on the record. "Tuesday morning [the day after the hijacking] Colson and Cochran were alone in the bedroom and I went in. That was when they told me all about the jam they had gotten into. I brought up the talk about the job the day before on the National City Dike. Looking at me, Colson said, 'Jerry, Cochran and I pulled that job.' "[7] Then Marty had related details of the spectacular holdup to his longtime buddy and fellow bootlegger.

In an interview after the hearing, Kearney labeled Colson "a wise monkey" and called Marty's silence a hoax "to beat the rope. Why, he can talk about anything, and as far as nerve is concerned, he's got it." Then Jerry modified his admiration saying that when in the Kearney home with a wounded shoulder, Colson "wanted someone to hold his hand all the time. I told him to go to hell. If he wanted to hold something, he could grab the bed post."[8] They were friends, perhaps, but only to a point.

From the stand, Kearney admitted his own role in the attempted cover-up, tossing weapons in the ocean and destroying the checks. He later said that he got a "funny feeling" about burning checks written for $75,000. "At first I thought I would bury them but what the hell? When a fellow is excited, he never does the right thing."[9] Jerry seemed relieved to learn that the casinos had records of the destroyed checks and would not lose a cent because of him. No remuneration would be asked, and he might avoid prosecution.

What Jerry Kearney was most concerned about, however, was his reputation. The *San Diego Sun* had labeled him a 240-pound squealer, "a traitor to his pals in the liquor business." He was reminded that he once had vowed "to go the limit for any of the gang."[10] Now he had turned stool pigeon. Kearney angrily countered that he and his wife cared for the wounded Colson because "it wasn't any more than I would do for any other fellow I had known like I knew Colson." Furthermore, Lee Cochran, from his jail cell, had urged him to clear his name and tell all he knew about the heist.

> I didn't squeal. I told about the whole business because Cochran advised me to in order to save my wife and myself.
>
> I've been nothing but a bootlegger, but an honest one. I've been handling the stuff for eleven years and never took a drink [from the haul]. A guy can go to a doctor and get a prescription for bum liquor. I'll sell him the same kind of [bum?] liquor without a prescription.

You tell the public I didn't have anything to do with the framing of this job and only got into it because I tried to help a friend. I've got several phony letters [from mobsters] threatening my life, but that's all hooey. When I get out of this, I will keep straight.

At least that's what I think now.[11]

MARTY'S REMORSE

One wonders what Marty Colson thought, if anything, of these legal proceedings. Perhaps his mind was in a different world; he was prone to despondency and depression. He felt the whole world unfair and against him. Now even his friend Jerry Kearney, his cohort in numerous hijackings, the pal to whom he turned when badly wounded, in whom he confided details of a murderous crime, had turned snitch—spilled his guts to save his own neck. What's the use? "Silent" Marty was at the end of his tether.

Early Tuesday morning, as the preliminary hearing was about to enter its second day, Colson borrowed a fellow-inmate's shaving outfit to clean up. Because of his aching shoulder wound, he normally let a fellow prisoner do the shaving, but this time he indicated to guards, without talking, that he wished to shave himself. No one thought that irregular, but Marty surreptitiously slipped the blades from the safety razor into his clothing and returned the kit. Around dawn the next day, about an hour before guards awakened prisoners, he slashed his wrists. Guards found him bleeding profusely; he had already lost a pint of blood. One blade lay on the cement floor of his cell, another on his bunk.

A jailer summoned the prison doctor, who stanched the wounds, declaring them not serious and finding the suicide attempt a "bungled job." No blood transfusion was necessary; Colson could continue his day in court. Marty, meanwhile, was placed under special around-the-clock guard.

Two days later, Colson "was carried into court in a chair. He sat through the proceeding as though in a trance and paid no attention to what was being said. Colson's wrists were heavily bandaged and H. H. Osborne, deputy sheriff, his guard, held up the prisoner's head throughout the two-hour court appearance."[12]

JERRY'S CURTAIN

In its rebuttal at the preliminary hearing, the defense strove mightily to break Jerry Kearney's story but could not dent it. The racketeer reiterated that he had come clean because, "Cochran told me to clear myself; that I had nothing to do with the affair and ought to get out from under." Still, Jerry stepped down with "a tired and worried look upon his face."[13]

His wife, next on the stand, confirmed much of what her husband had said. Surprisingly (or not), she was not queried about her gambling habits at Agua Caliente. The press noted Grace's comments about Colson's interest in psychology, which "would tend to give credence to belief expressed in some quarters that the accused slayer has been 'playing possum' in remaining silent at all times. What he expects to gain by this policy of silence is not apparent, unless it be to work on the sympathies of a future jury."[14] Without doubt, Marty had those surrounding him baffled, guessing, and concerned.

The defense called no one to the stand at that time, and Judge Daney remanded Colson and Cochran to jail without bail, pending trial in Superior Court. A hearing of accessory charges against Kearney and the two women was postponed, as the judge was going on vacation. Before he went, however, he freed Marian and Grace on their own recognizance. "Both women burst into tears and sought the refuge of their husbands' arms."[15] Furthermore, in recognition of Jerry's damning testimony for the prosecution, he cut the bootlegger's bail from $30,000 to a token $1,000, which Kearney made within three hours.

"Gee, but it's great to be out again," Jerry gleefully told reporters, "and tomorrow's my birthday."[16]

Police advised Kearney to remain in hiding for some time, "for in the eyes of the gang, he has been branded as a 'squealer,' and the penalty is usually death."[17] His attorney announced that Jerry might be provided a bodyguard.

A few days later, the state's star witness received another letter (the fourth) threatening his life: "Dear Sir: Just a little tip—there is some out-o-town gunmen just arrived in San Diego yesterday with the avowed intention of bumping you off. Take this tip and change your address quickly. This is from a party who knows."

Kearney laughed and crowed with typical bravado: "My address is 3559 Villa Terrace [where police captured Colson], and I'm going to live there as long as I can pay the rent or until my wife kicks me out."[18]

"Silent" Marty's Oration

The prosecution wanted to get the money-car robbery case over with; it feared public criticism, mob retaliation, or a Colson suicide. Its prediction that the defendants would plead guilty, avoid the noose, and take life imprisonment did not materialize, so they would have to go to trial. Authorities also speculated that heavy sentences levied against Colson and Cochran might entice any confederates still running free (specifically Marcel Dellon and Jeanne Lee) to surrender in hopes of a plea bargain. They needed to know the extent of the mob's activities, connections, and intentions throughout the region, California, the Southwest, and back East.

Time to proceed—and in a surprise move on the morning of July 11 they hustled the manacled and heavily guarded suspects into Superior Court, Judge Charles N. Andrews presiding. Only the defendants, their attorneys, regular court officers, prosecutor, and judge were present. Cochran, clad in a gray tweed suit, was smiling at his attorneys and court personnel; Colson, sullen, brooding, silent, stared blankly around the near-empty chamber.

THE JUDGE TAKES CHARGE

Judge Andrews, distinguished by his full, bushy mustache, was a fixture among the San Diego judiciary. At seventy, he was the Superior Court's longest presiding judge. Charles Nathaniel Andrews had come to the city from his home state of Minnesota in 1907, and four years later, California's Progressive governor, Hiram Johnson, appointed him to the court. Andrews was an outspoken individual with decided opinions about jurisprudence and the world. "While facing the courtroom, listening to counsel," wrote a historian of San Diego's judiciary, "he would spin a silver dollar continuously on the blotter before him. After argument he would spin his own chair 180 degrees, and with back to the room, communicate, apparently with his own soul."[1]

"He was no sheep, no follower of any legal bellwether. He didn't use precedents as authority, but as guides for his own thinking. When a legal argument was concluded . . . , he searched his own thoughts for the right answer. Sitting by appointment at times on the appellate bench, Andrews wrote decisions without citing a single authority (frequently contradictory to others that been based upon elaborate citation of earlier cases)."[2] That would hardly make him what today is called a "strict constructionist." He was, in effect, his own man, relying on his experiences with law and life to render judgments.

Judges at that time were not the specialists of today. They not only conducted civil and criminal trials and ruled on motions, but they also married and divorced couples and decided juvenile matters. As a result, Andrews had a lot of "experience" on which to base his findings, and his overly long, somewhat convoluted, and decidedly self-congratulatory exposition in the Colson-Cochran sentencing demonstrated that he meant to explore and explain them. He was, in short, a bit of a show-off and know-it-all.

He was also an "evolutionist," believing that human beings, over time, evolved from a lower to higher species, and in keeping with many evolutionists of his time, he also endorsed eugenics. In an address to the Bar Association of San Diego County in 1933, four years before his retirement, he advocated sterilization of habitual felons, the insane, and others deemed to be "sociologically unfit." Numbers of "unfit" (which he did not define beyond habitual criminals and the insane) were rising, he warned, threatening to assume numerical superiority, lowering the "scale of evolutionary progress," and bearing responsibility for increased crime. Besides, their incarceration cost taxpayers huge sums. Judge Andrews called for "a movement that would enlighten the public on the subject, and legislation that would serve both as a protection to the unfit and to society generally." And he had a model to recommend: "[Hitler's] Germany," he advised, "already is showing the way to the rest of the world in this respect."[3]

If I were "Silent" Marty Colson (with a minor criminal record) or a known bootlegger like Lee Cochran, I would not want to face *this* judge.

Cochran's plea was straightforward: "Not guilty!"

As for Colson: "As Judge Andrews read to him the charge, Colson first leveled his eyes upon the jurist and then turned his head slightly and stared blankly out the window."[4] His attorney informed the judge that Colson "could not or would not talk," and therefore he had no knowledge of what his client wished to plead. He asked that the court act for Colson.

Andrews did so, entering a "not guilty" plea—but then adding, *"By reason of insanity!"*[5]

The judge set trial for Monday, August 5. Ten days before that date, a morose Marty Colson again attempted suicide. Given that he scorned criticism of his intelligence, being declared mentally incompetent at the preliminary hearing might have triggered another death wish. First he broke a mirror with a tin cup, seeking fragments with which again to cut his wrists, but a guard heard the mirror break and wrestled it from the prisoner along with the cup. In frustration, Marty jumped from his cot and raced, full speed, twenty feet across his cell, smashed his skull as hard as he could against a steel door, and fell limp to the floor. He was conscious when examined by the police emergency doctor, who declared that Marty had not seriously injured himself, even if during the check up he "pretended nausea by rolling his eyes and holding his stomach."[6]

A few days later, Marty's mother begged her son not to attempt further suicides, and he promised her that he would not. Later, when finally talking at his trial, Marty recalled the covenant. The promise, he told the presiding judge, "was exacted of me by my mother, the saintly woman who suffered in bearing me into this earth and upon whom I have caused interminable shame. She exacted the promise that I would not take my own life."[7]

THE BOMBSHELL

Then a break for the prosecution. Hallelujah, its prediction came true. Colson and Cochran each wished to plead guilty. In exchange, the state agreed to drop the robbery charges, which might reduce the total weight of the crime, if not the heinousness of first-degree murder. The prosecution never softened its demand for the death penalty.

At the end of the workday on July 29, only five days before jury selection was to begin for the trial, Colson and Cochran, shackled and under double guard, marched into court with their attorneys, who informed Judge Andrews that their clients wished to change their pleas: guilty to the murders.

"Is that what you wish to do?" the judge asked Cochran, who was dressed in his customary gray tweed pants and a white shirt, open at the collar.

"Yes, it is," answered Lee solemnly, certainly not his customary carefree self.[8]

Judge Andrews then addressed the same question to "Silent" Marty, sulking, his face showing a week's stubble, who in reply used hand signals to indicate that he wanted a pencil and paper. He still would not talk to anyone of authority, even his own lawyer. The court concurred, and Colson hurriedly scribbled the word "yes" on the pad handed him.

The judge set ten o'clock the following morning for sentencing. Their plea change relieved the defendants of a risky jury trial, where conviction would most likely carry a death sentence, and placed the penalty phase squarely in the hands of Judge Andrews. The jurist, it was thought, would agree to terms of life imprisonment, although he still reserved the authority to decree the prisoners hanged. The press bellowed in headlines that the pair had switched their pleas to spare themselves the noose.

On the morning of July 30, "for the second time in as many days, the two gunmen were brought into court, heavily guarded by deputy sheriffs. Both were nattily attired and showed little trace of agitation when arraigned before the court. Colson still maintained his attitude of silence, but his keen black eyes flashed from court to counsel."[9] Tension in the courtroom was palpable, but the unaccountable absence of a defense attorney forced a second postponement, this one to Monday afternoon, August 5, the original trial date. The district attorney's office gave His Honor a copy of the preliminary hearing transcript to ponder over the weekend and prepare his remarks.

At the sentencing, character witnesses for the accused would be heard, rebuttals allowed, and the prisoners given an opportunity to speak. Then the judge would pronounce sentence and explain his reasoning for what he had just ordered, quite probably in florid language. The stage was ready, its set arranged, with spectators settled in place. Now the final act in this tragic drama began.

COLSON'S SURPRISE

On August 5 the court came to order before a thronged chamber. By agreement between lawyers, the prosecution dropped robbery charges against the two defendants. Character witnesses pictured Colson as honest, good-natured, convivial, smart, and hard-working. His mother, Antoinette (formerly Josephine) McDonald, stressed her son's kindness toward others and aversion to violence. Throughout her remarks, Colson, clean-shaven and dressed in coat and tie, sat with head down and never looked at her.

Through most of the proceeding he read a book—the judge did not order it taken away. (Alas, we do not know the title.) The prisoner's attorney, George Wicke, testified that he had known Colson for more than a year and that during that period Marty had always done legitimate work.

Cochran's short line of character witnesses followed. His wife, Marian, took the stand to state they had been married five years and that he had always been a "kind and loving husband and father."[10] Then it was time for closing arguments. The prosecuting attorney, Oran Muir, rose, ready to demand the death penalty for the pair.

But before he could speak, Colson passed a note to Wicke saying he wished to address the court. Wicke, stunned, somewhat embarrassed, and not knowing what to expect, informed Judge Andrews of his client's request, and the judge, confounded and wary, stammered—"ah, ah"—and after moments of reflection (possible trial error probably flashed across his mind), finally acceded. Even before the judge did so, Colson was on his feet and starting to *talk*.

What was this all about? "Silent" Marty had not spoken publicly or to authorities since his capture. Some doubted he could even speak English, but he immediately proved that he could—perfect English—both poignantly and eloquently with a fine vocabulary, effortlessly incorporating with unsuspected erudition words like "analogy," "syllogism," "ocular," "cultivated," "enumerate," along with "rectify," "despicable," and "ego." With no prepared text, not even written notes, he spoke an emotional soliloquy for almost an hour, mesmerizing all and moving more than a few spectators to tears.

Just listen to him:

> At this time, if the court please, I wish to make a statement. First, in consideration of the defendant, Robert Lee Cochran; second, a statement in respect and in consideration of this court itself, and thirdly, I have a request to make on behalf of myself, Martin B. Colson.[11]

Colson claimed to be suffering from paralogia, a disconnect in thought patterns (which today is connected to a form of schizophrenia), therefore:

> my statement may, seemingly, lack clarity. Nevertheless, if the court please to permit me—and consider this boy, Robert Lee Cochran.
> Here he [Cochran] is before this court awaiting sentence to be imposed on

him. Through the eyes of the world, he is seen as a murderer awaiting punishment, but the eyes of the world, as he is seen, in this case, as in any other legal case among the higher social classes [note Colson's prevailing class consciousness, seen earlier in his view of society]—the eyes of the world are blinded and suffer by a conspicuous lack of the truth.

Do the eyes of the world see Robert Lee as he is today—see that he would be willing to die and give his life, if by doing so he could undo the things he has done? Do the eyes of the world see him in his great shame and sorrow; see him as a young husband, and a young father? Do they see that as he is here, he would give his right arm, give his left arm, give his eyes—give his very all, if by so doing he could undo and rectify what has occurred? I ask you, do the eyes of the world see these conditions, those circumstances? Possibly not. Furthermore, the eyes of the world are blinded just as the eyes of Robert Lee Cochran were blinded when he was virtually led into this despicable affair. He was blinded and bound and led into this by the inestimable power of money—of gold to be gotten easily and quickly. And, who here doubts its power?

To further show how he was enmeshed, ensnared and entrapped into the tentacles of this octopus by the attractiveness of gold, let us see the plan by which it came about. Lee Cochran, being the ordinary youth that he is, and being a normal young man, is it unreasonable to expect that he desired the better things of life as does any other person? No.

Colson dramatically turned to face Cochran, whose wife, Marian, seated nearby with their three-year-old baby in her lap, began to weep.

The orator then laid out in detail the spectacular plan for robbing Agua Caliente's money-car and carefully explained how and why it had gone awry. He raised eyebrows, left jaws slack. Some internally probably jeered him, searched for his motivations in exposing the plot, thought him a liar in search of leniency, but that was a notion he was about to dispel. Whatever their judgment on Marty Colson, they could not fail to be impressed by the man's vigor, passion, and grandiloquence.

And as Colson concluded this phase of his speech, he asked that Cochran "be spared, and I sincerely believe that during his future life, although in prison, it will be such a future that the mercy of the court shall not go unrewarded."

Colson then said he wished to be sentenced to death. His overture to the court was close to a respectful demand.

First, I wish to forfeit my life so that no human being can say that Lee Cochran and Martin B. Colson did not pay their debt to society and by all that was in their power.

Secondly, I wish to forfeit my life as a sacrifice that the life of Robert Lee Cochran shall be spared.

Thirdly, I wish to forfeit my life as an act of contrition and repentance for my own personal satisfaction.

Fourth, I choose to die because I have educated and cultivated a desire for death.

Point four, he thought, required an explanation. How is it that a lust for death overcame a desire for life? Colson said he had no control over the process; it just happened, and he outlined a complex (and not totally coherent) analogy to prove his point. He requested the court to "picture, if you can, my mental state, my acute agony, my inestimable shame, disgrace, sorrow. Ignoble and broken spirit which all leans [toward] and adds to the pain of my mentality, the pain of which is so great, so very great that it actually deadens the nerves in the various parts of my body." He said his ego, his nobler self, died the day he was taken into custody. Now he pleaded for the "death of this physical hulk."

> Give me death—and permit this young man [Cochran] to live.
> I have nothing more to say."

Certainly, a good deal of Colson's mental state, his character and personality, are woven into his powerful, if at times illogical and rambling, statement with its references to "godliness," "unforeseen forces," the dearth of human will power, martyrdom, Cochran seen as a "boy," the fatal lure of quick money, and an unjust, class-driven society, but such savory tidbits are best left to psychiatry for juxtaposition and elucidation. More appropriate to Agua Caliente, the Border Barons, and the mob are the assertions that he and Cochran were victimized by a scheme that went afoul. Colson outlined that conspiracy in gripping detail that tests credulity but raises possibility.

BEST LAID PLANS

In their design to rob the treasure-car Marty Colson and Lee Cochran had not intended to kill the guards, but suddenly, unexpectedly, the carefully

designed conspiracy literally exploded in their faces. Under these unforeseen and calamitous circumstances, the shootings became self-defense and
the entire, fantastic scenario planned for the hijacking fell apart.

Roots of the entire affair, according to Colson, stretched back to Agua
Caliente itself. Six or eight months before the shootout on the Dike,

> [when] some of the "honest officials" of the Agua Caliente Company saw how
> much unrest there was in Mexico, and how much indecision and saw the con-
> tinued activity on the part of rebels in Mexico[,] they saw that under those
> conditions, they being more conversant with their [Mexican] manners and ways
> than others, they [the conspirators] saw that they would likely lose their money.
> They saw that because of the enormous amounts of money they paid to the
> [Mexican] government, they stood to lose, and a plan was fabricated by which
> the Agua Caliente gaming house was to be robbed . . . with the help of and effort
> of the officials and owners, as we understood it.

First, proceeds from the casino would have to be accumulated at the club
to ensure the largest possible take in the planned assault on the premises.
"It would be necessary to stop the money from crossing the line" and being
deposited in a San Diego bank. Those employees not participating in the
robbery needed to be frightened by a sensational security breach in the
transfer of funds into retaining several day's receipts at the casino. And they
also needed to appreciate how easy it was to hijack a money shipment.
While deliberating safer ways to transport proceeds, they would store millions at Agua Caliente. To emphasize the danger, then, revenue crossing the
border had to be pirated.

Initially, Cochran said, "it was arranged that we were to meet the guards
[transporting the money] and the guards were to hand over the money to us
and go back and report the robbery." But that plan was aborted, Colson
continued, "because too many of those interested in the Agua Caliente
Company were crooks and gamblers, and they would quickly see through
such a plan." So another scheme was designed.

> The man [whom Colson named only as Curley] who was the go-between
> ourselves [Colson and Cochran] and the [unnamed] officials of the Agua Cali-
> ente Company said, "Now everything is arranged and you have nothing to fear.
> You can't lose. Here is the plan.

"You shall meet the guard and you shall shoot off the tire of the car, and the guards will hand over the money to you, and you are to scatter some pepper in the car [causing eyes of the guards to smart and making the robbery look more realistic]. That is the whole plan."

Once cash had piled up at the resort following the staged robbery, the casino itself would be looted:

Just after some holiday, like the Fourth of July [when holiday crowds would guarantee huge proceeds], men dressed as [Mexican] rebels were to descend upon the gaming house, stop all communication and transportation, and under the excitement of the affair, fire would be set to the building, and they were to rob the gold and currency and silver and cash and even the valuables in the safe of the hotel . . . and then the building was to be blown up—blown up with dynamite.

And then the officials connected with it [Agua Caliente] were to collect the insurance and get out the best they could.

Then they would go to Miami, Florida, and open up a new gambling house. Meanwhile, others who wished to establish gaming in Tijuana "would have the field all to themselves."

Now to the fake holdup itself which would lead to the buildup of cash and the breathtaking, if unseemly, chain of events to follow.

We disagreed about the plan [to assault the money-car], but we were guaranteed everything. We said, "If we start shooting in public and some officer might come along there," [and the go-between person replied], "Don't worry. Everything is taken care of. There will be no interference on the part of the San Diego Police because of our political influence. They shall be held in abeyance." [Colson then explained this meant "they would be told to lay off."]

Furthermore, [the set-up man, Curley, maintained, testified Colson], there would be no interference . . . because there would be officers on the road who would protect us in the event that the plan fell through, if for example, a stray motorcycle officer came along, and furthermore, the men who were to hand the money over to us would not squeal because they had too much evidence on [against] them. They had taken too much [money in the past].

Besides that, Colson stated, the go-between assured him that U.S. customs officers knew the guards had political and police connections, that the couriers had been using the company money-car to bootleg liquor across the border, and that three years earlier they had been involved in the infamous Peteet rape-suicide case.[12] If the two guards driving the Agua Caliente money-car had been involved in the Peteet affair, Colson concluded they would be "all right."

As a final touch, as they robbed the treasure-car, the assailants "were to throw pepper into the car, and they [the guards] could [then] say that it got in their eyes, and they could report that their automatics jammed" when they tried to defend themselves and the money pouch. "We knew what kind of guns they were to have, because we understood they were in on the deal," Colson noted, then continued: "When that car came along, and according to our instructions, we shot the tire off, and then men in the car did not pull over to the side as they had been instructed. They immediately opened fire on us. . . . I thought at first that they were blank cartridges, and that they were making a demonstration for the benefit of the public."

Colson said he rushed to the side of the targeted vehicle, shouting, "Everything is all right, Curley sent us. We have the pepper here and everything, so just give us the money." The response was a bullet that knocked off his cap.

> At this time, I began to realize that they intended to kill us, that something was wrong—that some supernatural agency intervened—and we decided to shoot it out just enough to protect ourselves.
> And then this hideous thing occurred.

They slaughtered the guards.

Marty Colson's courtroom performance—for that is what it was, a performance—yields some speculative insights into his personality. First of all, his claim to paralogia makes no sense. Paralogia is a thought disorder. People with it are out of touch with reality; they are often delusional. If you encountered a person with paralogia, you would undoubtedly think the individual odd. None of this fits Colson, who despite his silence before authorities, knew where he was and why he was there. Why he professed to be suffering from paralogia is anyone's guess. Perhaps it was a tactic or a ruse—spectators would think him sick and excuse any shortcomings they spotted in his speech. Or they would marvel that a person with paralogia (even if they did not recognize the disease) could speak like *that*.

The oration itself was erudite. Marty Colson was smart, no doubt about it. Much of what he said probably went over the heads of those present. Its incoherence, furthermore, challenged comprehension. Even now it takes several readings of the transcript to decipher its meaning. During the presentation, Colson was unemotional and in total control of himself and the audience. Total control meant power over his listeners, and Colson may well have enjoyed his hold on the proceeding. He did not speak like an individual who is desperate or shaken. He was cool and collected in delivering his remarks. Was he trying to hoodwink people? His falsified arson story, his silence while imprisoned, the attempted suicides (gestures more than bona fide endeavors; for example, he did not cut his wrists as deeply as he easily could have with a bare razor blade) and now this—the spontaneous, adlibbed, philosophical talk—all add up to an aggressive manipulator fully in charge of his situation. Colson acted like a sociopath with disturbances but was not out of touch with reality. Better said, he was a crafty strategizer.[13]

So what to make of the orator's story about the plot to blow up Agua Caliente?

FACT OR FICTION?

Neither prosecutor nor judge believed Colson's account. His buddy, Lee Cochran, whose life he begged be spared, said he knew nothing of such a plan.[14] The press declined to follow it up. Public reaction is unknown. Agua Caliente officials, who admitted to having an employee named Curley, apparently cleared or fired him, but did not comment on further inquiry, if any, into Colson's allegations. But was Marty Colson's account true, or at least plausible? Do reactions to his commentary hint of cover-up?

Veracity

Many specific details of Colson's exposition before Judge Andrews dovetail with those discovered by authorities and reported in newspapers—the can of chili pepper, for example. Police said they found a container of such pepper in the rear seat of the crime car parked on Edgemont. Colson told the judge: "We were to throw pepper in the [company car] and they would say that it got in their eyes and they could report that their automatics jammed."[1]

"In accordance with our instructions, we shot the tire off," Colson claimed, "[but] the men in the car did not pull over to the side as they had been instructed. They immediately opened fire on us." Court records based on eyewitness accounts confirm this account. The hoodlums shot out a rear tire and were pulling alongside the money-car when the guards inside opened fire. In other words, in the exchange between assailants and defenders, the couriers fired *first*. The deluge of bullets followed. The defendant then ran behind the money-car, a move supported by court documentation, and says he shouted: "Everything is all right. Curley sent us," but the guards kept shooting. It will never be known whether or not Colson yelled anything at that hectic moment, but one of the couriers sure kept shooting.[2]

The affair as outlined by Colson raised the specter of double or triple cross with Marty and Lee Cochran as expendable scapegoats duped into making the danger of shipping money creditable while creating a pretext to retain mounting proceeds at the resort for the main conspirators to loot. The head schemers, he said, were owners and executives of the resort, but he did not name them.

CONDITIONS IN MEXICO

"When some of the 'honest officials' of the Agua Caliente Company saw how much unrest there was in Mexico," said Colson, "and how much indecision, and saw the continued activity on the part of the rebels in Mexico, they saw that under those conditions, they being more conversant with their [Mexican] manners than others, they saw that they would likely lose their money."[3] Was Colson implicating the Border Barons in a cabal to destroy their own resort?

Despite their harmonious public pronouncements, the Barons at the time were at serious odds with one another; in particular, Bowman and Crofton had fallen out with Baron Long. Crofton pointedly preferred not to patronize Long's Grant Hotel and instead leased an entire floor of the newer and even more opulent El Cortez Hotel ten blocks away on a hill overlooking downtown San Diego. Stockholders, moreover, soon began to question the whereabouts of promised dividends from the enterprise. They suspected corruption. Other millionaire syndicates, jealous of Agua Caliente's swift rise to prominence and reportedly fabulous returns, were pecking around to exploit fissures in the infrastructure of the company, and it was not long before the high-riding triumvirate fell apart. Authorities undoubtedly would have yearned to quiz Colson about his inferences, but following his statement to the court, he again turned silent, a loss to us all.

When noting the conspirators were "more conversant than others with the manners and ways" of Mexicans, Colson seemed to be pointing a finger at Wirt Bowman, close to President Calles, and almost family with Obregón, but once again the prisoner did not elaborate.[4] Nonetheless, when he mentioned unsettled conditions in Mexico, Colson knew what he was talking about.

Mexico was indeed seething during the years from 1926 to 1929. During his presidency, Calles relentlessly tightened screws on the Catholic Church, determined to drain its influence on politics, education, and the civil life of his countrymen. Blatantly challenged by Catholics every step of the way, in angry frustration the president precipitously tightened anticlerical legislation in 1926. The savage Cristero War followed, fought more ferociously in some regions than others, but seeping into and tearing at the seams and soul of the country. As in all such wars, not all unrest concerned the *cause*

célèbre. Opportunists also seized the handy banner of religion to settle old scores, eliminate rivals, seize property, denounce *amigos*, claim political power, erase social barriers, and tailor self-serving forms of justice. Martyrs were created (the Pope in the year 2000 canonized twenty-five village priests who died in the struggle), and to this day "Soy Cristero" ("I am a Cristero," conserver of the faith) is a badge of honor worn by a good many believers.[5]

Other adversaries of the regime who believed it had developed dictatorial tendencies also rebelled at this time, were defeated, and sought refuge in the United States to await a better day. The three years of strife around the Cristero War created an opportunity for exiles like Adolfo de la Huerta and Enrique Estrada to lead armed bands below the border to test their bases of support. Neither received much of a welcome, but their aggressions created banner headlines in an American press prone to exaggerations and anxious to chastise Mexico for its barbarism and backwardness and, not incidentally, to pave the way for American intervention, be it business, military, religious, political, or otherwise.

Forces of one forlorn revolutionary, José Escobar, actually took and held the Mexican half of the border town of Naco for a few days in the spring of 1928. They herded local authorities into the same Southern Club where the Border Baron James Crofton had earlier gotten his start managing a casino and nightclub. The revolutionaries hired an American crop duster to bomb federal positions with handmade missiles (dynamite, nails, bolts, and scrap iron crammed into suitcases), but his aim was atrocious, and as soldiers sniped away at him from the ground, he dropped two bombs on the U.S. side of the line, injuring four people. Mexican troops soon retook the town for good.[6] The invasion, nevertheless, fueled imaginations and made lively front-page news. We might ask how much less outlandish these sorts of mind-boggling events were than the plot outlined by Marty Colson to blow up Agua Caliente.

Then, just as Agua Caliente was celebrating its grand opening, a political bombshell exploded in Mexico City. A distraught Catholic seminary student murdered President-elect Alvaro Obregón on July 17, 1928, and the provisional presidency fell to the country's secretary of the interior, Emilio Portes Gil, a Calles appointee to be sure, but of unknown quality, temperament, program, and ambition. Wirt Bowman filled a place of honor at Obregón's funeral, but he also must have talked business while in the capital. The new regime, for instance, soon considered raising the already steep federal taxes on Agua Caliente, a move which sent the Barons scurrying to Mexico City for relief.[7]

Although Marty Colson professed to be a reader (most likely he learned of *paralogia* from a text), there was no way of knowing what he knew of these events. He was bootlegging and hijacking around Los Angeles when the arrest of Enrique Estrada's revolutionaries for neutrality violations around Tijuana made front-page news with pictures. The media aired and the public frequently discussed complaints of religious intolerance in Mexico. Obregón's assassination startled the general public in Southern California, which he had visited and where he was well known and liked. Mexican turbulence stirred the air, and it stands to reason that Colson caught a whiff, even if just enough to convince him that the plan to rob and destroy Agua Caliente had indeed been drawn.

AMERICA'S FINEST CITY

The entire cabal involving the fake robbery on the Dike depended upon the collusion of the couriers, San Diego lawmakers, and political contacts. Despite guarantees by the go-between that everything had been arranged, Colson pressed the crucial point: "If we start shooting in public, some officer might come along there." According to Colson, Curley quickly responded, "Don't worry. Everything is taken care of. There will be no interference on the part of the San Diego Police because of our political influence. They shall be held in abeyance." Colson explained to Judge Andrews that among mobsters "held in abeyance" colloquially meant, "They would be told to lay off."[8]

What of this alarming allegation surrounding San Diego government, alleged to be wide open to bribes and the assertion that anything could be "fixed" by payola? Colson seems to have taken that proposition for granted. He never questioned the existence of rampant corruption among officialdom, but only wanted assurances that protection money in his particular case was in the right palm. Such payoffs were, of course, common during Prohibition, but just what was going on in what many San Diegans (and others) have long considered to be America's Finest City?

Relentless boosterism has for more than a century proclaimed San Diego to be an attractive alternative to (or escape from) the stultifying traditions of the Midwest as well as the grime and crime of the East Coast. According to its puff sheet, the city offers unparalleled opportunities in commerce and real estate, while its everlasting sunshine and tempting, frothy surf cordially invite tourists and retirees. Truth is that the city has remained small-town rather than urban-big because city government has been dominated and directed by those who prefer and profit from such smallness (meaning growth designed for housing and modest commercial businesses) and because most San Diegans are content with their placid lot (they chatter incessantly about good weather as if they owned it) and do not care to consider alternatives. "Rest and enjoy" is their motto, long-term planning and political struggle far from their minds. They love their neighborhoods, but the overall city be damned, or more kindly said, ignored.

This state of mind and affairs is why San Diego fell behind Los Angeles in the early stages of Southern California development and continues to languish in the shadow of its pulsating, yet still laid-back, gigantic northern neighbor. Los Angeles aspired from the start of the last century to challenge New York's hegemony, or at least establish itself as "New York on the West Coast." Its leadership surveyed the big picture and assured itself, through scandal and treachery, a steady water supply from Northern California. Although twelve miles inland, the city constructed a world-class commercial harbor and complemented it with a sprawling international airport, not only to service the community and region but to reign as *the* cosmopolitan gateway to an ever-expanding trans-Pacific traffic. "New York West" had found its home, and as a bonus, there was Hollywood to provide glamour and advertising.[9]

San Diegans and their establishment, by contrast, thought (and still think) "village." Retired admirals settled into their grandiose homes on Coronado; real estate developers created neighborhoods of simple, comfortable housing, first on mesas close to downtown and then stretching far eastward across vast, open, and arid lands. A conservative city council, dominated by realtors, large business interests, and property owners, kept taxes low and public improvements and social services minimal.

City administrations over the years have battled the daily crises of government, but lacked more expansive foresight. As a result, the city for decades has debated but done nothing meaningful about a seriously threatened water supply, a horribly cramped airport, and a harbor that serves the Navy but not world-class shipping, the antithesis of what has occurred with

Los Angeles. Local specialists and outside advisors, political activists and interest groups have urged attention to the city's future. "But we don't want to be like Los Angeles," roars the response.

It has been this way for a very long time. The mayoralty campaign of 1917 pitted "Geraniums," those who favored a "village," against "Smoke-stacks," advocates of big-city infrastructure and growth. A "Smokestack" won, served a second term, declared the job "thankless," and retired to Los Angeles.[10] "Village" mentality returned to dominate city administration well into the Depression and there it remains.[11]

THE CROOKED CITY

In 1937 the Social Science Research Council studied municipal government in eighteen American cities, and concluded that while San Diego had "never had the corrupt machine politics that characterized the government of many American cities," or "any organization or clique powerful enough to control the city government," it suffered from "the lack of prestige of public office, the lack of coherent municipal policy, and the absence of effective leadership."[12] No Al Capone or Meyer Lansky ruled the town, but graft and corruption honeycombed a weak, inefficient, directionless city government. The "village" operated on deals and favors, payoffs and protection. Small-scale, much of it, but pervasive, just as Marty Colson seemed to understand.

All confidence in local government collapsed in 1928 when, at the council's behest, the public approved a $2 million bond issue to build a dam to enhance the city's water supply on an upper stretch of the San Dieguito River. To head the project, the city hired a renowned hydraulic engineer who had helped build Egypt's famous old granite "Low" Aswan Dam (1902), but the council rejected his recommendations, and he resigned. Plans for a dam, nevertheless, proceeded and construction began—*but* in the wrong place. The site was geologically unsafe, due to "a highly fissured condition of the foundation rock." The public simplified that assessment by saying the city was trying to build a dam on a gaping earthquake fault.

Planners, therefore, moved the dam a few hundred yards upstream, but that required a much longer structure. Cost estimates doubled, the public fretted and fumed, legal problems would have to be overcome, but building again started. In the next year concrete arches and abutments rose at the site. So did costs and new, intractable statutory issues. The council voted to abandon the entire plan. Taxpayers lost millions. "The prestige of the mayor and council never recovered from this episode," and the citizenry began its search for an entirely new form of government.[13] For twenty-three years the deteriorating arches stood like Sentinels of Silence at the miserable site. Then, in 1952, the voters approved a new bond issue to resuscitate the project. Final cost of the dam alone was $4,351,756.

In Colson's time, and probably today, the San Diego Police Department was the most demoralized department in city government. The mayor, council, and residents furiously and interminably debated what sort of "village" San Diego should be—shielded, moral, vice-free, and tightly controlled or, in recognition of its location as a seaport, naval base, and border town, more open, reasonable, tolerant, entertaining, and fun. Politicians took their stands one way or the other. Still, "no councilman can say publicly in San Diego that he proposes to permit illegal business like gambling and prostitution," said the Research Council, "and no councilman could be re-elected if the whole city took him seriously in an effort to eliminate it altogether."[14] It was a cul-de-sac from which the city has never escaped.

In this prolonged tension, police became fair game for press and politicians. "Many council members tried individually to influence the police department, either for favors that it could dispense or to induce it to enforce moral regulations more strictly, and the mayor was continually bickering with them over their attempts to give orders to the police," according to the Research Council. Amidst such contentiousness, police chiefs came and went, five of them between 1932 and 1934. Arthur Hill, who was in charge of the money-car case, lasted only seven months. In general, San Diegans felt their department "was allowing the city to become a place of cheap vice and a mere annex to the sporting places across the border in Mexico."[15] Police, however, were only minions plying both sides of the law. Fraud, extortion, bribery, and malfeasance seeped into many crevices of "village" life, most certainly allied to the national temper—Prohibition, fast money, loosened morals, heightened mobility—and to this particular place, Southern California, on the border and by the sea, with its get-rich-fast mentality spawned by tempestuous real estate booms and that romantic gold rush strain of the California Dream.

The *San Diego Herald* editorialized in 1926 that "Aside from bootlegging and banking there is not a profitable industry in San Diego."[16] (Notice the industry it put first.) Because of its location in the southwestern corner of the country and its proximity to an international border and the ocean, plus the fecklessness of city government (the *Herald* urged that the city council be recalled and the mayor put in chains), San Diego was a bootleggers' Arcadia approachable by land, sea, and air. All principals in the Dike money-car murder case were bootleggers and hijackers moving up the pay scale of such pursuits.

THE IRREPRESSIBLE BOOTLEGGER

The Treasury Department called the San Diegan Hugh McClemmy, "the most notorious border smuggler we have had to contend with." In 1925 McClemmy owned the Red Top Distillery, the largest of four distilleries in Tijuana, where he lived with his wife and children. Red Top produced three thousand gallons of whiskey a week, which McClemmy and his gang marketed across the line in trucks, Hudson sedans (which carried twenty-five gallon cans), and other cars with secret liquor tanks that carried fifteen to twenty gallons each, as well as in three airplanes and a large boat. McClemmy got caught in the act several times, paid fines of $300 to $500, and started out again. Most of the time, however, he bribed customs officials to let him pass unmolested. His business team included his wife, a local former deputy sheriff, a customs inspector who had been discharged for malfeasance, and an ex–U.S. Prohibition enforcement official.

McClemmy was not furtive. He was public, brazen, colorful, and well known to Southern Californians, especially thirsty ones. He claimed that he could fix any jury hearing a case against him, and he probably could. The government confirmed that "an undercover investigation of the jury panel [weighing a McClemmy case] does not look too good. We will probably only be able to get a hung jury," but the U.S. attorney's office vowed "to keep trying for conviction."[17]

The Treasury Department determined in 1926 to put McClemmy out of business and sent Prohibition agent Charles L. Cass to San Diego to develop a case against the bootlegger. A break for the government seemingly occurred on November 15, 1926, when Cass arrested Homer E. Eads, a prominent member of the McClemmy mob, with thirty gallons of rotgut alcohol and forty gallons of whiskey in his possession. "Cass, you are making a big mistake in arresting me. I have simply been getting evidence against McClemmy for you," the accused commented.[18] In exchange for leniency, Eads promised to help compile evidence against McClemmy, but never did so.

Snitches, however, did help the federal district attorney's office in San Diego to develop a thick file detailing McClemmy's widespread, highly profitable illicit operation. Then a spectacular reversal for the government; its entire file against Mc Clemmy suddenly disappeared from the DA's office, and an unnamed individual (the thief or a go-between) offered to sell McClemmy the expansive record of the government's case against him. The files were said to be in the hands of a former Prohibition enforcement agent.

Whether McClemmy bought the material or not, his knowledge of the theft provided the smuggler with a bright blue bargaining chip. McClemmy, brash and exuding self-confidence, voluntarily appeared on December 9, 1927, before the U.S. Attorney in Los Angeles saying that if a representative of the district attorney's office came to see him in San Diego, "he might be able to produce evidence indicating the party responsible for the theft of certain government files from the U.S. Attorney's office."[19] In exchange for the information, McClemmy demanded immunity from prosecution. The government did not take the bait.

Mexican authorities, meanwhile, also became fed up with Hugh Mc-Clemmy. Explaining that he did not pay duty on liquor he manufactured in Mexico and smuggled into the United States, they closed the Red Top, and declared him persona non grata. Furthermore, he had allegedly brutally beaten up one of his Mexican employees, accusing him of being an informant for investigating officials. These reasons for expulsion seem flimsy and invented. More likely he had not paid the mordidas demanded of him. McClemmy became especially cantankerous when he thought himself being flimflammed or extorted.[20]

The U.S. finally got a bootlegging conviction against McClemmy on February 1, 1928. He received a two-year jail term and $5,000 fine, lodged an appeal but then dropped it. That conviction essentially broke up the McClemmy gang, but another soon appeared to fill the vacuum.

As a fellow bootlegger and hijacker working much the same territory, Marty Colson may or may not have been aware of the Hugh McClemmy saga, but bribing officialdom during Prohibition was obviously routine for the times. In 1925 San Diego's elected district attorney, Chester C. Kempley, a former judge, prosecuted one of the city's councilmen, Harry K. Weitzel, for taking a bribe from the city's most aggressive and successful water and real estate developer, Ed Fletcher.[21] The next year, Kempley himself was being tried for accepting a bribe from a well-to-do Chicago mobster to fix the results of a sensational San Diego murder case. Colson, it seems, had plenty of reason to believe that payoffs would set up and protect his heist on the Dike.

FIXES

G raft and corruption were so prevalent, so open, in San Diego during the Twenties that the California State Attorney General lost confidence in the district attorney and in 1926 named a special prosecutor from Los Angeles to impanel a grand jury to probe the rot. That jury remained in session for a full year and called hundreds of witnesses, including the mayor and other city officials; a state senator from San Diego; a whorehouse madam; Baron Long, owner of the Grant Hotel and Sunset Inn; and Gene Normile, who was Jack Dempsey's former manager and had close connections to gaming activities in the area. Newspapers, day-by-day, session-by-session, listed on their front pages those being summoned to testify and had a field day speculating on the direction of the jury's investigation.

The press suspected tampering with witnesses. Several who had testified to the jury, according to the *San Diego Union*, "had been approached by an unnamed representative of persons supposed to be implicated in the investigation and asked to sign affidavits that would have nullified the effect of the testimony they had already given."[1] Dark, threatening clouds hung heavily over usually sunny San Diego. A good many locals welcomed the impending storm. City Hall needed a thorough cleansing.

Before long it became clear that among the jury's main targets were the San Diego district attorney himself, Chester Kempley, and his assistant, G. Guy Selleck. Ever since two Chicago hoods had been acquitted in March 1925 of the grisly murder of one of their own in San Diego, the sincerity and vigor of the district attorney's prosecution had been under suspicion, and the grand jury was sniffing about for evidence of bribery. For help, it hired a private detective agency to do the digging. Grand juries waged their own investigations in those days.

MURDER AND JUSTICE

On Saturday, February 28, 1925, two ladies, residents of Hollywood, were resting in their room at the Grant Hotel when a man knocked at the door. When one of the women answered, the man shoved his foot inside, pulled a pistol from his pocket, told the terrified women to keep quiet, swept diamond jewelry valued at $11,000 to $18,000 from a table into his pocket, and fled. The women gave police a description of the brazen thief.

The following day three children told their parents they had seen a dead man lying on a hill off Morena Boulevard, just outside San Diego's historic Old Town. Police found the corpse partially covered with bloody bath towels. A long knife protruded from the victim's chest at his heart. A coroner concluded the man had been beaten over the head with a dull-edged weapon, shot in the left temple with a small caliber pistol, and afterward stabbed with the knife "as a kind of decoration." A patrolman noted that this sort of ritualistic killing was a trademark of Chicago mobsters: murder the intended prey, stick a knife in his heart, and then dump him—sometimes in a secluded area, other times not.[2]

Investigators wondered if the unidentified dead man might have been the hoodlum who robbed the women in the Grant. Residents in the Morena neighborhood said they had seen a big car swing down the hill and stop about where the body was found. Solid detective work followed. Police traced a laundry mark on the dead man's shirt to the shop where it had been cleaned. The proprietor lacked the address of the customer, but a company driver remembered that the laundry bundle had come from the small, rather common Barbara Worth Hotel near downtown San Diego. A hotel clerk subsequently identified three Chicago men who had recently roomed there as Thomas A. Johnson, Hugh McGovern, and a George Byrnes or Frank J. Harrison (the last two turned out to be aliases for the murder victim, George McMahon). Authorities also learned that Johnson owned a house on nearby San Marcos Street. No one was there when police arrived, but neighbors earlier had seen Johnson and McGovern in the neighborhood. Police broke into the residence (with or without a search warrant) and "discovered the place to be a combined arsenal and charnel house, with pistols, shotguns and blood-stained clothing and rugs scattered or hidden within."[3] When Johnson and McGovern soon returned, they were met by police with leveled shotguns and pistols. Handcuffs and arrests followed.

When detectives later returned to the San Marcos address in search of additional evidence, they found a blood-stained coat that matched McMahon's trousers. They also discovered several suits stained with bloody blotches in the attic, and when deputies tried one on Johnson, it fit perfectly. An unnamed witness swore earlier he had seen both Johnson and McGovern wearing those same suits, minus the soils. Furthermore, a bathroom rug similar to the towels found wrapped around McMahon hung from a backyard clothesline, along with several shirts; all bore traces of blood, hurriedly washed but not eradicated. The shirts carried the same laundry mark as the garment found on the dead man.[4]

Checks with Chicago detectives proved Johnson to be a well-known mobster in the Windy City, with McGovern and McMahon his assistants. During one of those periodic cleanup drives in the crime-ridden city on Lake Michigan, they had come to San Diego, looking, Johnson admitted, to start a saloon business in Tijuana or farther south in Ensenada. When arrested, Johnson was wearing an Elks Club emblem set in diamonds and carried $500 in a pocket. The handsome and wealthy thirty three year old had numerous expensive suits, including a tuxedo, at the San Marcos address where he resided with his wife and young son.

Young McGovern, twenty-four, had been a laborer in Chicago before becoming Johnson's chauffeur. When arrested, he had only thirty-two cents on his person. McMahon had worked on a Chicago newspaper before joining Johnson, and his police record in the Midwestern metropolis noted a finger missing on his left hand, a physical defect which positively identified the body to San Diego authorities.[5]

With so much substantial, incriminating evidence in hand, the case against Johnson and McGovern today would be labeled a "slam dunk." At the time, most everyone thought the same. At that moment, however, Johnson's clever and well-heeled brother, William, also known to Chicago's underworld, arrived in San Diego to inquire about fixing the case. How could Thomas and his fellow-defendant, McGovern, be acquitted by a trial jury? Just whose palms needed to be greased? Who and how much?

The trial of Thomas Johnson and Hugh McGovern for the wanton, premeditated murder of their buddy, George McMahon, ran in San Diego Superior Court for six days in mid-1925 with District Attorney Kempley and his assistant, Selleck, for the prosecution. Evidence in their case had weakened. The bloody clothes which incontrovertibly linked the defendants to the crime now no longer fit them. The knife stuck in McMahon's heart had disappeared from the state's evidence box. Witnesses whose testimony could have supported the prosecution were not called. Defense lawyers claimed that their clients were nowhere near the murder site when the crime occurred. After one day's deliberation, the jury acquitted the defendants, and that night an exultant William Johnson staged a raucous party in his hotel room to celebrate the verdict. Baron Long and Gene Normile attended, which is why the grand jury subpoenaed them to testify about their connections to known Chicago mobsters.[6] Unfortunately, transcripts of grand jury interrogations are not public.

At the request of the defense attorneys, prosecutors returned all material evidence presented at the trial to the accused. Tom Johnson subsequently sold the blue-barreled .32-20 Colt revolver allegedly used to bludgeon McMahon to an officer of the San Diego Police Department, who meticulously cleaned matted blood and hair from the gun's rubber butt. In doing so, he noticed two notches in the butt, the sign often used by gunmen to tally up their victims.[7]

It was at about this time that the State Attorney General appointed a special prosecutor to investigate fraudulent and unscrupulous dealings among officialdom in the city "under the perfect sun."

PAYOLA

On December 1, 1926, Kempley and Selleck were brought to trial on charges of having taken a $40,000 bribe in the Johnson-McGovern murder case. The state's star witness was a flamboyant former bordello operator, Agnes Keller, transported from San Quentin where she was serving one to ten years for grand larceny, specifically for lifting $560 from a "visitor" to one of her establishments. Observers speculated that prosecutors had promised a reduction in sentence in exchange for her testimony against the defendants.

Agnes had organized prostitution and fostered gambling and bookmaking in various nondescript Tijuana and San Diego city-center hotels and houses since 1919, paying off police and other officials with money or a short stint with one of her workers, and shifting about when protection prices rose and authorities threatened her with closure. Questioned about her background at the Kempley-Selleck trial, she said that she could not remember the names of all her bordellos—there were too many of them to recall. The girls did not live in them; most came in for nightly business and then left for another abode. The city could have shut her down any time it wished but never did so. Indeed, a jury had acquitted Agnes of maintaining a disorderly house as recently as July 1925, even though two police officers and three young men testified that a taxi driver had brought them to her house for sexual adventures. The incensed policemen filed a civil law suit claiming that the entire jury system was unfair—that jurors blamed the police department when the court called them to jury duty, for which they received no pay, leading to spiteful acquittals, even when officers had defendants dead to rights. The officers did not get far with their complaint.[8]

Without doubt, Agnes Keller enjoyed an extraordinary relationship with officialdom that not only protected her business but afforded her entrée into its inner sanctum where she brokered deals and exchanged money.

Agnes knew both Kempley and Selleck before they became district attorneys, Kempley as a justice of the peace and Selleck as an attorney who once helped her son out of legal difficulty in Oakland. She gave presents to their families, so in March 1925, when Selleck, by then the assistant county attorney general, invited her to his office, she agreed to come and find out what was on his mind. "I have some work for you to do, want it?" he asked, and she consented to the task. Selleck (and Kempley) wanted her to pump the city coroner, Schuyler Kelley, for information about a $3,000 diamond stud and ring found on McMahon's corpse along with whereabouts of $3,000 that the victim was said to have stashed in a vault before his demise. Selleck then phoned the coroner to tell him that Agnes was dropping by to have a look at the murder victim. Her need and credentials to do so were never questioned.

The madam, according to her testimony, then went to the morgue, viewed the body, and afterward drove around town with the coroner casually passing the time of day and gleaning tidbits about McMahon's property. She did not reveal what she discovered at that time, but she testified that on a succeeding occasion Selleck told her that Johnson and McGovern had killed McMahon, and that Johnson's brother, William, was coming to San Diego "loaded with cash." The madam was to be go-between for the district attorney's office and the Chicago mobster.

Once William Johnson was in town, Selleck arranged a meeting between the wealthy gangster and Agnes Keller, during which (according to her testimony) William offered the district attorneys $10,000 each to fix the case against his brother and McGovern, and told Agnes she would be "well taken care of." She phoned Kempley to say she was doing her job.[9]

Agnes and William Johnson then visited the coroner and offered Kelley $10,000 for the thirty-four pieces of evidence held in the exhibits case for the impending trial. "Johnson met me one day and told me it would be well worth my while to turn over the exhibits," the coroner testified, "but I told him chances were mighty slim. Later, if my memory serves me correctly, it was Agnes Keller who offered me $10,000 for the evidence, particularly the knife found in McMahon's breast."

"Why did you not tell the authorities of this offer instead of keeping it quiet?" demanded the prosecutor. "Did you not know you were committing a criminal act in not making this known to the officials?"

"I knew it was not exactly right, but I didn't think much of it," came the response.

"Well, what about the people of California?" thundered the prosecutor.

Coroner Kelley admitted he had not paid much attention to the attempted bribe, since that same sort of thing frequently occurred, and "I can take care of myself."[10] He said that he put the evidence in a local bank because of William Johnson's and Agnes Keller's repeated attempts to get him to relinquish control of it.

Selleck never got the ring and stick pin from the coroner, but he did confiscate the dead man's $3,000 in cash. And he gained possession of those blood-stained suits belonging to the defendants and ordered Agnes to "shrink 'em." According to her testimony, she sent one suit to the cleaners to be shrunk and the other she soaked overnight in a barrel of gasoline. Indeed, they did not fit the defendants at the murder trial, causing doubt in the jury's mind and substantiating the defense contention that Tom Johnson and Hugh McGovern knew nothing of the murder. Yes, McMahon was their friend, and they had loaned him $50 for a date with a woman the night of the crime, but after he left the house, they never again saw him alive.[11]

As the Kempley-Selleck bribery trial moved into its fourth day, the defense relentlessly attacked Agnes Keller's damaging testimony. They impugned her character, assaulted her veracity, and challenged her memory of facts. Despite some uncertainties and hesitations, Agnes held her own, especially in detailing her meetings with Selleck and William Johnson. Even as the defense presented other arguments during the two-week trial, she remained "an interested spectator" seated in the courtroom "in a new coat of golden tint, an expensive black dress, and a large hat trimmed in lace and flowers. There was no trace of paint or powder on Mrs. Keller's cheeks."[12] Agnes Keller dressed like a socialite, even if only on temporary furlough from San Quentin.

Selleck testified from the witness stand that he had not seen or talked with Agnes Keller since a few days before the McMahon murder, that he "had nothing to do with the Johnson-McGovern case until some time after the murder, when he took it over as a matter of routine duty," and that he "co-operated as far as he could with the police department" gathering evidence for the prosecution.[13] As for Kempley, witnesses testified that he was out of town most of the time before the Johnson-McGovern trial, the period during which Agnes said she was in frequent touch with him to shuffle evidence and set up the bribe. The defendants admitted that William Johnson came to see them on behalf of his brother, Tom, but insisted he did not try to "fix" them.

The jury disagreed and took only a day and a half of deliberation to convict the district attorney and his assistant of soliciting and accepting a bribe to alter and otherwise suppress evidence in the first-degree murder prosecution of Johnson and McGovern. At the verdict, the defendants, confident of acquittal, "appeared dumbfounded. Their friends, making up the greater number of spectators in the room, were equally amazed."[14]

Appeals naturally followed, and in late 1928 the State Supreme Court reversed the convictions of Kempley and Selleck on grounds that Agnes Keller's "reputation for truth was bad, and her testimony was impeached in every way known to law." Furthermore, it was inadmissible under the law, which prohibited conviction based on the uncorroborated testimony of an accomplice. Keller had admitted her part in the scheme, but the testimony of others had failed to support her allegations. The court dismissed the charges against the defendants, who were freed from custody and reinstated to the California Bar.[15]

Kempley crowed that he had been vindicated. Still, the entire affair left a bad taste in the public's mouth and more doubt than ever in its mind.

A week after the stunning jury verdict against the district attorney and his assistant, the grand jury that had handed down indictments in the case rendered its report on a year's worth of hearings on graft and corruption in San Diego's government. "Grand juries," it said in part, "as a corrective body to curb public officials in acts of malfeasance are powerless if it so happens that your prosecuting attorney's office works hand in hand with corrupt persons. Financial assistance can be withheld so as to preclude the possibility of obtaining sufficient evidence. [Thus the grand jury had hired private detectives, at personal expense, though they hoped to be repaid.] Should indictable evidence be procured by personal funds, cases can be so apathetically prosecuted that acquittal is obvious. The only remedy is an appeal to the attorney general of the state."[16]

The challenge to San Diego was loud and precise, but the "village" had hardly caught its breath from the McMahon bribery scandal when another more contentious unveiling and a more widespread and deeper stain of corruption riveted the town's attention.

THE AMERICAN LEGION COMES TO TOWN

California's American Legion, twenty-thousand strong, came to San Diego for its annual convention in mid-August 1929. It was a momentous occasion for the city, promising both financial and patriotic profits. The Legion actually chose the town for its proximity to the amusements of Tijuana, but the conference planned its business and several formal banquets for less distracting San Diego. Legionnaires, as is well known, are a thirsty lot, and regardless of Prohibition they demanded their drink, and the city meant to be a good host. Their guests would know where they could readily, safely, and openly purchase bootleg whiskey. The Chamber of Commerce handed out folders advertising as much: "IMPORTANT CONVENTION INFORMATION," read the cover. And on the inside: "Attention! Arrangements have been made to protect your health and finances. Prices will be right. Taxicabs ordered through the calling of any of the following telephone numbers are absolutely guaranteed." The numbers followed. Then, "Beware of unofficial sources. Ask for representative's credentials. [Signed] The Committee."[17]

A couple of days before the arrival of the conventioneers, a group of San Diego bootleggers, among them several well-known civic and political activists, stocked a vacant store in downtown San Diego with 4,500 quarts of spirits they had acquired in Mexico. They lodged another 10,000 quarts at a three-story resupply house in an eastern suburb, where on upper floors, the booze received the "aging treatment": bootleggers colored, flavored, and bottled it. Everything had been arranged with law enforcement (as Colson thought in the Agua Caliente caper), official protection paid for and assured.

The Legion membership with family and friends began to stream into town on Saturday, August 17, for the official opening of the convention the following day. At ten o'clock that night the San Diego vice squad, acting on a telephone tip (it said), raided the liquor outlet in the city center, arrested five men and confiscated their banned holdings. Lawmen found the place ready for business, with six telephones hooked up for orders and a fleet of cars arranged for deliveries. It was called "one of the most elaborate [bootleg operations] ever uncovered here [San Diego]."[18]

"POLICE HALT PLAN TO INSURE AMPLE SUPPLY OF LIQUOR," the *Union* headlined the bust, and the five men taken into custody immediately began to talk. "What's going on?" they asked, claiming they had paid $2,000 in protection money to people high up in city administration who had assured them they had "fixed" the deal with the police chief and mayor. The arrested dealers then conferred with their "inside contacts," who told the bootleggers not to worry, for another $2,000 they would be guaranteed protection and could have their confiscated liquor back. The whiskey peddlers did not fall for that line. One double-cross was enough.[19]

ANATOMY OF A FIX

Charles Mulock, who organized the operation and was arrested in the raid, later turned state's evidence and detailed the entire setup to a *San Diego Union* reporter. There are few better dissections of U.S. bootlegging during Prohibition. "I was first approached on June 15th," he began. "Arrangements were made for me to furnish the boys with their drinks. A week later, individuals who identified themselves as representatives of the Legion, told me that they would furnish the protection. I never gave a dime to anyone. It was my understanding that [Police] Chief Hill and the sheriff [Ed F. Cooper] had been seen. [Congressman Phil D.] Swing was to tend to the government end of it through Washington."

"But weren't you nervous? Didn't you want to know how the alleged protection was to be arranged?" the reporter asked.

"I was not worried," Mulock replied.

There has been liquor here before when conventions were in progress. There has been liquor at conventions throughout the United States. Never has the law interfered. Other associations were shown courtesies. Naturally, I thought the American Legion would be given this same courtesy.

I do not know all the details of the "fixing." I do not know if there was any money passed. I paid nothing. The Legion was to attend to that, according to my information. The men I dealt with furnished me with cards. I gave these to my men and kept some. These cards were passports. If I was stopped by an officer, I was to show this passport. It identified me as a member of the official committee. . . .

I was given official stickers for my automobiles. The stickers allowed me to park double, go where I wanted to, and other traffic courtesies.

Ready to move his "stock" downtown, Mulock suggested that his contacts phone Chief Hill to ensure that "a copper who was o.k. be put on the beat. I suggested, too, that this officer be kept on the beat until the convention closed." As he was unloading the liquor, "a police officer walked up. He was a different one than the one I noticed on the beat before. I thought he was the okay cop—the new one that would mind his own business."

Mulock said the policeman asked, " 'That's pretty hot stuff, isn't it?' I told him it was and went on working."

That night police raided the store.

When I was arrested, I pulled the passport card. It didn't work. I was double-crossed. I was made the goat. When I was arrested and my liquor confiscated—several thousand dollars worth—it didn't dry up the convention.

There are six other outfits working. They didn't get knocked over. Why? I was double-crossed.

Even before the raid on his business, Mulock said, he had been receiving orders for booze, but, "before I could fill the orders, someone had filled them. They were my orders, and sometimes I had to run around the corner to a hotel to deliver the booze. Nearly always, however, someone else got there before me."

Now, he lamented, "I have lost all I had. I'm in debt. I have told [authorities] all I know, but there is still more to be found out."[20]

Someone squealed to police about Mulock's operation. It could have been a competitor bootlegger serving the Legion. The "fixers" in the case never were established. Were they Legionnaires or imposters posing as Legionnaires? Just what arrangements did the Legion's hospitality committee make with bootleggers? Was the patrolman who witnessed unloading of the liquor "fixed" or "straight"? Why did Chief Hill choose to terminate Mulock's business and not others serving the visitors? Tentacles of corruption wriggled every which way.

EXPLANATIONS AND EXCUSES

The populace struggled to gain perspective on events roiling about them. At a mass meeting attended by more than a thousand excited, perplexed, and anxious locals, Wayne Compton, a blunt-speaking attorney and an ardent civic reformer, tried to focus concerns:

> Circumstantial evidence is about as good as direct evidence. The little liquor seller is not a menace. But $100,000 worth of liquor didn't accidentally find itself here. Those who brought it in thought that they had it "fixed." But something went "hay wire." The little men were arrested. They said they had been double-crossed. They said $2,000 had been paid for protection.
>
> Who got it?[21]

That is what everyone wanted to know.

The assertion—"fixed"—threw city hall into a tizzy. So many officials were under suspicion. Denials flew. Police Chief Hill said the raid made by his vice squad proved that his department was not part of any fix. Mayor Harry Clark asserted that on the day of the raid he had received a dozen phone calls, but "no effort was made to get anything that bordered on 'protection' from me." Later, when sharply questioned by reporters, he admitted that on other occasions he had been offered bribes, specifically $2,000 to protect Chinese lotteries in town and $50,000 to urge President Herbert Hoover to keep the border crossing with Mexico open twenty-four hours a day. (Gaming interests in Tijuana had been lobbying for the extension ever since the Peteet case led to early closure on the U.S. side.) Mayor Clark asserted, of course, that he had turned them down. He said he talked to the police chief about them, but "regarded the attempted bribes as no different from those which might confront any public official." The chief also had rejected bribers, he insisted.[22]

The mayor's remarks about bribes and border crossings stung John P. Mills, a testy millionaire San Diego real estate developer with deep investments in Tijuana sporting, including Agua Caliente. "Of all the people in San Diego, I was the only one who came out in the open and championed the change in the border regulations." If the mayor could prove that Mills offered him a $50,000 bribe to contact President Hoover, "I'll give $25,000 to a local charity," said Mills, who eagerly pledged another $25,000 for a political campaign to recall Mayor Clark.[23] Investigation of bribes surely makes folks nervous and starchy.

Councilman J. V. Alexander proposed that the council itself investigate the scandal "to take the stigma off of many innocent officials who were not guilty of those charges and to make it possible to see that the people who were guilty of trying to give protection to bootleggers and other vices in this town are prosecuted to the full extent of the law."[24] The *Union* noted that the councilman's resolution mentioned protection for "other vices in this town" and called for a probe of the city's entire underworld. Councilman Edward R. Dowell opposed, saying it would only amount to "mixing up a lot of whitewash for the council to spill over its own head."[25]

"Well, there's one good thing about it [the bust]," said Councilman Louis G. Maire. "If something had not slipped and the police had not found the booze, a large number of the people who would have drunk it would have gone blind."[26]

With careers, reputations, and jail time in the offing, officials wrangled, maneuvered, and dodged over the proper legal office to handle formal investigation of the sensitive case. San Diego's current district attorney begged off, saying he had neither the finances nor personnel to do the job, at least that is what he announced. Secretly he was conducting his own investigation, undoubtedly concerned about what might be discovered and insisting on screening it first.[27]

As the scandal involved both state and federal anti-liquor laws, an investigation could fall under state or federal jurisdiction, or both. Some, however, had no confidence in the local U.S. Attorney's office and thought the county grand jury most qualified to conduct the inquiry; others felt that a county probe brought matters too close to home and was liable to seek a cover-up. To satisfy all, prosecutors decided on two grand jury investigations convening at the same time, the regular county jury and a special federal jury that would sit in Los Angeles. Over the next few months, each relentlessly pursued its task, calling hundreds of witnesses from mayor and police chief to petty bootleggers, known sportsmen, and Legionnaires. Speculation soared as the media announced who was to be interrogated, and in exit interviews witnesses swore they had told all. The inquiries promised fireworks but few crackled, at least in public.

In the end, when the county jury indicted no one and turned its evidence over to its federal counterpart, only the relatively small-time bootleggers netted in the original raid on the downtown store, plus eleven others with whom they were connected, were indicted, tried, and convicted. The alleged "fixers" were never identified nor were any of the city officials who supposedly received the bribes. Most everyone thought the findings inconclusive, and it was generally conceded that graft and corruption continued to permeate "village" government.[28]

The Legionnaire bribery scandal came to public attention hardly a month after Marty Colson stood in the dock before Judge Andrews and related his version of why the Agua Caliente money-car robbery had gone so wrong. Obviously Colson could not have used it as direct evidence for the sort of police and political fixing that he claimed for the Dike job, but the Legionnaire morass was only the latest scandal that served to dramatize and confirm the lawless and duplicitous atmosphere permeating the air Colson breathed and life he lived before the crime he committed. These were giddy Keystone cop cases where highly publicized, flagrant corruption in the city's highest offices went unpunished and society sank more deeply into resignation, an attractive backdrop for wanton crime.

Sentencing and Censuring

On August 6, 1929, before expectant but subdued spectators in an overly packed courtroom, Judge Charles N. Andrews, noted for his grandiose treatises, if not grandiloquence, sentenced Martin Colson and Lee Cochran for their killings on the Dike. One of the pompous jurist's greatest productions, it lasted almost an hour as he weighed his duty and responsibility; the nation's state of mind and crime rate; the origins of mankind and human morality and sensibilities; capital punishment; the defendants' motivation; circumstances (depravities) surrounding the murders; and finally, in a few short words, the sentences. That adds up to a lot of palaver, and soon after, it inspired rebuttal.

"The Courts are always faced with serious problems," he began.

> Into their keeping are committed the property rights, the liberties and lives of citizens, law and order, the peace and welfare of society, the welfare of the state and of the individual citizen are all within their keeping.
>
> Perhaps no more stern responsibility could come to a court than when it is called upon, in its discretion, to fix a penalty which involves life or death.[1]

Judge Andrews then referred to an analysis of America's rising crime rate by a former U.S. attorney general, up 350 percent since 1900, fifty times greater than in Great Britain, costing $13 billion annually, matching the national debt. But why should this be? He set the upheaval of the First World War and Prohibition aside, but excoriated greed, "the presence on every side of loose and easy and abundant money which men are seeking to get without relation to how, or whom it belongs to."[2] Andrews noted that Marty Colson had described the same sort of unfettered avarice to explain the participation of his partner, Lee Cochran, in the holdup: "He [Cochran] was blinded and bound and led into this by the inestimable power of money —of gold to be gotten easily and quickly."[3]

Death penalty cases might more fairly be decided by a jury, the judge continued. "Every individual, whether he knows it or not, has those weaknesses that are common to human nature. He may have prejudices of which he cannot dispossess himself." So what is a judge to do? "I believe it is the duty of the court to seek as far as possible to find what the idea and sentiment of the *public* is with reference to this crime," an excellent example of this judge's propensity to rely on general knowledge and experience rather than case law to formulate his verdicts.[4]

Judge Andrews then reviewed the public debate over capital punishment. Some believe that "this life is a life of probation and that a man is entitled to live out that life to the end . . . ," which represented a spiritual approach to humanity. But Judge Andrews placed more confidence in science, which allowed him to expound on evolution "yet going on developing man to a higher degree." Evolution for all, but still he believed some humans more evolved than others.[5]

HEREDITY AND FREE WILL

Colson's request for death, coupled to his explanation, "I have no will or volition in the desire [to die]. It is only an existing condition," caused the judge to ponder man's relation to nature and the power of heredity, "so dominating and so controlling a force in this world, that we scarcely have the right of the freedom of will," he offered.

"Who knows the forces and experiences which enter into our inheritance and the forces which were born and formed in our pre-natal existence? There may be in any young man that which we call dementia praecox and which was a pre-natal fixing of a mental condition [that] made his acts beyond his control." So free will was expunged from human behavior, responsibility diminished or made of no consequence. It is doubtful that the feckless Cochran could follow this line of thought, but the more perspicacious Colson could, and the judge, without doubt, aimed his remarks at him:

"While I am not seriously considering the matters disclosed here by the defendant [Colson's setting up the money-car holdup as a prelude to robbing and destroying Agua Caliente], it may be that the strange conduct of the defendant, it is scarcely possible, if not easily believed, indicates a mental condition and an hereditary strain that we may not fully understand. . . . It is one of those considerations which, perhaps, may enter into the fixing of the death penalty."[6]

Sensing his remarks too abstract for his listeners, Judge Andrews explained, "I think it is my duty to arrive at an estimate of public sentiment by a somewhat more direct expression upon the question [of capital punishment, in this case], and I have not been left wholly without direct expression by my fellow citizens." One confidant had told him, "Judge, if you don't hang those lousy bandits, you are lying down on your job. These men are part of an organized gang that are raiding society; they are killers. . . . If you haven't the guts to hang those men, then you had better send them over to Mexico whose citizens they killed and property they took and let them deal with them there. They know what to do with such cattle."[7]

On the other side, a "good woman" had remarked, "Judge, don't hang those boys. They are young fellows with a wrong slant on life just now. They are some mothers' sons; they are human beings." To sentence them to death would be "a reversion to the old idea of the barbaric age of an eye for an eye, and you are false to the civilization of which you are part, if you take the lives of those boys."[8]

What His Honor was doing in discussing the case with a "confidant" and a "good woman" seems forgotten in the flowery rhetoric, but the conflicting positions appear to be more self-invented to make a point than genuine specimens of public opinion which the judge said he sought. Between these two extremes, he said, lay a "mass of public opinion that is not voiced," but if it were heard, he assured, it would express its faith in the court system and urge the judge to do his duty. Judge Andrews then turned to Jesus for help.

CHRIST'S EXAMPLE

"What should be the verdict of the Savior if He sat in this seat of judgment?" Andrews asked himself out loud. "He would have the wisdom to know all the influences and all the bearings and all the consequences which have preceded and followed their [Colson's and Cochran's] acts, and as He looked upon them with his gentle eyes, I am wondering if He would say, 'They shall die,' or 'They shall live.'" The judge then pondered selected Biblical stories—those without sin casting the first stone, "I was naked and you clothed me," the good Samaritan—all of which stressed *mercy* as Christ's word.

Mercy "droppeth like the gentle dew of heaven alike upon the just and upon the unjust . . . ," he said. Mercy has "some part in the divine plan and the plan of man fashioned upon that divine plan, [and] seems to be a recognized fact in our civilization."[9] Judge Andrews clearly embraced "mercy" as a concept, if not for all his legal decisions. It depended upon the crime committed, and for him even first-degree murder possessed degrees of heinousness.

"There are crimes like the crime which so arouses the south as well as the north where some brute takes some gentle, helpless woman, ravishing her and killing her, and there is a reaction which is irresistible in the human heart and that man cannot live, and communities break down jails and do the things [public lynchings] which are unseemly to civilization because of this reaction to that crime."

Or the example "of one man finding an old couple in bed and believing that they had their life's savings with them, killed them with an axe and rolled them off their mattress where he searched for their wealth."[10]

Then there was the William Edward Hickman case, just two years earlier, "where this little girl [Marion Parker, age 12] was taken from her school, kept in confinement and choked to death; where her body was dismembered and placed in a satchel, and then eyes sewed open and her trunk [her torso] sold to her father for $1,500." (A week after the kidnapping, police in Oregon arrested Hickman, who confessed, and the following year he was hanged at San Quentin.)[11]

Judge Andrews found these horrifying cases incompatible with "our civilization," repugnant to mankind, and worthy of the death penalty. "It is the one safety valve to society."[12]

BUT THE MURDERS ON THE DIKE?

In his extraordinary exposition, with no reference to statutory law whatsoever, but only the judge's personal views on life, history, and religion, all moderated by nineteenth-century evolutionary thought (and by attributing his ruminations to the public at large), Andrews found the slaughter on the Dike "not so shocking."

And while not exactly inferring extenuating circumstances, he alleged to know the psychology of the crime: "They [the accused, Colson and Cochran] admit the holdup, and perhaps the psychology of it is that they felt that being in the hi-jacking game, those games at Tijuana [open gambling, specifically at Agua Caliente] were crooked, and that they [the Border Barons] were a band of legalized robbers, and that they had accumulated $80,000 or $90,000 over the weekend by that kind of process, and [therefore] that it was legitimate to take it from them."[13] In other words, thieves mimicked thieves, like hijackers hoisting liquor from bootleggers.

"Of course, they were in error," the judge continued, " but I am not surprised that it should occur to some [mobsters and others] that know that place [Agua Caliente and Tijuana at large] which is so tremendously potent in the influence upon men and women and the public, and it brings to this court house here so much of the crime and misery that it might be charged with a conspiracy such as was charged [by Colson] in court here yesterday."[14]

Here is the judge venting his scorn on Tijuana and Agua Caliente and charging those who profited from them with complicity—as Colson had explained—in the money-car robbery. Again, it was essentially a matter of filchers looting filchers. Vice-ridden Tijuana provided at least the context for the crime and made it understandable. Colson's story may or may not have been true, but given the contingencies, it was conceivable.

But Judge Andrews dared not pursue that line of thought too far. It invited recriminations best avoided. "I do not credit that [Colson's] story," he added with no further explanation, but he used the opportunity in an unctuously patronizing way to spit more venom on Tijuana. "I believe that the time will come when that awful danger spot to mankind which is now comparable to Sodom and Gomorrah before their fall," he sermonized, "will be morally wiped from the face of the earth, though not physically, and I look for this to come from the moral awakening of the great Republic to the south, and that the order [which] emanates for that removal and for the suppression of the dangerous plague center of gambling, drunkenness, prostitution, and crime will come from the President of Mexico himself."[15]

There was some prescience in the judge's final comments about the future of Tijuana, but for now, sermon ended, back to sentencing.

SENTENCES

After some additional pomposity, Andrews got around to passing sentence on the self-confessed defendants. "I walk, and it is my duty to walk the path which the light of my reason and my conscience [ignoring case law and judicial precedents] dictates and so far as I can determine my own views in this matter, I have arrived at the conclusion that so far as the defendant Cochran is concerned that this is not a case for capital punishment. Arraign Mr. Cochran for judgment."[16]

The clerk read the charges against Cochran. As he rose to hear the verdict, his wife burst into tears, as did the couple's three-year-old daughter. Marian's "sobbing was plainly audible above the voice of the judge as he pronounced sentence."[17]

"As punishment for this crime it is the judgment and order of the court and of the law [the judge's rare reference to the law], that you stand committed to the State Prison of San Quentin ... [for] your natural life."[18] Life in prison for Cochran, but subject to parole.

Lee showed no outward sign of emotion at the decision. "The muscles of his face did not move as he looked Judge Andrews squarely in the face and listened intently to the sentence."[19]

Colson's arraignment followed, but then a query: "Mr. Colson, you yesterday expressed in court the desire that the court impose upon you the death sentence. Do you still desire that the court order you to be hung?"

Suspense gripped the courtroom. Colson did not immediately answer; he stared at a stack of papers on the court clerk's desk. Then he faced the judge and in a clear voice which penetrated every corner of the crowded courtroom said, "Your honor, in as much as I left it to the discretion of the court yesterday, I, today, as yesterday, at this time I leave my fate in the hands of the Court."[20] Newspapers reported that a faint smile crossed the judge's face, as if to say, "I thought so. I knew all along that you did not want to die."[21]

Judge Andrews then sentenced Colson to life imprisonment in Folsom Prison. There was a difference between San Quentin and Folsom at the time. San Quentin held first-time, less notorious offenders, who had a better chance for early parole. Hardened criminals and recalcitrants went to Folsom, with much less chance of parole.

Court adjourned (after taking, for the record, some brief personal history data from the prisoners).

REACTION

At the verdict, there was so much commotion in the courtroom that the bailiff and deputy sheriffs had to clear it of spectators. The press never reported the sense or content of the buzz. Cochran seemed dazed as deputies escorted him away; he did not smile at his wife, as he so frequently had done at previous hearings. Colson, his chest shaking, bowed his head, perhaps because, per his request to Judge Andrews, he had anticipated a lesser sentence for his partner. Before leaving for prison, authorities grilled the two convicts about Colson's electrifying comments about the scheme to blow up Agua Caliente. Cochran denied any knowledge of such a conspiracy; Colson swore to say no more about the subject, and did not.[22]

En route to San Quentin, Cochran again exonerated Jerry Kearney of any participation in the crime. "Jerry was good to us in a time of need and because he took us in, he is in a jam."[23] Marty Colson again turned silent. They arrived at their respective penitentiaries without incident, Cochran slated to repair boat motors and Colson to do plumbing, but it was not the last heard of them.

Satisfied or not with the court's verdicts, San Diego seemed to consider the matter finished. There was no outcry that the mobsters had escaped the noose nor any that the sentences were unduly harsh. But the entire case was hardly concluded. Two suspected major confederates in the affair—Marcel Dellon and Jeanne Lee—yet ran free, and the state still intended to prosecute Jerry Kearney as a co-conspirator in the crime. Many questions concerning the crime itself, its perpetrators and their purposes, the connection of Agua Caliente personnel, remained unanswered, but official investigation of the Dike affair was simply set aside in order to concentrate on more current police inquiries, or so it was said.

The *San Diego Tribune* editorialized that the matter allowed people to see the "realities of Prohibition first hand. . . . It clearly demonstrates how the liquor crusade functions as a nursery for the type of criminal that has made contemporary American 'Civilization' the laughingstock of the world." When would America wake up? "No self-respecting nation can continue a condition in which such crimes multiply" due to "the blind prejudice of a minority [anti-liquor supporters]." Prohibition was not the issue per se for the newspaper, but "the retention of some measure of national self-respect is essential."[24]

The judge's vigorous attack on Tijuana, though, garnered more vehement responses, some for, others against.

Ever anxious to smear and defame Tijuana for its tourist-attracting entertainment and recreation, the *Los Angeles Examiner* weighed in with another of its scurrilous attacks against the Devil's haven. "Judge Andrews of San Diego may or may not prove a true prophet as to the fate of Tia Juana at the hands of the Mexican Government," the newspaper editorialized, "but his description of the place fits the facts, and all the facts."

And those *facts*, neatly listed:

> There is no viler hole; no deeper sink of iniquity than this city of sin and crime so near our border.
>
> It is a plague spot in which all manner of moral diseases are developed.
>
> It is the home of crooks, cutthroats, fiends, and degenerates of every known variety.
>
> It is the base of dope dealers and machine gun operators. . . .
>
> The crime for which the bandits were given life imprisonment, though brutal and cowardly to the last degree, was almost merciful as compared with other fiend crimes of frequent occurrence in Tijuana. . . .
>
> Sodom and Gomorrah were destroyed because of sins. Tia Juana and Agua Caliente are destroying those that go there. They are also spreading destruction in many American homes and families.[25]

So indicated one side of the coin.

On the other side, the *San Diego Herald* ridiculed His Honor: "Superior Judge Andrews of America, but living now on probation in San Diego before he goes to Heaven, says Tijuana is a rotten spot comparable to Sodom." If Tijuana goes, it sarcastically asserted, it would be hard on Los Angeles and San Diego, "for millions of people will go dry [without liquor] and become violently wicked. Many will lose their souls . . . [and] go 'into perdition' with Satan. That's happened more than once."[26]

Tijuana's Chamber of Commerce, however, was hardly satirical and certainly did not joke or mince words in its published open letter rebutting the jurist's slurs against their entire city. If Judge Andrews meant to condemn certain businesses, he should have said so; he was entitled to his opinion,

> but he is not entitled to involve a whole community, . . . ignoring the fact that there is good and evil, not only in Tijuana, but in all Mexico, the United States and the whole world.

It cannot be denied that there are here, commercially and socially speaking, people that are as decent, clean and honest as elsewhere, [and for their sake] we indignantly raise this protest against the abuse which unfortunately is being cast upon this community.

The Chamber demanded the same sort of respect and square treatment for Tijuanenses "that those who vilify us demand and expect for themselves with so much zeal."[27]

A BARON'S BARK

No one defended the vitality, commercial flair, and pleasures of Tijuana with more zest than Border Baron Wirt Bowman. While the Agua Caliente robbery story was still unfolding, San Diego's Mayor Harry Clark (soon to be entangled in the Legionnaire scandal) referred in a public speech to U.S. businessmen invested in Tijuana as "renegade Americans." Bowman, who had national political aspirations, erupted, calling the mayor's remark "unfair and reckless."

"Your public position enables your voice to reach the people and the press with a facility that you could not do as a private citizen," he said. "Therefore, it would seem that the responsibility of your position would dictate that you temper your utterances with tolerance, temperance, and truth."

Bowman reminded the mayor that while he [Wirt] did business in Mexico, he lived in San Diego, where he paid county taxes on over $100,000 worth of property, as well as $200 a month to the city's Chamber of Commerce, of which he was a director, and to which in 1927 he had donated $5,000 to relieve it of debts. On behalf of Americans doing business in Mexico, and the Mexican people at large, Bowman forcefully protested the mayor's politics and remarks: "American citizens go in great numbers to every country in Europe and to Canada for diversions, comfort, and pleasure of the same identical nature as those you condemn, for going to Mexico. . . . But because there are resorts in Mexico which Americans enjoy equally with European and Canadian resorts, you would continue to impede, restrain, or suppress travel to and from Mexico for every reason."[28]

Given his thirty years of collaboration in Mexican business ventures, Bowman's censorious remarks could be expected, but the mayor's statements were especially stinging because Agua Caliente's bud was about to blossom, and no one could predict how the money-car robbery might affect business. Despite the horrors of the crime and the accusation of conspiracy, it seemed to hold true in this instance that any publicity is good publicity. Entertainment and sports celebrities, prominent politicians and socialites, along with crowds of curious oglers flooded the resort, spending freely on the sumptuous cuisine and luxurious lodging, losing thousands in the opulent casino, and eagerly anticipating first call at the new, beautifully honed world-class thoroughbred horse track, due to open in only a few months. Most anyone who was anybody desired to experience, to see or be seen at posh, casual but still dignified Agua Caliente, so distinct from the exclusive resorts back East and abroad.

Agua Caliente was *our* place for *our* times.

Let's go!

Hollywood's Playground

O ff on its meteoric flight, Agua Caliente soared into the 1930s. Hype surrounding it broadened, but basic themes, captured in newspaper headlines, remained the same:

AGUA CALIENTE RISE MARVELS

Famed Resort Below Border Still Mere Infant

Millions Spent in Building Great Pleasure Spot

Western Rival of Deauville and Nice Ultramodern

And in December 1930 the *Los Angeles Times* declared:

> Only a baby, a trifle more than two years of age, to be exact, yet Agua Caliente, a pleasure resort deluxe, nestling in the valley of Tia Juana, in Old Mexico, eighteen miles below San Diego, has attained international fame comparable with the great fashionable watering places of Europe.
>
> Here are found, in an atmosphere of gaiety, tempered with the refinements of polite society, all of the pleasures of the Old World. The loveliness and completeness of the place is beyond compare. Everything is ultramodern. Monte Carlo, Nice, Deauville have moved to the doorstep of Uncle Sam. A spacious hotel offers the same things to be had in New York, London or Paris.[1]

Indeed, in 1929, eleven million American tourists crossed the border at Tijuana and Calexico. Thirty thousand passed through customs daily. How many moved on to Agua Caliente (three miles south) is not known, but enough to earn the Barons $5 million their first year of operation.[2] Wirt

Bowman called that figure exaggerated, but like all casino owners, he never admitted the enormous profits realized from his gambling enterprises, and deliberately left such amounts vague to enhance their mystique, encourage the public to inflate the sum into awe-striking fantasy, and confound tax collectors. (The Bureau of Internal Revenue was already auditing Wirt's tax returns for fraud.)

Little is known of Agua Caliente's profits and losses. Miscellaneous records of the organization appear now and then in the hands of an artifacts collector or for sale on eBay, but they are piecemeal and impossible to assemble into a coherent whole. Bowman, Long, and Crofton each invested $50,000 to get building underway and then went public with 500,000 shares at $10 each. They, along with Abelardo Rodríguez, each kept 100,000 shares for themselves and sold the remaining 100,000 in increments, first to friends and insiders at the initial $10 a share, and then at $45 and finally $60 a share to others. Those with at least $100,000 (today a million) worth of shares included motion picture magnates, nationally famous boxers such as Jack Dempsey, film actors, a few bankers, and, of course, the Border Barons themselves.[3] Wayne McAllister, the main architect on the project, remembered how he and his wife, then in their early twenties invested all their savings, $1,500, at the $10 level and then in a short period saw it balloon at least six times higher: "All of a sudden, we were doing pretty good."[4] And so was everyone else connected to the venture, especially the Barons, millionaires many times over.

Shares floated freely, as Bowman loosely delivered stock beyond the total approved by the corporation's directors. When Wirt sent Abelardo Rodríguez an additional ten shares of company stock in 1928, the governor reminded him that the company was already fully subscribed, that no new stock could be issued without calling a general meeting of the stockholders, and warned him, "You are entangling yourself in something that may be of very serious consequences." Rodríguez returned the stock, requesting that Bowman comply "with the provisions of the law."[5] Given his propensity for shady dealings, the governor's insistence is surprising. Bowman was a banker; he knew corporate business and the law, but he searched for loopholes, stretched statutes, played his "contacts," covered missteps, and masked his finances and ambitions.

The value of Agua Caliente shares increased nine-fold the first year of

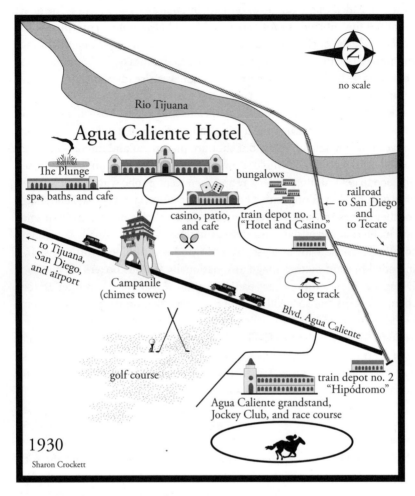

Agua Caliente, 1930. Sharon Crockett

operation, and the company paid more than a million dollars in dividends on an original capital investment of $1.2 million.[6] Another 400,000 shares financed the new racetrack. The early years of the Great Depression, however, greatly diminished crowds, revenue, and stock dividends; they also precipitated a managerial shake-up, briefly closed the track, created labor unrest, attracted new threats from mobsters, caused the Barons to beg for relief from the Mexican government, and endangered the entire operation. Still, despite the deepening crisis, the Barons maintained a glamorous, carefree front.

WONDROUS SIDELIGHTS

Special events packed the resort's calendar, not only with championship bridge and golf tourneys, but also a festive carnival of creative attractions, all subject to betting. Ostrich races became a favorite on the track normally reserved for greyhounds. (Ostriches are the fastest creatures on two legs, and in short bursts can run up to forty-three miles an hour.) "The birds are to be ridden by negro boys as jockeys [the jockeys were Mexican lads], and they will guide the birds by means of their wings. Hoods will be placed over the animals' heads at the start, so the riders may get aboard and then the race will be underway." Sponsors noted that ostriches do not like to run over a set course but whether or not the birds liked the race, "there would be plenty of laughs." Names of the trained birds in the final race in July 1933 were Abyssinia, Sadie Sahara, and Abdul the Turk, and a picture advertising the race showed a jockey being tossed from his fast-strutting, feathery mount.

Place your bets! Five hundred spectators roared. Sadie won with Pedro on top, hanging on for dear life to the bird's neck, wings, or whatever he could grab. Abdul was second; Abyssinia finished third—but riderless.[7]

The crowd wildly cheered the man who trained the birds. He had recently staged a horse race at the same track with monkeys as jockeys.

The resort, meanwhile, staged the "Kentucky Derby of Greyhound Racing" and the world's richest golf tournament ($15,000 total prize money) and handicap horse racing (originally $100,000 but reduced to $50,000 by the Depression); planned an international bridge Olympiad for 1932 which guaranteed the winners $10,000 to $50,000; and vowed to get the German heavyweight Max Schmeling to box there at a new ring seating forty thousand, either against Jack Dempsey (the Manassa Mauler) or the popular Irishman "Sailor Tom" Sharkey.[8] Dempsey promised to fight any contender but preferred the current "Black Menace," George Godfrey, because Godfrey had proved to be such a good draw in California.

"They said that I drew the color line [would not fight blacks]," crowed the champ. "Well here's where I will make somebody swallow those words."[9]

The boxing world went wild, and such bombast further embellished the magnetism of the resort, even if the Dempsey-Godfrey fight never came off, and New York got the Schmeling-Sharkey bout.

Agua Caliente's powerful private radio station, located at the site, bally-hooed these happenings along with the arrival and departure of notables, such as former Mexican president Plutarco Elías Calles, so instrumental in founding the complex and one of its chief financial beneficiaries, along with Lázaro Cárdenas, the somewhat taciturn army general who would ascend to *jefe máximo* in 1934. Following their visit to the resort, Baron Long ferried Calles and Cárdenas in his sumptuous yacht, the *Norab*, from Ensenada to Guaymas, and Cárdenas later said that the ostentation of Agua Caliente had deeply impressed him. When he became president, the Barons learned to their dismay just how much.[10]

Swanky fashion shows, featuring strikingly unusual and highly expensive furs, rugs, and tapestries along with stylish Parisian gowns and renowned imported perfumes; beauty pageants showing off Hollywood's starlets; business conferences, such as the "Hands across the Border" banquet, organized by Mexican and American shippers advocating more favorable trade relations between the two countries; and lavish, dressy luncheon parties, extensively reported in the society pages of Southern California newspapers, abounded at the complex. Tony duty-free shops offered, at a one-third to one-half price discount, exquisite millinery, gentlemen's fine accessories, and an astounding assortment of alcoholic beverages, including Aquavit (also called Akvavit; the "National drink of Denmark, Sweden. Should be served cool. Powerful . . . can be drunk straight . . . with beer chaser . . . or with charged water in highballs . . . straight is preferred"), or Spanish Tarragonan chartreuse ("When you sip Chartreuse . . . you are transplanted to the romance of stone flagged cloisters . . ."), or China's popular drink, Naskapi ("from which many strange concoctions are made: 'Celestial Sunbeam,' 'Shanghai Gesture,' 'Fu Manchu Elixir'").[11]

The long list of both well-known and exotic whiskies, cordials and liqueurs, and wines fairly shouted: "To Hell with Prohibition."

ANODYNE (OR, RELAXATION)

Vogue's correspondent, Eleanor Minturn James, visited the resort in December 1930, gushed over the spa, and perpetuated the hype:

> Here in the cloistered patio is peace. There is peace in the soothing chimes of the campanile bells, an echo of the old world of Spain and its cathedrals. There is

anodyne in the soft Mexican names, slurred and rhythmical,—*Agua Caliente, gallería, vestíbulo, avenida escalera, campanile.*

So, there is anodyne for the heart and mind, and cure for physical ills at the luxurious new spa. Help for high blood pressure, help for low blood pressure. For the abstemious and anemic, a quickened circulation: for the overindulged, a beneficial slaking of over-active appetites. . . .

The gymnasium has multiple devices for exercise—a huge ship helm affording a nautical air . . . and an electrical horse for reducing. I almost forgot the tonic baths—for the thin, better than the Turkish. There are ovens, filament lined, where your head is packed in cold towels and you are considerately given ice-water, not for your comfort, but to make you hotter. Then the needle spray, followed by cold water.[12]

Hollywood's gossip columnists reveled in the fantasia. Agua Caliente's skilled and industrious publicity agent, Harry Pollock, in April 1933, invited two of filmland's most famous and vituperative gossip columnists—Hedda Hopper and Lilyan Tashman—to judge the Easter fashion show at the resort. What Pollock did not fathom was the spitefulness coursing between the two prima donnas, the result of Hopper's failure in one of her columns to include Tashman among the three best-dressed women in Hollywood. With that marvelous bitchiness to which they both were accustomed, and in a world where jealousies are often draped in flattery, the columnists declined the invitation, Hedda sarcastically saying, "[I] Resign in favor of Miss Tashman who will fit the glamour and flamboyancy of your casino to a dot," and Lilyan allowing, "Sorry, have a cocktail party Sunday. Miss Hopper qualified to judge anything passé."[13]

WHERE HOLLYWOOD MAKES WHOOPEE

Agua Caliente and Hollywood fit hand in glove. The resort's deluxe surroundings, its flamboyant display of gambling, thoroughbred horse racing, and cocktails, proved tailor-made for movie magnates and stars reveling at the zenith of their public acclaim. Moguls who had schemed and worked hard to rise above their humble and deprecated backgrounds, stars whom upper society and sophisticates considered to be superficial, false (only actors, after all), thinly gilded, poorly bred, crass money machines who had hypnotized the hoi polloi with their tricks and illusions, now had the opportunity to be seen as they "really were"—wealthy, urbane, intelligent, demanding, charming, a crowd apart, royalty in their own right.

At Agua Caliente aristocrats took a step down and Hollywood a step up. They met and fell in love, albeit in the ambiance of their era, when the *nouveau riche* everywhere flooded into cavernous voids created by collapsing traditions, and people deliberately broke the "laws" and norms of a former society in order to create a new one for themselves.

A pictorial review published on the West Coast in 1932 featured Agua Caliente and perfectly captured the atmosphere and new blend of high taste. It reflected a mood not only distinct to the pleasure site itself, but evidenced in much of America.

There sat the famous resort in the "Land of mañana. . . . A dreamer's paradise, nestling in a scented valley." "A touch of Old Spain" pictured flamenco dancers, and the "culmination of a Mexican romance," a young, smiling couple—Charles and Anne Morrow Lindbergh, who had met in Mexico, where her father, Dwight, was U.S. Ambassador.

"Agua Caliente where all nations meet and speak the tongue [English] and happiness [reigns]" headlined a montage of "greats" mingling at the spa: England's Sir Henry and Lady Wood; opera's famous Wagnerian, Ernestine Schumann-Heinck; the U.S. Secretary of the Navy; Johor's Sultan and Sultana; the Scottish songwriter and singer Sir Harry Lauder (*Roaming in the Gloamin'* and *I Love a Lassie*), said in the late Twenties to be the highest paid entertainer in the world; Hollywood's Clark Gable; the French wine king, Monsieur Cruse; Sir James Currie of England; Australia's Major General Johnson; and Prince Zurlo of Italy. The review's following page displayed golf idols at the resort: Gene Sarazen, Olin Dutra, George Von Elm, Glenna Collett Vare (Queen Glenna), and "The Haig," Walter Hagen, the most flamboyant golfer ever.[14]

Bugsy Siegel also dropped in on several occasions and picked up ideas for the concept of a luxurious, star-studded casino-resort elsewhere, maybe in the desert outside Las Vegas, but first the East Coast mobster wanted to survey the organized crime scene on the West Coast and hobnob with movie stars such as George Raft, known for his gangster portrayals (*Scarface*), an actor who did not discourage rumors about his own mob connections. It was also said that the epoch's famous bank robber, Harvey Bailey, who masterminded raids with Machine Gun Kelly and Ma Barker, briefly hid out at the resort.[15]

While much of his country lay deeply mired in Depression, President Franklin Roosevelt's soil conservation chief, Big Hugh Johnson, vacationed for a week at Agua Caliente in 1934 and left an appreciative letter to Baron Long. "You know that I am no stranger in this [Pacific Coast] country," he wrote, "but must say to you that I was perfectly astonished at what I found here. I have been in most parts of the world and have squandered my money in most parts of its hostelries, but for what you can get here [Agua Caliente] in perfect cuisine, efficient service, and decent surroundings, I do not know its equal in the world. Considering the heat and drought in the Middle West, I leave here for there with considerable regret."[16]

Without doubt, it must have been difficult for the soil scientist (and flamboyant showman) to leave the enchanting resort for the raging Dust Bowl. To his credit, however, he soon became nationally esteemed for the reclamation of lands ruined by howling dusters.

A *Los Angeles Times* reporter later revisited the spot's halcyon years and vividly recaptured Hollywood's frenetic rush to Agua Caliente. "Caliente clicked immediately [with movieland]," he wrote. "For the first time in their quixotic careers, the glamour girls and boys from Hollywood found a place where they could play in the manner of emperors and czars and in keeping with their large salaries. Their patronage naturally attracted other people with more dollars than sense."[17]

MOVIEMAKING

The film industry was so enthralled with Agua Caliente it was only natural that studios would want to utilize the resort as a setting for movies. It became a kind of hotspot for making "quickie" movies. As film plots involving horse racing were then in favor, many scenes were shot at the spa's gorgeous new racetrack. Such motion pictures were essentially morality tales. Fixed races abound. Crooked, Runyonesque jockeys befriend an innocent, down-and-out young lad and are morally reformed. Mickey Rooney (then Mickey McGuire) played such a boy in *Fast Companions* (1932). In *Racetrack* (1933) Joe (Leo Carrillo) gets a young jockey to throw a race, then tells the track's judges about the fix so that the boy gets disqualified from (corrupt) racing, returns to his mother, and becomes an honest bookie. Jackie Searl plays "Gimpy," an eleven-year-old orphan with a bad leg whom no one wishes to adopt in *The Unwelcome Stranger* (1935). A friend allows the cripple to jockey a horse, and he is winning the race when a rival rider grabs Gimpy by his bad leg, tosses him off his mount, and wins the race. Judges, however, disqualify the cheater and declare Gimpy the winner. He is then adopted by a racing stable owner (Jack Holt).[18]

All of these pictures gave thoroughbred horse racing a decidedly black eye. One wonders what audiences learned from them, how closely they may have approximated those corrupt practices in movies with what they knew (or suspected) of the real racing world, and whether or not they compared these sordid motifs with conditions at Agua Caliente's premier new track.

The film that took most advantage of Agua Caliente's sleek surroundings was the romantic comedy *In Caliente* (1935), starring the stunning and classy Dolores del Rio; the hardy Irishman Pat O'Brien; the stereotyped Hispanic, Leo Carrillo; the fine character actor, Edward Everett Horton, forever the talented bumbler; and the pigeon-holed dizzy blonde, Glenda Farrell. The movie also featured musical dance spectaculars choreographed by Busby Berkeley. The plot: a magazine editor (O'Brien) is engaged to a gold-digging woman (Farrell). To save him from a fall, his wealthy fuss-budget of a buddy (Horton) takes the editor to Agua Caliente, where he promptly becomes enchanted with a beautiful dancer (del Rio). When she learns the editor has written a savage magazine review of her dancing without ever having seen her, she plots revenge—pretend to be romantically interested and then drop him—but (predictably) they fall in love. (It is thought that Dolores del Rio wears the screen's first two-piece bathing suit in the pool scene.) The gold digger abruptly arrives on the scene, causing the dancer to flee in a car. The editor jumps into the auto to apologize and explain. His nervous, well-meaning friend follows with the gold digger in another car. When the money-minded woman realizes the man next to her is rich, she decides to marry him, leaving the editor and the dancer free to make up and then get married.

One can hear the corn crackle around the storyline, but Berkeley staged two spectacular dance revues in the motion picture, one which introduced the still well-remembered "The Lady in Red," and the other, a typical, sprawling Berkeley extravaganza which magnifies Dolores del Rio's attractiveness but, with misguided sensationalism, sends horses bounding up a staircase. The *New York Times* rated the picture "fair entertainment" and then panned it: "The story [line] is so inconsequential that its four writers and adapters should blush for their salaries." The lyricists "hit below the Equator with one little classic which begins, 'Muchacha, at last I've gotcha where I wantcha, muchacha." Even Busby Berkeley caught a dose of disdain for transforming the resort's charming patio into a bandit cave with roaring campfires and a rodeo of white horses backed by a mountain range crudely painted on a tarpaulin. In other words, *In Caliente* was a stinker but seen today still garners a lot of laughs and humming along.[19]

Movies made Agua Caliente look like no other place for gaiety and romance, even when the real action took place elsewhere. In *One Way Passage* (1932), two strangers, Dan (William Powell) and Joan (Kay Francis), fall deeply in love on a sea voyage. En route, they gleefully toast one another by ritually smashing their cocktail glasses after finishing a drink. But their hidden pasts are dark: Dan is a convict being transported to prison, and Joan, a wealthy heiress, is fatally ill. Bit by bit, the truth becomes known. Dan schemes to escape when the ship docks in Honolulu, but Joan's illness deters him. Still, she rallies to bid him goodbye, but not before they agree to meet at Agua Caliente on New Year's Eve, though they know this will be impossible. At midnight on New Year's Eve with Agua Caliente in the midst of raucous celebration, a bartender hears the sound of breaking glass and turns to find the shattered stems of two glasses just as Dan and Joan used to break them—but no one is there.

A MOGUL'S PARADISE

Joseph M. Schenck, the likeable, hard-driving, high-roller chairman of the board at United Artists and in 1933, a co-founder of Twentieth Century–Fox, was Hollywood's biggest investor in Agua Caliente, which he eventually came to control. Schenck, vigorously ubiquitous in his early fifties, even shoved around the Border Barons—except for Abelardo Rodríguez, who, as state governor and then president of Mexico, had the political power to veto any of the resort's operations or even its existence (its governmental concession).

Agua Caliente fit Schenck's lifestyle of prodigious, frequently frivolous spending on lavish parties, gambling, and flowers for preferred ladies, along with expensive gifts for personal friends and business targets. He enjoyed posing for publicity shots with celebrities other than Hollywood notables, such as the golf wizard Craig Wood and the high-flying Ruth Elder, the audacious pioneer female pilot triumphing in days when many thought that women could (or should) not fly planes. Incredibly, this extraordinary man still awaits the biography he deserves, although in 1952 the Academy of Motion Pictures honored him with an Oscar for long and distinguished service to the film industry.[20]

Much of the daily entertainment and the pageantry provided for special events came from Schenck's studio, arranged by the magnate's "yes man," Lou Anger. All studio heads had their yes men, loyal lapdogs who assured their insecure and frequently indecisive bosses that "this picture is just right for us," so and so "is just perfect for the lead; the audience will love her" (or him). And most important, "The film is going to be a blockbuster. We'll make a lot of money on this one." Even the moguls needed their ravenous, vulnerable egos bolstered.

The *Hollywood Reporter* gleefully reported an encounter with one of these highly paid, smarmy sycophants resting up at Agua Caliente.

> A familiar studio personality was spotted at Agua Caliente doing an elbow-lifting act [boozing it up]. As each beaker was emptied, the "Lone Wolf" was heard to exclaim in a stage whisper: "No, no, a thousand times no."
>
> Finally someone asked him what the meaning of the gag was—or if it was just the unaccustomed head [headache]—to which the solo performer replied:
>
> "I'm just a yes man on vacation, having a good time."[21]

No names mentioned, but when it came to arranging an anniversary party at Agua Caliente, or entertaining guests at a conference, staging a cabaret, or a beauty contest, Lou Anger normally remained in charge.

Joe Schenck was fourteen when he and his family emigrated from Russia to a tenement on New York's lower East Side and then moved to Harlem, where he did odd jobs for three years until he could scrape together enough money to take a pharmaceutical course that led to a clerk's job in a local drugstore. For fun and play, he and his younger brother (by two years), Nicholas, regularly visited the magical Fort George Amusement Park with its toboggan slide, Ferris wheel, and two dance halls located at the Washington Heights end of the trolley line. There the Schenck boys saw concessionaires making substantial, quick profits and eventually opened a beer stall called the Old Barrel, where they performed vaudeville to attract customers. Their showy energy caught the eye of Marcus Lowe, a regular customer at the park, who owned a number of penny arcades ("electric vaudeville"), nickelodeon parlors (open-front parlors with machines), and theaters in various East Coast cities. Together they installed new rides and games of skill in a section of Fort George they called "Paradise." From there, the trio transferred their interests across the Hudson River to somewhat shabby Palisades Amusement Park in Fort Lee, New Jersey, where they gradually filled concession spaces with upgraded, inviting, moneymaking entertainment. Soon they owned and renovated the entire park.

Lowe liked the young, aggressive, imaginative, and inventive Schenck brothers. As he expanded his theater operation, he hired Joe, the more outgoing of the pair, to book his movie houses and Nick, more businesslike, to run the company office. Joe soon left to produce motion pictures, while Nick stayed on to become president of Lowe's Incorporated, the parent company of Metro-Goldwyn-Mayer.[22]

Both Schencks experienced a scintillating rise to power, but in Hollywood, luck, success, and failure occur in just such leaps and bounds, which is why so many movie people are inveterate gamblers. Their lives are a gamble, and one much more tenuous than the cliché, "all life is a gamble." Motion picture producers and directors gamble on this movie or that one, performers on one acting job or another. They play hunches more than logic, so it is no wonder they are attracted to roulette wheels, dice tables, and poker games—and why in the late Twenties Agua Caliente became their nirvana.

Joseph Schenck was a womanizer (Marilyn Monroe became an intimate friend), financially generous to his friends, and the biggest and best-liked of all movieland gamblers. He once bet $100,000 (a million today) on a single horse race, and on another occasion lost more than $30,000 in a day. His gambling losses of 1937 ran to $70,000. Another year he lost almost $20,000, including $12,000 to Herbert Bayard Swope, a famed journalist and newspaper editor, who regularly played poker and bet horses with the country's upper crust, as well as nearly $4,700 to Harpo Marx, and $2,400 to Darryl Zanuck, his partner at Twentieth Century–Fox.[23]

An acquaintance remembered that "Joe was a philosopher who had a comic sense. He was not opinionated, and he gave good advice, such as, 'If four or five guys tell you that you're drunk, even though you know you haven't had a thing to drink, the least you can do is to lie down a little bit.' "[24] And when a good friend, also a chronic gambler, asked Schenck how to quit the habit, the movie magnate frowned (he wrinkled his brow more than he smiled): "Be on the other side of the table if you are going to suffer those kinds of losses—build a casino."[25]

THE PATRONS

A hotel's service booklet not only tells visitors about the place in which they are lodged, but what is expected of them while there. Most often the rules are annoying and ignored, and Agua Caliente was no exception. Yet they remained a potential threat of expulsion and embarrassment. First came the amenities listed in the handout: dining, dancing, room and taxi service. The parking garage cost $1 a night and included an auto checkup and dusting. Activities incorporated rides on five-gaited saddle horses and en-trée to championship tennis courts "finished in green." The hotel offered a tobacco shop and newsstand from which telegrams could be sent. The hotel manager, the house physician, and the valet (who guaranteed that "delicate fabrics and intricate gowns [would] receive special attention") could be quickly summoned through the telephone operator. "The Spa offers the same beneficial treatments with more luxurious surroundings than the famous spas of Europe . . . bathing suits [rentals] 50-cents." A taxi ride to the racetrack or the golf course cost 25 cents.[26]

Now for the "House Rules."

Police required all guests to register on arrival. By signing in, guests bound themselves to the hotel's regulations. Those who did not comply, could be asked to leave along with "anyone whose conduct conflicts with the morality of the Hotel."

Those who wished to retain servants must obtain management's permission.

"Children must not be allowed to leave their rooms without an adult person to watch over them to avoid damage or trouble."

No dogs, birds, or other animals.

No wandering from rooms to pool in "Bathing Costumes."

"No guest is allowed to share his room with anyone without first notifying management. . . . It is prohibited for men to receive visits of women and for women to receive visits from men in their rooms. . . ."

"Guests without baggage are requested to pay in advance. . . ." Those with baggage who did not pay at checkout had to leave the baggage as guarantee of payment.

Those wishing to cash checks must fill out a credit card at the front desk, "giving us time to investigate" one's background and credit standing.

By all accounts, some of them scandalous (a Mexican army general sup-posedly murdered his girlfriend at the hotel), the rules were there but rarely invoked.

Most guests remembered delightful times at the resort, but not all. One night, the silent screen star Mabel Normand (an artistic comedienne impli-cated in 1922 in the mysterious slaying of the Paramount film director William Desmond Taylor) decided to take a swim *au naturel* in the resort's pool. As she rushed across a lawn toward The Plunge, she stumbled into a heap of horse manure piled there to fertilize the span before dawn when the smell might be less offensive.

A servant found an incredulous Mabel sitting in the smeary stuff.

"It is shit," she said, "common horse shit."

"Oh, no, Madam," the worker replied. "It is the very best grade available, I assure you."

"Thoroughbred shit," Mabel said sourly. "Well, it still stinks."[27]

THE SERVANTS

Payroll records show that more than 90 percent of the workers at Agua Caliente were Mexicans, or at least had Hispanic surnames, which is all one can go by in this case; some undoubtedly were Latinos from border towns on the U.S. side. The complex employed 339 individuals in 1932. Most were locals, which meant that a great many families in Tijuana (pop. 11,000) had at least one member working at the resort, by far the largest employer in town. Some Tijuanenses who were employed there now say that almost all laborers were *Americanos*, but that sort of remembrance only proves how today's political fashions shape yesterday's memories.

And Mexicans not only did menial jobs at the resort, but they were administrators, head cashiers, lawyers, doctors, section chiefs, and croupi-ers. The heavy employment of Mexicans was due less to the largesse of the Barons than to the governor's mandate that at least 80 percent of those working at any establishment in the territory be Mexican. Furthermore, when the Barons needed a favor from the government, they were quick to point out how dependent the entire community had become on a flourish-ing Agua Caliente: the $30,000 monthly that the corporation paid in district taxes, the many public improvements—schools, roads, water mains—that it had donated to the town, and the jobs it had provided at the request of government officials up to the president. It was true. While the Barons lined their own pockets with proceeds from the resort, they also helped keep Tijuana afloat.

Nor were the Mexican employees at Agua Caliente underpaid. In fact, for the specific work that they did, they received among the highest wages in the country: telephone operators and bartenders, $232 a month; bellboys, $92.80; maids, $100; cooks, $324, their aides, $174; and waiters, $100. Musicians received $250 and gardeners, $174, as did golf and laundry assistants. Farther south, Mexican *campesinos* earned a dollar a day and artisans not much more.[28]

The salaries of ordinary employees at the complex did not, of course, approach those of management: the chief administrator, A. V. Aldrete, earned $1,000 and James Crofton's brother, E. H., who oversaw the casino, $830. But monthly remuneration for all workers was substantial (the payroll totaled $65,474.70 in February 1932), especially for those who received tips from guests, many of whom were exceptionally good tippers. Al Capone, it was said, once gave a hat check girl a $50 tip, but even if that story is apocryphal, it sets the tone for the place. Clara Bow, Gloria Swanson, and Charlie Chaplin were especially remembered for their large tips, which could come in unexpected, spontaneous ways. Winning and superstitious gamblers also tipped well, and a streak of luck could bring a waiter serving them drinks a pile of silver dollars along with a request not to leave the site. A dealer made from $500 to $600 monthly extra in tips. One winner gave the floor manager $2,700 to divide among workers on duty, a substantial offering, but not uncommon.

The Barons recognized that their enterprise depended upon good relations with both the town's authorities and its general populace, and designed facilities and events (separate but equal) to keep any charges of favoritism or racism at bay. With blacks and Asians it was not difficult; in those cases, Tijuanenses harbored the same harsh prejudices toward them as did Anglos. (Concessions granted for nightclubs frequently stipulated the particular race permitted.) Mexicans, however, could be demanding of Anglos working their terrain for gain, and the governor often sided with his laboring countrymen in their conflicts with Agua Caliente.

A particularly nasty exchange occurred between the Barons and unions over tourist transportation rights from the border to the resort. Tourists did not like changing from U.S. to Mexican carriers at the border. Wirt

Bowman received complaints and feared losing business. Bowman begged Governor Rodríguez that American transit companies be permitted to tote customers from downtown San Diego directly to Agua Caliente. In the process, Mexican taxi drivers might be losing fares, but Wirt promised them monetary compensation.[29]

The *taxistas* rejected Bowman's bargain; tourist taxi fares were the staple of their business. Governor Rodríguez, mindful of his politics, agreed with the union. He could not chance angry striking unionists mass-marching through Tijuana, fists raised, flags waving, demanding justice against foreign favoritism. His present position and political future depended on maintaining order and stability in the district. Under the circumstances, Rodríguez formally, rather curtly, denied Bowman's overture, though Wirt never stopped trying.[30]

To defuse nationalistic and racial anxieties, the Barons staged golf tournaments and beauty pageants "for Mexicans only" at the resort. They provided a motion picture theatre, lounge, community center, and basic education classes for jockeys and stable help, most of whom were Mexican. Furthermore, they built a swimming pool for Mexican employees just off the premises. Someone questioned what might have happened if a dark-skinned Mexican dishwasher had decided to swim next to Gloria Swanson in Agua Caliente's glorious, 300-foot-long Plunge, but the possibility drew only nervous chuckles. Still, a mist of racial anxiety pervaded the complex, and Tijuana's labor syndicates knew when to strike for most effect.

Indeed, striking laborers almost wrecked the opening of James Crofton's magnificent new racetrack, heralded as the world's greatest, and applauded by racing enthusiasts everywhere. Unionized workers had complained in the early fall of 1929 that overbearing foremen had kept the pay of unjustly discharged laborers, but it was the hiring of American blacks from Los Angeles to assist in work before the grand opening that created the crisis. Mexicans wanted those jobs for themselves. The unionized workers demanded immediate satisfaction and set a time limit, and when that was not met, they struck. With work on the track yet to be done and the aristocracy of American racing poised to participate in lavish initiation rites for the Sport of Kings, the syndicalists threatened to mix some of that blue gringo blood with Mexican proletarian red. The workers ran on a short fuse, ready to be lit.

"Place Your Bets!"

The Great Depression hardly slaked American tastes for betting on chance and counting on luck. Just the opposite. People rationalized it better to bet what you had in hopes of hitting the jackpot than to fret about limping along on less. Besides, West Coast cities were far less damaged by the catastrophic downturn than eastern industrial centers. San Franciscans and Southern Californians still found Agua Caliente within reach and a delightful diversion from depressing realities elsewhere and doomsday talk everywhere.

OPENING JITTERS

James Crofton's glistening new $2 million racetrack opened with dramatic fanfare as scheduled on December 28, 1929 (two months after the market crashed), to capacity throngs and widespread acclaim. Its luster had looked in danger of being tarnished the previous day, when the track's three hundred unionized maintenance workers went on strike, protesting the hiring of that handful of black laborers. The unions could not have picked a more propitious time, from their point of view, to argue their case. Cleanup tasks remained only half-done, and the opening was in jeopardy.

Crofton's hurried call to the mayor's office brought two truckloads of soldiers who descended on the strikers with rifles in hand and bayonets unsheathed. They arrested three "agitators" (not union members) and kept strikers away from the track itself, but allowed them to march downtown (under wary military eye), fists raised, red-and-black anarchist flags waving amidst angry shouts and handmade placards demanding justice and "Down with Agua Caliente."

Union sympathizers joined the demonstrators in the town center. In one gigantic, threatening protest, five blocks long, they paraded, banners flying, to the border crossing, where they angrily demonstrated against foreign entries until the 6 P.M. closing. No incidents occurred; the unionists molested no tourists but vociferously and steadfastly proclaimed "Mexico for Mexicans" and then dispersed.

That night, the usually ribald downtown tourist area fell nearly silent. In sympathy with their brethren from the track, unionized musicians refused to play at the bars, clubs, and cabarets (so owners put phonographs and radios to work); taxi service went dormant; bartenders and waiters refused to serve (although some later relented); and barbers declined to cut hair. *This* was not the Tijuana known to tourism, although worried authorities urgently proclaimed the town as safe as ever.

The unusually quiet *centro* contrasted with a vibrant, anticipatory hum at the track. Nonunion employees, reinforced by jockeys, trainers, concessionaires, bookies, and some hundred strikers who had been promised protection against recalcitrant comrades by the town's mayor, teamed up all night long and far into the next morning, the day of the opening, to put final touches on the enterprise. They sang lusty *corridos*, ate tacos, drank beer, and enjoyed an only slightly subdued *pachanga* (lively party) while getting the premises in shape. Crofton himself, in suit and tie and fine spirits, urged them on and himself proudly whisked a broom.

On the afternoon of December 28, as a full house of fans ardently cheered their favorite pony in the eighth race, twelve union leaders met with track officials in one of the turf club's swanky offices, resolved their differences, and ended the strike to the relief of all.[1]

Patrons had booked solid the Agua Caliente Hotel six weeks before the track opened. To accommodate the overflow, fifteen Pullman sleepers occupied tracks at the resort's train station. San Diego's downtown hotels were full, as was the gaggle of motor courts along the coastal route stretching southward from Los Angeles. At the inaugural moment, a throng of more than twenty thousand overflowed the grandstand (seating capacity 5,600) and standing room lawn areas for the opening of an eighty-one-day racing season. Special guests and luminaries packed the adjoining Jockey

Club, women in their cloche head-huggers and flapper-style dresses (although hems were dropping by then) and men in their tweed jackets, flannel trousers (or baggy knickerbockers), and homburg or bowler hats.

Club guests watched the races while eating a connoisseur's luncheon on the manicured, shaded patio facing the track, or repaired to the upstairs gaming parlor, through which one passed to collect winnings on a race. The spacious, beautifully appointed room was an architectural masterpiece. Winners could cash in their tickets, turn around, and promptly lose their windfall at a high-stakes card game, all in sophisticated elegance.[2]

HOLLYWOOD AT THE RACES

Hollywood, long stricken by horse-race fever, was, of course, present in legions. Al Jolson acted as master of ceremonies on opening day, and his wife, Ruby Keeler, crowned the handicap winner. Racing is not only recreation for celebrities; it is *the* place to be seen and gain social status. The film stars' attachment to horses and tracks is tied to their unbounded quest for prestige. Movie czars buy stables to fly their colors and allow horses to be named for themselves. A minor scandal erupted in 1935 when con men convinced movie stars to permit their names to be affixed to supposedly promising, but yet unproven, race horses. In return, the promoters promised the film people an oil painting of "their" thoroughbred. But when the artwork arrived, express and collect, at the address of the star, it turned out to be an innocuous rotogravure picture of almost any nag.[3]

Once California allowed pari-mutuel betting in 1933, the sluice gates opened, and movie money poured in. Santa Anita opened near Hollywood in 1934 with the beloved multimillionaire crooner Bing Crosby, along with W. S. Van Dyke and Henry King, heavily invested. Crosby, who owned horses and a breeding ranch, was also the major stockholder in the profitable Del Mar Racetrack ("where the turf meets the surf," twenty miles north of San Diego), which opened in 1937. Racing commenced at Hollywood Park in the Los Angeles suburb of Inglewood the following year, with Jack Warner of Warner Brothers, Jolson, and Raoul Walsh on the founding board. As these three tracks staggered their racing seasons, Hollywood stars packed (and still do) their respective clubhouses at a whim.

Movie people say they indulge and invest in horse racing and its surroundings because they love the well-bred animals, or for a tax break; they list their holdings as a business and deduct losses. Much more, however, is at play here. Races lure a distinguished, cosmopolitan crowd to the track, and as the Sport of Kings, it couples filmland's famous with traditional aristocracy. Agua Caliente did that more than most.[4]

Indeed, thanks to imaginative management in perpetual search for clientele, renowned horses, and ever-widening public acclaim, Agua Caliente brought genuinely significant innovations to the American racing game: movable electric starting gates; German photo-finish cameras, a French automatic timing device that clocked time to one-tenth of a second, instead of the usual one-fifth; large purses up to $100,000 (a million dollars now), races called on a public address system, a huge pari-mutuel betting ("Tote") board allowing all to see exact amounts wagered on each horse along with totals; Sunday races, wetting the track with a sprinkler car (to keep choking dust down); and extended free-admission ladies' days.[5]

Despite its flashy overlay and newfangled wrinkles, however, overall ownership and management of the new track foundered in dark suspicion and vicious rumor. Infighting among the directors for control, stockholder concerns about inadequate returns, falling patronage due to the Depression, reports of fixed races and profit skimming, tax problems with the Mexican government, all hinted at collusion, bribery, malfeasance, and cheating. An unsavory, fetid air fouled the glamorous track.

TEMPEST AT THE HELM

Agua Caliente's track opened only two months after the stock market crash, the impact of which was immediately catastrophic for some but still took time to settle into the dazed and skeptical American mind inclined to denial. By the early spring, however, people more forthrightly began to ponder finances, disposable income, job security, and future safeguards, and their hesitations reverberated on the racetrack. Patronage slumped and betting tailed off—amounts wagered lessened. The Barons, in particular James Crofton, who managed the track, publicized their intention to hang on, and predicted better times for the 1930–31 racing season. Then a snarl occurred. Agua Caliente's projected program coincided in part with the popular Tanforan track outside San Francisco, and many horse owners, including many of the best known, had already committed to Tanforan. Crofton asked the northern track's administrators to adjust their schedule to Agua Caliente's needs, but Tanforan's executives declined. Tough times were met with tough stands.

Crofton's solution was to move his track's 1930 opening from Christmas to Thanksgiving, and between the two holidays he staged a 24-day truncated session which was a disaster. The dark mood of Depression had settled in, racing fans stayed home, and the track lost $100,000 (now a million), virtually overnight.

Then, a second hammer blow. The Mexican government announced it intended to raise taxes on the enterprise. The precise amount of increase was not publicly stated, but it must have been considerably above the $20,000 monthly stipend formerly charged Coffroth. Crofton paled; his favorite project was going bankrupt. He hurriedly consulted with Mexico City, but relief was not immediate, and so on December 23, he suspended operations, vowing to reopen on New Year's Day.[6]

The closure put more than six hundred people associated with the track suddenly out of work: owners, trainers, jockeys, ticket-takers, concessionaires, stable help, and "swipes" (grooms). Including their families, about one thousand people were stymied, forlorn, and bitter. On Christmas Day the Barons staged a gala turkey dinner in the exclusive Jockey Club for the owners, trainers, and jockeys, track management, racing officials, and stockholders, where Crofton explained the track's dilemma, the need to refinance the entire enterprise and sharply cut costs. The owners, meanwhile, tendered the stable help and "swipes" an equally sumptuous meal in other, much plainer quarters. Throughout the suspension, management provided meal tickets for horsemen in need, and donated hay and feed to those unable to purchase food for their horses.[7]

Truth is, despite movie moguls and celebrities, relatively few horse owners, then and now, are glamorously wealthy and swagger in high society. Most, while perhaps mired in such pretensions, are barely hanging on in a hugely expensive sport. More than a few have to bet on the horses to survive. Beyond the enhanced handicap and stakes races at Agua Caliente in the early 1930s, winners' purses ran a paltry $400–$800, barely enough to make expenses unless a horse wins regularly. Jockeys were contract hires and treated like indentured servants. Closing tracks, even for short periods, spelled calamity for many underpaid hands working to sustain the Sport of Kings.

With the assistance of Tijuana merchants who feared loss of business if the track collapsed, Crofton managed to negotiate tax relief from the Mexican government, and Baron Long donated $100,000 (later repaid by Bowman) to get the track back on its feet. When Tanforan ended its season on January 1, it released some four hundred horses to race at Agua Caliente. Purses were sharply reduced and handicaps halved, but the enterprise limped along for the remainder of a profitless season. Stockholders grumbled and demanded better for the following year. Crofton, again strong-willed and self-confident, promised to reward them, and he did.[8]

Agua Caliente's 1931–32 season augured something especially suspenseful and exciting for racing fans everywhere, as Australia's greatest mount, the beloved, feared, and fiery "Red Terror," Phar Lap (pronounced "farlap"), was coming to Tijuana's track for his first (and, as it turned out, last) race in the Americas.

PHAR LAP

Phar Lap was a big, five-year-old gelding, a racing machine standing 5′8″ at the shoulder with a stride of over twenty-three feet. His name meant "lightning" or "lightning strike" in Thai, but people called him "Bobby" around the stables. Before coming to North America, the horse won twenty-two of twenty-five races, including some of the sport's richest purses in Australia. Crofton wanted him at Agua Caliente to bolster sagging attendance, and paid the horse's shipping fare to get him there. Publicists at the resort labeled the mount the "Anzac Antelope," which does not speak well of their inventiveness ("Anzac" originally referred to the Australian and New Zealand Army Corps), but the press adopted the nickname anyway.[9]

Phar Lap arrived at Agua Caliente in February 1932 and began a secret training regimen that confounded sports writers, fans, and competitors who yearned to get a glimpse of the newcomer in action. All they saw, however, was the horse walking or jogging, which led to speculation that the animal was injured, or accustomed to running on grass and so did not take well to Agua Caliente's dirt track. Touts (devious tipsters) reported they had seen Phar Lap casually cantering through predawn exercises at the track, but when the touts left and the grandstand was empty, Phar Lap's trainer pushed the horse to full gallop. The owner and trainers deliberately shrouded the animal's preparation in mystery to raise the odds on him, but when the race began, Phar Lap was six-to-five, a decided favorite.

March 20, 1932: "They're off!"

Phar Lap was one of the last away from the starting gate, and three other horses briefly cut him off. His jockey, Billy Elliott, maneuvered him to the outside where he had plenty of running room, and the big horse took off, sending the packed house into delirium, cheering the Red Terror on. In the back stretch, Phar Lap took the lead, never relinquished it, and won by nearly three lengths, breaking the track record. When the jubilant jockey climbed down from his mount, he grabbed the course announcer's microphone and shouted, "Hello Australia! Hello mother! Your last letter spurred me on. This is a great victory!"[10] That night in the casino, Al Jolson sang to the melody of *Tipperary*:

> It's a long way to Caliente,
> It's a long way to go.
> It's a long way across the ocean,
> For the richest purse I know. . . .
> It's a long way to Caliente,
> And Phar Lap knows the way.[11]

England's King George V sent a telegram: "Heartiest congratulations on great victory of Phar Lap." One of the racing world's most respected officials, Marshall Cassidy, proclaimed the gelding "the greatest horse I have ever seen," and another revered racing judge, Francis Dunne, when later asked which horse was better, Man O' War or Secretariat, replied: "Neither. I saw Phar Lap." James Crofton was ecstatic; Agua Caliente, it seemed, was back.

The day after his memorable victory, the horse's owner, David Davis, shipped the champion to the ranch of a prominent racer and breeder in Menlo Park, just south of San Francisco, to await the next booking. Filmmakers courted Davis, but on the journey, the horse's trainer noted the animal was "not himself." Within a few days, on April 5, the Red Terror was dead—reportedly of arsenic poisoning.

Unbelievable! Not possible!

Who had poisoned this great horse? Rumors tabbed mobsters in the service of American horse owners, who would tolerate no challenge to their supremacy. Others thought that fervid, anti-racing reformers might have done the truculent deed; some American preachers thought Phar Lap the reincarnation of the devil, enticing innocents to bet and leading them to perdition, so the Good Lord had struck the gelding down.

Such far-fetched conspiracy theories are to be expected in the wake of any such unforeseen, seemingly unexplainable tragedy, and they continue to take root and mutate. In the 1940s the journalist and writer Damon Runyon received a letter from an American soldier stationed in Australia who wrote that when in a bar with some Aussie buddies, "pretty soon one of them is sure to say, 'Ho, you Yanks murdered Phar Lap.'" In response, Runyon extolled the great mount and his enviable racing record, and related that when American horsemen saw Phar Lap race that day at Agua Caliente, they concurred that the horse "was out of the equine world." "No, Sonny," Runyon stated, "no one in this country would dream of 'murdering' a horse like that."[12] Runyon, of course, was a folklorist given to colorful hyperbole.

Doctors who examined the horse soon after death concluded that he had died of acute enteritis (inflammation of the intestines) caused by a toxic substance, but they were unable to explain the origins of that poison—hence the conspiracy theories and other malicious inventions. Modern veterinary science, however, now indicates such toxins can be produced by a kind of bacterium which produces the symptoms of stomach disease and kills 70 percent of the horses it strikes. Phar Lap was the victim of a horrible sickness that in April 1932 had not yet been diagnosed. He probably contracted it contentedly nibbling the bark of a tree or bush in his pasture. The precipitous loss, nonetheless, was horrendous, and racing still laments it.[13]

Taxidermists stuffed the body of the "Red Terror" and sent it back to Australia, where it proudly stands today in Melbourne's Victoria Museum, well loved and memorialized as a national legend, along with that country's renegade bush wrangler Ned Kelly.

THE SHAKE-UP

A month after Phar Lap's death, with a moderately successful winter season ended at Agua Caliente, the directors and stockholders of the corporation met to chart their future. The company had not paid a dividend in its three years of operation; Crofton explained that over that period, the books showed a profit of $900,000, but the money had gone to pay off construction costs of the main plant and to reduce the debt incurred during the disastrous period before Christmas 1931. That debt still stood at $250,000 and kindled an internecine struggle between Bowman, Rodríguez, and Joe Schenck on one side versus Crofton and Long on the other.

Crofton's intentions and activities had become suspect in September of the previous year when, without telling others, he went to Mexico City to consult with ministry officials about a new casino being constructed outside Monterrey. He also expressed interest in investing in the famous La Selva casino in Cuernavaca. Furthermore, he and Bowman had bought and were operating the California Club (casino and cabaret) in Tijuana. Rodríguez wanted to know why he had not been informed of the purchase, and Crofton nonchalantly replied that he had not done so "out of carelessness."[14] He was sorry for the slip-up; all along he had intended to divide the profits from the club four ways—among the four Barons. The former governor, soon to become interim president of the republic, had doubts, noted that the new California Club would reduce patronage at the Foreign Club in which he held a financial stake, and demanded to receive his share of revenue from the California cabaret. Jimmy Crofton had always been a loose cannon, but these latest audacious, furtive maneuvers went too far. It is no wonder that Rodríguez and others aimed to squeeze Crofton off the racetrack at Agua Caliente. But then, all along the Barons had been partners in name only.

Perhaps Crofton saw the contest coming and was in search of an acceptable refuge, a profitable substitute, but at this stage in his peripatetic life, he was hardly a financial planner. Jim, instead, was a spontaneous and instinctive buyer, out to impress others with his wealth and élan. Even as the track he managed foundered, he announced plans to open a new, multi-million dollar racetrack outside San Francisco, which he insisted would not interfere with Tanforan, the track with which he had earlier squabbled.[15] Did he intend to run two tracks, or flee from endangered Agua Caliente to the northern venture? So much of what James Crofton proposed never came to pass, including a casino in Panama, but he had the brashness and money to dream schemes and give some of them a try.

Wirt Bowman was equally intractable and unpredictable. In the midst of the crisis in the winter of 1931, he quit the board of the Jockey Club but returned as its president a year later.[16] Wirt had a lot on his mind. He had been named the Democratic Party's committeeman from Arizona, and if Franklin Roosevelt became president, Bowman saw himself in line for a major appointment, most likely ambassador to Mexico at a time when his friend, Abelardo Rodríguez, would be the acting president.

There were, nevertheless, perilous barriers to be overcome. The ownership of gambling halls is not an especially good recommendation for a politician. Nor are tax issues under scrutiny by the Internal Revenue Service. Nor is a personal record in federal government files which speaks of un-American activities during the First World War, and Wirt was tarred with them all.

Bowman moved aggressively to clean up the stains. He paid a well-known Washington lawyer $5,000 to arrange an appointment with FBI Director J. Edgar Hoover to discuss the allegations concerning violations of wartime embargos on shipments of weapons and other banned goods into Mexico. Hoover said he was "impressed with the honesty and sincerity" of Bowman and found that the complaints against him "are without any valid foundation." Wirt breathed easier. He asked the FBI chief to have the offending material removed from his personal file, but all Hoover would do was to enclose his own conclusions in the thick folder. Wirt was never able to get those damning remarks removed from his record, which is why we know about them today.

About the same time, Bowman began tense and vituperative negotiations with Internal Revenue inspectors, who charged specifically that in the years 1926 and 1927 Bowman had understated his net income by nearly a quarter of a million dollars and owed the government almost $50,000 in additional taxes, plus penalties. The IRS focused on Bowman's ownership of the Foreign Club but hesitated to take the case to court because of expense, not the certainty of evidence it held against Bowman. Wirt, however, drove a hard bargain and it took years to resolve the case. Still, if Bowman hoped for a political appointment (to enhance his image and ego), he needed to get out of gambling, at least its public face.[17]

As a result, Bowman sold his shares in Agua Caliente to Long, Crofton, and swashbuckling Joe Schenck on June 1, 1932, but retained ownership of the remunerative Foreign Club. Schenck became president of the Jockey Club, which ran the racetrack, while as head of the umbrella Agua Caliente Corporation, Crofton ran the casino, and Long, a director in the corporation, managed the hotel. Official titles in these sorts of interlocking companies are shuffled about like cards in a deck, and outsiders can never be sure how much authority goes with each label. Bowman, while retaining gambling interests in Tijuana and Mexico City and substantial real estate in

San Diego and southern Arizona, along with banking and other businesses in Nogales, opted for politics in his home state, hoping for appointment to a national office. Crofton, who had lost the confidence of the racetrack directorate, returned to casino responsibilities while free to pursue other interests in gaming, thoroughbred horse raising and racing, Oklahoma oil, and vast cattle ranches in central California. The shake-up hardly implied setback for handsome, roving, money-hungry Jim Crofton.[18]

Rodríguez took office for a two-year term as Calles's approved interim-president of Mexico on September 4, 1932, but maintained an active interest in Agua Caliente, including a lengthy, diversified, growing list of substantial investments.

Faced by changes in betting laws that led to new racetracks in Southern California, plus the impending end of Prohibition throughout the United States, Schenck successfully used his flair, power, contacts, and money to prop up and maintain the resort's reputation as the most luxurious, diversified, exciting, and entertaining in the hemisphere, if not the world.

Baron Long, meanwhile, very nearly self-destructed.

THE LINDEN TREE SCANDAL

As the owner of premier hotels and one of the finest thoroughbred breeding ranches in America, as well as profitable shares in gaming and cabarets, plus unparalleled connections in sports and entertainment, puff-cheeked and boastful Baron Long thought he could not be touched. So riding atop his game in 1932, he decided to put one over on the bookmakers, especially the flush ones on the East Coast. He meant to "punish them" for their irksome practice of "plugging," which meant stuffing betting machines at the last moment to bend odds on horses on which clients had bet more to the bookie's chances. It was a common practice, and Long intended to give bookies a taste of their own medicine. He was so proud of his scheme that he detailed it to the press the day following its success, January 7, 1932. In his own remarkable words, he admitted, "For years I have observed the bookmakers of the country sending money back to the racetrack, apparently for the purpose of cutting the prices of the horses their clients had bet on. Remembering the day when because of this 'come back' money I was forced to take one to ten on a legitimate six to one shot, I got to wondering what would happen if conditions were reversed. From the furor caused by the Linden Tree [the crack two-year-old gelding Long bet on] incident, it seems to make a lot of difference whose ox is gored."

Long set things in motion with $1,000 on Linden Tree to win, placed with an Eastern betting commissioner too late, of course, for him to send the money back to the track and bet it at the mutuel price. As the horses were going to the post at Agua Caliente, that same day,

> I took a position near the mutuel window which closes last, and when I saw the calculator jotting down the final figures, I turned and asked [the teller] whether I could lay a bet.
> "Is it too late to make a bet?"
> "No," he replied.
> So I handed him $3,500 split between all the horses in the race except Linden Tree, including a $500 wager on my own entry. [Long had two horses in the race and placed $500 on each.] The net result of my venture was to win $9,700 and lose $3,500, a profit of $6,200.[19]

As the result of Long's calculated maneuver, odds on Linden Tree, a heavy favorite that won by five lengths, jumped from three-to-five to nine-to-one. Bookmakers all over the country lost their shirts, and smaller ones went broke. One heard their wail from coast to coast.

Bookies controlled the flow of money into their books by the carefully considered raising and lowering of odds being offered. If too much money was being bet on the favorite, a bookie lowered the odds so that the horse became unattractive to bettors. Or if wagers ignored a mount, he might raise the odds to attract backers. Bookies, overall, manipulated the odds to guarantee themselves a profit regardless of the winner.

Bookies had to have good judgment and be fast thinkers. Their clients were often astute horse players. If an experienced bettor noted that a bookie had misjudged a horse and held the odds high, they pounced. If too many players won big, the bookie was ruined. Earlier in racing—the last part of the nineteenth century and into the early twentieth—bookies strove to overcome the hazards of their "profession" by paying for tips on the condition of horses, posting their own clockers at training sessions, and, on occasion, trying to fix a race. One of their ploys was to enter a "plow horse" in a race, post spectacular odds on it, and lure the gullible and naïve to bet on the inevitable loser. Bookies eyed one another between races trying to tease out hints to give them an advantage. They were a storied bunch, these bookies, more so because moral reformers tried so hard to corral them, while writers and journalists glorified their misdeeds. The do-gooders had little success; it was the parimutuel machines that slowly put the colorful characters out of business.

Stewards at Agua Caliente noticed the last minute change of odds on Linden Tree, but because Long had two horses in the race (they finished last and next to last), they suspected no shenanigans. When the ebullient Baron so euphorically revealed his scheme to the press, however, the stewards recoiled at his lack of ethics. They noted that racing people thought (still think) it unprincipled for an owner to bet against his own mounts, because it could lead observers to believe the horses were not trying; it creates suspicion and doubt. Agua Caliente, moreover, had already experienced its share of talk about fixed races. Jockeys could be paid to lose (holding the horse back a few seconds at post, or restraining him during a race, or committing flagrant fouls like "pocketing" [crowding] or "locking" [riding close to pin a rival's leg against his mount]). Scuttlebutt persisted about tampering with mounts before the starts (overfeeding a horse to slow him down, leadening his shoes toward the same end, sitting on a stabled horse all night to tire him out, or feeding him a narcotic to make him sluggish). Owners, in another fraud, renamed horses and otherwise obscured the animals' identities to bilk bettors. Allegations of these sorts were not uncommon to horse racing elsewhere, but they were so prevalent at Agua Caliente that the track's own judges and officials threatened to quit if a thorough housecleaning was not undertaken.[20]

Fearing more adverse publicity for their already troubled oval, a week after the Linden Tree affair, the stewards at Agua Caliente banned Baron Long from racing on his own track, citing "acts prejudicial to the best interests of racing in general and Agua Caliente Jockey Club in particular."[21] Long was stunned. "What I did in the race in question was a joke," he plaintively explained, "and I did not think at the time that I was violating any code of ethics. As it turns out, my joke has become a boomerang."[22]

The racing world was astir, for and against. Furious and chagrinned, Long brooded, and in early February he impetuously announced his intention to quit racing altogether and to sell his magnificent breeding ranch at Valle de las Viejas. In a more than symbolic act, he burned his famous jade-and-orange racing colors in disgust. Friends counseled against the rash decision but could not influence Long to reconsider. The stewards quaked; racing was about to lose one of its most prominent patrons, the man credited with keeping California racing alive during the recent bleak period of prohibitions against betting on the sport. Better to reinstate Baron Long—and they did so on March 10, less than two months after the suspension began.[23]

Long overtly expressed pleasure at the turn of events, but continued to swear off horses and racing. He retained management of the Agua Caliente hotel along with the Grant in downtown San Diego. He leased the famous but failing Biltmore Hotel in downtown Los Angeles in 1933, which he then refinanced, refurbished, and stamped with his unique personality as the fashionable center of city and Hollywood high society.

Turmoil and travail, back-stabbing, shifting alliances, and jockeying for advantage marked these unsteady years at Agua Caliente. An even more ominous threat, however, hovered over the Barons. Mobsters never let them forget that they were watching and waiting and poised to strike. In short order, Bowman received a series of extortion notes threatening him and his family, and in a spectacular display of bravado, Crofton met and negotiated with a seedy extortionist in San Diego's main downtown train terminal. Most ominously, the snarling, daring clutch of hoodlums cobbled together by Ralph Sheldon, a veteran of Chicago's gang wars, still plotted to kidnap and ransom the Border Barons. The Barons had been warned of the danger and took precautions. Besides personal protections (guns and guards), they bought an armored car to transport funds between the resort and San Diego. To avoid any stoppages or weak links, customs officers routinely waved the vehicle through the border crossing.[24] The slaughter on the Dike still weighed on their minds.

And, as one more dark remembrance of mob presence, Marty Colson was back in the headlines.

NEWS FROM FOLSOM

When remanded in the autumn of 1929 to the forbidding hard-liner Folsom Prison for life, Colson again turned "silent"; prison authorities called him "defiant." For them, silence meant contempt. Addressed by guards, he returned only a hard, unnerving stare; he hated giving in to authorities. No one knew what was on his mind. Prison officers labeled him a "loner," and judged that he confided in no one, not even his fellow inmates.

Guards need to be sensitive to moods and mood changes in prisoners, which might indicate that an inmate is thinking hard about something, perhaps escape. "If a prisoner who routinely says hello to you suddenly stops," explains Jim Brown, a longtime guard at Folsom, "you suspect something is up and you keep an eye on him. Vice versa is true too. If a normally silent prisoner starts chattering a lot, trouble is up." Authorities considered Colson a "trouble maker." For guards who used his moods as signposts, he kept them busy—and guessing.[25]

When the warden thought Colson acted especially odd, he placed him in solitary confinement, "removed from the general prison population for observation." This was the way prison authorities treated non-talkers, meaning recalcitrants. Lock them in solitary for a spell for fear their "defiance" might spread to other inmates. Marty had been lodged there several times. "Solitary" at Folsom meant an old cell block where a prisoner could be watched or, more ominously, consignment to the Dungeon—a dark hellhole where the inmate slept on a straw mattress on the floor and had his meals tossed through a door. It is not known to which confinement Colson was assigned—the old cell or the Dungeon—documentation only states "solitary."[26]

Released from solitary in July 1930, Marty gambled on freedom. A swift flow from the American River, which borders the prison, had been diverted into a canal that flowed inside the prison grounds to power the penitentiary's electrical plant and then emptied back into the river. Inmates eyed the canal as an improbable but still inviting escape route, if only one could stay under water long enough to avoid detection.

No one noticed (or fellow inmates declined to report) when Marty slipped into the canal with a length of hose in hand for underwater breathing (in prison parlance, a "breather"), but after a distance, the hose apparently clogged. Colson probably tried to hold his breath, but failing, he gradually glided into unconsciousness. His inert body floated to the surface, where inmates in the exercise yard spotted him and excitedly pulled him from the water, barely breathing.

Rushed to the prison hospital, Colson received oxygen. In his pocket, doctors found a note: "I have $125 in the prison bank, mother dear, and it's yours. [Signed] Martin," which led the warden to label the affair "attempted suicide."[27] He noted that the prisoner had a history of such attempts, even if they did not appear to be serious endeavors to kill himself. Wardens routinely denigrate attempted escapes on their watch. Marty, moreover, had promised his mother that he would try no more suicides. When he plunged into the canal, Colson, most likely, meant to escape, but in case of failure and death, he wanted his mother to have the money earned working in prison industries. Gangsters often display a sentimental side, even if it is only feeling sorry for themselves.

Marty Colson recovered—and would be heard from again.

Determined to build the world's most glamorous racetrack featuring the most modern racing accoutrements and innovations, four of Agua Caliente's ranking officials, (left to right) Marshall Cassidy, a highly respected starter of races; John Mills, a multimillionaire real estate developer and heavy investor in Agua Caliente; Wayne McAllister, the chief architect of the complex; and the Border Baron James Crofton, in 1929 toured racetracks in the United States and Cuba, looking for novel ideas and potential pitfalls.
Andre Williams Collection

The crowd arriving for the day's activities at the track, many on the infield to weigh early betting odds with bookies. The ornate Jockey Club is to the left. University of Southern California Special Collections

The ceiling of the dining room at the racetrack carried a spectacular Art Deco cosmic design, reflecting the high spirits and optimism common to the Jazz Age, at least among those who frequented places like Agua Caliente. California State Library Special Collections

Murals in the Jockey Club mirror the essence of Art Deco and its age: gracefully stylized racing horses, left, and a swinging jazz orchestra, right, supported by pillars with a reed motif topped with geometrical sunburst floral designs. California State Library Special Collections

Passes to the grandstand and Jockey Club,
plus a decal for one's car or luggage. The movie magnate
Joseph Schenck, an inveterate gambler who owned a large share
of the horse track and became its president in 1933,
signed that season's passes to the club.
Andre Williams Collection

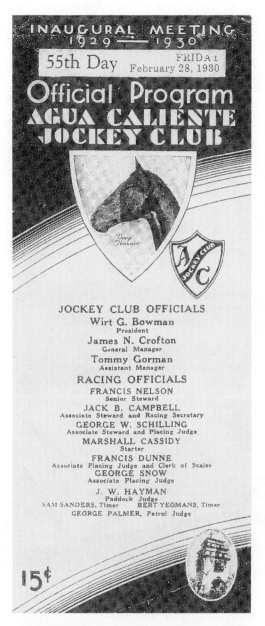

An official program for Jockey Club guests in 1930 pictured the horse Deep Thought owned by two of the Border Barons, Wirt Bowman, club president, and James Crofton, general manager. All the Barons regularly raced horses they owned at the track. Andre Williams Collection

257

Hollywood czars and stars flocked to the races.
Wallace Beery founded an exclusive club
for filmland's elites on the premises.
Andre Williams Collection

Betting was with bookies in the infield at the track,
although a large tote board quoting odds faced spectators
in the grandstand, one of several important innovations
introduced to racing at Agua Caliente.
Andre Williams Collection

The Barons created publicity stunts
for the winners' circle and recruited movie and
sports stars to crown the victorious.
Andre Williams Collection

AGUA CALIENTE HCP,
(Agua Caliente, Mexico, 20/3/1932)

Phar Lap 1st (9.3 W. Elliot) .... Reveille Boy 2nd .... Scimitar 3rd .... Won by: 2 len .... Time: 2:2.8 (Course record)

The biggest race in early track history brought Australia's "Red Terror,"
Phar Lap, to Agua Caliente in March 1932 for his first and only appearance
outside of his homeland. The event created unprecedented fervor
among racing enthusiasts. Andre Williams Collection

Phar Lap, the winner by two lengths, set a track record.
Tragically, the gelding died of mysterious causes soon after.
Notables of the racing world called him the greatest horse they had
ever seen run, surpassing even America's beloved Seabiscuit,
the great Man O' War, and his offspring, War Admiral.
Andre Williams Collection

The classic Mission Revival–style casino with Art Deco
chevron designs worked into the cupola top and framing the window
at left. Architects freely experimented with a variety of
patterns, especially in tile work, during the period.
California State Library Special Collections

Customers stood three and four
deep during peak hours at the casino's
exquisite bar paneled in precious woods and surrounded
by highly stylized Art Deco ornamentation under an incredible
ceiling of geometric design and fine workmanship,
all befitting the epoch's cocktail culture.
California State Library Special Collections

Another bonus for patrons: cheap gas. Savings on
gas provided a subtle nudge toward the casino.
Andre Williams Collection

Beauty and the Birds . . .
At Agua Caliente's
Wishing Well
[Esther Ralston]

Bing

Dick Powell

Ruggles Family . . .
Birthday Party

HOLLYWOOD
AT PLAY
lured by a foreign
land, Old Mexico

La Joyce

Helen Twelvetrees

Jean Hersholt

Constance Bennett

Kibbee

Uncle Carl

El Hardy

Joseph M. Schenck

Buster Crab
Goes Mexi

ISHED BY
ACIFIC
ICTORIAL
LTD.

"Hollywood's Playground:" the resort's publicity agents,
fashion magazines, the industry's trade publications, and gossip
columnists for the daily press played the moniker to the hilt,
as did Agua Caliente's own powerful radio station.
Andre Williams Collection

The casino's dining room was a showcase of Art Deco geometric themes:
replicas of an Amerindian past in zigzag designs on the upper borders of the room,
a fountain pattern at bottom center, a feast of various fashionable lighting fixtures, and in
the upper center, a mural with a partially obscured classical runner followed by a
graceful greyhound in full stride. Sensational archaeological discoveries in Egypt
and Mesoamerica in the 1920s influenced Art Deco designers to
incorporate themes from those cultures into their work.
California State Library Special Collections

Classical art scenes revived from Greek and Roman mythology,
albeit with modern interpretations, highlighted the ceiling of the Casino's
Gold Room, where only pre-approved, wealthy special guests with gaming fever
could play for enormous stakes. Note the modern machine on which the main
male figure is leaning, meant to honor the epoch's advances in technology and
industrial might. California State Library Special Collections

A handsome playboy smitten by filmland's glamour,
Border Baron James Crofton divorced his first wife, who
had been his teenage sweetheart, and married a vivacious
movie star, Mona Rico, known as his "Mexican spitfire."
University of Southern California Special Collections

Paraphernalia from the resort: poker chips
of various denominations, a watch fob medallion from
the racetrack, a passkey to hotel rooms, and a pin-on button
for admittance to the spa's international golf tournament in 1931,
which offered the sport's largest purse to that date and
attracted the world's most renowned players.
Andre Williams Collection

PATIO SPECIALS
Clicquot Champagne Cocktail 25c
Clicquot Champagne Cup $1.50 (Serves Four)

LUNCHEON
$1.00
Including bottle of Mision de Santo Tomas wine
or bottle of "O. K." Beer

French Field Salad Cumberland Marinade

Chicken Noodle Soup Old Fashion
Cream of New Asparagus Saint Valier

Selection of:
Whole Boned Rockbass fried in Butter white wine sauce
Joinville
Beeftenderloin Slices en Casolette with Fresh Mushrooms
& Parisian Vegetables

Mexican Specialty
Tortillas Enchiladas de Pavo estilo de la Casa
Colache de Calabaza - Frijoles Refritos
Home made Turkey Enchiladas with Mexican Squash & Fried Beans

Special Top Sirloin Steak, Burgundy Wine sauce
with Marrow a la Bordelaise

Milkfed Chicken saute sauce Castellane

Fresh Vegetable Selection, Baked stuffed Tamato D'Uxelle

Cold Boiled Fresh Lobster Mayonaise Cambridge

Cold Roast Prime Beef Ribs, Potato Salad

Potatoes Gratine Del Rio - Buttered Garden Peas

French Macaroon Slice
French Fraisia Ice Cream or Frozen Roman Punch
with Pecan Wafers
Coffee

Sunday, November 25, 1934.

Patio dining was for people-watchers and haute cuisine
with French touches. The menu also included a traditional
Mexican dish, as well as old-fashioned chicken noodle soup . . .
plus some spelling errors. Andre Williams Collection

BOTTOMS UP *!*

Y Como!

■

— to DRINK

—How
—What
—When
—Where

■

(El Catecismo de la Libación)

■

A GUIDE FOR EVERYONE

ASK - FOR - VAL.

COMPLIMENTS *of*

AGUA CALIENTE *In Old Mexico*

WHERE DRINKING NEVER CEASED

Zeke Caress, the track's dapper betting commissioner and himself a heavy gambler, was kidnapped and held for ransom in 1931 by the Sheldon mob. They planned to do the same with the Border Barons. University of Southern California Special Collections

When Prohibition ended in the United States, Agua Caliente, "where drinking never ceased," offered many of the world's most lauded alcoholic liquors at reduced prices. *Bottom's Up!*, the resort's comprehensive guide to drink, revealed the favorite libations of past emperors along with recommendations for treating unpleasant hangovers.
Andre Williams Collection

In mid-1940 Bugsy Siegel modeled his ritzy Flamingo Club, the first such sprawling resort on the Las Vegas Strip, after the Agua Caliente complex, which he had periodically visited a decade earlier. University of Southern California Special Collections

When Agua Caliente closed in 1936, thousands of locals lost decent-paying jobs. Workers and their families took to the streets in raucous protest against the government's ban on gambling. Rioters, at one point, burned public buildings. Bloodshed ensued, and the military imposed martial law on the town. University of Southern California Special Collections

Lee Cochran, at seventy-four.
Despite a strong recommendation for pardon
by the state parole board, Governor Ronald Reagan
in 1973 denied clemency, ruling Cochran's crime
on the Dike too heinous to be forgiven.
California State Archive

Get the Barons!

The Ralph Sheldon gang was a *bona fide* mob, but California style. It was a pickup group. Fleeing Chicago after a murderous career with Capone in the beer wars of the 1920s, Sheldon had assumed the alias Ray Short and cut hay with his wife for two years on a 40-acre ranch in Antelope Valley, outside the desert city of Lancaster, in southeastern California. There he had his nose altered to change his appearance, went to Roman Catholic mass every Sunday—and kept in touch with criminal activities in Los Angeles, fifty miles south. He also relived old times and planned new ones with compatriots "just moving through" the ranch. Meanwhile, he built up an arsenal of deadly weaponry.[1]

Nothing tied the Sheldon mob together but criminal intent and underworld experience. Louis Frank was a fellow Chicago mobster, but never had worked with Sheldon. Ray Wagner had "taken people for a ride" in St. Louis. William Baillie was a Hollywood racketeer. Les (Pat) Bruneman, a Los Angeles gambler and bookmaker, had fallen from favor because he had "muscled" into territories of similar crooks. Jessie "Cheesey" Orsatti, a petty criminal looking to move up, was "fingerman" for the group; he knew Southern California and could identify targets. Jimmy Doolen, a feckless fellow, perhaps insane, aimed to be a big shot in the criminal world and thrilled to "blasting coppers." All in all, they resembled those late-nineteenth-century happenstance gangs so imbedded in American lore, or even more, the nondescript, unremembered outlaws that came together out of desperation, boredom, fate, chance, and fantasy, and rambled around the open West about the same time and afterward. Local histories are full of their failed, pitiful (but still human, and occasionally poignant) escapades.

The early, but already legendary, reputation of Agua Caliente as the repository of free-flowing and easily gained wealth, an image cultivated by the Barons themselves and their propagandists, could not fail to tempt mobsters interested in a quick strike and big return. As the Sheldon gang began to survey kidnapping potentials in 1929, the Barons (minus Rodrí-guez) headed their list of targets. Long, Bowman, and Crofton would be kidnapped from their respective dwellings, blindfolded, driven by separate routes to a hideout in suburban Los Angeles and held under threat of physical harm for at least $50,000 (half a million now) each. The exact amount to be demanded of the Barons would be settled by the outcome of a trial run, the abduction of Zeke Caress, the betting commissioner at Agua Caliente's track. Sheldon, in other words, first wanted to know what the ransom market would bear, perhaps up to $100,000 per victim. He would extract the ransom by having his victims write checks made out to some of their friends, who would then be compelled to cash the checks in Tijuana and give the money to go-betweens. Once the ransom money was delivered, the undoubtedly shaken, but otherwise unharmed, victims would be re-leased along some out-of-the-way road. Then the gang would break up and its members disappear into hiding.[2]

THE TRIAL RUN

Ezekiel L. Caress, "Zeke" to everyone, was well known throughout Southern California as a big stakes gambler who had reaped millions in gaming ventures. As Agua Caliente's betting commissioner, he oversaw the often tumultuous betting ring, where clever and devious bookies took wages and set odds at the resort's new racetrack. He also handled the betting book at Bowman's Foreign Club casino. It may seem strange that an inveterate gambler be hired to police betting, but in this topsy-turvy ambiance, suc-cessful gamblers who knew the game often became enforcers in the same way that for centuries bandits became police. Casinos hired card sharks and dice cheats to police their games, and in 1906 the owner of the New Orleans race course employed Frank James, brother of Jesse, to be his betting com-missioner.[3]

Zeke, accompanied by his wife, Helen, had spent December 20, 1930, at Agua Caliente discussing the suspension of horse racing there. After travel-ing by rail from San Diego to Los Angeles, the couple got into their auto-mobile to return to their Hollywood home. Inside the depot, Jesse Orsatti pointed out their quarry to the gang, and, as the Caresses drove home, mob-sters followed. When they parked in their garage, their pursuers dashed toward them. Helen saw them first. Startled, then terrified, she thought them robbers and offered her purse. "Two men, masked and with guns, rushed up to us in the garage of our home and told us to stick 'em up," she later testified in court. "Then they put [blindfolds with] adhesive tape and dark glasses over our eyes and drove us away in our own car."[4]

Inside the house, the couple's Japanese servant heard his employers returning, went to greet them, but caught only a glimpse of the assailants before they put on masks, rolled up their collars, and pulled down their hats. When the kidnappers spotted the servant, they also took him captive and affixed a blindfold, secured with tape.

After ransacking the house for jewelry, furs, and small artifacts that looked valuable (they took several thousand dollars' worth of goods), the mobsters drove their victims to their rendezvous hideout in the Los Angeles suburb of Alhambra. There they forced Zeke to write four checks totaling $50,000 and designated Les Bruneman to carry them to the bustling gambling barges offshore at Long Beach, where he could verify Zeke's signatures (the gamblers knew one another) and cash them.[5]

Four conspirators drove to a Long Beach dock early the next evening, December 21—Sheldon and Doolen up front, Bruneman and Wagner in back—to catch a ferry headed for the gambling barges. On suspicion, nothing more than that, two local patrolmen drove up, demanded identification, and began to search the car and its occupants for weapons. "That's when we busted them," Doolen later said.

A wild shootout erupted. One patrolman was hit below his left shoulder, the missile lodged in his spine, and he collapsed, near death. Other nearby officers heard the commotion and came to the rescue. Wagner staggered off into the darkness with a bullet near his heart, while Doolen leaped into the bay, clung to an anchor boom, and escaped. Sheldon's pistol misfired, and deputies captured and shackled him along with Bruneman, who protested his innocence. Gang members holding the Caresses and their servant recognized their plan had gone amiss and next morning freed their unnerved victims on a deserted city street, and precipitously fled town.[6]

While authorities held the mob's confident and uncooperative kingpin, Ralph Sheldon, they hunted the others. After two months, they netted Frank and Wagner in a secluded cabin in mountains north of Phoenix, "a sort of outlaw hospital, where wounded members of the crew may be treated by friendly and silent physicians."[7] Wagner was recovering from his serious chest wound. Another gang member, William Baillie, also had been at the Phoenix den but fled south into Mexico before the raid.

Now officials held four men associated with the kidnapping, but the decision was made to bring charges of assault to commit murder—for the shootout with the police. A judge set trial for March, but multiple impediments interfered. Los Angeles and Long Beach wrangled over jurisdiction— where should the high-profile case be tried? Both cities wanted the publicity, while the defendants preferred Long Beach, but the courts would decide. Shadows of corruption crept in. A shady individual, presumed to be a henchman of Sheldon, offered a Long Beach police officer connected to the case $10,000 to vanish from town. Rumors flew that sympathetic mobsters would try to rescue the four in custody, causing police to reinforce an already overwhelming security contingent.[8]

With public angst concerning Eastern mobs permeating town, heightened by the Caress kidnapping, law enforcement announced the roundup of all hoodlums in Los Angeles. "In fact, we are going to start a gangster census," authorities announced.[9] Vagrants and street people, as usual, bore the brunt of the cleansing, but the drive netted no threatening mobsters. District Attorney Buron Fitts (facing reelection), however, pursued bigger game. Calling them "a rendezvous of thugs and hoodlums," in January 1931 he conducted spectacular raids on two gambling ships anchored off Long Beach, the *Johanna Smith*, once a majestic, four-masted schooner, and the *Rose Isle*. According to Fitts, the heavily patronized barges carried machine guns and armed guards capable of "blowing right out of the water" any investigating law officers, and, naturally, authorities found a conglomeration of weapons on the boats. What casino does not possess its cache of firearms? Seven arrests followed, owners and their employees, but hundreds of patrons, among them celebrities and elites, were herded into water taxis and sped ashore to escape notoriety.

One barge operator claimed the right to run offshore gambling and produced a map to show that his boat lay in international waters (three miles offshore), outside the jurisdiction of Los Angeles County. "In my opinion," Fitts responded, "both ships are within the county lines. We will fight them through the courts and make every effort possible to obtain convictions. . . . If we can't get them legally," he added, "we'll go after them so hard, we will make their operations unprofitable." Just to play safe, the barge owners had tug boats shove their casinos a mile or so farther out to sea. The spirited contest of government versus barges-of-chance continued for another decade along the California coastline, another exciting and enchanting story yet awaiting its author.[10]

THE TRIAL

Long Beach won the legal right to try the Sheldon gang, but as authorities had for security reasons housed the defendants in the Los Angeles County Jail, they had to be transported to and from the proceeding. Crowds jammed the streets to witness the spectacle. "With all the thrills and frills of an underworld motion picture," the trial began on March 18, 1931. "Machine guns guarded every inch of the road as the four men were conveyed this morning from the County Jail to Long Beach. An escort of motorcycle officers cleared the way. Officers, all armed, stood watch in the courtroom during the day and the same heavily weaponed fleet took the prisoners back last night to Los Angeles."[11] It was not quite a Rose Bowl Parade, but....

To observers and commentators the state's case seemed unassailable, defendants' alibis easily demolished. Jurors toured the crime site, and most details of the shootout related by witnesses confirmed what already had appeared in newspapers—with one extraordinary exception. In an astonishing aside, Zeke Caress testified that even after the kidnapping and release, members of the gang still at large (Doolen and Bruneman) continued to harass and extort money from him. They threatened to cut off his wife's ears if he did not give them $20,000 needed as a defense fund for those under arrest. Zeke had paid the money and another $10,000 to pay for Doolen's escape to Hawaii.[12]

Deputies subsequently arrested Bruneman and charged him as a gang member. Doolen returned from Hawaii during the trial, surrendered, and confessed to authorities. Then he copped a deal; authorities dropped the assault charge in exchange for information and assistance in arresting other uncaptured members of the mob. Doolen, a childish, unpredictable, and treacherous hoodlum, later boasted of being an "undercover agent" for police.

After a month of "dime novel thrills," punctuated by reports of witness and jury tampering, attempted bribings of law enforcers, and swirling rumors of the mob's intent to free their comrades, on April 17 the case went to the jury. After twenty-two hours of deliberation, during which it once split six to six and requested additional information from the judge (which he refused to give), the panel found the four defendants *not guilty!*

Unthinkable, puzzling, absurd.

Confusion wracked the courtroom, and the judge had to rap spectators back to order. Acquittal: the verdict exonerated and freed Sheldon and the other mobsters. Not possible, but it occurred. A juror explained that the tribunal could not decide who had fired first—police or hoodlums—that fog-shrouded night on the docks. In other words, the jurors had "reasonable doubt" about who assaulted whom. And as the released defendants left the courtroom, jurors shook their hands and embraced their relatives while prosecutors fumed in disbelief.[13]

Pandemonium burst among prosecutors, public, and press. "I consider the acquittal a blot on the judicial record of the Southland," railed District Attorney Fitts, who in a moment of careless frustration ranted that the verdict "amounted to either miserable cowardice or incredible stupidity. The word has already gone throughout gangland in the United States that Los Angeles is a safe place in which to operate."[14]

Noting that in their hometown Chicago gangsters have "hog tied the law," a popular *Los Angeles Times* columnist summed up public opinion: "With this verdict California is closer to coming under the sway of the gangs. It would be charity to believe that this Long Beach jury was merely below normal intelligence."[15] In other words, it had been fixed by the mob.

In a short conversation with detectives, Sheldon said he intended to return to his ranch in Lancaster. "We will be keeping an eye on you," an officer warned. Sheldon thought a moment and replied, "Well, if you give me a few days to settle things up, I'll clear out and go back East."[16] Few relaxed at *that* promise.

The stunned prosecution, however, did not surrender its litigation against the mob. It only needed a short period to reassemble its case, this time on kidnapping charges. While a grand jury investigated possibilities that the mob had intimidated the Long Beach jury, police rearrested Sheldon for perjury committed during the trial, and a judge set his bail at an insurmountable $100,000. On appeal, however, another jurist sliced the amount in half, and Sheldon's defense team quickly posted it. The state, meanwhile, held Frank on charges that, as a formerly convicted criminal, he again broke a state gun law by possessing a firearm, and over the next year the district attorney relentlessly and meticulously rebuilt his case against the Sheldon mob, even if three members (Baillie, Bruneman, and Wagner) were not in custody.[17]

THE SECOND TRIAL

The new trial began in January 1932, with Sheldon and Frank as defendants along with Jesse Orsatti, who had surrendered and confessed his role to authorities. The state's star witness, Doolen, gleefully used gangster language in his testimony and then translated it for the trial judge and jury.

> Doolen: "And then Sheldon told me [during the kidnapping] to slam the broad [Helen Caress] with my rod if she kept peeking under her cheaters [sun glasses]."
> Judge: "Just what do you mean by that language?"
> Doolen: "Well you see, broad means woman and rod means revolver."

The witness continued, "They [Sheldon and Frank] told me to get a croaker and a mouthpiece," and then explained that "croaker" meant doctor and "mouthpiece," lawyer.

And finally, "We saw an automobile coming [toward them on the Long Beach dock] and it looked like a squad car with a lot of fuzz in it." "Fuzz," he explained, meant police.[18]

Summing up Doolen's testimony, a news reporter wrote that he had "poured the heat" on his former companions. Indeed, he had. Otherwise, statements by witnesses replicated those heard in Long Beach.

The trial lasted three weeks, but it took the jury only two hours and thirty-five minutes to return guilty verdicts. The mobsters received sentences of ten years to life with the judge's recommendation against any chance of parole for Sheldon. Fitts felt vindicated: "By the conviction of Ralph Sheldon and his companions, the trial jury has rid this community of the most dangerous group of kidnappers ever to operate in Los Angeles County. We have in the files of our office the names of several outstanding business men [including the Border Barons] who were scheduled to be kidnapped by this mob."[19]

Mopping up took another two years and then some because of legal appeals. In June 1932 officers found Bill Baillie working as a barber in Panama's Canal Zone and returned him to Los Angeles. After one mistrial, a jury took only four hours to convict him of complicity in the kidnapping. A judge sentenced the "three-time loser" to life in prison.[20] Raymond Wagner, recaptured following his acquittal in Long Beach, was in December 1932 found guilty of participation in the Caress abduction and given twenty-two years to life in San Quentin.[21] Pat Bruneman, who hid out on the Canadian border while continuing to protest his innocence through a spokesman, surrendered to authorities in February 1934. He was convicted in May and sentenced to ten years to life, but won a new trial on grounds the judge had erred in jury selection. At his second trial, in October 1935, the judge found Bruneman only a contact man between Caress and the gangsters and dismissed the kidnapping charge, but the hoodlum hardly went free. Bruneman, at the time of his initial arrest, had told police that he expected to "be taken for a ride" by mobsters who resented his intrusions into their territory. "Unless things break, I haven't long to live. I might just as well be in jail, because I'm on the spot anyway." He was right. On release, he returned to bookmaking, got wounded in a shootout with competitors, and settled into running a small gambling parlor on the beach outside Los Angeles. In July 1937 the sheriff's office denied him a gun permit. "Gosh, I'm living on borrowed time as it is," he pleaded. "It looks like you would give me a chance to help prolong that time. They'll get me for sure, and it won't be any more than six weeks." Three weeks later, hired gunmen killed Bruneman while he was promenading with his blonde girlfriend on a popular beach boardwalk just south of Los Angeles.[22]

COPY CATS

Initial reports that the Sheldon gang aimed to get the Border Barons led to an electrifying spate of audacious extortion threats against the ostentatious owners of Agua Caliente, who all hired bodyguards. James Crofton received a menacing ransom note on January 30, 1932, delivered to his swanky suite that covered an entire floor in San Diego's new El Cortez Hotel: "It is your time to make a donation to me. You can take the easy way, if you are smart," the mobster wrote.

> The hard way may not be good for you. You do as we tell you, and no one will get hurt. Otherwise, you can blame yourself for what happens. You have been on the list [of ransom prospects] for quite awhile but don't know it.

You've been lucky.

Get $7,500 in $100 bills and have them ready to deliver when we tell you to. When you are ready to pay, put ad in the *Evening Tribune* three days straight reading:

"William, that deal is OK with me, Signed, Roy."

A Mr. Houston will phone you where to deliver the money. Give envelope containing the money to your negro butler but tell him nothing. [Involvement of the butler never materialized.] For this consideration, your safety will be assured. We will move away. No frame [frame-up] goes [will be tolerated]. Try to frame us and may God help you.

A bad move and you will pay with something besides money.

Report this to police or any of your friends, and your lights will go out. We warn you to make no false moves.

[Signed] HOUSTON.[23]

With the recent Caress experience in his mind, Crofton resolved to keep the matter secret, "handle it my way," and make no false moves. He would meet with the extortionist and try "to talk him out of the extortion idea." Jim placed the requisite ads in the newspaper and, when "Houston" phoned, made plans to meet him the following night at 10 P.M. by the newsstand inside the city's downtown railroad station. But Crofton hesitated to arrive unprotected; he carried a pistol in his pocket and wore a steel, bulletproof vest, "in case I was double-crossed."

Less than one hour before the scheduled rendezvous, Crofton began to sweat; maybe he was in deeper danger than first thought. "Houston" could be a member of the Sheldon gang back at work. Jimmy needed help fast, and he phoned Baron Long at the nearby Grant Hotel to relate his predicament.

Long feared for his fellow Baron, or perhaps hoped to forestall a similar plot against himself. In a decision that soon roiled the entire city, Long phoned his friend, Fire Chief Louis Almgren, and then the sheriff's office (and notably *not* the police department, which he did not trust), and together they devised a hasty plan to protect Crofton and catch the mobster along with the rest of his gang.[24]

A mysterious automobile carrying two women shadowed Jim as he drove with a girlfriend (he was separated, but not yet divorced from his first wife) from the El Cortez to the spacious, Mission-style Santa Fe Depot.

When he arrived, shortly before 10 P.M., he noticed a tall, thin, well-dressed man (long tan overcoat, gloves, and fedora) in his mid-thirties loitering at the newsstand. "Are you looking for someone?" he asked the stranger. "Are you Crofton?" came the response, and they sat down together on a wooden bench in the terminal with Jim's lady friend (never identified) nearby.

"I need the money," the extortionist explained, jabbing an automatic pistol into Crofton's ribs for emphasis. "I have only six months to live because of tuberculosis, and I don't care what happens. You can plug me, but if you do, my gang will get you." Jim tightened his grip on the pistol in his pocket.

"I do not have the money with me," Crofton replied. "I am not a millionaire [he lied], but I have a friend who is," implying the money could be secured, "but all I can get is $2,000." "Houston" was dissatisfied, angry, and threatening, but agreed to meet and pick up the cash two nights later at the same site. Then the hoodlum hurried off, out of the station, and into a car. Jim's girlfriend got the license plate number of that vehicle, but could not see the driver.[25]

Watching this incredible drama were Chief Almgren and a squad of firefighters armed with shotguns (such weapons were standard equipment on fire engines at the time), along with Oliver Sexson, second in command at the sheriff's department, plus six armed deputies; Baron Long; and, incongruently, Crofton's middle-aged father. Several posed as ticket-sellers in their booths, others stood in shadowy corners, trying to be inconspicuous, and the remainder found "other places of advantage." As "Houston" was the only mob member in sight, they did not pounce; better to wait until the scheduled reunion of the extortionist with Crofton in hopes of capturing the entire gang. Success, however, depended upon keeping the planned ambush secret.[26]

They could not do it. Someone leaked the sensational story to the press, and "blew up the plan to capture the gang." Banner headlines citing indecision and incompetence inflamed officialdom and the general citizenry alike. Ground through the gossip mill, the Crofton affair became the talk of the town. Most simply put, San Diego showed its colors—better said, its dirty linen—as another sorry (but still verging on hilarious) episode in the city's scandal-ridden, topsy-turvy political life unfolded.

THE POLICE REVIEW

The morning after the tense melodrama in the depot, Acting Mayor James V. Alexander (Mayor Austin Smith was in Washington on city business) called Police Chief H. H. Scott on the carpet for failing to hunt down Crofton's criminal enemies and "letting the town fall into sinful ways, generally." (He echoed the debate over what kind of city San Diego should be.) The dressing-down flabbergasted and outraged Chief Scott; he had not even heard of the incident until confronted by the acting mayor. "It seems funny to me," Scott said, "that the fire department would know about the situation while the chief of police is kept entirely in the dark. I don't see how people can expect the police department to do much, when it can't get any co-operation."[27]

Scott went further, saying he intended to ask the district attorney to swear out obstruction of justice warrants against Baron Long, Fire Chief Almgren, and others who refused to give information to the police. It made sensational newspaper copy, but nothing came of his pique.

The implausible circumstances, nonetheless, gave the *San Diego Union* the opportunity to editorialize for an efficient police department. The ransom demand had "confronted a well-known citizen with the choice between trusting to the efficiency of the local police, and putting his faith in the efficiency of the extortionists who threatened him," the editor wrote. "He and his friends decided that they had better play ball with the extortionists—and there is not one citizen in a hundred who would have made the opposite choice.... We are confronted with a very definite choice. Shall we police this city adequately, at whatever cost, or shall we turn it over to the racketeers—also at whatever cost?"[28]

San Diego's city council handled the immediate crisis by ordering the formation of a special police squad assigned to round up all "Big Shot" mobsters in town. Five patrolmen went to work and arrested twenty-seven "suspicious characters," once again, mostly homeless vagrants and street people, but netted no gangsters. A few days later Chief Scott cut the squad in half saying, "There are no gangsters, so why have a large gangster detail. There is the usual run of stickups and so on," he admitted, "but as far as gangsters are concerned, they are not here." Besides, the sweep for suspicious folk had scored a return: Seven of those arrested confessed to burglaries, allowing authorities to sponge a number of petty robberies from their dockets.[29]

Meanwhile the sheriff's office announced it was working on a "hot lead" in the Crofton case, but conspiracy theories abounded. What the newspapers and authorities said happened simply was not believable to the public. One of the most prevalent rumors labeled the entire affair a hoax, alleging that politicians had conspired with Crofton to embarrass the mayor and police for political advantage. The mayor himself called it "the work of a [movie] scenario writer."[30] In other words, the extortionist was a phantom, his plot a fabrication.

As it developed, the mobster was hardly make-believe and certainly meant business.

AN ARREST

Undersheriff Sexson, who had witnessed the gangster's exchange with Crofton, thought he recognized the extortionist as a young man he had helped send to San Quentin for armed robbery a decade earlier, a crime-bent, arrogant youth named Howard J. Abbey. The license plate on the extortionist's getaway car showed the vehicle registered to Abbey in Los Angeles, so the search quickly focused there.

Jimmy Crofton, meanwhile, had taken refuge with bodyguards at Agua Caliente, where he refused to discuss the case, further frustrating Chief Scott. The extortionist remained in touch with Crofton through his address at the El Cortez, warning him that he would be punished for his failure to keep their exchange secret. In another message the hoodlum claimed to have eight members in his gang, which had come to California from Brooklyn, and said they would be going back East "as soon as we get the money." Handwriting experts checked the messages. As they were hand-printed, identification was difficult, but the signature, written out, yielded a likeness to Abbey's hand.[31]

A week after the anxious encounter in the Santa Fe depot, Sexson had his suspect. Howard Abbey, now thirty-two and a hardened ex-con, had been trailed (thanks to a snitch) to a Los Angeles apartment, where police found him with two automatic .38 caliber pistols "well-oiled and ready for use." Nearby lay ammunition—dumdum bullets, the kind that break into four parts and spread when striking a target, creating savage, tearing wounds. Abbey had been sent to prison for one to ten years in 1921, but lost his parole chances when he tried to help another felon escape, and therefore had finally been released only four months before confronting Crofton.[32]

Under interrogation the prisoner called himself Eddie Hayes, denied knowing anyone by the name of Abbey or Crofton, said he had not visited San Diego in years, and called the case against him one of "mistaken identity." Fingerprints, however, confirmed him as Abbey. His trial, which began March 14, 1932, lasted ten days, much of it in jury selection. The brassy defendant smiled sardonically as witnesses, one after another, testified against him, and Abbey broke out laughing when a detective remarked, "If I had been on my own, I would have arrested him or blasted him." The defendant's alibi was a transparent fabrication, and the jury took less than three hours to find him guilty. The judge gave Abbey five years in Folsom prison.[33] He was lucky, for at the time of his trial, the entire nation had been captivated by the far more odious, and still unsolved, Lindbergh kidnapping, a drawn-out tragedy that eventually led to strict laws and heavy penalties for abductors.

Jimmy Crofton, meanwhile, was not certain his ordeal had ended. During the Abbey proceeding, another mobster sent him threatening notes, one saying that if he did not drop the charges against Abbey, "we will take care of you no matter how many guards you have." Another stated, "We'll be in power in San Diego soon, and we have plenty of money, so you have to act wisely."[34] Investigators tried to establish the origins of these communications, but never could do so. Nor did they develop sufficient evidence to arrest any accomplices in the Abbey extortion plot.

Crofton worried about other mobsters pursuing him and retained additional personal bodyguards. They came in handy on March 20, when a disgruntled employee fired two shots at the Baron in a private room off the Agua Caliente casino. The shots narrowly missed Jimmy and lodged in the ceiling and a wall. His guards quickly subdued the assailant, while just next door a thousand or more patrons spun roulette wheels and tossed dice, oblivious to the nearby shooting spree.[35]

WIRT'S TURN

Deprived of success with Zeke Caress and James Crofton, gangsters turned their sights on another Border Baron, Wirt Bowman. Bowman boasted that no mobster could touch him, but he kept a private bodyguard just in case. Known Sheldon gang members were still free of the law, as were unidentified members of the Abbey pack. There was no telling how many other kidnappers had planned capers in the region, and the sensational Lindbergh case had raised the nation's blood pressure. Abductors knew of each other's escapades through banner news headlines, if not personal networks, and referred to them in their ransom notes, thereby underlining their demands with proven examples. The Caress and Crofton failures hardly deterred them, and on April 5, in lead pencil on cheap notebook paper, they turned to Bowman in a bizarre mishmash of Italian-English:

> Wirt Bowman—I write you to say u gonna die soon. U hava big time much money. Now you won't live [to] have more big time. You pay us $50,000. You no pay, u no live. U get money in bigga bill and hava ready alla time. You carry in pocket. U get surprise how quick it happen. We miss [Crofton] ona time at depot. No miss this time. We tell you secret soon [as] we see what happen to your partner for no pay us. Tell him he gonna die quick. He [surrendered] no money, no good now [the deal is off with him]. He only x [double-crosses us] ona time. He little company. We big good company.
>
> This letter you no show no one. You do [and] three in your family get hurt bad. . . . U tell police, he [the police] no keep you live. When Crofton die, police he scratch his head. You will see mine friend. You will hear from us again soon. Pay or else we will give papers something to write about beside the Lindy [Lindbergh] baby. Be ready.
>
> [Signed] The Cobra.[36]

Two days later, Bowman received another short note so indecent that police later refused to reveal its contents to the public; it not only threatened the life of Bowman, but those of his wife and two daughters.

The Baron hesitated to inform police of the threats. Perhaps he thought the fulminations a hoax not worthy of attention, or Wirt could have been frightened and seriously considering demands of the mob. A week after receiving the notes, however, he conferred with the sheriff's office, and Undersheriff Sexson, flush with success in the Abbey case, promised, "Just give me three or four days, and I'll have my man. I got Abbey all right."[37] The next day Sexson hurried to Los Angeles to check out clues—or just on a hunch. Underground criminal contacts in that city had led to Abbey's whereabouts and arrest, and the sheriff hoped for the same for Bowman's aggressor, but nothing developed. Canaries knew or said nothing about abductor gangs who wrote ransom notes in broken Italian.

Wirt, meanwhile, went into seclusion with his family under heavy guard at his estate, even if he publicly protested (in vintage Bowman), "I am out in the open, and I will meet those rats anytime."

Sexson had lost some of his cockiness by the time he returned from Los Angeles. "Just when we will get them, is hard to say," he told the press. "It takes a little time to uncover these things." One thing for sure, "the letters are believed to have come from one of the largest kidnapping gangs on the [West] coast," but handwriting experts could not find a match.[38]

Bowman upped his assertiveness: "I'm not afraid of any rats who send me anonymous letters. They don't mean a thing, and it is a certainty that I am not afraid."[39]

The police file on the Bowman extortion case remained open for several months, but no new leads developed, and the paperwork slid into "unsolved crimes." The same occurred with investigations involving mobs across the land. Once authorities had the gang leader in hand, or those members directly connected to a crime, detectives spent little energy pursuing accomplices. They bragged about breaking up the mob, but those hoodlums who escaped prosecution soon melded with other cliques of gangsters. For most, it was the only life they knew, and there were always newcomers willing to chance a try. Police blamed the revolving door on soft judges and early parole, and investigators claimed a lack of time and money, but unbridled corruption, weak-kneed politicians, and widespread taxpayer indifference were much more at fault. Then there are those who admire others who have the gall (courage) to tug the beards of the rich and thumb their noses at authority.

CLEANING UP DETAILS

When Marty Colson and Lee Cochran went to prison in August 1929, two members of the gang remained free: Marcel "The Greek" Dellon, said to have masterminded the holdup and commandeered the $5,000 in stolen cash, and his companion, the spunky "Rumrunning Queen," Jeanne Lee. Police had searched futilely for the pair from San Francisco to Ensenada and

out to sea, but with Cochran and Colson behind bars, the fugitives forthrightly stepped forward (separately) and surrendered to police in August
1929. Much of the time they had been hiding in San Diego, and each denied
complicity in the crime. "Because I am innocent," said Dellon, "I am anxious
to give myself up and have the law clear me in open court. I did not know
anything about the assault until it was all over and in the newspapers."[40]

Jeanne Lee, her naturally red hair now dyed black, approached the sheriff
with a faint smile on her face: "I am Jeanne Lee. I understand that you want
me in connection with the Agua Caliente holdup. Well, here I am."[41] She
admitted helping a wounded friend (Colson), but claimed she knew nothing
at the time of the crime he had committed. The state charged both as
accomplices and a judge set bail, but neither ever went to trial and prosecutors soon dropped the complaints against them, as they did for those
against the wives of Cochran and Jerry Kearney.

Big Jerry himself was not so lucky. His lawyer argued that, "after his arrest,
Kearney made a clean breast of everything he knew about the case," but
Police Chief Hill countered, "We have three confessions on record regarding Kearney's extensive part in covering up the murders in the case, and I
see no reason why he should not be brought to trial on the charges." The
district attorney agreed, and in a packed courtroom (interestingly, mostly
women) on March 17, 1930, the trial began. Lee Cochran, transported from
San Quentin, served as the state's star witness. Lee reiterated that Kearney
knew nothing of the attack itself, but detailed how Jerry had covered up evidence—burned checks and hurled weapons into the sea. It was damning
evidence against a former buddy, but by cooperating, Cochran helped to
build a record for his own early parole. Rejecting a plea for probation, the
judge sentenced Kearney to a year in county jail.[42]

COLSON'S GRAND FINALE

In 1932 two "lifers" were scheming to break out of Folsom Prison—Marty
Colson and Lloyd Sampsell, the notorious San Francisco "yacht bandit" (he
had fled in a stolen yacht after robbing a bank). It had taken them a year to
assemble lethal homemade pistols from scraps and tools—nuts, springs,
drills, and bolts from the prison's industries—but now on February 27 they
were set. All night they struggled to drill through doors of their cells, and

when that failed, next morning they feigned sickness and were taken to the prison hospital on the third floor of the administration building. There they overpowered two guards and forced them at gun- and knife-point to accompany them downstairs to the main offices of the complex, where Colson covered the guards along with prison trustees at work in the offices (other employees locked themselves in a closet). Sampsell, meanwhile, went to the nearby telephone switchboard, then manned by Sherman Powell, a member of the warden's staff.

Powell stayed calm and lit his pipe.

"Never mind the pipe," Sampsell said. "Call the warden and tell him to come down to the office."

"A little smoke won't hurt, will it?" Powell asked.

"I wish I was as cool as you," replied Sampsell, who resembled a Caspar Milquetoast but struck his victims like an aroused rattlesnake. "Call the warden . . ."

Powell phoned the warden, Court Smith, at his home. The convicts planned to take the warden hostage and to use him as a shield against tower guards as they walked out the front gates of the penitentiary to liberty in the surrounding farmlands and ultimately refuge in the nearby Sierra Nevada.[43]

Smith took the call; he was needed on urgent business in his office. A few minutes later he phoned back to ask the captain of the guard if any trouble had arisen, but the call did not go through; the switchboard did not answer, because Sampsell had taken Powell to the warden's office. Warden Smith suspected a disturbance and ordered armed guards to surround the administration building. Sirens shrieked warnings of trouble. Rumors had the warden held hostage with inmates in control of the hospital and new cell building. Colson and Sampsell heard the wailing sirens and talked over their chances of escape. Maybe this was the end of their venture.

"Well, I am going to bump myself off," Colson said. "I stood this around here as long as I can."

"Don't be a damn fool," Sampsell replied. "Let's shoot it out; let's go as far as we can and get as many of them as we can while they are getting us, perhaps."

"No," said Colson, "there's a chance that I might get all crippled up and live around here for the rest of my life. I am going to kill myself."

To humor his partner, Sampsell said, "If that is the way you feel about it, if you promise me to go as far as we can, I will bump off with you."

"All right, I will do that," remarked Colson—halfheartedly.[44]

Sampsell took Powell back to the switchboard and told him to phone the warden.

A muffled shot echoed in a side room.

On the phone Warden Smith told Sampsell the game was up. The two convicts should meet him outside in the prison yard, where they must disarm, undress to prove they carried no weapons, and surrender. Sampsell agreed. He also told the warden that he believed Colson had killed himself.

Guards took Sampsell into custody. They found Colson dead in a pool of blood in the lavatory next to the warden's office. He had shot himself with the homemade pistol; the bullet passed through his head and embedded itself in the door. Marty had broken his promise to his mother never again to attempt suicide, but as the intended escape failed, he had had enough of life.

The homemade guns, resembling .45 caliber automatic pistols, had been fashioned from pieces of pipe and fittings with a sheet metal drill which the convicts had acquired while working in the prison granite quarry. Folsom was built in the 1880s near the quarry, so that prisoners could be put to hard work there. Match heads, saltpeter, and perhaps other ingredients were used for powder inside the fifteen hand-crafted bullets found on the prisoners. Convicts were always making explosive devices. In one celebrated case a few years earlier at San Quentin, an inmate about to be hanged blew off his own head with a homemade bomb made from a section of pipe from his iron bed, match heads, and cellulose scraped from playing cards.[45]

Today the ingenious pistols wielded by Colson and Sampsell are on display at the prison museum. "We still can't figure out exactly how they did it," said the curator, John Moore, a former guard who later knew Sampsell in Folsom. "He'd exchange pleasantries with me. When I took a vacation and returned, he'd ask how my family was doing. But I knew his attitude could change in a minute, and, if he could get ahold of me, he'd kill me and try to escape. Very dangerous man, that Sampsell."[46]

Colson died unlamented at the age of twenty-nine. "So far as the records show," wrote the *Los Angeles Times,*

> Martin Colson never did but one helpful thing in his life; that was when he killed himself during an attempt to break out of Folsom. He has been a vicious beast of prey and has cost the public a lot of money . . . not to mention costing two men's lives.
>
> Armed gangsters should have special prisons and special discipline in prison. And most of them should be hanged. No reason why the public should pay taxes to guard and support them. Cheapest thing this State could buy would be a lot of rope.[47]

Marty Colson would have expected that epitaph.

Fools and Thieves

In a bet there is a fool and a thief.
—Proverb

Even as I approach the gambling hall, as soon as I hear, two rooms away,
the jingle of money poured out on the table, I almost go into convulsions.
—Fyodor Dostoevsky, *The Gambler* (1867)

Son, we are sorry about the tuition funds. . . . Your mother and I
did not know that you are not supposed to split tens.
—Letters from parents visiting casinos

Your best chance to get a Royal Flush in a casino is
in the bathroom.—V. P. Papy, gambler

Agua Caliente's opulent and glamorous casino was by far the resort's star attraction. Everything else around it played a supporting role. Enormous
proceeds from the casino financed losses elsewhere and stuffed the coffers of
the Barons. Because their betting odds cannot be beat, casinos always make
millions, or more. At the time that Agua Caliente flourished, there were few
hindrances to flagrant corruption and unbounded profiteering in management, and even among the lower echelons. It stood as a symbol of the Jazz Age.

THE SETTING

The structure itself set the stage, with its classic Mission Revival style:
graceful arches, an array of painstakingly landscaped patios, entryways accented by elaborate tile work and swirling, Churrigueresque molding, all

topped by a traditional red tile roof. Out front was an enchanting wishing well with underwater lighting and a decorative tile bottom into which patrons tossed coins for luck. Two dark-skinned Mexicans of imposing stature (said, for effect, to be fearsome Yaqui warriors), wearing simple native dress, greeted guests (and kept order—they weeded out drunks).[1]

Inside was breathtaking in its rich sophistication. A diversity of decorators and expert craftsmen were given an open checkbook to add their specialties to the interior. Close inspection revealed a hodgepodge of styles and designs, but the overall impression was of Moorish royal wealth and splendor. Floors in the gaming hall were of domestic marble, as were the columns that rose to an intricate, delicate filigree ceiling (ornamental openwork through which casino supervisors could watch gamblers below and spot shills). Imbedded in the filigree was a large, oval painting by the Dutch muralist Anthony Hinsburgen, which added a classical touch, as did the cast bronze statuary on pillars and in niches in the main gaming room, lit by ornate fixtures finely crafted especially for the club and an immense chandelier from Milan, said to be the most exquisite and expensive in the hemisphere, which generated 2,500 watts of brilliant light. Gamblers delight in such magnificence; it makes them feel rich, important, and honored, and creates a devil-may-care sensibility which loosens purse strings. Give them a free drink and a cheap meal and they will gamble it all away.[2]

At one end of the main hall patrons took three steps up to the bar, where on a busy night customers stood four deep to order imported Scotch at 25 cents a shot. "On a Saturday night," wrote the film director William Wellman, "the huge barroom was loaded up and so was everyone in it. . . . It was so noisy that everyone had to yell and everybody had the floor."[3] Behind the bar stood two majestic cast-bronze griffins, those legendary creatures with the head and wings of an eagle and the body of a lion, a protective symbol exuding strength and vigilance. The Barons had them there for a reason; they were emblems of medieval barons, lords of the manor.

Two alcoves branched off the main gaming hall, one for dining, the other for dancing on a shining parquet floor. The dining area was posh, tables set with stemmed glassware and heavy genuine silverware on Irish linen tablecloths. On special occasions management brought out a unique, specially designed gold service, dishes with massive moldings etched in gold and carrying the Agua Caliente crest. The regal salver (serving tray) with its jeweled cover was the *pièce de résistance*, reflecting the verve and color of seventeenth-century Spanish art, its handles suggesting traditional crowns of royalty. When these items were in use, guards patrolled the room.

Adjoining one side of the casino was the famous Gold Room, preserve of the highest "plungers," which required formal dress, tuxedo or gown. Silk brocade tapestries from France cloaked the walls amidst solid walnut paneling and trim. The movie titans Joe Schenck and Carl Laemmle regularly gambled there and at times had it to themselves and a few gaming friends like Sid Grauman, the theater owner, the movie lawyer Edward Loeb, or Sam Bartlett, Los Angeles insurance man. Bets of $1,000 were common, and losses for an evening reached $30,000 to $50,000 (the latter equals half a million today), substantial amounts for casino play even if they never approached the $3 million won by a Syrian ex-carpet salesman at Deauville in 1920 or the $400,000 divided by two baccarat players nine years later at a French casino for the fabulously rich in Nice. After that noteworthy triumph on the French Riviera, one of the winners nonchalantly remarked, "It was all in a night's play. As a matter of fact, anybody with courage, some luck and plenty of money can always win against the baccarat bank."[4] Experience, of course, has taught others otherwise.

For movieland's moguls, however, gambling was much more than a display of wealth. It tested the will power and judgment of these highly insecure and competitive executives in a small coliseum where they could bluff and intimidate one another, and prove their mettle and worth. Play for high stakes marked their rank in Hollywood, and the Gold Room at Agua Caliente reflected an ambiance to which they were accustomed: risk-taking, hunches, sudden changes, luck (good and bad). As one producer said, "Making movies is like shooting dice all day."[5]

THE CLIENTELE

Celebrities and elites certainly roamed the casino and placed their bets. Raul Walsh, the film director, took away $18,000 in 1930, but, as is normally the case, most who gambled were teachers and realtors, store managers and their families, small business bosses and professionals, druggists, stenographers, off-duty firemen, and better-paid clerks—in other words, middle Americans, who left behind an average of $45 (now $450). "By their looks," said a writer surveying the scene, "many—nay, most of them must have even voted for [President] Hoover and Prosperity." Nor were they inveterate gamblers. They were ordinary people "out to find out what there was about the darned racket, [even] if it cost them money to do it. They go at it like a set of high-school kids out for a straw ride." Even today, "the majority of casino players leave too much to chance," a gambling author advises. "To put it bluntly, they don't have a clue as to how to play."[6]

So what? Naïve or inexperienced about gaming, it did not matter. People played for fun and (hopefully) fortune. At Agua Caliente a young woman sauntered up to a chuck-a-luck table (three dice are placed in a shaker and tossed on a table with various betting options) and asked her companion, "Oh! Will, will they let me bet?" Of course, they would. Nearby, "a large, motherly woman in [a] sprigged print [dress], was speculating, a dollar at a time, with exactly the same expression that she would have shown in frying doughnuts," and a gray-haired man wished to cash in a substantial pile of chips, yet "knew not their worth." Then there was the woman at a roulette wheel suddenly surprised by her husband: "I thought you had gone to bed," she said. "The baby? Is he awake again? Why didn't you go in quietly like I told you? Wait here till I run up—put down a dollar for me on thirty-five."[7]

Of course, the occasional spoilsport, like Eleanor González of Los Angeles, spoke up angrily. In a letter to the interim president Ortiz Rubio, González charged that the Border Barons were running "an infamous gambling joint, not a 'casino,' as they call it, and are causing the ruin of thousands of people each year. The games are unfair, and not a particle of sportsmanship is shown. They (or this man Bowman) refers to *their* investment of $7-million. [Truth is,] every nickel was stolen from poor fools who go up against their skin games—blood money."[8] Gamblers chuckle at such sentiments.

Hollywood's hordes who frequented the casino provided grist for their industry's gossip columnists. "You've all heard about that 'last dollar' plunge that's supposed to make you even," wrote the *Hollywood Reporter*, "well, listen to what Mel Baker's wife did at Agua Caliente last week. They went for three days, and by the end of the first, had given all they'd planned on at the gaming tables. Came the last night and Mary Baker found she had $20 left and figured she might as well be absolute broke as take that home with her, so she went over to the craps table and plunged . . . and made seventeen straight passes." Her husband took the winnings and handed Mary her original $20, which she bet when the dice again came her way. This time she rolled off twenty-four straight passes. "If you think that's not true," the journal continued, "ask Wally [Wallace] Beery, who was willing to bet it could never happen." Beery was a habitué at Agua Caliente, where he founded an exclusive club, limited to one hundred film people.[9]

MANAGEMENT

Casinos should be thought of as a business that deals almost exclusively with money. (*Casino* literally means cash.) They exist only to separate players from their currency and to maximize profits for the owners while creating the illusion that customers can win. "Suckers have no business with money anyway," is the way one card dealer put it. If the casinos can't be beat, why do patrons keep trying? Luck is the temptress. Luck blinds players to statistics.

It is not easy, however, to run casinos, which appear to be more organized than they really are. Managers face the usual problems of any large business, plus those unique to an operation based on chance. The inventory of a casino is its money, and a steady flow of coins and bills passes through the fingers of many employees before reaching the owner's bank account or pockets. Under these circumstances, the goal of a casino manager is total control through a system of regularity and vigilance, an arrangement bound to have its chinks.

Cheaters abound, not only players determined to beat the house by hook or crook, but also employees. Today's casinos have elaborate electronic equipment—cameras everywhere—to catch cheaters, but in Agua Caliente's day surveillance could only be done with a sharp eye and mirrors. There was a hierarchy of vigilance: the casino manager watched the shift manager, and the shift manager watched the pit boss, and the pit boss watched the floor men, who supervised the dealers. Employees followed rules; dealers wore aprons over their pockets to prevent them from filching chips and clapped hands when departing their table to prove they were not carrying chips away. Dealers called out every $100 bill changed at their tables so the pit boss could see them stuff it into a slot. Chips had to be stacked by color to facilitate counting, and blackjack dealers learned to cup their hold card against cheats. (Hustlers search out weak dealers, sit behind them, and signal partners playing the game.) "An experienced stickman at a craps table is trained never to take his eyes off the dice, especially when the noisy drunk at the end of the table spills his drink on the felt, drops his chips on the floor, or takes a swing at his wife."[10] At moments of diversion, phony dice can be slipped into the game, marked cards placed on a poker table, or card-dealing shoes slyly exchanged at blackjack play.

Big winners are always suspect, and their backgrounds checked. Managers work to keep such clients in the house. "The worst nightmare of a casino manager has always been the spot player, the individual who bets large, gets lucky and leaves."[11] Give the lucky winner a dinner ticket, comp the bell-ringer a room, anything that keeps the person close by and gambling, so the house can recoup its loss. Winners, of course, understand this ruse, but Lady Luck often seductively lures them back.[12]

Short of insurance against cheaters, managers insist upon the loyalty of their employees. Of course, they do not always get it. As a casino manager at Agua Caliente, James Crofton hired family, relatives, and school friends from his hometown, The Dalles, to work the most important and sensitive positions in the gambling hall. His older brother, E. H., for instance, administered the "count room," the vulnerable heart of the operation, where a tight knot of the most-trusted counted and packaged daily proceeds. In all, thirty-five young men and their families came from The Dalles to serve the casino, none with experience in gambling, or even an aptitude for it, but they were people whom Crofton could trust, and none (as far as is known) bilked him. Jim also courted The Dalles's police chief, but citizens of the little Oregon town raised the chief's pay $50 a month to keep him home. Still, Crofton's enterprise threatened to drain The Dalles of its young men, as more than a hundred of them applied for jobs at the casino. The fellows had a choice: farming and manual labor in an eastern Oregon town well past its heyday, or steady employment at good pay among movie stars and other celebrities, and as a bonus, proximity to a ribald town with an unsavory (but inviting) reputation. Maybe not the best place to raise a family— but most actually resided in San Diego.[13]

SKIMMING

Managers found it difficult to follow money through the house, and their biggest foe was not thievery nor connivance by shrewd patrons but out-and-out stealing from the till (skimming) by employees. For a long time, it was accepted that casino workers from dealers to top management received a cut of casino money on its way to the count room. Everyone took home a little extra. No doubt, a good deal of that practice occurred at Agua Caliente, and management could do little about it. Mexican labor laws were too tough. Dismissal of a Mexican employee for any cause could bring protest and legal claims, and then strikes and violence. On the other hand, pay-plus-tips was so advantageous at the casino that ordinary workers took fewer risks with the skim. They did not want the town's major employer to pack up and leave.

Besides, most skimming does not take place on the casino floor, but in the operation's inner sanctum, the counting room, where stacks of bills and tons of coins must be counted and packaged every day. The owners permitted no strangers in Agua Caliente's counting room. Even so, Jim Crofton stood duty there, pistol in hand, with armed guards nearby. On occasion, he took his nine-year-old niece to the cage-like room just to see the stacks of bills and innumerable bags of coins.[14] So much money pours into some casino count rooms that it cannot be counted; it has to be weighed. "Coins are poured into specially made . . . coin weighing machines. A million dollars in quarter slot machine winnings weighs twenty-one tons."[15]

Casino owners and workers do not report their skim as taxable income to the Bureau of Internal Revenue (the 1927 Sullivan Law made illicit income taxable), but Internal Revenue agents have little difficulty spotting the gaping difference between a reported moderate income and lavish living. That disconnect is what raised suspicions about Wirt Bowman, who owned Tijuana's Foreign Club, substantial shares in Agua Caliente, a bank, a hotel, and vast real estate in Arizona. Where was Bowman getting *that* kind of money? His tax returns certainly did not reflect it.

WIRT'S SKIM

A complaint by an unidentified party ignited the probe against Bowman in the late 1920s. Investigators noted that in the wake of Carlie Withington's death, Wirt incorporated the Mexican Development Company, which controlled Tijuana gambling. "The retention and operation of the gambling concession held by the Mexican Development Company was a difficult task," the tax men wrote. "The necessity of paying tribute to diverse and sundry Mexican officials of high and low estate is freely admitted by all." It was and is the way business is done in Mexico.[16]

The long, detailed commentary discovered Bowman conducting his company business "in a remarkable manner. The company issued its checks either to cash or to Wirt G. Bowman, charged the amount to [a] 'Concessions Fund,' and thereafter neither received or required substantiating vouchers or information as to the recipient of the money. Mr. Bowman, in turn, cashed these checks and disposed of this money without making a record of it. The nature and purpose of these currency payments explains the secrecy with which they were handled."[17]

The Bureau of Internal Revenue Intelligence Division presumed rampant skimming occurred. (Bowman was fortunate that the Treasury Department's aggressive, unyielding special intelligence unit, which had just put Al Capone in prison, did not intrude into his case. Later it netted Joe Schenck.)

Bowman paid mammoth bribes, which pointed to the profitability of his casinos. Forty checks ranging from $550 to $65,000, totaling $769,817 were charged to the "Concession Fund" in 1926. The following year the amount equaled $802,400 in thirty-two checks worth $400 to $50,000.

As the Bureau noted, "Mr. Bowman has no record of the disposition made of this money."[18]

The Bureau calculated Bowman's taxable income for those two years at $381,805 (it was almost certainly much larger), and noted that he reported only $137,728 earned. No one, however, could be sure of Wirt's gains. "During the years 1926 and 1927, Mr. Bowman did not maintain books or records reflecting his many and varied financial transactions. He opened his first regular set of books about June, 1929."[19]

The dam burst in the fall of 1930, when revenuers learned from their unrevealed source that a concession or political fund of $550,000 had in 1926–27 been divided among owners of the Mexican Development Company: Bowman, Baron Long, Frank Beyer, Marvin Allen, and Joseph Zamansky, none of whom had reported his share on his tax return. Bowman and Long alleged they only borrowed money from the fund and therefore it was not taxable. The other three claimed they had never received any income at all from the deal—which suggests who might have snitched to the Bureau.[20]

Tax agents followed the money: "It was further disclosed [in the Bureau's investigation] that Mr. Wirt G. Bowman had acted as cashier in the transaction, and that the money could not be traced beyond him."[21]

Confronted in his Palm City home by revenue inspectors on April 23, 1934, Bowman squirmed and sputtered, saying he had been so busy with his various business ventures that he had not been able to keep proper records, had allowed others to handle his tax matters, and admitted it was possible that mistakes had been made on the 1926 and 1927 returns. He agreed to pay any additional taxes due: $49,000.[22]

The Bureau, however, also demanded interest on the amount and 50 percent fraud penalties totaling $12,000. For the next three years, Bowman, a multimillionaire with a political reputation at stake, fought the interest and penalty charges. He had the help of his close longtime friend, Arizona Senator Carl T. Hayden, but each time Wirt pleaded for a reduction in his due, the Bureau questioned his ability to pay. Bowman dared not allege poverty at this juncture.[23]

Internal Revenue also noted that other infractions piled up. Investigation for the year 1932 disclosed that Bowman failed to report an $11,400 dividend received from the Foreign Club, that he improperly claimed a $30,000 loss from his personal holding company (La Mexicana Comercial), claimed a $5,000 expense deduction for bribe money, and farm losses of $12,000 when half of that went to pay cooks, maids, and caretakers.

In June 1936 Wirt tried an amazing ploy (even for him) to reduce his tax liability. He produced for the Bureau an affidavit signed by ex-president Calles, saying that in the latter part of 1925 or early part of 1926, the Jefe Máximo had loaned his friend, Wirt Bowman, $150,000 in cash. The document stated no terms for repayment. Bowman contended that the amount did not constitute taxable revenue and should be subtracted from his total estimated income for those years.

The Treasury Department sent a representative, W. Williams, to interview Calles about the affidavit. According to Bowman's correspondence, the conversation went like this:

> Williams: "The Department of the Treasury has commissioned me to ask you if this document [the affidavit] is authentic, signed by you in which you recognize that you loaned Wirt G. Bowman $150,000."
>
> (Williams took the document from a file folder and handed it to Calles.)
>
> "Indeed, what the document says is correct," the ex-president replied.
>
> "Can you be precise about the date and place that this document was prepared?"
>
> "I do not remember exactly, but probably in November or December, 1925, or in January or February, 1926, at my house in Mexico City."
>
> "In what currency was this loan made?"
>
> "The biggest part was in American dollars and the rest in American gold."
>
> "Was any document signed that guaranteed [repayment of] the loan?"
>
> "No, Señor, I did not sign another document. Señor Bowman is an old and good friend of mine to whom I owe some personal services, and for this reason, I did not demand any signed document from him. I believe that my money is well-placed in his hands, and when I need it, if Mr. Bowman does not have it readily at hand, he will make whatever sacrifice is necessary and pay me immediately."
>
> "Was interest set on this loan?"
>
> "No, Señor. This loan will gain no money."

"Within six or seven months, Bowman will be asked by the Tax Board to further clarify this matter. Do you expect to be a witness at the hearing?"

"I do not know whether or not I will testify in this matter."

"This is all I have to ask of you, General, and I thank you for the interview and the kindness with which you treated me."[24]

But Williams suspected during the interview, and the Treasury Department quickly verified, that *Calles read no English*. Since the loan document was written in English, he could not have read it, and so tax investigators ignored it as part of Wirt's defense.

Avoidance of taxes is legal; evasion is not. Situations can be created to legally avoid taxes (e.g., charitable contributions and business expenses), but illegal tax avoidance becomes evasion. Wirt Bowman, skimmer and schemer *par excellence*, did not seem to understand the difference—or chose to ignore it. In either case, he got caught for evasion. In Nogales it is still rumored that Bowman donated $25,000 to the Roosevelt presidential campaign to have the tax charges against him dropped. While the contribution cannot be verified, it would have been in character.

The devastating summation of Bowman's tax record concluded: "For the years 1927 to 1931, Mr. Bowman reported dividends totaling $985,000 [now $10 million] from Mexican corporations which operated gambling clubs. . . . It seems clear that Mr. Bowman made himself a millionaire as a result of gambling operations in Mexico. . . . Further investigation might disclose that Mr. Bowman is liable for additional taxes from this source [his personal holding company]." The Bureau sought criminal charges against Wirt, who was by then Arizona's Democratic National Committeeman, but prosecutors declined "for the reason that they [the accusations] were considered inadequate." One wonders what "inadequate" meant.[25]

Negotiations continued, a compromise was reached at $25,817.87 (with no fraud penalty), and on August 13, 1938, Bowman paid up. Case closed, but political future jeopardized or ruined.

MEXICO'S GRASP

Mexico's government meant to control the casinos, especially those in Tijuana, so close to the international line. Foreign dominance of border territories could only fuel annexationist conspiracies persistently being hatched to the north. If Americans like the Border Barons aimed to profit in Tijuana, they would have to pay heavy fees, taxes, and bribes, and contribute to civic improvements for local inhabitants. Concessions outlined the fees and taxes to be exacted—not only the immense monthly amounts for general operations, but supplementary charges for every roulette wheel spun and each horse race run. The Barons also paid police and soldiers to maintain security around their enterprise, agreed to build the critically needed Tijuana-to-Ensenada highway, and helped to finance the town's newest civic attraction, its first secondary school, an impressive, stately structure of classical design and proportion on a high bluff overlooking city center.[26] Overall, the financial demands appeared to be a gigantic shakedown, but at the same time, they highlight the fruits of the Agua Caliente enterprise. The skim, tariffs, taxes, and announced profits came from one massive pot of money.

A deliberately bewildering network of rules, regulations, and laws covered gaming in Mexico and established controls: only certain games, those supposedly dealing more with skill than luck, could be played; no more than fifty people could gamble at one time, and individual losses could not exceed (an unrealistic) $5.00. Police agents and uniformed military people could not play, and only visitors of good character and decorum were to be admitted. The contract placed a limit on profits: the club could keep no more than 10 percent of all money bet, and there had to be easy access to an exterior door so that fiscal inspectors could enter surreptitiously to survey conditions and file complaints against offenders.[27]

Almost everyone, of course, ignored or broke the rules, but the regulations still left owners and managers vulnerable to accusations and the extortion of hush money. Many untraceable checks that Bowman wrote undoubtedly went to inspectors and their superiors, and there is no knowing how many palms he greased with cash. Tijuana then was like Las Vegas today: a city of deals.

The presence of inspectors from Mexico City was a nuisance to owners, or potentially much worse. The officials received payoffs but could also render a report which could shut down a casino, a frequent occurrence in Withington's time. Or the threat of closure could come from the opposite direction, from the Barons themselves. At one point in 1929, Bowman, poor-mouthing, called fines levied at Agua Caliente for alleged missteps "additional taxation" which the resort could not tolerate, hinting that, short of relief, the resort would lock its doors.

Governor Rodríguez, hardly an impartial observer, came to the resort's defense, reminding Mexico City of what gambling taxes meant to the district—everything—and also cleverly appealed to the government's nationalistic instincts. Casino funding had helped both to rescue and to distance the territory from foreign hands. "We have been able to buy large tracts of land, divide and colonize them with Mexicans," he wrote. New roads, schools, and the gigantic dam under construction on the Tijuana River have helped the territory to become self sufficient, he continued. "If inspectors continue to charge gambling places with legal infractions, they will close, and we will hardly have funds to pay public employees, and development of the district will cease."[28]

The governor wrote directly to ex-president Calles: "Bowman is headed to the capital to discuss matters connected to his business. Please help him. He continues to be the good friend you knew in Sonora and has been disposed to help the government in cases as in March of 1929, when he aided us pecuniarily in a very efficient matter." The governor was referring to a barracks rebellion which occurred at Nogales. Rodríguez had rushed to the scene, and from his suite in Bowman's Moctezuma Hotel, paid off the rebels to lay down their weapons with money borrowed from Bowman's bank. That same year, Wirt loaned the government $100,000 (one source says $15 million, but that seems exaggerated) to help quell the more dangerous Escobar uprising, and the previous year had loaned Obregón a similar amount to finance his reelection campaign.[29] As a successful banker, Wirt knew when and where to lend money and received much more than simple interest in return.

Unfortunately, we are not privy to the conversation that Bowman had with government officials in the capital, including the new president, Pascual Ortiz Rubio (1930–32), who though under the sway of Calles remained his own man. They certainly discussed taxes and inspectors, but a more urgent concern also demanded attention. In their gambling concessions, casino owners like Withington and then Bowman received monopolies over gaming in Tijuana. Competitors used their own political influence to challenge those rights, went to court, but were beaten back by judicial politics and presidential fiat. The Ortiz Rubio administration, however, granted new gaming concessions to construct a resort resembling Agua Caliente below the international line on the sea, where it would attract the affluent yacht crowd, and a second to a syndicate represented by a cousin of the president, to be located just north of the established Agua Caliente, aiming to siphon off clientele headed toward the complex.

The Border Barons howled in protest. Their Mexican representatives urged Ortiz Rubio to close down unauthorized casinos in Tijuana and cancel concessions for new ones. The president's cousin fought back, however, saying he would lose the $8,000 commission paid him to consummate the deal should the license be revoked. The give-and-take showcased the machinations surrounding casino permits at the highest levels of government. Ortiz Rubio claimed he favored competition among casinos; Calles was heavily invested in Agua Caliente's welfare and meant to shield it from rivals. Wirt Bowman had his work cut out, but long experience had taught him when to open his wallet (or bank) and make deals.

The negotiations which followed remained private, but on his return to the United States, Bowman had a cheerful announcement for the press: "President Ortiz Rubio assured me that the Mexican Government would not only protect our twenty-year [reduced from seventy-five] concession but would alter the document to encourage us to make further improvements at the track and hotel."[30] "Alter the document" meant lower taxes to support development, and one can be sure that the president's cousin lost no money in the settlement.

Agua Caliente thereby survived the threat of nearby competition, and when Rodríguez became president, the resort had one of its own as protector. There was, nonetheless, a paramount lesson in all this. Changes of administration in Mexico could spell trouble for vice lords and new elections were set for 1934. The new president might be handpicked by reigning políticos, but that alone did not guarantee a smooth transition, as each político had his own agenda to promote, his own debts to pay.

Truth was that the casinos had always been held hostage by the Mexican government, which issued and canceled gaming concessions at whim, for political purpose, or financial gain. The "game" was in *its* hands. Even the Border Barons had to play by Mexico's rules. Unpredictability reigned, luck changed, and the Princes of Vice knew to skim while they could.

A Dead Cock in the Pit

In his stern inaugural address on December 1, 1934, President Lázaro Cárdenas vigorously deplored the cavernous pockets of poverty in his homeland; the lack of basic, practical education, which contributed to personal lassitude and irresponsibility; the general dependency on priests and fate; and the overall deleterious resignation common to so many of his countrymen. Although his election had been assured by his country's rigged political system, Cárdenas had campaigned widely throughout the nation's inner cities and vast rural hinterland, and the tour convinced him that Mexicans most needed to be weaned from vice and superstition and taught to become productive wage-earners and thereby satisfied citizens (beholden to his government).

CHANGING TIMES

Cárdenas vowed radical reforms, which followed fast and furious. The administration expropriated land from gigantic haciendas and divided it among ordinary *campesinos*, created a curriculum for schools that emphasized scientific (at least, more modern) approaches to collective farming, preached a lessened dependence on God's will, and promoted sanitized living habits. The government also whipped up patriotic civic activities and urged proletarians to unionize and forcefully demand, through strikes and fierce protests, their due from management. Certainly the fervent crusade was meant to right wrongs, but also to build the new regime a broad political base and to force resistant regional strongmen into the fold. To be sure, the whirlwind of rectifications stirred not only passions, but also resistance, a good deal of it armed, wanton, and terrifying. Concerned by ideologies then circling much of the globe, many at home and abroad thought Mexico was fast turning communist; others recognized strains of fascism, while outraged capitalists and proponents of democracy cringed.[1]

Changing Mexican nature (and cherished traditions) was at the heart of the Cárdenas crusade. Among other things, Mexicans had to be weaned from drunkenness and gambling (prostitution was largely ignored) and endemic corruption curbed throughout society. Such admonitions had been heralded in past moralization campaigns but more for political effect than application. Cárdenas, however, meant business, and within a month of that first emphatic presidential speech (even if he was hardly a mesmerizing orator), the president by fiat closed down the country's gambling casinos in all but Baja California Norte (Tijuana), a border district he recognized as dependent upon casino tax revenue and resistant to mandates from the far-off capital. Agua Caliente thereby survived the initial moral cleansing and still prospered. In its last five years it had paid an appreciable $2 million in dividends, and its 500,000 shares of stock were worth $27,500,000.[2] Still, warning flags flew.

The Border Barons thought their renowned resort untouchable, too important for the region's budgetary demands, too lucrative for official profiteering, and safely protected by national officialdom, including two ex-presidents. The hammer fell, however, on July 20, 1935: *This* president intended to be his own man, and only seven months after he took office, Cárdenas decreed the district's casinos also be closed.[3] The day before the announcement, Abelardo Rodríguez warned his fellow Baron, Jim Crofton, that the guillotine was about to fall, so Jim and his brother, Ernest, rushed to drain the company's money vaults. As they could not quickly lay their hands on briefcases or the usual money pouches—and they wanted no one to suspect what they were up to—they stuffed $2 million, maybe $3 million, into gunnysacks and headed for a San Diego bank. Wirt Bowman also had been forewarned and urged to protect his assets. All knew that without its casino, Agua Caliente was "a dead cock in the pit."[4]

The thunderclap reverberated throughout California's Southland, and on to New York, Paris, and Shanghai. Telegrams from throughout the world requested information about the reported closure. "It's time," Baron Long replied. "Our number is up." Of the other Barons, Rodríguez was traveling and had "no comment." Feisty James Crofton was also free of the tempest. In 1932 he had nearly been killed in a small-plane crash outside Mexico

City. Relatives said that "every bone in his body was broken." Not "every" bone perhaps, but ribs, and a leg, arm, and collarbone, along with torn joints and numerous cuts and bruises. A mystery woman seated next to him also barely survived but was facially scarred. She turned out to be his new, but still secret, wife, Monica Rico, the beautiful Mexican movie star whose career ended with the mishap. Following the horrific accident, which killed the pilot, Carl W. Gilpin, a well-known American West Coast airline owner, Crofton ceased active participation in everyday affairs at Agua Caliente (but retained substantial business interest in the racetrack), invested in a San Diego brewery, managed his enormous cattle ranches in central California, raised thoroughbred horses which he raced, and lived with a leisurely rustic touch like the socially prominent multimillionaire that he was.[5]

The departure of Rodríguez and Crofton from the original Baron foursome left the casino closing crisis up to Bowman and Long. (Joe Schenck still hovered in the background but was mainly connected to the racetrack and resigned six months later.) The Barons decided there was insufficient profit in running either the hotel or the golf course and shut them down, pending gaming clarifications from the Cárdenas government. Horse racing was suspended at the nearby track, and six hundred horses readied for shipment to other venues. A full house of downcast patrons packed the resort for the last hours of gambling and final serenades on the now wistful patio of the hotel. At midnight on December 18, 1937, the famous tower bells chimed a last farewell. Bowman, meanwhile, sponsored a lavish final banquet for his employees and then padlocked the Foreign Club. Disbelief and sadness reigned, along with expectation that the hiatus would be brief. So much remained unknown.

Managers emptied out the refrigerators and storage bins the next day at the club and resort, giving away food—eggs, butter, bread, vegetables—and other perishables to local residents but favoring the poor. It was the first time these people had tasted French pâté and Russian caviar, and, in general, they turned up their noses at such bourgeois delicacies. They gladly took home, however, meats, fowl, and fish to prepare as more accustomed fare with tortillas. Laid-off workers received one month's compensation but soon demanded three in accordance with law. Conflict ensued over such obligations, as the Barons hesitated to pay.[6]

The closing appeared to be an unmitigated disaster for Tijuana's economy. Some fifteen hundred locals lost decent wages, including some of the best-paid work in town. It immediately affected every household. Husbands worried about their families; union bosses cried foul, telegrams urging a reprieve flooded the capital, while municipal and union delegations headed to Mexico City for conferences with the administration.

Baron Long and Wirt Bowman also went south to confer with Cárdenas, but publicly vowed to adhere to the president's demands and kept doors to the resort locked tight. "The President's word is law," said Long, "and we are abiding by the order which will be carried out in full." Employees called it a lockout and blamed the Barons as much as the national government for their plight. Truth was that for seven years, and despite the Depression, the casino had financed the resort and generated vast profits for its owners. Without the casino, the complex became a white elephant. So management packed up the gaming paraphernalia along with furnishings from the hotel, secured them in storage along with the resort's storied and carefully inventoried liquor supply, turned off all water and most electricity, surrounded the grounds with a barbed-wire fence, posted signs—"*Se Prohibe Entrada. Keep Out*"—and hired guards to enforce their will. Newsmen reported the seemingly deserted place now inhabited by ghosts.[7]

A PUZZLEMENT

Observers, then and now, have debated just why Lázaro Cárdenas shuttered Agua Caliente. Any single explanation seems too simplified for an act that assuredly carried many strains. Politics were doubtless involved. Cárdenas had broken with his predecessor, Calles, over the depth and rapidity of the latest reforms, was about to send his critic packing into exile in the United States, and needed to sever the ex-president's substantial financial ties to Tijuana's casinos. Cárdenas, furthermore, wanted to crack the hold that combative labor unions which supported his predecessor's regime held over places like Agua Caliente. The new president, in that regard, endorsed an even more aggressively militant confederation of syndicates, and the two were soon in hostile competition.

The president, moreover, asserted that despite their significant contributions to annual budgets, no nation can survive on gambling proceeds (even if the territory of Baja California Norte had done so for years, and such income is vital to many state coffers today). In an apparent contradiction to this notion, however, the administration supported the National Lottery for Public Benefit, an important source of federal revenue. What's the difference, Agua Caliente's workers asked, between a Mexican buying a 50-cent lottery ticket and an American playing roulette for a dollar? The administration did not reply.

Cárdenas may genuinely have felt a deep personal responsibility for what he called "the moral regeneration" of Mexicans, even if few of them, especially more ordinary ones, ever gambled at casinos, which catered to the affluent and excluded the poor. In this role, he played the *gran patrón*, promising protection and demanding loyalty. Disgruntled workers mounted the grandstand in Tijuana's main park, renewing their cry, "Why, if he [the president] stops gambling for Americans in Tijuana, does he permit the national lottery to operate? What is to become of us?"[8] Anger mounted.

Closure of the border city's casinos was undoubtedly a major measure in the regime's overall plan to make Mexicans less dependent on magic, grace, fortune, "*Que será, será*," and the mysterious power of luck, and make them more subject (subservient) to government direction and welfare. Such intent is the hallmark of systematic national intentions to centralize government. The world of chance is masterless, and a centralized, more powerful government seeks to conquer and control it, to create one single, orderly scheme. The contest is on: control versus chance, and culture mediates the outcome. As a whole, but certainly with notable exceptions, Americans (and undoubtedly other, but mainly Western cultures) by tradition tend to feel more comfortable in a managed world, one of responsibility and personal choice, which is why random, seemingly inexplicable events like 9/11 so shake their security.

Mexicans, and many others, find inspiration and consolation in forces outside of human control—in roulette wheels, dice and card games, *peticiones* to miracle working saints (including those canonized by themselves), and in "God willing." Gambling, of any kind, may alleviate the dullness of one's everyday life and with a win, make a nobody a somebody, if only for a moment.[9]

Cárdenas did not intend to scrub clean the Mexican soul; his lottery represented a peephole into the world of kismet and fortune. But his administration, among other better-known goals such as those concerning land, labor, and educational reform, aimed to lessen the people's affinity for chance, its bent toward spontaneity, and to encourage more willingness for human control—meaning in great part his government's projects and proposals. Closing Agua Caliente planted his standard in treacherous ground well seeded with the folkways of customary life. Culture breathes, lives, and changes, but over time. Many still believe it is better to be lucky than good.

UNCERTAINTIES

The sudden and dramatic lockdown of Agua Caliente stunned the sporting world. "One can imagine the plight of uninhabited lumber towns, of similar deserted communities where industries might have failed and stopped all activities," wrote the *San Diego Sun.*

> It's hard to conceive of all this tiled, gold splendor going to ruin. But the owners know there is little chance of anything but a stilled, boarded place. . . .
>
> The aims of the reformers may appear lofty. Yet the actual execution of the reform is in itself an ugly, tragic thing.
>
> You realize that when you think of gleaming Caliente going to waste, of its five thousand actual and allied workers being cut adrift to settle their debts, make their existence from other sources.[10]

The *San Diego Union* pondered a proper response to the termination. A good deal was at issue. San Diegans earned some $300,000 monthly supplying Agua Caliente, and many of the resort's employees spent earnings in town. Should the city implore the Mexican government to ease its ban, or might San Diego start its own gambling industry? The newspaper answered its second question first: "Our choice is an emphatic No. The profits of a nothing-for-something industry—no matter how fascinating and colorful the industry, and no matter how extensive the profits—are unhealthy for the community in which they are exploited. San Diego should seek no part of them."

As for urging the reopening of Agua Caliente in Tijuana, "There is no easy answer to that." The editorial lamented the plight of the laid-off workers, but continued, "In the final analysis, though, gambling is a doomed industry, and to postpone its doom in any place is merely to prolong an illusion. The closed paradise was a fools' paradise, deriving its vast profits out of revenue from a picturesque lie. Revenue is only one side of the picture of this paradise. Ruin is the other."[11]

Given the prevalence, and prosperity, of casinos today (including their proliferation in San Diego County), one wonders if such editorials are foolish or prophetic.

When Agua Caliente closed, civic leaders in Las Vegas, claiming their town to be the "most liberal and progressive community in the West," urged the Border Barons to move their entire enterprise to the fledgling desert town where gambling and prostitution had been legalized.[12] With their sights already trained on other ventures, however, the Barons demurred, but a handsome young fellow with Hollywood tastes and links to organized crime, took notice.

A decade later, in 1946, Bugsy Siegel, who had sampled the delights of Agua Caliente, opened the Pink Flamingo Hotel and Casino, the first luxury resort on what became The Strip. He followed the flamboyant, anything-goes script written by the Border Barons: "Get them there, keep them there (with diverse and seductive sideshows), take their money."

And there gaming halls thrive today, reminders of an even more glorious, if short-lived, ancestor.

SHAKY GROUNDS

Mexican officials confirmed the administration's hard line, squelching rumors that Agua Caliente would soon reopen. "If Agua Caliente opens again, you can shoot me—six times," said Fernando Villaseñor, Baja California's fish and game commissioner. "President Cárdenas told me three months ago that gambling would be stopped soon in Caliente and Tijuana. Purging Mexico of vice was part of his campaign for office. All the millions of dollars Mexico might receive in taxes from gambling, and all efforts of influential persons are not enough to change President Cárdenas' plans."

The same report also quoted the president's personal secretary, who told Tijuana's union leaders that "under no circumstances would President Cárdenas rescind or even modify the order. Agua Caliente and Tijuana gambling resorts are closed for good."[13] Such statements further frustrated and infuriated discharged workers. Employees in the habit of earning $25 to $30 a day suddenly faced common labor jobs at $1.50 daily. Managers accustomed to buying Stetson hats, Florsheim shoes, and Hart, Shaffner, and Marx suits were suddenly without work. People who thought the money would never stop discovered that it had and demanded relief.

Cárdenas appreciated their plight, and sent a new governor, the renowned Zapatista general Gildardo Magaña, to the district with orders to design a relief plan. Magaña found Tijuana $100,000 in debt and in need of civic improvements costing another $300,000, sums that could only be covered by tourist dollars or a massive government subsidy. As the nation's treasury ran dry, tourism seemed to be the only answer. Mobbed by adoring, hopeful, jobless workers, the general hinted that gambling might once again be allowed in town. The U.S. consul in Mexicali wired Washington on October 21, 1935: "It is reported on good authority that Gov. Gildardo Magaña, who left for Mexico City to consult with Cárdenas on economic situation in Baja [California] will offer his resignation unless he can secure reopening of gambling in Tijuana and Mexicali."[14] Details of the conversation that followed between the president and the governor are unknown, but the result was clear: the territory received a new governor, another military general, a product of the Revolution, Gabriel Gavira.

Gavira was another disaster, though for opposite reasons. When the newcomer immediately appointed his friends to public office, he enraged local unions and other well-rooted political groups. His response to unemployment was to offer workers a measly $10 to leave Baja California and find jobs elsewhere, which led to the accusation that he was trying to depopulate and abandon the district to America's territorial appetite.[15] He lasted only four months, and the president replaced him with yet another general, Rafael Navarro Cortina, who curried favor with his constituents by allowing them to operate gambling houses with prohibited games of chance. "It has been a matter of general knowledge for some weeks," wrote the U.S. consul at Ensenada, "that gambling houses equipped with all kinds of the prohibited games of chance have been in operation publicly in Tijuana. . . . Thus, the administration [of the district] seems to be reverting to that of former times when governors have used their office largely to advance their own economic position."[16] The president's own officials were undermining his moralization campaign, and governing the northern district had become a revolving door.

Cárdenas tried once more, this time settling on yet another general, Rodolfo Sánchez Taboada, whose only apparent blemish lay in his complicity in the assassination of the national hero, Emiliano Zapata. As an offering to restless laborers, the president also announced a "New Deal" for Tijuana, jobs in public works and relief payments for their families. At the same time, he stationed additional federal troops in town to dampen thoughts of disturbance. Finally, he hinted that limited gaming might be allowed at Agua Caliente—at least, he was thinking about the possibility.[17]

SIDE EFFECTS

Closure of Agua Caliente had caused a temporary dip in Tijuana's tourism, but buoyed by the exuberant, well-attended international exposition of 1935 in neighboring San Diego, whose visitors relished a detour to foreign exotica, the Mexican border town's restaurants and bars, curio shops and dance halls, girlie and jazz joints once again boomed. The surge involved, as usual, only four or five "tourist" blocks along both sides of Avenida Revolución, but it was enough to sustain the community.

Mexicans, too, made adjustments. While labor unions continued to cry "foul" and demand recompense from the government and severance pay from the resort, workers opened their own small services—gas stations, car repair garages, barbershops, taco stands, laundries, liquor stores, and shoe repair, picture frame, and tailor shops. Street vendors peddled trinkets, *cigarros*, and *chicles*. Rather than sink into despair, they relied on their own ingenuity to start over in new opportunities. These folks appreciated the milieu of their border town and noted that when a person moved from one interior town to another, it usually took eight or so years to get reestablished, but in Tijuana, with its flux of population and job possibilities, an energetic individual needed only three years to own a house and a car. Others felt that if recent events had curtailed vice, driven out indigents and ne'er-do-wells, so much the better.

With the passing of casino gambling south of the border, San Diego police braced for a surge of illegal gambling in their city. They expected gaming paraphernalia (roulette wheels and dice tables) to be secreted across the line and operated in clandestine halls on the U.S. side. Politicians and law enforcement vowed that nothing of that sort would be tolerated but, being who they were, also insured that with proper remuneration it would be.

Less than a month after Agua Caliente shut down, police raided a "palatial residence" imaginatively named the Hoomama Ranch outside Imperial Beach (which abuts the international border in San Diego County) and confiscated Agua Caliente gambling equipment valued at $15,000. Four men arrested as owners of the operation were former employees of the Tijuana resort. All ten rooms in the house featured hand-carved furniture from the resort and, to diminish noise, were heavily draped and carpeted with plush Agua Caliente trappings. Each room was outfitted for a specific game—roulette, blackjack, poker—and when officers arrived, they found each game "banked" for $500 to $700 and ready to receive wagers. Big winners received payment by check to reduce the amount of cash on hand.

A lookout guarded the house, which was surrounded by a high fence topped with barbed wire. Officers captured him in the raid. But it was not as if the lavish gambling hall were tucked out of sight or clients (or law enforcement) needed special instructions or a map to find it. At one corner of the compound stood a tall pole with a blue light on top which, when lit during working hours, could be seen for two miles.[18] Police saw the beacon as well as customers. Judging by the circumstances, no snitch caused this raid. Most likely it resulted from a missed or contested payment to officialdom. With Agua Caliente's demise, more modest but still swanky replicas of its casino continued to sprout up on both sides of the international line.

COUP DE GRÂCE

For the next two and a half years, Agua Caliente struggled to stay alive. In news accounts, Cárdenas seemed to waffle on the resort's future. He never intended to change course, however, and only wished to ease the pain of those discharged and avoid their hostility. To onlookers, he may have seemed indecisive, but, after all, the president had more pressing challenges on his mind. Armed insurgencies dotted the country's interior, while other rebels threatened invasion from the U.S. border. His experiment with socialized, practical education (including some classes on sexual reproduction) had reignited the bloody Cristero war, while powerful foreign oil companies brazenly resisted union demands endorsed by his government. Other labor-management negotiations erupted in violence, and the nation's economy flagged. Moralization squabbles in tiny Tijuana paled by comparison. Yet the president in early 1937 offered some relief to the border town. He would allow Agua Caliente to reopen but with restricted gambling. Roulette, craps, and blackjack—the most profitable games for owners —remained outlawed, but he approved other betting.

Baron Long thought the president's idea worth a three-month experiment. To him it was the camel's nose under the tent, a prelude to the resumption of all accustomed gambling. Horse and dog races would be resumed on Labor Day weekend, along with legal games of chance such as billiards, chess, bowling, and dominoes, which involved human skills rather than pure luck. Long settled money issues with the unions, agreed to a closed shop, rehired hundreds of employees, poured $100,000 into refurbishing the plant, and opened on schedule to swarms of movie celebrities, political dignitaries, business magnates, and social elites, along with more ordinary sightseers and gawkers.

The bud, however, did not blossom. Without gambling's big money-makers, Long claimed the resort could not make a go of it, and at the end of the month he reclosed the premises. Laid-off workers demanded severance pay in accordance with law, but owners claimed the place had been re-opened only as an experiment, not as employment defined in codes. The case went to labor arbitration courts, and the outraged unions threatened violence and hounded the president for help.

Then, in the midst of escalating turbulence, Long boldly announced an agreement with the government to allow unrestricted gambling in Agua Caliente's casino. With whom he pulled strings, if anyone, is not known. Bribes remained commonplace, or the daring declaration could have been one of his periodic trial balloons. Regardless, an exasperated Cárdenas stated he knew nothing of any such arrangement.

The president ran out of patience. Enough was enough. He put his foot down on December 18, 1937, and expropriated in the name of the nation all but the racetrack at the troubled resort and ordered the entire complex redesigned as an industrial trade school meant mainly for sons of low-income workers who had lost their jobs at Agua Caliente. Mexico would pay off the owners in bonds over the next ten years. As far as he was concerned, the world-famed resort was without question or hope of further review a dead cock in the pit.[19]

The final curtain, however, had not yet fallen on this astonishing drama.

REBELLION IN TIJUANA

Following the expropriation, Tijuana seethed and then, on the day after New Year's 1938, exploded. Some four hundred of Agua Caliente's shutout workers took matters into their own hands, occupied the resort, and pro-posed to make a living by running parts of it themselves. As described by the sympathetic *San Diego Sun,*

> The workmen, their wives and children trailing after them, marched into the spacious grounds and said they would hold the resort until they were provided new jobs in protest to the government seizure.

Eight men were posted at the padlocked gates to the ground, and they told reporters that they intended to stay until removed forcefully by soldiers. Carrying their possessions in bandana handkerchiefs, the workers and their families trudged along the three-mile route from Tijuana [town center] to Caliente last night [January 2, 1938] and turned into the grounds.

Waving from staffs a few carried were the flaming red flags of CROM, a labor union [a confederation of the town's syndicates]. They forced entrance to numerous small bungalows, laid down their bundles, and made themselves at home.

The small, expensively furnished cottages became the temporary homes of people of whom some have lived all their lives in windowless, dirt-floored huts along the Tijuana River bank. Bare feet of scores of children pattered over the thick rugs. Soft, heavily cushioned chairs held in comfort men who formerly entered the cottages with trays on their hands.[20]

The unions proposed to run the bar, dining room, spa, and souvenir shops as a cooperative. The government could use the golf links as a landing strip for military aircraft. Should their demands not be met, the workers threatened to loot every building on the grounds, and they professed no fear of the army: "Let the army come. They have only twenty eight soldiers. We have 400 people here and 5,000 more in [downtown] Tijuana."[21]

Then they began to dismantle the premises. The company had planned to remove a million dollars' worth of liquor and furnishings from the holding, but the workers beat them to it. During the first week of occupation, they consumed $4,000 worth of food and liquor. The government tried to assuage their fury by offering them work in converting the complex into the technical high school ordered by the president, and afterward guaranteed them farms or jobs in public works. The proposition split the protesters: some wanted immediate work to support their families, and others demanded more benefits and stood firm.

Cárdenas recognized the split and squelched any idea of a cooperative; he wanted Agua Caliente closed for good and a school at the site. When visited by a delegation of dissidents, the president cordially received them but paternalistically advised them to turn to farming. The workers chafed at the rebuke; they did not want to farm.[22]

Then a second heavy blow fell. On January 24 Tijuana's labor conciliation board rejected the union's request for severance pay, agreeing with Agua

Caliente's management that the brief reopening had been designated a trial period, not subject to severance rules. The decision solidified working-class people throughout town. Four days later, some five thousand irate union people, headed by "mourners" carrying a coffin draped in black which bore the sign, "Labor laws in Mexico are dead," paraded to a mass meeting in the center of town where speaker after speaker excoriated the government for its failure to assist Agua Caliente's former workers. They called for the resignation of the labor board and a general strike. Union members should not pay taxes, or utility bills, and should not send their children to school. They would demonstrate day and night, shouting slogans, firing firecrackers, banging on pots and pans outside the municipal building. The strident challenge to authority could not have been more clarion.[23]

Cárdenas counseled patience for the rank and file but his own had worn thin. He gruffly told disgruntled workers throughout the country that he could not attend to all their issues, "because there are many problems in the nation; not only labor but some of international scope," meaning the titanic battle with international oil moguls. Then he scolded the proletarians: "You laborers do not realize that yours is not the only problem in the country, and that the peasant class lives in the same situation that prevailed years ago—a situation of misery."[24]

Tijuana's workers listened but scoffed at the brush-off. They were not bluffing. Workers occupied the main interior patio of the town's city hall (municipal palace) on February 9, 1938. Fidgety soldiers patrolled the fringes of the contentious crowd but dared not interfere. The town approached open rebellion against the state.

The general strike never materialized as envisioned by the militants, but workers set up camp in one corner of the city hall's quadrangle, where their red-and-black battle flags staked out their territory and emphasized their defiance. During the daytime supporters sent in food, bedding, and other supplies to the women and children stationed there, while men manned the post at night. Further fissures in union membership developed over such a blatant challenge to authority, but the leadership held firm.

Then a ghastly tragedy intensified strife, and much blood flowed.

On Sunday evening, February 13, 1938, an eight-year-old girl was savagely raped and murdered in Tijuana. The killer nearly decapitated her with a shard of glass. Next day, authorities arrested a twenty-four-year-old Mexican soldier garrisoned in town as the main suspect. Urged on by disgruntled union leaders, an outraged mob stormed the old military fortress near the center of the city where the soldier was being interrogated, vowing to lynch him. Fire bombs ignited the interior of the structure, but with fixed bayonets the army held protestors at bay. Authorities announced the soldier had confessed but that hardly dampened the ardor of the crowd. Night fell with the army in only tenuous control of an insurgent populace.

The conflagration reignited the following morning when, after warning union demonstrators in the quadrangle to leave, the mob marched on city hall, ransacked the premises, set the structure afire, and then withdrew. Soldiers retook the smoldering, largely destroyed building and formed a cordon around its perimeter, facing the rioters, who tossed rocks and insults, surging forward then backing off, while the army threatened to shoot them down if they got too close. Then the soldiers opened fire.

Rioters fell, dead and wounded; comrades dragged them up side streets and into homes, so a body count became impossible. The firepower of the army, however, soon sobered the rioters, and an uneasy calm settled over town. Meanwhile, the nation's security apparatus, up to the president himself, readied a response: the power of the national government must be demonstrated, and the murder case quickly resolved. The administration accomplished both with an orchestrated execution of the soldier.

In every way, this was an extraordinary execution. It took place in a federal territory where capital punishment had been abolished and was a staged outdoor, public execution, in a country which, in an earlier nod to "civilization" and "modernity," had banished such gruesome public displays. Executioners, furthermore, fulfilled the ritual using the detested, extralegal, and internationally damned *Ley Fuga*, whereby a prisoner is shot down from behind while allegedly trying to escape. Many authorities used the *Ley Fuga* to rid themselves of a popular outlaw, to spare themselves a potentially embarrassing political trial, or, more simply, as a terror tactic, but they normally did so at some hidden, out-of-the-way spot where the deed could not be easily traced and blame assigned. In this case, however, the state broke the mold.

As more than a thousand people gathered to watch and newsmen took pictures, soldiers forced the terrified soldier to run "for his freedom" across a municipal cemetery where firing squads composed of his military comrades obediently shot him down. Three times the mortally wounded soldier struggled up and staggered forward only to be knocked down by yet another volley of shot. Then he pitched forward in death. Some in the silent crowd thought that manner of execution unnecessarily cruel and unjust.

The execution had a peculiar aftermath. Within the next few days onlookers visited the soldier's grave and reported "signs" they construed as Divine presence: blood oozed from the site, and the soldier's *ánima*, his spirit, protested his innocence and cried out for revenge. According to their faith, those who die suddenly and unjustly sit closest to God, and the soldier, whose name was Juan Castillo Morales, even if guilty of rape and murder, had suffered a hurried trial and an unconscionably merciless execution. The devoted thought him blessed and erected a shrine at the site, renamed the victim *Juan Soldado* (John the Soldier), and asked him to intercede with the Lord for help and favors. Miracles occurred, they said, just as pilgrims continue to claim at the shrine today. "*Juanito*" is said to be "*muy milagroso*" and represents one of the most remarkable popular canonizations in all Christendom.[25]

This confluence of exceptional events tolled a final death knell for Agua Caliente. Within months of the heartbreaking death of the little girl and the subsequent ceremonial execution of the soldier, Cárdenas poured sufficient relief and public works money into Tijuana to create jobs for union members and soften their animosity toward his regime. Despite the demise of the casino, the racetrack floundered along under new ownership headed by Gene Normile, a well-known entrepreneur in racing circles, attracting the immortal Seabiscuit for its 1938 season. Tourist dollars steadily flowed to Tijuana, even if the spenders lacked the star quality that had surrounded Agua Caliente. Some lamented the passing of the *Grand Dame*, because she had put the town on the map; others were just as glad to see such a flashy gringo showgirl disappear.

Prohibition, The Border, Mobsters, Reformers, Refugees from Klondike Fever, Cars and Radios, Naughty Tijuana, Westward Migrants, Changing Values, Outlandish Fads and Fashions, Breaking Old Bonds, Imagined Prosperity—all generated in a specific epoch—melded to create a fantasia called Agua Caliente. As with all such ventures, it concealed warts, wrinkles, and blemishes under the glitzy makeup. Even Camelots carry a timeline with a closing date.

Agua Caliente's end came so abruptly—thriving one day and shut the next —that it was bound to create shock, disbelief, protest, a yearning for its return as well as welcome goodbyes. The splendid resort's time, nonetheless, had come. Prohibition had ended, along with bans on racetrack betting in California and elsewhere. Casino gambling at Palm Springs (illegal but countenanced) satisfied Hollywood's gaming needs, while plans for a legal Las Vegas strip only awaited big-time investors. Not surprisingly, organized crime showed interest. The Depression had quelled many enthusiasms of the Twenties as new war clouds gathered over Europe, diverting attention and creating new concerns. Although masked by a glimmering façade, when closed by presidential edict, Agua Caliente was already fading into comforting nostalgia.

What Ever Happened To?

The passing of Agua Caliente left hardly a ripple. Patrons pursued their pleasures in other newly inaugurated, equally attractive venues around Los Angeles and Las Vegas, where movie stars and other entertainers still shone. Tourists visited those joy palaces and yet remained within easy striking distance of the riddles and delights of bawdy Tijuana. Elites simply crossed one gathering spa off their lists and added another. Tijuanenses, meanwhile, turned the page to the next chapter. Once the shock of their destructive rampage had worn off and dissipated and their outrage with government been ameliorated, they settled into the satisfactions and woes of daily routines.

Of course, Agua Caliente was not forgotten. It faded softly, instead, into remembrance nourished by imagination, where it resides today.

MOVING ON

Transformation of the resort into a technical school occurred overnight, as if the government sought to certify the closure, dramatize its practical education program, and provide the border town with a new symbol of which it could be proud. If the once stylish, lush grounds of the resort retreated somewhat into their original high desert terrain and scrub vegetation, the structures, built to be permanent (as opposed to the temporary buildings of most world's fairs), remained in reasonable physical condition. With the knocking out of some walls, the string of distinctive hotel rooms became a plain student dormitory, and the expansive car garage a vocational classroom for prospective tinsmiths, auto mechanics, carpenters, and electricians. Workers refitted the casino as the student center—a sumptuous one at that—for hanging out and amusement (dominos, pool, and cards, minus any reminders of high-stakes gambling). Comfortable bungalows became temporary housing for faculty; the first-class laundry and modern kitchen still served the complex, while groundskeepers converted the greyhound oval into soccer, baseball, and other sports fields. The only new structure on campus housed a dozen modern classrooms; all else on the "Técnico" campus was fashioned from what had once been called the Monte Carlo or Deauville of the Americas.

The Instituto Tecnológico de Tijuana opened in October 1939. Some eight hundred students joined a faculty which included distinguished Spanish academics who had fled fascist persecution in their homeland and been welcomed in Mexico. Cárdenas himself asked the refugees to help out at the new Técnico. Mexicans everywhere enthusiastically praised their president for transforming a North American gambling den into a Mexican educational and cultural center.[1]

The Border Barons already had one foot out the door when the closure edict arrived. They hardly felt the sting of expropriation. By then, or soon after, they had sold their stock in the company. All along they had been laundering their earnings in real estate, cattle, breweries, mercantile and movie houses, hotels, banks, and myriad other businesses that caught their attention. The Barons attempted to enlist the U.S. State Department in recovering their losses, but in accordance with the spirit of the Good Neighbor Policy, heightened by the outbreak of the Second World War and the necessity to maintain amicable relations with its southern neighbor, the government declined any assistance. The company sold off what remained of the resort's furnishings and liquor for a bargain $140,000. Stockholders lost everything, lawsuits proliferated, but few settlements resulted. When the enterprise tried to sell its gaming equipment to outlets in Los Angeles, local law enforcement objected and blocked the sale, so the owners donated the entire batch to Hollywood studios for props in movies. Some are still in use for period pictures.[2]

WIRT'S HANDICAPS

While he also juggled numerous real estate properties in Southern California, Wirt Bowman concentrated on business holdings around his hometown of Nogales, Arizona, where he bought sizable cattle ranches to the north. After his first wife committed suicide in 1934, he married a pretty young dancer from one of his cabaret shows, a union unannounced until the dancer was about to give birth to their first child.[3]

Wirt was wealthy, but also anxious and frustrated. He had long been a leader in the state's Democratic Party, a delegate to the party's national convention with close friends like Jim Farley, patronage chief and postmaster general in the new Roosevelt administration, but the ultimate appointment he sought—ambassador to Mexico—eluded him. He was already in his mid-sixties and time was running out.

The controversial case for and against the self-assertive Bowman undoubtedly seeped into many crannies of party politics, but his stubborn standoff with the Bureau of Internal Revenue over taxes due certainly did not help him. The Calles "loan" that explained additional income turned out to be bogus and comical. Arizona's senator, Carl Hayden, tried to intervene on Bowman's behalf with the Bureau's commissioner on several occasions, with no success. The agency suspected additional tax evasion by the Democratic National Committeeman from Arizona and yearned to investigate, but party politics deterred them. Delinquent tax claims, however, continued to dog Wirt's political ambitions.

So did inferences that he had traded with the enemy during the First World War. Although J. Edgar Hoover had cleared him of such duplicity, Bowman could not get the charges expunged short of a special act of Congress. Therefore, every time he sought an appointment from the administration, his record was reviewed and the taint reemerged. Wirt pleaded that he had a family (six children by his two wives) and that he did not want his peccadilloes to tarnish their legacy. Despite contacts in high places around the nation's capital, he never could get his dossier cleansed.

Underscored by Bowman's $10,000 donation to the new president's successful campaign, supporters flooded the White House in 1933 with recommendations for the ambassadorship, mentioning his fluent Spanish and long dealings with influential Mexicans. Wirt's friend and fellow Border Baron, Abelardo Rodríguez, now president of Mexico, also endorsed him. Where he ranked, if at all, on Roosevelt's list of candidates for the post is not known. Certainly, his attachment to gambling was generally well known, and the tax and trading charges were part of his official record. They alone were enough to disqualify him, but they probably did not matter. Tradition (and common sense) had it that no ambassador to Mexico should come from territory carved from the southern republic as a result of the Mexican War. Bowman argued that harsh sentiments caused by that catastrophic conflict had been ameliorated by time, but he knew differently.[4]

Roosevelt, who insisted on naming his own ambassadors, soon asked his former Navy boss, Josephus Daniels, to take on the significant and sensitive post, and during his tenure Daniels defused much of the tension between the two countries and otherwise distinguished himself as one of America's finest foreign ambassadors. Bowman was left a disappointed bridesmaid, but defeat did not bank his ambition.

When Daniels indicated in 1940 that he might soon resign, Bowman again pushed for the appointment. Hayden once more spearheaded the drive. Wirt wrote the senator in his quest for vindication and recompense:

> You know, Carl, what I have been to the Party in this State since 1904. I believe I have given the Party at least $30,000 since 1932. . . . I have never had one iota of recognition from the National Democratic Party.
>
> You know, Carl, of the dirty work that has been done by government employees and others against my reputation in Washington since 1918, all of which [he wished] has finally been cleared up; I also paid a large amount of income tax that I did not owe [the BIR proved differently], which I presume squares me with that department, too
>
> Nothing better could be done for me than receive this appointment . . . , just to show that the work I have done for my Party and for the State of Arizona has not been ignored.[5]

The campaign for the appointment was strident. Bowman visited Vice President Henry Wallace several times; petitions from civic and political groups, Washington insiders, and Democratic Party leaders inundated the administration. Hayden pulled strings, but Roosevelt did not bend. Wirt's good friend, Jim Farley, wrote him frankly, "I feel the President will not appoint you to the position. I have nothing to base this on except that my own guess is he will appoint someone more nationally known. . . . In this particular crisis [the Second World War], he will want to appoint a national character."[6] Farley misjudged the basis of the appointment, but the result was the same for Wirt.

Bowman's relentless bid for the ambassadorship ended in March 1941 when Hayden had a private conversation with the president. The senator reiterated Wirt's qualifications for the position, and Roosevelt replied that he had "no doubt about the truth of what I said but that an Ambassador to any foreign country was his personal representative and that in these critical times he is compelled to rely on men that he deems best fitted to express his views to foreign governments." The president seems to have known more about Bowman than expressed to the senator. In sum, he did not want Wirt as his "personal representative," and added that he had "fully made up his mind as to whom he was going to appoint" and it was not going to be Bowman.[7]

Wirt, disgruntled but resigned, retreated as gracefully as he could and announced that he was no longer a candidate for the ambassadorship, and when Daniels resigned, Roosevelt transferred his Cuban ambassador, George S. Messersmith, a career foreign service officer, to Mexico.

The Democrats tossed Bowman a bone two years later and named him Collector of Customs in his hometown of Nogales. Even that proved controversial. Some thought the appointment was like putting a fox in the henhouse. When considering Bowman for the job, the administration asked the renowned intelligence unit of the BIR to check into and update Bowman's financial background. The agency responded with a scathing report. After outlining Wirt's lengthy, contentious struggle with the Bureau, it found "reason to believe that improper returns may have been filed by this taxpayer for the years 1936 to 1941, which were not examined by revenue agents." It recommended that consideration of the customs appointment be shelved and that the case be referred back to the intelligence office for investigation of the later returns. Criminal proceedings beckoned but were not pursued.[8]

In "other information" about Bowman, the unit noted that in a personal letter to Roosevelt, a resident of Phoenix had asked that the customs appointment be barred because Wirt had made his fortune "running gambling and brothel houses in Mexico." Furthermore, the nation's war censorship board reported Wirt in touch with John S. Alessio, manager of a Tijuana bank, who "is reliably reported to be currently receiving Nazi propaganda." (Alessio, popularly acclaimed "Mr. San Diego" and "Mr. Tijuana," in 1953 became director of the refurbished Agua Caliente racetrack and eighteen years later went to prison for tax evasion. Any earlier suggestion of a Nazi connection was disproved or forgotten.)[9]

Regardless of his obvious shortcomings, this time politics prevailed, and Bowman received the customs post, which he resigned after three years.

His vanity had been served and party loyalty rewarded. He died on April 20, 1949, of a heart attack at the age of seventy-five in Tucson, where he had retired, one of the wealthiest men in Arizona.[10]

CROFTON'S REPOSE

Jimmy Crofton's body, so broken in the plane accident, never healed, yet he kept working with that sort of boundless, youthful energy that had made him one of California's six millionaires.[11] With casino as well as racetrack ventures behind him, he formed a partnership in a San Diego brewery, invested in Oklahoma oil and gas, as well as cattle ranching in central California, and zealously pursued his accustomed womanizing, luxurious automobiles (Cadillacs were his favorites), stately living, and big-name socializing. He also bought, sold, raised, and raced thoroughbred horses. His best mount, Special Touch, ridden by Willie Shoemaker and Johnny Longhren, earned more than $1 million around 1950. Then he lost $80,000 on a 24 to 1 shot, for him more a boast than a regret.[12]

Ranching became Jim's passion in the 1930s and 1940s. The self-taught rancher owned seven tracts outside Bakersfield totaling more than one hundred thousand acres, where he ranched thousands of cattle, cut timber, and prospected for oil. He got started in the cattle business by bribing border agricultural agents to turn the other way while he railroaded herds of tick-infested cattle from northern Mexico across the Arizona line and on to Bakersfield. Once on his land, he drove the animals into pools laced with DDT to kill the ticks, pastured them for months on grassy slopes, and then transported the cows to his ranch below San Diego for fattening on highly nutritious dregs (soaked barley seeds) from his brewery. The cattle gained 200–500 pounds a month (good for flavor, bad for arteries) at a time when they sold by the marbled pound. Some called it force-feeding; others, good business.[13]

Ranch workers remember him as a tough taskmaster who demanded a full day's work but paid minimum wages. When one hand stood before him with his forlorn wife and three grubby children and asked for a pay raise, Jim said, "I don't know that I could do that. I didn't make them kids. Why should I pay for them?"[14]

Many lads driven west by the Great Depression found work on Crofton's ranch. They complained that their boss cut costs on their food and billeting, and refused to replace worn-out gear and equipment with more modern, automatic implements. "If it's not running well, buy the part that will fix it," was his motto.[15]

Maybe Crofton was not cheap, but just had his priorities. He threw raucous parties for celebrities at the ranch, although Jim drank only an occasional whiskey; his niece remembers riding horseback with Clark Gable. Intellectuals were not especially welcome; he distrusted educated people, and thought formal learning, along with politics, a waste of time. Jim read little, only the *Wall Street Journal* to review business trends. He did not know a van Gogh from a Picasso, and the only painting in his house was a portrait of his last wife, Loretta.[16]

Jim treated his women lavishly, if not always well. He married three times but had no children. When divorced from Vera, his childhood sweetheart, he wed the Mexican movie star, Mona Rico, who was so frightfully injured with him in the plane accident. He bought her an exquisite platinum and diamond bracelet for $2,000, but, typically, had to be sued by the jeweler for payment. Jim called Mona his "Mexican spitfire," but she proved too fierce for him, and they divorced after a year of sparring. Then in 1939 he married a Ziegfield girl, Loretta, more than twenty years his junior, and they remained together for the rest of his life. Vera received half his property in her divorce settlement, and Mona Rico agreed to $500 monthly alimony as her due.

In 1948 Crofton bought an idyllic 40-acre ranch in California's San Fernando Valley, near Northridge. He paid $48,000 to the cantankerous movie producer Samuel Goldwyn and his wife, the vocalist Gloria Simms, and settled into a gentrified semi-retirement. His home was not sumptuous but a dignified, two-story ranch house with stables, a barn, and a racetrack he no longer used. Elizabeth Taylor frequently visited. Jim sold off most of his thoroughbreds to save the cost of their upkeep and sold his cattle ranches because he detested paying taxes on them. Crofton had not turned frugal but spent according to his moods and judgments.[17]

As his legs, broken in the plane crash, deteriorated, he installed an elevator to carry him between floors of his home. His health failed further by 1960, and a stroke confined him to a wheelchair. His family spent $60,000 to $80,000 a year to keep him alive, but on June 21, 1968, he died of heart failure at seventy-three. Under the terms of his will, eighteen blood relatives received annual payments from a trust he established for them until their deaths; two still do so. Loretta inherited half the estate and died in 1995 with property worth $12 million.[18]

THE PITCHMAN

Baron Long retained his role and reputation as an innovative, glad-handing promoter with a touch of class and a colorful past. He leased the struggling, $15-million Los Angeles Biltmore, largest hotel on the West Coast, for twenty-five years in 1933. The Baron then proclaimed (as only he could) the Depression over, the country healed, and turned the Biltmore into a lustrous magnet for celebrities, politicians, social elites, and foreign dignitaries—the same sort of crowd attracted to Agua Caliente. He envisioned a chain of hostelries dominating Southern California: the U.S. Grant, the Biltmore, and the Tijuana resort. The latter ran afoul of Mexican politics, and he squabbled with the Grant family over ownership rights and in 1944 sold his stake in that grand enterprise for $3 million to another hotel magnate.[19]

The Baron's special touch was immediately felt at the Biltmore. He lowered room rates and opened the Rendezvous, a daytime dance hall, from noon to six P.M., with $1 luncheons. It flourished, even if at the expense of his customers' afternoon work habits and obligations. Evening diners filled the even more attractive Biltmore Bowl (capacity one thousand guests), which at opening featured Hal Roberts and his Student Prince Orchestra, along with vaudeville acts and song and dance extravaganzas. It was Long re-creating his Vernon Club days only on a much grander stage. The hotel became famous for its Hollywood Nights, charity fundraisers, masked balls, and Academy Awards evenings.[20]

At the Vernon, Long had ballyhooed the Hawaiian Room with its hula girls and luaus. At the Biltmore, he created Little Paris, with French furniture, imported French food, charming French checkroom girls and waiters. A French chef with an unusually high hat, carried raw cuts of meat on trays around the dining room and invited customers to take their pick.[21]

Ever the grandstander, he leased his 120-foot yacht, the *Norab* (Baron spelled backwards), to the military for a dollar a year during the Second World War. General Douglas McArthur used it as his Pacific headquarters. Afterward, it became a hospital ship for Australians.[22]

Long was well known among patrons of Deauville and the Grand Prix auto race, but most recognized for his early escapades—racing a jalopy against Barney Oldfield, promoting boxing matches for Jim Jeffries, bringing semi-pro baseball to the West Coast—all recorded and often exaggerated in Damon Runyon's columns or the *Los Angeles Times*'s popular "In

Other Times." Baron Long told stories about those "Other Times" like no one else and made you wish you were there. He died on February 18, 1962, at seventy-eight in the Biltmore and, as was his wont, in his will left monetary gifts to 106 relatives and friends.[23]

THE RICHEST BARON

The "behind the scenes" Baron, Abelardo Rodríguez, discreetly dropped out of national politics in the decade following his brief presidency and turned to a life of travel, leisure, and property management. One of his trips took him to the Soviet Union, and he later likened communism to slavery. He scorned Fidelismo (he called Fidel Castro "crazy and irresponsible"), which endeared him to most American diplomats and Latin American dictators. The United States awarded him its Legion of Merit; the University of California, Berkeley, an honorary doctorate; and the City of New Orleans, its Theodore Brent Award as Latin America's outstanding leader. The *San Diego Union* tabbed him "Freedom's Champion." Throughout the accolades, Abelardo keep fingering his investment portfolio.[24]

Rodríguez was the most entrepreneurial of all the business-minded generals spawned by the Revolution. (Looting, confiscation, forced loans, filching, kidnapping, rustling, and wanton lawlessness seem to energize the entrepreneurial spirit.) With investment capital garnered from Tijuana vice while a Border Baron, Rodríguez developed a thick investment file. He founded forty-one new companies from 1940 to 1950 alone, and in the next decade twenty more, some of which resulted from mergers and reorganizations. In all, by then his name was connected to eighty-four firms, mostly in fish, cinema, and banks, but also hotels, wineries, and airports. Armed with a government concession to develop Mexico's fishing industry from Ensenada halfway down the Pacific coast to Manzanillo, in 1941 alone he bought nine trawlers from Puget Sound dealers, built a dozen more in Guaymas, established fish-processing plants and canneries on Cedros Island in the Sea of Cortez and at El Sauzal, just north of Ensenada, founded refrigeration plants in Guaymas and Topolobampo, and refitted a ferry boat that once plied San Francisco Bay to serve as a shrimp factory.[25]

The ex-president and businessman extraordinaire sold off most of his Mexican investments in 1955 (it was said to have been the biggest banking transaction in the country's history), and concentrated on expanding and modernizing his crown jewel, El Sauzal, overseen from his nearby stately family mansion (now a school). The boy who grew up not unlike any other kid on the block, who made pennies beating other lads at shooting marbles and spinning tops, and quarters selling homemade handicrafts to the children of elites, became a millionaire many times over thanks to Agua Caliente's bounty and Mexican-style business acumen, both his own and that of his advisors.

In 1943, with his political party's dynasty every more firmly grounded, he was appointed governor of his home state of Sonora. There he founded the state university and favored his birthplace, Guaymas, with public works, but the citizenry generally vilified him for his failure to do much else. Abelardo's heart was in business, mainly his own.

Citing poor health, he retired from the governorship in 1948, and for the next two decades he managed his investment folder. When he died in 1967, at seventy-seven, he was said to be the wealthiest individual in Mexico, and among the richest in the world. The eulogies at his funeral attended by thousands were expansive and magnificent.

None of them mentioned Agua Caliente or called the deceased a Border Baron.[26]

JOE SCHENCK REVEALED

Although not one of the founding Barons, the movie mogul Joe Schenck had large stockholdings in the venture, regularly gambled for high stakes there, and with the departures of Bowman and Crofton became president of the Jockey Club and a board member of the hotel.

He was president of Twentieth Century Pictures when it merged with Fox Films in 1935 to become gigantic Twentieth Century–Fox. The transaction produced significant capital gains for Schenck, and his annual salary as chair of the board of the new combine hugely increased, creating a substantial tax liability. The film czar paid no federal taxes in 1933 and only $7,136 the following year, but his taxable earnings for 1935 were $242,005 and for the next year, $321,834. Faced by enormous tax payments, Schenck and his chief accountant cooked the books. They claimed $275,970 in losses for the sale of Agua Caliente stock and another nearly $90,000 in unreimbursed business expenses.[27]

Red flags waved at the Bureau of Internal Revenue, and following several years of investigation, indictments led to closely watched trials. The government showed that Schenck never really disposed of his Agua Caliente racetrack stock but sold it for minor amounts to two longtime friends and even forwarded them the money to buy it. He later voted his holdings through proxies.[28]

As for the business deductions, they financed Schenck's gambling, his outlays at yacht and country clubs, bills at spas and resorts, flowers and dinners for girlfriends, day-to-day living expenses (groceries, hardware, laundry bills, plumbing and carpentry repairs, salaries to servants, and drugstore bills for toothpaste, playing cards, aspirin, and razor blades). Most of these "business" expenditures had been repaid by Twentieth Century–Fox. "Schenck's entertaining was closely confined to his relatives and intimate friends [like Harpo Marx], including gambling and women companions," the government charged, "and his frequent trips were vacation jaunts to resorts for the benefit of his health or mere recreation."[29] He claimed in 1936 to be making a movie on his yacht, *The Caroline*, but brought no camera aboard. He listed his guests as crew, claiming them as a business expense; Irving Berlin and wife, Marx, and Douglas Fairbanks Sr. and wife supposedly had swabbed the decks.

In the end, Schenck did himself in. His office kept detailed records for all expenditures, including receipts. Only the gambling winnings and losses were in cash and escaped mention in his detailed account books. The court sentenced Schenck to three years in prison in 1941 and fined him $20,000. His appeal failed. But Joe vowed never to go to jail. His escape was a plea bargain that laid bare the mob's hold on Hollywood.[30]

THE MOBSTERS

In 1934 a Russian immigrant named Willie Bioff, friendly with Lucky Luciano, Frank Costello, and the Los Angeles mobster Jack Dragna, had grabbed control of the weak International Alliance of Theatrical State Employees and began to pressure the movie moguls for favors and protection money. If his demands were not met, the union could shut down Hollywood production, and the Depression-burdened industry already trembled on an unsteady foundation. When it came to profits, moviemaking was never a sure bet.

Bioff levied $50,000 a year per major studio and $25,000 for each independent. Joe Schenck entertained the corrupt labor leader at his home, bought him stock in Consolidated Oil, Continental Can, and Twentieth Century–Fox, and gave him $95,000 to buy a picturesque Southern California ranch for himself and family. The deals resembled extortion, but they bought labor peace.

The government indicted Bioff for tax evasion and asked Schenck to testify about a $100,000 check he had given the defendant. Payment for what? Joe testified he knew nothing of the check or of Bioff's activities, and the prosecution promptly cited him for perjury. Facing twelve counts of perjury and about to go to prison for tax fraud in 1942, Schenck admitted his ties to Bioff and organized crime (he claimed that he and other studio heads paid the mob out of fear), and had the three years for tax evasion reduced to three year's probation to be served after a year in jail on one count of perjury. A presidential pardon released him after four months.[31]

Schenck paid $432,050 in back taxes and fines. The Academy of Motion Pictures honored him with a life service Oscar in 1952, and he has his star on Hollywood Boulevard. He died at eighty-three in 1961.

COLSON'S PRISONMATE

Lloyd Sampsell, the scholarly looking, highly intelligent bank robber who surrendered in the attempted Folsom Prison break with Marty Colson in 1933, served time in The Hole and then in high security. During the Second World War Sampsell was among prisoners placed in outlying encampments to work on farms; he knew how to work the system. Security was sufficiently lax that Lloyd visited a girlfriend in San Francisco and, when caught, admitted enjoying "unusual privileges" that allowed him to travel unescorted to any number of central California cities on "personal business." The scandal cost Folsom's warden his job.

After spending more than twenty-two years in prison, Sampsell was paroled in 1947 and soon returned to bank robbing. The next year he made the FBI's Ten Most Wanted list for killing a teller while robbing a credit union in San Diego. He celebrated the notoriety by robbing a Los Angeles bank of $8,700. Phoenix police soon identified and arrested the killer. The state tried and the court sentenced Sampsell to die in San Quentin's gas chamber.[32]

Lloyd Sampsell, however, was not yet done with the law. Consulting on the same death row with one of the most famous of all jailhouse lawyers, Caryl Chessman, he wrote brilliant legal briefs that were argued before both the California Supreme Court and the U.S. Supreme Court. He won stays of execution in classic appeals that even won the admiration of prosecutors. "One of the best pieces of work I've ever seen," said Clarence Linn, assistant state attorney general for California. Judges agreed.[33]

His expertise and cleverness, however, ran out on April 25, 1952. "He remained calm to the end, and even showed curiosity about the straps used to pinion his arms and the pellets which release the deadly gas." The execution room accommodated forty spectators, but double that number crowded in to watch Lloyd Sampsell die at age fifty-two.[34]

A CAGED TIGER

Ralph Sheldon was not as brilliant as Sampsell but still a competent jail-house lawyer who challenged the legal bureaucracy forcefully, if with no success. First he appealed his kidnapping conviction, alleging trial errors, but a judge rejected his claims and soon after a prison board denied his plea for parole. He asked the governor in 1939 to commute his sentence and grant him a pardon on grounds of "cruel and unreasonable punishment," specifically that he had received ten-years-to-life, while his accomplices got much lesser terms for the same crime. The governor's Advisory Pardon Board, however, recommended denial, citing the opposition of police chiefs, the district attorney, and the trial judge involved in the Zeke Caress kidnapping case. That judge, Charles S. Burnell of the Superior Court, was vehement: "I believe that this man should no more be turned loose than should a man-killing tiger afflicted with hydrophobia; that he is a menace to the community and should be kept in confinement as long as he lives."[35]

With that sort of vitriol in hand, the governor's executive secretary on August 26, 1940, sent Sheldon a one-line communication: "I regret to inform you that Governor [Culbert L.] Olson has denied your executive clemency, in view of the unfavorable recommendation of the Advisory Pardon Board."[36] No further explanation necessary.

The prisoner, two years later, once again futilely applied for parole. Sheldon undoubtedly would have continued to seek freedom, one way or the other, but on July 4, 1944, he died of a heart attack at Folsom. He was forty-five years old.[37]

ABSOLUTION

Marty Colson's partner in the Dike holdup, Robert Lee Cochran, was by all accounts a model prisoner at San Quentin, where he worked in the boiler and machine shops and fashioned gifts for the prison store; he also contracted tuberculosis during his incarceration. After four denials, the parole board approved his application in 1943, and Cochran went to work as an engineer for the U.S. Army Transport Service. He earned $3,418 a year as a boat captain in the Pacific theater of operations. While he was in prison, his wife, Marian, divorced him, and in 1945 at Port Adelaide, Lee married an Australian, Matija Jean Luketina.[38]

On return to the United States, Cochran worked for a Los Angeles tug-boat company, then in 1960 established his own ship-towing business. He sold it five years later, rejoined his previous company, but was forced to retire in 1972 due to stomach complications from a prior colon cancer operation. Three weeks after new surgery, he was back playing golf.

Throughout these Los Angeles years, his wife did secretarial and administrative work, at one point for the Los Angeles district attorney's office. They had a son, joined the Episcopalian Church, invested in stock, played bridge, and took car vacations. On one occasion Cochran was the luncheon guest of the San Diego sheriff's deputy who had arrested him in the money-car caper, Capt. A. Blake "Blackie" Mason. Lee called Mason his "friend."[39]

Cochran sought executive clemency—the cleansing of his criminal record —from Governor Ronald Reagan in February 1973. "My main reason is my son, who is 17 years old now," he wrote in his petition, "and I am thinking of the effects of my past may have in his future of employment. So far my past has only caused me to try harder to make a fine young man of him and teach him to be a good law-abiding citizen. I coached Little League baseball here for several years, and I tried to teach those boys sportsmanship, as well as how to run the bases and hit. I am thankful to be able to look back on a pleasant relationship with everyone since my big mistake, the arresting officers, Judge, prison officials and all the many Parole officers that I have worn out and caused to retire."[40]

Parole officers reported that "Cochran's adjustment on parole has been exemplary. He has maintained steady employment throughout the years and his wife remains employed as a legal secretary. He has been carried under minimal supervision through his years under parole supervision and there have been no adverse reports. It has been noted that his adjustment during the past number of years defies any criticism, his attitude has been outstanding and his cooperation likewise."[41]

Letters in support of Cochran's request were submitted:

> United Towing Company: "Mr. Cochran was hired to work for our company on December 3, 1946, and is working on a call-in basis at the present time. Mr. Cochran is a gentleman of extremely high integrity, is loyal, dependable, honest and a hard worker."
>
> San Diego County District Attorney: "It was noted that notwithstanding the seriousness of the offense of which the defendant was convicted and im-

prisoned until 1943, that since that time his conduct has been exemplary and constructive. . . . It is the recommendation of this office that the defendant's application for executive clemency be granted."

Gloria Bonadonna (Lee's daughter by his first wife): "I have to tell you that my dad is one great guy who has paid his debt to society and should have this burden removed from his back. . . . As your records must show, I am now 47 years old and I grew up without him. I would like my [half] brother who is 17 years old to have this cloud removed from him, as these things have a way of coming up and his friends may find out which would not be fair to him. I have three children, two boys and a girl, which I have not told. They adore their grandfather, as he has always been good to them and was able to do things for them he was never able to do for me."[42]

Governor Reagan referred clemency requests to the state's Adult Authority board for recommendation. Regarding Cochran, the board wrote the governor on July 17, 1973: "The Adult Authority recommends that Mr. Robert Lee Cochran be granted a pardon on the grounds of rehabilitation: The Adult Authority noted the extended number of years in which Mr. Cochran has maintained an excellent employment program, obtained financial security and has lived crime free."[43]

Some five months later, Cochran received a stunning letter from the governor's legal affairs office:

Governor Reagan has been informed by the Adult Authority that at its meeting held on May 21, 1973, your application for executive clemency was given consideration. It has been determined [by the governor's legal office] to deny your application at this time because of the extreme seriousness of the case.

In view of the foregoing, the Governor will not consider your request at this time.[44]

Note that nothing was said to Cochran about the board's decision to recommend a pardon.

Too little is known of the machinations and considerations given the Cochran appeal by Reagan's legal office, but lying, arrogance, and probably politics were part of the process. The official record includes only two pages, one a brief, undated, unsigned, handwritten summary of the case, with a recommendation to deny, and the other an undated, intra-office memorandum containing short, hand-scribbled comments by members of Reagan's legal staff to James D. Garbolino, the governor's assistant secretary for legal affairs, who then wrote the carefully manipulated letter to Cochran.

The unnamed legal staff member assigned to review the case concluded: "Recommendation. Deny. AA [Adult Authority] recommends grant. The seriousness of the offense accompanied by the sheer brutality and manner in carrying it out—demonstrates total disregard for life of others. Sentence of life imprisonment is mercy enough."

These comments were then circulated to other members of the staff. One, with the signature Jim, wrote cryptically, "There is probably more here than meets the eye" without explaining what "more" meant.

An unsigned comment replied to Jim, "I deny. Don't you think that denial is appropriate?"

"Herb," who sent the memo to Garbolino, wrote the fullest comment: "RTA and I agree we should not pardon or commute. Seriousness of initial offense is the reason. This was a cold-blooded, gangland-type slaying. I sense ties to Johnny Alessio stemming from Agua Caliente and Banco del Pacífico and Bank of Italy."[45]

Herb did not know what he was talking about. There were no ties between Cochran, Colson, and Alessio, who at the time of the money-car heist in 1929 was a seventeen-year-old shoeshine boy in San Diego; he might have just taken a job (the precise day and month is not known but the year was 1929) as a messenger boy at Banco del Pacífico in Tijuana. Fifteen years later he was director of the Agua Caliente racetrack, heavily invested in banking, real estate, cab and tuna companies, hotels, and shopping centers, and was rumored to have mob connections. In 1973 Alessio was convicted of massive tax evasion.

When Herb mentioned Alessio in the memo, that millionaire was serving three years in federal prison and recently had been in the news for bribing guards to permit him unauthorized leave from jail, but nowhere along his twisted way had he been involved with Lee Cochran, who was still faithfully reporting to a parole officer.

For their own reasons, perhaps to protect their boss, the governor, against adverse publicity, or to maintain the administration's hard-nosed image toward crime, or because repentance, rehabilitation, and absolution were concepts beyond their worksheets and political vision, they denied Lee Cochran (who died in 1993 at eighty-nine) the chance to clear his name.

Ghosts

Strolling today across the grounds of the once internationally acclaimed Agua Caliente—Playground of the Western Hemisphere—not much visible evidence of its glorious and celebrated past remains. There was a concerted effort in 1975, endorsed by the then president of the republic, Luis Echeverría, to restore the complex—not all had yet been dismantled. But those bent on its destruction as a symbol of foreign vice and exploitation sacked the place before preservationists could act. Its remaining carved doors, sculpted fountains, staircases, elaborate wall lamps, and marble mosaics found their way into private homes and hands where they now serve as trophies.

Time, scavengers, souvenir hunters, urban encroachment, and the needs of the Técnico for expansion and renovation have taken their toll, but the aura surrounding the place is spellbinding and profound. Scattered touches of its heralded past still kindle one's imagination and curiosity about the fabulous enterprise and its renowned patronage. The tall, thin minaret-like steam plant tower with its brilliant tile work (now restored) at the top, for example, still marks the location, and the oversized swimming pool (now being refurbished for public use) has been rimmed with lovely new tile designs. Artistic, intricately hand-painted tiles imported from Spain still adorn a few decayed walls. Several of the original bungalows which housed distinguished guests are yet in use as modest homes, and, if they have a deep well, these latter-day inhabitants can tap into the primeval waters of Agua Caliente flowing below.

In remembrance of a bygone world, the trademark of Agua Caliente, its elaborate gateway of mixed architectural grandeur, has been reconstructed according to blueprints, but at three-quarter size. It stands as a proud sentry on a steep hill overlooking the old entranceway. No grave marker, it reminds us that what was once a scruffy, little, inconsequential border town, now a pulsating metropolis, has an enduring history.

Many Tijuanenses still consider the resort as it was in its heyday, the city's most memorable historical benchmark, and they honor it at periodic gourmet dinners prepared from one of the hotel's special menus at which guests, including the city's political and cultural leaders, recall the impressiveness and scope of the conglomerate and speak longingly of renovation. Tales told on these commemorative occasions are frequently hilarious, politically piercing, nostalgic, exaggerated, fictitious, poignant, and mysterious. Some say, for instance, that when Agua Caliente closed to patrons, ghosts remained and continue to haunt the premises. How could it be otherwise?

The ghost of a petite, graceful ballerina who danced at Agua Caliente is still said to be shadowing the premises. In one of many versions of her provenance, she was murdered there by a Mexican army general. The precise circumstances are unknown, leaving the entire tale to the mercy of the tellers' imaginations, and since then she has been seeking justice and revenge for the unpunished crime, a common concern of ghosts. Students at the Técnico swear she is still seen, anguished and resolute, appearing first as a wisp of drifting fog, then swirling and transforming into human form, an enchanting ballerina, who beautifully dances for seated guests (also ghosts) dining on one of the resort's former charming patios. She is ethereal.[1]

Not as fanciful and considerably more variable (at times frightening), La Enlutada, the lady in mourning, also prowls the former resort's grounds as well as other sections of Tijuana. She is said to have been the daughter of a Chinese merchant, Zarco, who around 1930 prevented her from marrying the man she loved. She therefore willed herself to die, and in a state of *artículo mortis* (the moment of death), she married her beloved and then died. In her funeral procession, headed by a young girl dressed as an angel, she rode in a handsome horse-drawn coach and was buried with pomp in the town's public cemetery.

The deceased was not heard from for twenty years, and then in 1951, La Enlutada appeared to a taxi driver, as well as to several people on the street, and two or three times in cabarets. What she said, if anything, is not known, but why this sudden restlessness? Perhaps we know: her father, who had frustrated her marriage, died Christmas Day that year.

The story, however, did not end there. A local newspaper in 1963 reported residents mysteriously dying at night, their faces eaten away to the bone. It seems that one evening a lady had answered a knock on her door and encountered the famous La Enlutada, a phantom woman dressed in black, her face hideously eaten away by some malady. The shocked respondent fainted, and La Enlutada hurried away. Soon, however, there were knocks on other doors, and the unwelcome visitors had become two women, and then two women and a man, all with horribly disfigured faces.

Police paid no attention to the outburst until one night the ghostly trio confronted the pregnant wife of the commandant himself at her front door. The woman swooned but did not lose her baby. Investigation led authorities to two women and a man who had recently escaped from a nearby leprosarium (actually a miserable mental hospital) who explained they were starving to death at the hellish institution and had come to town to beg for food. Ashamed of their appearance, they did so at night and ate in hideaways during the day. The conclusion to this particular pitiful drama is unknown, but Las Enlutadas in various guises continue to roam the imagination, and on occasion, the city's streets and the old terrain of the spa.[2]

Ghosts flourish at Agua Caliente in the labyrinth of old tunnels beneath the grounds, once conduits for water, electricity, heat, and now for phantoms. Al Capone's gangster limousine is said to be there, long sought but never found. Técnico students formerly probed the tunnels, but now the underground passages have been placed off-limits. It is also said that the Barons built tunnels from their premises up to and then under the border to outlets in the United States as avenues to transport liquor, revenue, and other taxable or illegal items back and forth, evading the eyes of officialdom.

Wirt Bowman's stately Palm City home was reported to have been connected to Tijuana by a special tunnel, an improbable five-mile stretch. Nonetheless, because of the spectacular tunneling accomplished more recently by the area's narcotics dealers, inhabitants suspect such diggings honeycomb the border region, and that many of today's underground routes are refurbished corridors originally dug in Prohibition's bootlegging days.[3]

Ghosts frequent tunnels, where they hide out to await reappearances among the living, and it is no wonder that Agua Caliente's elaborate underground system harbors them and sustains their mysteries and menaces along with reminiscences of the legendary resort.

Tijuana is much changed since the Jazz Age days of Agua Caliente, but honky-tonks on Avenida Revolución continue to amaze and excite tourists, and Donald Trump started to build a $200-million luxury condo-hotel resort—three twenty-six-story towers—on the Pacific just south of El Monumento, a site once favored by the Border Barons for an extravagant gaming complex. Speculation had it that Trump's Tower One would someday house an elegant casino, but the entire deal collapsed and is now in colossal litigation. Trump and his clients had gambled and lost, but there was never any chance that his project would have attained the grandeur and panache of the former Agua Caliente. Farewell to all that, although a regal image of the sprawling resort is embedded in common remembrance.

Assuredly, the world of the Border Barons is forever lost. Nevertheless, an aura of these colorful, unscrupulous go-getters, along with that of their vain habitués, the mob, and airy wraiths, still hovers over the scanty remnants of the once resplendent, world-famous spa. And it is true that, despite the crafted pretentiousness of the place and the insatiable self-glorification of its owners and most celebrated patrons, one rather wistfully recalls Agua Caliente as a playground one wishes to have known.

Notes

1. THE MOB STRIKES THE BORDER BARONS

1. One mobster outlined the plan when on trial. See County of San Diego Superior Court, Records Division, Civil and Criminal (1929), No. 60783 (microfilm reel C-428), 406–12; hereafter cited as "trial transcript." The plan is fully discussed in chapter 12 and analyzed in chapters 13 and 14. The trial judge's comments on the plan are in chapter 16.

2. *San Diego Union* and *Los Angeles Examiner*, May 22, 1929.

3. The company not only cashed checks for a substantial fee for gamblers but also took personal drafts for liquor to be smuggled back home and for the purchase of luxury duty-free imports sold in tony retail shops on the premises. A good number of checks in this stolen batch represented stock purchases at $10 a share in the fast-growing, high-profit Agua Caliente enterprise. It was commonly thought that management at the complex cashed checks for most anybody, even strangers—"no questions asked—because whether or not the check was good, the company was bound to get its money back from the gaming tables." Actually, the resort maintained an elaborate card-index credit system on its check-cashing clientele. The rule remained, however: make it comfortable for patrons to lose their money. See H. L. Davis, "Three Hells," 264–65.

4. The holdup and its aftermath are reconstructed mainly through detailed accounts in five daily newspapers: *San Diego Union, San Diego Sun, San Diego Tribune, Los Angeles Times,* and *Los Angeles Examiner.* No Tijuana newspapers for the period still exist. In a letter to the author dated March 1, 2005, Steven J. Barard, manager of the Records and Identification Division of the San Diego Sheriff's Department, reported there are no records on the case in police files. The trial transcript has details as does a remembrance piece in the *San Diego Union,* July 28, 1962. A *San Diego Union* reporter, William G. Cayce, covered

the affair from start to finish. He had extraordinary access to the principals involved and later wrote an interesting overview, "The Case against 'Silent' Colson," for *True Detective Magazine*, which ceased publication years ago. A copy of the article, however, exists in the Arthur Hill files of the Pliney Castanian Papers at the San Diego Historical Society.

5. *San Diego Union*, June 22, 1929.
6. Ibid.
7. *San Diego Sun*, May 21, 1929.
8. *San Diego Union*, May 21, 1929.
9. The history of the machine gun is from Helmer, *The Gun That Made the Twenties Roar*, 80–81, 89, and *passim*.
10. "Talks with Readers," *San Diego Sun*, May, 22, 1929.
11. *San Diego Union*, May 25, 1929.
12. *San Diego Tribune*, May 23, 1929.

2. MOBS

1. Repetto, *American Mafia*, 39–40, 46–48, 54–55, 82, 103. Rappleye and Becker, *All American Mafioso*, 61–62. Albert Nathan, "California's Home-Grown Racketeers," *Los Angeles Times*, May 24, 1931. Joe Domanick, *To Protect and Serve* [LAPD], 46–48.
2. *San Diego Union*, June 22, 1929. *San Diego Evening Tribune*, June 28, 1929.
3. "Are Gangsters Building Another Chicago Here?" *Los Angeles Times*, March 29, 1931.
4. *San Diego Union*, December 26, 1930. *Los Angeles Times*, December 25, 1930, and May 9, 1934. *San Diego Evening Tribune*, December 25, 1930.
5. *Los Angeles Examiner*, May 28, 1929.
6. *San Diego Union*, May 25, 1929.
7. *San Diego Union*, June 22, 1929. *San Diego Sun*, June 22, 1929.
8. *San Diego Union*, June 22, 1929.
9. Ibid. *San Diego Evening Tribune*, June 28, 1929.
10. *San Diego Union*, June 22, 1929.
11. *Los Angeles Examiner*, May 28, 1929.
12. *San Diego Union*, June 22, 1929.
13. *Los Angeles Examiner*, May 25, 1929. *San Diego Union*, May 27, 1929.
14. *Los Angles Times*, May 25 and 26, 1929.

3. PLAYGROUND OF THE HEMISPHERE

1. Information about Crofton from interviews with Alvin "Bunker" Daniels, Crofton's nephew, April 30–May 2, at his home in Grass Valley, Calif.
2. Estimates—and that is all they can be—of profits garnered at Agua Caliente

vary but were generally considered to be enormous. Entrepreneurs interested in building luxurious gaming resorts at Rosarito and Ensenada (south of Tijuana on the Pacific coast) used profits at Agua Caliente to make their cases to investors. They claimed that in 1929 the Border Barons and their stockholders had invested $2 million in improvements at the resort, and every dollar spent had resulted in a dollar profit. Stocks had quadrupled in value and $750,000 had been declared in dividends. Bowman's Foreign Club, they said, earned $150,000 monthly, and predicted that with their proximity to the Pacific Ocean, these new ventures would do even better. See "Playas Ensenada y hoteles y lugares de recreo afiliados en Baja California . . . ," 26–27. Maestro Jorge Martínez, researcher at the Instituto de Estudios Históricos at the Universidad Autónoma de Baja California (UABC, Tijuana) kindly loaned me his personal copy of this rare document. I thank him for his generosity. Other estimates of earnings at Agua Caliente appear in Davis, "Three Hells," 259, 266, and in a *Los Angeles Examiner* series that began in mid-August 1929. See also chapter 17.

3. Neil Morgan developed the concept of "tumble weeds" in *Westward Tilt.*

4. There is no substantial single printed account of the ambiance at Agua Caliente, hence the necessity to weave the image from interviews as well as newspaper accounts, magazine articles, pamphlets, photographs, and memorabilia lodged in personal and archival collections. The patio scene described here, for example, is drawn from a photo with cut lines located in the San Diego Public Library, California Room, Vertical Files, Regions: Baja California. The patio is also featured in many Southern California pictorial magazines of the period, most prominently in *Pacific Pictorial* (Los Angeles: Pacific Pictorial Ltd., [1930s]). The *San Diego Union* pictured the splendid patio on September 22, 1929. The best, but still extremely brief, overview of the resort is in Ortiz Figueroa and Piñera Ramírez, *Historia de Tijuana, 1889–1989,* vol. 1, 104–5, 115–18, 123–28; vol. 2, 168–69.

5. *New York Times,* May 16, 1987. Proffitt, *Tijuana,* 170–71. There is a lovely photograph of Rita dancing with her father at Wirt Bowman's Foreign Club in *Southern California, Pictorial Life* 4, no. 4 (1935–36), located in the San Diego Historical Society archives, pictorial files, 1930s.

6. Menus from the resort are in the extensive personal papers and memorabilia on Agua Caliente held by Andre Williams in Tijuana.

7. The liquors and prices are from a booklet, *Unwritten Wonder: Baja California, Territory Mexicana,* published by Agua Caliente in 1933. A copy may be found in San Diego State University Love Library, Special Collections, Vertical Files, "Agua Caliente."

8. From the booklet, *Bottoms Up! Y Como!,* 6, and inside back cover. A copy exists

in San Diego State University Love Library, Special Collections, Vertical Files, "Agua Caliente."

9. Walter Donaldson, "There's a Wah Wah Gal in Agua (A-Wah) Caliente," Donaldson, Douglas & Gamble music publishers, New York, [n.d.]. Ms. Lorna Elliott, assistant at The Dalles (Oregon) Public Library found this musical sheet and a vinyl disk of the melody, while cleaning out the basement of her parents' house being readied for sale. Joanne Ward, an artist and local historian in The Dalles, had the tune transferred to a compact disk and then generously forwarded these items to me.

10. *San Diego Union*, December 26, 1929. *San Diego Sun*, December 29, 1929.

11. Milnor's advertisement is from the Andre Williams collection cited above. See also San Diego Historical Society, Pictorial Files, 1930s, *Southern California, Pictorial Life*, especially 3, no. 4, and 4, no. 2 (1934), and 5, no. 1 (1935).

12. Interview with the niece, Barbara Gunning, March 18, 2005, in her Oceanside, Calif., home.

13. These examples of ballyhoo are from the *San Diego Sun*, December 28, 1929; *Los Angeles Times*, December 19, 1930; Baron Long, "Charm of Old Mexico Idealized at New Agua Caliente Hotel," *San Diego Magazine* (March 1928): 12+; *San Diego Union*, January 1, 1930; and *San Diego Herald*, June 7, 1928.

14. *San Diego Union*, January 1, 1931.

15. *Unwritten Wonder*, booklet, [p. 1].

16. *Bottoms up*, booklet, [p. 1].

17. James, "Agua Caliente: Heaven of the West," 156, 158.

18. Ibid., 158.

19. Davis, "Three Hells," 258–61.

20. San Diego Public Library, California Room, Vertical Files, "Mexico/Baja California, Business Enterprise, Hotel Agua Caliente, *A Trip through Agua Caliente*. Also *San Diego Union*, January 1, 1930; *Los Angeles Times*, March 1, 1929, and December 19, 1930; *San Diego Herald*, September 15, 1932; *Daily Transcript* (San Diego), July 23, 1936; *San Diego Evening Tribune*, August 16, 1939.

21. For one of the many examples of virulent racism in Tijuana see *The Rounder*, the town's English-language newspaper. It wrote on April 9, 1927, "A negro [seen in the tourist area] claims to be Hawaiian and seems like a familiar type of old Kentucky or Louisiana. Police should walk him over the bridge [to the U.S.] for keeps. Eddie [the black's name] cross the line tonight and stay put with your dark skinned wife who is yours and whom you trick rottenly in your attempted daily consorts with white women of diseased minds. Get out!" And in an editorial the same day, "*The Rounder* will not tolerate the appearance of white women with diseased minds to be seen in public with negroes in Tijuana. If

these unfortunate lewd women wish to practice their trade, they must find other places. The Mexican people are against these methods, not to say how Americans feel about it. These smart coons who are under the impression that Mexicans will tolerate them are badly mistaken and the quicker they get away from Tijuana the better for their necks."

Additionally, from the *Calexico Chronicle*, February 16, 1915, "General [Esteban] Cantú [territorial governor of Baja California Norte] appeared to have a special antipathy toward the chocolate-colored race, the majority of the immigrants [U.S. workers coming to Mexicali] being dusky-hued, and walking with a shuffle. . . . The Ethiopians were not alone in their abdication of the Mexicali joy palaces, being accompanied by several Asiatics, among whom figured Chinese and Hindus. Among the polyglot crew was found a Hungarian who got lost in the shuffle."

Finally, a *Nogales* (Arizona) *Herald* headline read on March 16, 1922: "Jap Caught in Nogales (Mexico) with U. S. girl." According to the newspaper, the "Jap," Chicahura Honda, 29, operated a pool room and barbershop in Yuma, Arizona. The lady, Juanita Furst, 25, was from Chicago. They went together to Nogales, Sonora, and U.S. Immigration arrested them returning to the United States. The authorities released her but threatened to charge the "Jap" with a Mann Act violation.

22. *Los Angeles Times*, December 28, 1929.
23. Wayne McAllister videotape. On March 6, 1995, Wayne McAllister's son, Don, videotaped a detailed interview with his father about his experiences as architect of Agua Caliente. Wayne at the time was eighty-seven, animated and sharp, still working as an architect. The interview was conducted at Wayne's home in Pasadena, Calif. Wayne died on March 22, 2000, in Arcadia, Calif. Hereafter the valuable video is cited as "McAllister videotape."
24. McAllister videotape.
25. *San Diego Union*, December 29, 1929. Beltrán, *The Agua Caliente Story*, 35–44.

4. FORTUITOUS BREAKS

1. Cayce, "The Case against 'Silent' Colson," 4.
2. *San Diego Union* and *San Diego Sun*, May 23, 1929.
3. *San Diego Union* and *San Diego Sun*, May 23, 1929.
4. California State Archives (Sacramento), Governor's Office Records, Prison Papers, Corrections-Folsom, Identification Cards, Martin Colson.
5. Trial transcript, 396.
6. Ibid., 395–97.
7. Ibid., 396–97.

8. *Los Angeles Times*, June 19, 20, and 24, October 1, 1924, and February 3, 1925. *Los Angeles Examiner*, June 20 and October 1, 1924.

9. *Los Angeles Times*, June 19, 1924.

10. Ibid.

11. Trial Transcript, 393.

12. Ibid., 394.

13. Ibid., 371. The sentence of "one to twenty-five years" was an indeterminate sentence. The judge left it up to the state parole board to decide when Colson was sufficiently rehabilitated to reenter society. When released, however, he remained on parole for the remainder of his sentence. Colson was thus still on parole when he committed the Dike crime, but there is no indication that he had been reporting to any parole officer since his release from San Quentin.

14. Ibid., 392–400.

15. *San Diego Sun*, May 23, 1929. *San Diego Union*, May 25, 1929.

16. *San Diego Evening Tribune*, May 24, 1929. *San Diego Union*, May 24 and 25, 1929.

17. *San Diego Union*, May 23, 1929.

18. *San Diego Union*, June 22, 1929.

19. *Los Angeles Times*, January 20, 1925.

20. *San Diego Union*, May 25, 1929.

21. Ibid.

22. *Los Angeles Examiner*, May 25, 1929.

23. *San Diego Union*, May 25, 1929.

24. *Los Angeles Examiner*, May 25, 1929.

25. *San Diego Evening Tribune*, May 24, 1929.

26. See chapter 1, n. 4, above.

27. Cayce, "The Case against 'Silent' Colson," 6–7.

28. *San Diego Sun*, June 27, 1929.

29. *San Diego Union*, May 26, 1929.

30. With their sleek lines and extreme accuracy, Lugers ranked among the most famous firearms of the twentieth century. While the German army regularly used them in the Second World War, the American military found them prone to jamming. Semi-automatic pistols could be switched to "automatic," and were at times referred to as "machine guns."

31. *San Diego Evening Tribune*, May 30, 1929.

32. *San Diego Union*, May 25, 1929.

33. Ibid.

34. *Los Angeles Times*, May 30, 1929.

35. *San Diego Sun*, May 27, 1929.

5. BORDER BABYLON

1. Shaffer, "Aunt Jane: The Old Lady from Hell," 7–10.
2. Ibid., 7.
3. Quoted in Ridgely, "The Man Who Built Tijuana: Part 1," 58. This is part of a lively and informative eight-part series that ran in the magazine in 1966–67.
4. Summers, *Buenos Días*, 13–14.
5. *Los Angeles Times*, May 7, 1888.
6. *Los Angeles Times*, July 23, 1899.
7. Ibid.
8. Ibid.
9. *Los Angeles Times*, April 6, 1889.
10. José A. Castillón, dir., *Diario oficial, Estados Unidos Mexicanos*, 93, num. 36 (México, 12 de diciembre de 1907), Secretería del Estado y Despacho de Gobernación, Sección Tercera, "El Presidente de la República ha tenido a bien aprobar el siguiente: Reglamento de juegos para el Territorio de la Baja California," 560–62. Sincere gratitude to my longtime friend and history colleague, Dra. Eugenia Meyer of La UNAM for tracking down and sending me a photocopy of this fascinating gambling law.

    For a fine overview of the early development of Tijuana's "vice industry" see Taylor, "The Wild Frontier Moves South," 204–29.
11. *Los Angeles Times*, May 3, 1915.
12. *Los Angeles Times*, April 6, 1915.
13. Cantú deserves but has yet to be the subject of a full biography. Among works that mention his life, work, and antics are Hall, *Oil, Banks, and Politics*, 9–16, 54–58, 166–67; Schantz, "From 'Mexicali Rose' to the Tijuana Brass," 65–67, 171–74, 180–224, 238, 231, 346, 551, 557; Sandos, "Northern Separatism during the Mexican Revolution," 191–214; Buffington, "Prohibition in the Borderlands," 19–38; Werne, "Esteban Cantú y la soberanía mexicana en Baja California," 1–30; Rodríguez González, "La Figura y época de Esteban Cantú (1914–1924) en el Archivo General de la Nación de los Estados Unidos," 163–70; and Rathbun, "Facts about Lower California," 9, 17. In 1919 the Mexican federal government sent a member of its treasury department to the district to report on the region's economic development. For his report, see Rolland, *Informe sobre el Distrito Norte de la Baja California*.
14. Gómez Estrada, *Gobierno y casinos*, 57–60.

6. KING OF BORDER VICE

1. Morgan, *History of Kern County, California*, 1294–95.
2. On oil strikes and boomtowns, see Bailey, *Heart of the Golden Empire*, 77–80; Kirk, *A Flier in Oil*, 57–59, 71.

3. *San Francisco Chronicle*, June 29, 1910.

4. Gia, "If Christ Came to Bakersfield."

5. Gia, "Death of the Tenderloin." Shaffer, " 'Aunt Jane,' " 9.

6. Schantz, "All Night at the Owl," 559.

7. "Jack Tenny Autobiography," 5 vols., typescript., vol. 1, *passim*, University of California, Los Angeles, Herrick Research Library, Special Collections.

8. Schantz, "All Night at the Owl," 562–67, 576–80. *Los Angeles Times*, April 20, 1919.

9. F. C. Spayde, "Plan Great Casino below the Line," *Los Angeles Times*, April 20, 1919.

10. Ibid.

11. *Los Angeles Times*, September 27, 1919. *San Diego Union*, February 7 and July 2, 1933. San Diego Historical Society, Archive, Vertical File 288.1, "Hotels/ Motels/Agua Caliente"; Shaffer, " 'Aunt Jane,' " 9.

12. *California of the South*, 251–53. *Los Angeles Times*, September 27, 1919. *San Francisco Chronicle*, February 16, 1931. *San Diego Union*, February 16 and 17, 1931, February 7, 1933. San Diego Historical Society, Archives, Vertical File 288.1, "Hotels/Motels/Agua Caliente." Ridgely, "The Man Who Built Tijuana," Part 4, 116; Part 5, 3; Part 6, 46; Part 8, 99.

13. For a scholarly analysis of the 1915 Exposition see Bokovoy, *The San Diego World's Fairs and Southwestern Memory*, chaps. 1–4.

14. *San Diego Union*, April 19, 1915.

15. *Los Angeles Times*, April 28, 1915. *San Diego Union*, January 1, 1917. *Calexico Chronicle*, May 1 and June 10, 1915.

16. *San Diego Union*, January 1, 1917.

17. *Los Angeles Times*, July 6, 1915; Gómez Estrada, *Gobierno y casinos*, pp. 49–50, 81–83.

18. *Los Angeles Times*, July 6, 1915.

19. *Los Angeles Times*, December 15 and 28, 1915; *San Diego Union*, December 1, 1915.

20. For more on Coffroth, see chapter 7.

21. For more on Long, see chapter 11.

7. "THEY'RE OFF!"

1. San Francisco Public Library, Special Collections, Coffroth Scrapbooks. The two large scrapbooks, amassed by a Coffroth relative, contain mainly newspaper clippings about James Coffroth's life and times. Hereafter cited as "Scrapbooks," with volume number, newspaper article, and volume page number. Scrapbooks, 1: *San Francisco Bulletin*, 45; *Oakland Tribune*, 282. Albertanti, "Saga of Sunny Jim Coffroth," 8. Ridgely, "The Man Who Built Tijuana," Part 1,

58–59. *Los Angeles Times*, February 7, 1943. *San Diego Union*, February 7, 1943. *San Francisco Chronicle*, June 9, 1940. The *Chronicle* ran a fifteen-part series on Coffroth, mainly in his role as a boxing promoter, in January and February 1940.

2. Nat Fleischer, "Coffroth Was Tops," 25. Albertanti, "California's Great Sportsman," 42.

3. Ridgely, "The Man Who Built Tijuana," Part 2, 54. *San Francisco Chronicle*, December 14, 1913.

4. Scrapbooks, 1: *San Francisco Call*, June 30 and July 1, 1907, 39; January 12, 1908, 306–7.

5. *San Francisco Call*, March 22, 1909. For other such mentions see *San Francisco Call*, February 3, 1907, July 5, 1908, and August 30, 1912.

6. Beltrán, *Agua Caliente*, 14. *San Diego Union*, January 2, 1916.

7. The marvelous Hatfield story is well told in Higgins, "Hatfield's Flood"; Patterson, "Hatfield the Rainmaker"; and "Rainmaking, 1916–1951," *[Union] Title-Trust Topics*, 5, no. 2 (March–April, 1951): 12–13.

8. Quoted in Patterson, "Hatfield the Rainmaker," 2.

9. Ridgely, "The Man Who Built Tijuana," Part 1, 98.

10. *San Diego Union*, January 2, 1916.

11. Ibid.

12. Patterson, "Hatfield the Rainmaker," 2; "Rainmaking," 12.

13. Patterson, "Hatfield the Rainmaker," 15.

14. Ibid., 19.

15. Ibid., 21.

16. Ridgely, "The Man Who Built Tijuana," Part 2, 52.

17. Ibid., 52–53.

18. Ridgely, "The Man Who Built Tijuana," Part 3, 68–70.

19. *Los Angeles Times*, February 15, 1920. Gómez Estrada, *Gobierno y casinos*, 81–83. Elía Flores Estelo, "La última de nos vamos: Una opuesta de reflexión sobre el campo de diversión," in Castillo Udiarte, García Cortez, and Morales Lira, *La Revolución también es una calle . . .*, 38.

20. For San Diego's development as a Navy town see Shragge, "'I Like the Cut of Your Jib.'" Also Shragge's fine Ph.D. dissertation, "Boosters and Blue Jackets."

21. Davis, Mayhew, and Miller, *Under the Perfect Sun*, 48.

22. U. S. National Archive, Department of Justice, RG 60, Class 23, "Liquor Violations," 23–12–53–2, F. W. Becker, United Veterans of the Republic, to C. B. Slemp, Secretary to the President, April 17, 1924. Hereafter cited as: "Liquor violations," plus file no., correspondents, and date.

23. Vincent Z. C. de Baca, "Moral Renovation of the Californias," 55–56.

24. Kenamore, "What Is Germany Doing in Mexico?," 343.

25. *San Francisco Chronicle*, April 12, 1918.
26. Aikman, "Hell along the Border."

8. PROHIBITION'S BOUNTY

1. Merz, *The Great American Band-Wagon*, 1.
2. *Los Angeles Times*, July 1, 1919.
3. Ibid.
4. The national mood created by Prohibition has been well recorded and documented. For starters, see Asbury, *The Great Illusion*; Cashman, *Prohibition*; and Merz, *The Great American Band-Wagon*.
5. *San Diego Sun*, January 5, 1927.
6. *San Diego Union*, January 1, 1917. *Los Angeles Times*, February 15, 1920.
7. Woods, "A Penchant for Probity," 107.
8. De Baca, "Moral Renovation of the Californias," 75. Ridgely, "The Man Who Built Tijuana," Part 4, 117.
9. Jim Heimann, *Out with the Stars*, 51–53.
10. Ibid., 51.
11. Ibid., 53. Gómez Estrada, *Gobierno y casinos*, 49–50.
12. Quoted in Heimann, *Out with the Stars*, 53.
13. De Baca, "Moral Renovation of the Californias," 55–56. For Tijuana's general gaming atmosphere in 1920 see Ridgely, "The Man Who Built Tijuana," Part 4.
14. *Nogales Herald*, July 20, 1920.
15. Graciela Sández de Gutiérrez, "Nuestra cocina, un *collage*," in Ortiz Figueroa and Piñera Ramírez, *Historia de Tijuana*, vol. 2, 407–10. The original Caesar salad recipe called for: 1 cup French bread croutons, 1/3 cup olive oil, 2 garlic cloves, 1–2 tsp. anchovy paste, 1 bunch romaine lettuce, salt and pepper to taste, juice of one lemon, 1 tsp. Worcestershire sauce, and 1 coddled egg. See also Heimann, *Out with the Stars*, 53; *Historia viva de Tijuana*, 16, 33, 69, 131; and Summers, *Buenos Días, Tijuana*, 40.
16. This and the quotes that follow are from Chambers's article, *New York Times*, June 6, 1920.
17. Fideicomiso Archivos Plutarco Elías Calles y Fernando Torreblanca (Mexico City; hereafter cited as Calles Archive), Gav. 9, Exp. 16, Inv. 569, Leg. 1, des. Becker, F. W. [memorandum to Mexican government], n.d. [1922].
18. Gómez Estrada, *Gobierno y casinos*, 91–96. Samaniego Lopez, *Los Gobiernos civiles en Baja California, passim*.
19. Calles Archive, Gav. 49, Exp. 127, Inv. 3316, Leg. 11/12, des. Lugo, José I., Obregón to Lugo, March 2, 1923, and Lugo to Calles, March 12, 1923.
20. U.S. National Archives, Department of Justice, RG 60, Class 23, Liquor violations, 23-12-53-2, Becker to Slemp, April 17, 1924.

21. *Los Angeles Evening Express*, June 6, 1916.
22. Ibid.
23. *Calexico Chronicle*, February 10, 1920. See also *Los Angeles Times*, February 10 and 11, 1920.
24. "Tenny Autobiography," vo1.1, 46–48.
25. Rev. John Wood, *California Christian Advocate*, December 7, 1922.
26. Ibid.
27. For one example among many see Archivo General de la Nación (hereafter cited as AGN), Fondo Obregón/Calles, vol. 168, Exp. 425-T-7.
28. Rogers, *Will Rogers Weekly Articles*, vol. 2. 163–66.

9. THE NEW WAVE

1. AGN, Presidencials, Gav. 84, Fondo, 02; Serie, 08, Exp. 798, Rodríguez to Calles, 1926. Ridgely, "The Man Who Built Tijuana," Part 3, 143. Rodríguez again solicited presidential influence for Bowman in 1929: Calles Archive, Gav. 66, Exp. 189, Inv. 5010, Exp. 7/11, Rodríguez to Calles, June 10, 1929.
2. Rodríguez, *Autobiografía*, 31–119. Martínez Assad, Horcasitas, Ramírez Rancaño, *Revolucionarios fueron todos*, 284–86. *San Diego Union*, February 14, 1967. Gómez Estrada, *Gobierno y casinos*, 102–12.
3. AGN, Presidenciales, Gav. 84, Fondo, 02, Serie, 08, Exp. 798, Rodríguez to Calles, 1926.
4. Calles Archive, Gav. 66, Exp. 189, Inv. 5010, Leg. 5/11, des. Abelardo Rodríguez, Rodríguez to Edmundo Moneda, Secretaría de CROM, October 14, 1925.
5. Ibid.
6. San Diego Historical Society, Archive, Oral Histories, Leonard Rottman, interview conducted by Bob Wright, June 18, 1972, transcript, 5, 12–13. Hereafter cited as "Rottman interview."
7. Gómez Estrada, *Gobierno y casinos*, 82–83.
8. *San Diego Evening Tribune*, September 12, 1923. *San Diego Union*, September 12 and 13, 1923.
9. Martínez Assad et. al, *Revolucionarios fueron todos*, chap. 7. Gómez Estrada, *Gobierno y casinos*, chap. 3.
10. *San Diego Union*, October 14 and 24, 1925. *Los Angeles Times*, October 14, 1925. *San Diego Evening Tribune*, October 13, 1925, and August 27, 1929. *San Diego Sun*, October 23, 1925. *Calexico Chronicle*, October 14, 1925.
11. The material on Bowman's early life is from a variety of sources, but principally from an unfinished autobiography he wrote covering the background of his parents and his birth to October 12, 1894, when he took a railroad job in Sonora, Mexico. Bowman's daughter, Ms. Georgia Allen of Sacramento, kindly furnished me with a typescript of the document and through telephone inter-

views and e-mails gradually filled in details of The Baron's life. Her contributions were invaluable. Ms. Allen admitted her prejudices. She said her father "was my hero and always will be. He was a true patriarch—our world was best when he was in it."

Additional biographical material on Bowman came from Wirt's vertical file in the archive of the Arizona Historical Society in Tucson. Bowman filled out a biographical sketch for the Society, and his file also contains printed materials about his life.

My thanks also to Bowman's nephew, John Bowman of San Diego, Calif., who in an interview on December 3, 2005, provided personal observations about The Baron.

Axel Hom, president of the Pimería Alta Historical Society in Nogales, Ariz., maintains a personal scrapbook on Bowman's life and allowed me to review its contents. His hospitality is greatly appreciated. The Society itself has a vertical file on Bowman, which I utilized along with its invaluable local newspaper collection.

For printed sketches of Bowman's life, see "Pioneer Arizonan, Wirt Bowman: A Real American Whose Life Story Sounds Like the Pages of Horatio Algier," *The Magazine Tucson* (February 1949): 18–19; King, *Pioneer Western Empire Builders*, 226, discusses the rail system on which Bowman worked; and Ready, *Open Range and Hidden Silver*, 155, calls Bowman "a self-made man and a millionaire" and notes he "was a politician, and exceptionally shrewd businessman and promoter. In him were represented—and certainly exaggerated—the qualities characterizing the men who had been able to build and perpetuate the dynamic little commercial center called Nogales."

12. Aguilar Camín, *La Frontera nomada*, 320–29.

13. For example, on January 20, 1921, the *Nogales Herald* reported on page 1 that Bowman and two other Nogales men, Henry Levin and Joseph Polin, had incorporated "one of the largest commission and brokerage houses in Mexico. It will handle some of the largest accounts in U.S. and Central American cities." Polin was Obregón's son-in-law.

14. U.S. National Archives, Justice Department, Investigative Case Files of the Bureau of Investigation, 1908–1922 [file] OG18765, microfilm roll 62, agent Don S. Rathburn (Nogales) to Bruce Bielaski, Bureau chief, Washington, D.C., July 9, 1918. Hereafter cited as "Bureau of Investigation" plus file number, correspondents, and date. Details of Rathburn's and other such reports were repeated (and denied) in correspondence and conversation that Bowman had with federal agencies, including FBI chief J. Edgar Hoover in 1932. Bowman relayed much of the same information to Wade H. Ellis, a powerful lobbyist

and lawyer in Washington and paid Ellis $5,000 in fees to have his record expunged of any peccadilloes. Those records are in the Franklin Delano Roosevelt Presidential Library and Museum in Hyde Park, N.Y., Collection Title: Morgenthau, Henry J., Box 89, Folder/File, "Confidential Report about People: Bowman, Wirt G."; hereafter cited as "Morgenthau Collection."

15. Bureau of Investigation, OG 18765, Rathburn to Bielaski, July 9, 1918. Also, Don Smith, *Nogales International*, November 25, 1988. "Pioneer Arizonan" quotes Bowman: "I resigned from the railroad in 1912 because I'd become interested in the movement of cattle out of Sonora. The revolutionary situation there made all cattlemen anxious to get their herds over the line." The article concluded that Wirt's ranching experience "provided him with the know-how to handle big deals in the big way."

16. Bureau of Investigation, OG 18765, Rathburn to Bielaski, July 9, 1918.

17. Ibid.

18. Bureau of Investigation, OG F320583, from (signature illegible on microfilm) to E. M. Bowling, U.S. military telegraph censor (Nogales), May 13, 1918.

19. Bureau of Investigation, OG 18765, Rathburn to Bielaski, July 9, 1918. See also, *Nogales Herald*, October 12, 1918.

20. Bureau of Investigation, OG 18765, Rathburn to Bielaski, July 9, 1918. See also, *Nogales Herald*, October 12, 1918, and Ready, *Open Range*, 99.

21. Bureau of Investigation, OG 18765, Rathburn to Bielaski, July 9, 1918. See also, Morgenthau Collection, Statement of Wirt Bowman to FBI, March 7, 1932, and fourteen-page memorandum to (Elmer Lincoln) Irey (chief of the Bureau of Revenue Service Investigative Division), March 16, 1943, and Bowman to Wade H. Ellis, March 12, 1931.

22. Morgenthau Collection, Statement of Wirt Bowman to FBI, March 7, 1932.

23. *Nogales Herald*, April 6 and 23, May 24 and 27, June 3, 1918, and June 1, 1921. *Border Vignette* (Nogales), September 24, 1924. Ready, *Open Range*, 110, 115.

24. *Nogales Herald*, April 6, 1915, January 20 and March 2, 1921. *Border Vignette*, June 22 and July 15, 1922; May 19, 1923; May 31, 1924; and April 4, 1925. Ready, *Open Range*, 110, 138. Universidad Autónoma de Baja California (Tijuana), Instituto de Investigaciones Históricas, Archivo, Colección Abelardo Rodríguez, expediente 105/22, Secretario particular de Rodríguez, F. Javier Gaxiola, to Bowman, November 10, 1934; hereafter cited as Rodríguez papers, plus file number and correspondents.

25. Calles Archive, Serie 11030500, Inv. 3080, des. Wirt G. Bowman, Bowman to Obregón, August 17, 1920.

26. Calles Archive, Serie 11030400, Exp. B-09/88, Inv. 2104, des. F. A. Bórquez

(acting governor of Sonora). Telegram, (Adolfo) de la Huerta a Bórquez, July 30, 1920.

27. AGN, Presidenciales, Obregón/Calles, vol. O-C C266, Exp. 808-B-14, June 7, 1924.

10. AGUA CALIENTE IN GESTATION

1. Calles Archive, Serie 11030500, Exp. 204, Inv. 3080, des. Wirt G. Bowman, Bowman to Obregón, September 25, 1920.
2. AGN, vol. C248, Exp. 803-B-12, Bowman to Obregón, January 29, 1921; Obregón to Bowman, April 9, 1921. Gómez Estrada, *Gobierno y casinos*, 170–72.
3. AGN, vol. C248, Exp. 168, Exp. 425-T-7, Bowman to Torreblanca, August 30, 1923; and C230, Exp. 771-B-21, Bowman to Obregón, September 30, 1923.
4. Elmer, "Thomas N. Crofton," *An Illustrated History of Klickitat, Yakima and Kittitas Counties*, 442–43. May, "A Kid's Eye View of Centerville." Atwell, *Early History of Klickitat County, passim. The Oregonian* (Portland), July 25 and October 6, 1929. *Sunday Oregonian*, May 25, 1930. Harris, "The Dalles," *The Wasco County History Book*. The Dalles Public Library, Vertical Files, "Lula Crandill's Newspaper Clippings," "Razing of Umatilla," from *Dalles Weekly Chronicle*, July 4, 1929; *Dalles Weekly Chronicle*, July 28, 1911.
5. Daniels and Gunning interviews. *Dalles Weekly Chronicle*, April 15, 1910, and March 18, 1933.
6. *San Diego Sun*, December 27, 1929.
7. Ibid. Pourade, *The Rising Tide*, 130.
8. Rottman interview, 5.
9. *Border Vignette*, December 1, 1923, and March 8, 1924.
10. *Border Vignette*, December 8, 1923.
11. *San Diego Sun*, January 3 and April 4, 1927, November 20, 1928, and December 27, 1929. *San Diego Union*, December 1, 1928, and January 8, 1929. *Border Vignette*, May 10 and December 27, 1924.
12. *Daily Transcript* (San Diego), July 23, 1936.

11. BUILDING CAMELOT

1. *San Diego Evening Tribune*, October 9, 1994. Antonio Padilla Corona, "Entrevista a Wayne y Corine McAllister . . . el día 17 de Septiembre de 1983," typescript, Tijuana, 4. Padilla comes from an architectural background and is a researcher at the Instituto de Estudios Históricos, Universidad Autónoma de Baja California. He earned his Master's Degree in history at San Diego State University and has written well and extensively on early city planning in Tijuana. I am extremely indebted to Mtro. Antonio for furnishing me a transcript of the interview, which has now appeared in print: *Agua Caliente: Oasis en el Tiempo*.

See also, "Pioneer's Visions Fulfilled," *San Diego Magazine*, November 28, 1928, 32; Gómez Estrada, *Gobierno y casinos*, 81, 173–76; and Rottman interview, 7.

2. Gómez Estrada, *Gobierno y casinos*, 116, 119, 124–26, 156–57, 174–76.

3. *San Diego Union*, January 2 and March 5, 1934.

4. *San Diego Tribune*, February 19, 1962. San Diego Historical Society, Vertical File, Joseph L. Howard, Category, "Baron Long: The Man and the Legend," typescript [no author], 1988, 1–2.

5. *San Francisco Chronicle*, May 10, 1908. "Long: The Man and the Legend," 3.

6. *San Francisco Chronicle*, February 19, 1962. "Long: The Man and the Legend," 3. *Los Angeles Times*, April 21, 1918, March 1, 1929, and February 19, 1962. William Hamilton Cline, "When Night Life Started in Los Angeles," *Los Angeles Times*, May 23, 1937. Damon Runyon, "Shades of Dear Old Vernon," *Los Angeles Examiner*, December 22, 1931.

7. Heimann, *Out with The Stars*, 11–13.

8. *San Francisco Chronicle*, February 19, 1962.

9. *Los Angeles Times*, May 22, 1937.

10. *Los Angeles Times*, February 21, 1962., Heimann, *Out with the Stars*, 11.

11. *Los Angeles Times*, January 28, February 26, and October 26, 1915.

12. *Los Angeles Times*, June 18, 1916.

13. *Los Angeles Times*, December 5, 1919.

14. Long's prominent role in American thoroughbred horse breeding and racing is recounted in Montague, "Baron Long" and a four-part series, Cochran, "The Baron Long Story."

15. *San Diego Union-Tribune*, October 9, 1994.

16. Bransburg, "Remembering Agua Caliente."

17. McAllister interviews, July 9–10, 2004, at his home in Corvallis, Ore. For a scholarly overview of the Spanish Colonial, or Mission Revival, architectural movement in Southern California, see Gebhard, "The Spanish Colonial Revival in Southern California." Also helpful are "Adobe . . . Gingerbread . . . and Glass"; McWilliams, *Southern California*, 70–83; Merz, *American Band-Wagon*, 126–30; and Perry, "Expo Buildings Keep Art, Beauty in Restoration."

18. The physical layout and design of Agua Caliente is best discussed in Padilla Corona, *Agua Caliente: Oasis en el Tiempo*. Pablo Bransburg, an Argentinean architect, interviewed McAllister in 1994, and his report, "Remembering Agua Caliente," appeared in the *San Diego Union* on October 9 of that year.

The best way to appreciate the grandeur of Agua Caliente is through photographs of the resort. The finest collection of such photographs is archived at the California State Library in Sacramento. Gary G. Kurtz, curator of Special Collections at the library, wrote of them in "Agua Caliente: A Gambler's Paradise in Old Mexico." My thanks to Mr. Kurtz for allowing me to review the photographs plus several splendid watercolor architectural renditions of tiles used at the resort. Wayne McAllister used photographs of Agua Caliente to explain architectural details in "McAllister videotape."

David Marshall, the president of Heritage Architecture and Planning, mulled over copies of photographs of Agua Caliente with me in his San Diego office and used his formidable expertise to elaborate on architectural styles, designs, and motifs used at Agua Caliente.

19. Calles Archive, Fondo Soledad González, Gav. 82. 01, Exp. 691, Inv. 618, Leg. 212, Rodríguez to González, March 29, 1928. Also, Gav. 66, Exp. 189, Inv. 5010, Leg. 7111, Abelardo L. (Gral), Rodríguez to Soledad González, March 29, 1928.

20. For descriptions of Agua Caliente at its inauguration and plans for future development see "Agua Caliente Hotel and Casino Will Make Tijuana World Famous Resort," *San Diego Herald*, June 7, 1928; "Charm of Old Mexico Idealized at New Agua Caliente Hotel," *San Diego Magazine*, March 1928, 12; *Los Angeles Times*, December 19, 1930; San Diego Public Library, California Room, Vertical Files, Mexico/Baja California/Business Enterprises/Hotel Agua Caliente, "A Trip Through Agua Caliente [1929]."

21. *Los Angeles Times*, February 28, 1962. Beltrán, *Agua Caliente*, 40

22. Rottman interview, 8.

23. *San Diego Union*, June 6 and 11, 1929.

12. CAPTAIN JERRY'S DAY

1. *San Diego Union*, May 28, 1929.

2. *San Diego Union*, June 18, 1929.

3. *San Diego Union*, June 21, 1929.

4. *San Diego Union* and *San Diego Sun*, June 21, 1929.

5. *San Diego Union*, June 21, 1929.

6. *San Diego Union*, June 22, 1929.

7. Ibid.

8. *San Diego Sun*, June 27, 1929.

9. Ibid.

10. *San Diego Sun*, June 22, 1929.

11. Ibid.

12. *San Diego Union*, June 29, 1929.

13. *San Diego Union*, June 22, 1929.

14. *San Diego Tribune*, June 28, 1929.

15. *San Diego Union*, June 22, 1929.

16. Ibid.

17. *San Diego Sun*, June 22, 1929.

18. *Los Angeles Times*, May 27, 1929. *San Diego Union*, July 4, 1929.

13. "SILENT" MARTY'S ORATION

1. Leland G. Stanford, "Footprints of Justice . . . ," *San Diego and Profiles of Senior Members of the Bench and Bar* (San Diego, 1960), 63. An Andrews obituary appears in the *San Diego Union*, July 9, 1937.

2. Leland G. Stanford, *San Diego's Legal Lore and Bar* (San Diego, 1968), 221.

3. *San Diego Union*, September 5, 1934.

4. *San Diego Union*, July 12, 1929.

5. Ibid. Emphasis mine.

6. *San Diego Union*, July 25, 1929.

7. Trial transcript, Colson's statement, 413.

8. *San Diego Union*, August 1, 1929.

9. *San Diego Union*, August 2, 1929.

10. *San Diego Union*, August 6, 1929.

11. All of Colson's remarks are from the trial transcript, 405–18. A portion of his comments concerning the plot to rob and blow up Agua Caliente was reported in the *San Diego Union*, August 6, 1929.

12. The two Peteet daughters, Clyde, twenty, and Audrey, nineteen, went to Tijuana with their parents in February 1926. The father and the girls did some barhopping, the father wandered back to their hotel, but his daughters stayed out and returned the next morning claiming they had been raped. The girls implicated seven Mexicans, including Tijuana's police chief. While local authorities investigated the charges, the Peteet family returned to their home in San Diego and committed suicide. The case reached the highest levels of government in both countries, and as a result, the United States imposed a temporary 6 P.M. border crossing deadline, which seriously cramped Tijuana business until 1933, when the curfew was lifted. A Mexican jury acquitted the accused. Much has been written about the case, most recently a revision: Cabeza de Vaca and Cabeza de Vaca, "The 'Shame Suicides' and Tijuana."

13. My sincere gratitude to Ms. Marjorie Millstein, licensed clinical social worker, for her assistance in drawing a personality sketch of Martin Colson. Besides her private practice, Ms. Millstein teaches her specialty in the School of Social Work at San Diego State University.

14. *San Diego Sun*, August 8, 1929.

14. VERACITY

1. Trial transcript, 410–11. The entire plan runs 406–12.

2. Ibid., 410–11.

3. Ibid., 406–7.

4. Friction among the Barons themselves and between the Barons and stockholders in the enterprise is related in chapter 18.

5. Literature on the Cristero War is vast. For an overview in English see Meyer, *The Cristero Rebellion*.

6. *New York Times*, April 7, 1929. See also the websites of the city of Naco, and the U.S. National Park Service; search on "history." Dolan Ellis, billed as Arizona's official state balladeer, sang an ode to the Naco bombing with symphony orchestra backing on April 15, 2005, in Sierra Vista, Arizona. For other revolutionary outbursts in Mexico during this period, see *San Diego Sun*, August 17, 1926; *San Diego Union*, September 3 and November 24, 1926.

7. Rodríguez papers, Caja (1921–28), Exp. 12, "Wirt R. Bowman," Rodríguez to Bowman, January 15, 1929.

8. Trial transcript, 409–10.

9. A good book examining how Los Angeles development outdistanced San Diego is Erie, *Globalizing Los Angeles*. Shortcomings in San Diego development and leadership are detailed in Davis, Mayhew, and Miller, *Perfect Sun*, 21–59.

10. Ports, " 'Geraniums vs. Smokestacks.' "

11. A risk management team from New York surveyed San Diego's current financial problems and suggested a fix in August 2006. "The evidence demonstrates not mere negligence," it stated, "but deliberate disregard for the law, disregard for fiduciary responsibility, and disregard for the welfare of the city's residents for an extended period of time." See *San Diego Union*, August 9, 2006. For the entire report see Arthur Levitt, Lynn E. Turner, Troy A. Dahlberg, audit committee, "The Kroll Report." August 8, 2006, Mayor's Office, City of San Diego. The report may be accessed online on the city's website.

12. Stone, Price, and Stone, *City Manager Government in San Diego*, 69. The report underscores the abysmal failures of San Diego city government in the 1920s and 1930s.

13. Ibid., 13–14.

14. Ibid., 31.

15. Ibid., 14.

16. *San Diego Herald*, July 29, 1926.

17. U.S. National Archives, Department of Justice, RG 60, 23–12–197, S1–5435, Cornelius, special agent, Los Angeles, to Chief J. M. Doran, intelligence unit, Washington, D.C. November 27, 1927; hereafter cited as "McClemmy file, Justice Department," plus date of communication. This file details and summarizes the Justice Department's case against McClemmy. See also Walker, *One Eye Closed, the Other Red*, 201–5.

18. McClemmy file, Justice Department, November 15, 1926.

19. McClemmy file, Justice Department, December 9, 1927.

20. McClemmy file, Justice Department, November 18, 1927.

21. *San Diego Union*, August 5, 1927. *Los Angeles Examiner*, January 6, 1928.

15. FIXES

1. *San Diego Union*, December 4, 1926. *San Diego Sun*, December 7, 1926.
2. *San Diego Union*, March 2, 1925.
3. *San Diego Union*, March 3, 1925.
4. *San Diego Union*, March 4, 1925.
5. *San Diego Union*, March 5, 1925.
6. *Los Angeles Times*, September 16 and November 26, 1926. *San Diego Sun*, December 6, 1926. *San Diego Union*, December 7, 1926.
7. *San Diego Sun*, September. 15, 1926.
8. *San Diego Sun*, July 21, 1925.
9. Agnes Keller's testimony is from *San Diego Sun*, December 21, 1926.
10. *San Diego Union*, September 2, 1926.
11. *San Diego Union*, December 10, 1926.
12. Ibid. *San Diego Sun*, December 3, 192.
13. *San Diego Union*, December 14, 1926.
14. *San Diego Union*, December 17, 1926.
15. *Los Angeles Examiner*, November 1, 1928.
16. *San Diego Union*, December 21, 1926.
17. *San Diego Union*, September 16, 1929. *San Diego Sun*, August 16 and 17, 1929.
18. *San Diego Union*, August 24, 1929.
19. *San Diego Sun*, August 18, 1929. *San Diego Union*, August 19, 1929.
20. *San Diego Union*, November 8, 1929.
21. *San Diego Union*, September 16, 1929. At the same meeting a Baptist pastor, Dr. John B. Smith, condemned liquor and praised Prohibition, which he said had its inception in the church, noting that "God never intended men to drink alcohol. Had He, He would have given man a cast iron stomach. Amen!"
22. *San Diego Union*, September 15 and 17, 1929.
23. *San Diego Union*, September 15, 1929.
24. *San Diego Union*, August 23, 1929.
25. *San Diego Union*, August 27, 1929.
26. Ibid.
27. *San Diego Union*, September 16, 1929.
28. Castanian, *To Protect and Serve* [SDPD], 53.

16. SENTENCING AND CENSURING

1. Trial transcript, 431. All the judge's comments are from the trial transcript.
2. Ibid.
3. Ibid. (Colson's statement), 406.
4. Ibid., 433, 434.
5. Ibid., 434, 436.

6. Ibid., 436, 438.

7. Ibid., 439.

8. Ibid., 439–40.

9. Ibid., 441, 444.

10. Ibid., 446.

11. Ibid.

12. Ibid.

13. Ibid., 447.

14. Ibid.

15. Ibid., 447–48.

16. Ibid., 448.

17. *San Diego Sun*, August 6, 1929. *San Diego Union*, August 7, 1929.

18. Trial transcript, 449.

19. *San Diego Sun*, August 6, 1929. *San Diego Union*, August 7, 1929.

20. Trial transcript, 450.

21. *San Diego Evening Tribune*, August 6, 1929.

22. *San Diego Sun*, August 6, 1929.

23. *San Diego Union*, August 11, 1929.

24. *San Diego Evening Tribune*, August 8, 1929.

25. *Los Angeles Examiner*, August 10, 1929.

26. *San Diego Herald*, August 22, 1929.

27. Statement published on August 13, 1929, in *San Diego Union, San Diego Sun,* and *San Diego Evening Tribune.*

28. *San Diego Sun,* June 11, 1929.

17. HOLLYWOOD'S PLAYGROUND

1. *Los Angeles Times,* December 19, 1930.

2. *Los Angeles Examiner,* August 18, 1929; from one in a series of five long articles, all extremely hostile to Agua Caliente, that the *Examiner* printed at the time.

3. *Los Angeles Examiner,* August 16 and 17, 1929.

4. McAllister videotape.

5. Rodríguez papers, Caja 1, File, "Agua Caliente," Exp. 2, "Predio denumerado Agua Caliente," Rodríguez to Wirt Bowman, June 18, 1928.

6. *Los Angeles Examiner,* August 16, 1929.

7. *San Diego Union,* July 30 and 31, 1933.

8. *San Diego Union,* July 18, August 8, 1929, April 14, 1932. *Los Angeles Times,* November 28, 1928, January 26, 1930.

9. *Los Angeles Times,* June 4, 1929.

10. *San Francisco Chronicle,* July 13, 1933. *Los Angeles Examiner,* July 17, 1933.

11. *Unwritten Wonder, passim.*

12. James, "Agua Caliente," 156.

13. *Hollywood Reporter*, April 14, 1933, 2.

14. *Pacific Pictorial*, 1932. This issue is in the personal collection of Andre Williams. Similar rotogravures titled *Southern California* and *Pictorial Life* are in the San Diego Historical Society, Research Archives, Pictorial Titles, c. 1930s, 1931+, vols. 1–8.

15. Wilkerson, *The Man Who Invented Las Vegas*, 66, 68. *San Diego Union*, February 25, 1962.

16. *Los Angeles Examiner*, August 1, 1934.

17. Harry Haller, "What's Become of Caliente," *Los Angeles Times*, December 13, 1936.

18. Films are all from the American Film Institute Catalogue: Patricia King Hanson, executive editor; Alan Gevinson, associate editor, *The American Film Institute of Motion Pictures Produced in the United States* (Berkeley, 1993).

19. *New York Times Film Reviews, 1913–1928*, 6 vols. (New York, 1990); *In Caliente* reviewed in vol. 2, *1932–1938*, 1187 (June 27, 1935).

20. For a glimpse of Schenck, his gambling, and his relationship to Agua Caliente, see Gabler, *An Empire of Their Own*, 257–62. The best detailed source is the trial record of Schenck's income tax evasion and perjury cases with the U.S. government: see U. S. District Court for the Southern District of New York, RG 21, Criminal Case Files, Nos. C-107–440, Box No. 945 (322544) (29506), and RG 276, U. S. Court of Appeals for the Second Circuit, Case Files 17851–17854, Archives Box No. 5205, and Case No. 17847–17851, Archives Box No. 5204. The records are located at the Lower Manhattan, New York City, branch of the U.S. National Archives. Hereafter cited as "Schenck tax case" or "Schenck appeal case."

21. *Hollywood Reporter*, August 13, 1931, and June 21, 1933. On "yes men" in Hollywood, see Leo Rosten's excellent *Hollywood*, 44. See also *Mexican Herald*, June 23, 1929.

22. Gabler, *An Empire of Their Own*, 112–13. Rosten, *Hollywood*, 222. French, *The Movie Moguls*, 148–49. Margaret L. Talmage, *The Talmage Sisters: Norma, Constance, Natalie. An Intimate Story of the World's Most Famous Screen Family by Their Mother, Margaret L. Talmage* (Philadelphia, 1924), 49. See also *Los Angeles Times*, March 12, 1941.

23. Rosten, *Hollywood*, 222.

24. Gabler, *An Empire of Their Own*, 113.

25. Wilkenson, *The Man Who Invented Las Vegas*, 12.

26. Andre Williams generously provided me with a copy of the service booklet from his personal collection of Agua Caliente memorabilia.

27. Messick and Goldblatt, *The Only Game in Town*, 116.

28. The original payrolls researched were for October 1930 and February 1932. They are from the personal Agua Caliente Collection of Luis Tamés León, a Tijuana chemist and local historian.

29. Rodríguez papers, Caja 1, File "Agua Caliente," Exp. 7, "Predio Denominado Agua Caliente," Wirt Bowman to Rodríguez, June 13, 1927. Marco Antonio Samaniego López wrote a first-rate article on labor militancy during this period: "Formación y consolidación de los obreros in Baja California."

30. Rodríguez papers, Caja 1, File "Agua Caliente," Exp. 7, "Predio Denominado Agua Caliente," Abelardo Rodríguez to Wirt Bowman, June 17, 1927. There are numerous examples of the governor's refusals of Bowman's requests. When, for example, Wirt proposed to build a hospital for Agua Caliente employees and deduct payment for health services from the workers' paychecks, Rodríguez told him to forget the hospital and build them instead affordable housing, as formerly proposed. See Rodríguez papers, Caja 1 (1921–1928), #12, Bowman to Rodríguez, June 7, 1929, and Rodríguez to Bowman, June 10, 1929.

   On another occasion, the governor did not mince words when Wirt asked to be relieved of the agreement to hire Mexican security guards for the racetrack: "I am not able to fulfill your requests," Rodríguez wrote, "because I have already made many concessions to the Empresa de Hipódromo [racetrack] at the expense of government and only through a desire to help you profit from your enterprise." See Rodríguez papers, Caja 1 (1921–1928), Leg. #12, Rodríguez to Bowman, June 4, 1928.

18. "PLACE YOUR BETS!"

1. *San Diego Union*, December 28 and 29, 1929. *San Diego Evening Tribune*, December 28, 1929. Davis, "Three Hells," 259.

2. *San Diego Sun* and *San Diego Evening Tribune*, December 28, 1929. *New York Times*, December 16, 1929. *Los Angeles Times*, December 22, 28, and 29, 1929. *San Diego Union*, December 15, 28, and 29, 1929.

3. *Hollywood Reporter* 28, no. 6 (July 8, 1935): 3.

4. Hollywood's love affair with horse racing is admirably covered in Rosten, *Hollywood*, 108, 212, and 220. The fervor is also mentioned in Sklar, *Movie-Made America*, 262–63.

5. Bob Owens, "Caliente," *The Reader*, 12, no. 28 (July 21, 1983): 17. Beltrán, *Agua Caliente*, 33, 45, 62. Davis, "Three Hells," 260.

6. *Los Angeles Examiner*, November 13, December 24, 25, 1931. *Los Angeles Times*, November 17, 1931.

7. *San Diego Sun*, December 24, 25, 26, 30, 1930, and January 17, 1931. *Los Angeles Times*, December 25 and 26, 1930. *New York Times*, December 24,

1930. Rodríguez papers, Caja 1 (1921–28). Leg. 12, Exp. "Wirt G. Bowman," Rodríguez to Juan R. Platt in Mexico City, September 9, 1931.

8. *Los Angeles Examiner*, January 16, 1932.

9. The Phar Lap story is best told in Armstrong and Thompson, *Phar Lap*. See esp. the chapters "It's a Long Way to Caliente," 139–54, and "Who Killed Phar Lap?," 155–65. See also *Los Angeles Times*, March 27, 1932; and Beltrán, *Agua Caliente*, chap. 6.

10. Armstrong and Thompson, *Phar Lap*, 147.

11. Ibid.

12. Damon Runyon, "Death of Phar Lap," in *All Horse Players Die Broke*, 18–22.

13. Armstrong and Thompson, *Phar Lap*, 164–65.

14. Rodríguez papers, Caja 1 (1921–1928), Leg.12, Exp. "Wirt G. Bowman," Rodriguez to Juan R. Platt in Mexico City, September 9, 1931.

15. *Los Angeles Times*, June 2, 1931.

16. *Los Angeles Examiner*, December 16, 1931; January 26, 1932. When Mexican officials threatened to confiscate and auction off the track in 1936, Bowman denied interest in regaining control of the enterprise. "Why, what kind of fellow would they think I am," he asked, "if I let these rumors stand that I am hanging around Tijuana trying to get control of the track [from the original stockholders] by means of this action?" *Los Angeles Examiner*, January 31, 1936.

17. Bowman's wartime troubles are discussed in chapter 19, and his tax problems in chapter 20.

18. *Los Angeles Times*, April 19, 1929; April 22, 1931; May 3, 25, and 26, June 1 and 2, 1932. *San Diego Evening Tribune*, January 16, 1932. *San Diego Union*, January 17 and 18, 1932. *San Diego Sun*, January 23 and 27, March 1, 1932.

19. *New York Times*, January 9, 1932, and November 16, 1972. *San Diego Evening Tribune* and *San Diego Sun*, January 8, 1932. *Los Angeles Examiner*, January 13, 1932. *Los Angeles Times*, January 16, 1932, December 12, 1934. Beltrán, *Agua Caliente*, 66–67.

20. For scandals at Agua Caliente see *Los Angeles Examiner*, March 26, 1931; *San Diego Union*, January 11 and 12, 1931.

21. *San Diego Union*, March 11, 1932. *Los Angeles Examiner*, January 16, 1932. *San Diego Evening Tribune*, January 15, 1932.

22. *San Diego Sun*, January 15, 1932. *New York Times, Los Angeles Examiner, San Diego Union*, all January 16, 1932. *Los Angeles Times*, March 11, 1932.

23. *San Diego Sun*, January 15 and 16, February 11, March 23, 1932. *San Diego Evening Tribune*, January 15 and 18, March 11, 1932. *San Diego Union*, January 16, 19, and 24, March 12, 1932. *Los Angeles Times*, January 17 and 24, 1932. *New York Times*, January 24, March 11, 1932.

24. Rodríguez papers, Caja 1, Exp. 2, H. E. Anthony to Rodríguez, August 22, 1929; Exp. 12, Bowman to Rodríguez, June 8, 1929. Extortion notes to Bowman and Crofton, as well as Sheldon's plans, are detailed in the next chapter.

25. Interview on May 3, 2005, with James Brown, a retired Folsom guard who served thirty years at the prison and now volunteers to manage the institution's museum. My appreciation for his illuminating observations on prison life.

26. *Sacramento Bee*, July 3, 1930. San Quentin had an especially notorious solid-rock Dungeon, where a convict was made to sit on a wet spot in the nude and not move. Lime tossed on the spot emitted acrid fumes and burned the inmate's bottom; Brown interview.

27. *Sacramento Bee, San Diego Evening Tribune, Sacramento Union*, July 3, 1930.

19. GET THE BARONS!

1. *San Diego Evening Tribune* and *San Diego Sun*, December 24, 1930. *Los Angeles Times*, April 21, 1931.

2. *San Diego Evening Tribune*, December 25 and 26, 1930. *San Diego Union*, December 26, 1930. *Los Angeles Times, Los Angeles Examiner*, December 25, 1930.

3. See www.fairgroundsracecourse.com/about/history.html.

4. *Los Angeles Examiner*, February 9, 1932. *San Diego Evening Tribune*, December 22, 1930. *San Diego Union*, December 22 and 24, 1930. *Los Angeles Times*, December 23 and 24, 1930.

5. *Los Angeles Times*, April 7 and 8, 1931.

6. *San Diego Evening Tribune* and *San Diego Sun*, December 22, 1930. *Los Angeles Times*, December 1 and 3, 1931.

7. *Los Angeles Times*, December 1 and 3, 1931.

8. *Los Angeles Times*, February 12, 14, 16, and 25, March 8, 1931.

9. *Los Angeles Times*, January 30, 1931.

10. *San Diego Union*, December 28, 1930.

11. *Los Angeles Times*, March 18, 1931.

12. *Los Angeles Times*, April 9, December 2, 1931, February 17, 1932.

13. *Los Angeles Times*, April 19, 1931.

14. Ibid.

15. *Los Angeles Times*, April 25, 1931.

16. *Los Angeles Times*, April 21, 1931.

17. *Los Angeles Times*, April 22–25 and 28, 1931.

18. *Los Angeles Times*, February 11 and 12, 1932.

19. *Los Angeles Examiner, San Diego Evening Tribune, San Diego Union*, and *New York Times*, March 5, 1932. *Los Angeles Times*, March 5 and 17, 1932.

20. *Los Angeles Times*, June 21–23, October 12 and 22, 1932 and August 4, 1933. *New York Times*, July 21, 1932.

21. *Los Angeles Times*, December 21and 24, 1932.

22. *Los Angeles Times*, February 21, May 18 and 26, June 25, October 16 and 22, 1934; June 25, October 16 and 22, 1935; July 22, October 26, 1937.

23. *San Diego Sun*, February 3, 1932.

24. Ibid.

25. Ibid. *San Diego Union*, February 4, 1932. *Los Angeles Times*, March 23, 1932.

26. *San Diego Sun*, February 3, 1932. *San Diego Union*, February 4, 1932.

27. Ibid.

28. *San Diego Union*, February 5, 1932.

29. *San Diego Union*, February 4, 1932. *San Diego Sun*, February 5 and 10, 1932.

30. *San Diego Union*, February 14, 1932.

31. *San Diego Sun*, February 26, 1932.

32. *Los Angles Times*, February 14, 1932. *San Diego Union*, February 14 and 27, 1932.

33. *San Diego Union*, February 14, 15, and 27, 1932. *San Diego Evening Tribune* and *San Diego Sun*, March 24, 1932.

34. *Los Angeles Times*, February 27, 1932.

35. *Los Angeles Examiner*, March 21, 1932.

36. *San Diego Call*, April 14 and 16, 1932. *San Diego Union*, April 15, 1932. *Los Angeles Times*, April 16, 1932.

37. *San Diego Union*, April 15, 1932.

38. *San Diego Call*, April 15, 1932, *San Diego Union*, April 16 and 17, 1932.

39. *Los Angeles Times*, April 15, 1932. *San Diego Union*, April 18, 1932.

40. *San Diego Sun*, August 15, 1929. *Los Angeles Times*, August 16 and 17, 1929. *San Diego Tribune*, August 15, 1932. *San Diego Union*, August 16, 1932.

41. *San Diego Sun*, August 28, 1929. *San Diego Union*, August 29 and 30, December 29, 1929. *Los Angeles Times*, August 30, 1929.

42. San Diego Superior Court, Records Archive, Civil and Criminal, 1930, No. 62715, Kearney, Gerald E. (Jerry) Trial, Probation Officer's Report. *San Diego Union*, August 8, December 20, 1929, and February 24–26, March 17, 1930. *San Diego Sun*, February 25–27 and 28, 1930. *San Diego Evening Tribune*, February 24, 26, and 27, 1930.

43. *Sacramento Bee*, February 27, 1933. *Sacramento Union*, February 28, 1933. Sacramento Archives and Museum Collection Center, History and Science Division, Coroner's Inquest into the Death of Martin Colson, held at Folsom Prison, March 17, 1933, case no. 2503. Also, Coroner's Record, case no. 2503.

44. Coroner's Record, case no. 2503.

45. *Sacramento Bee*, February 27, 1933. The homemade pistols are pictured in *Sacramento Bee*, February 28, 1933, and *Los Angeles Times*, March 1, 1933.

46. John Moore interview, May 3, 2005, at Folsom Prison.

47. *Los Angeles Times*, March 8, 1933.

20. FOOLS AND THIEVES

1. Davis, "Three Hells," 261. McAllister videotape. *San Diego Herald*, September 15, 1932. Pileggi, *Casino*, 91.

2. McAllister videotape. Rottman interview, 8–9. Alejandro F. Lugo Jr., "El Casino de Agua Caliente," in Jesús Ortiz Figueroa and David Piñera Ramírez, *Historia de Tijuana*, 116. Luis Tamés León, "El Casino de Agua Caliente," in David Piñera Ramírez, *Panorámico Histórico de Baja California* (Tijuana, 1983), 452. Engstrand and Crawford, *Reflections*, 91.

3. William Wellman, *A Short Time for Insanity* (New York, 1974), 184. Chapin Hall, "Where Gambling Flourishes along the Mexican Border," *New York Times*, September 28, 1930.

4. *Los Angeles Herald Examiner*, August 23, 1920. *San Diego Sun*, December 31, 1929. *San Diego Herald*, September 15, 1932. Gabler, *An Empire of Their Own*, 74, 258–59. The Andre Williams archive provided information on the gold service.

5. Rosten, *Hollywood*, 58, 156–57, 222–23. Sklar, *Movie-Made America*, 229.

6. Davis, "Three Hells," 261. A *New York Times* reporter, T. J. C. Martyn, rendered another view of the resort's patrons: "The people who go to Tia Juana and Agua Caliente come from every walk of life, as is evidenced by their cars, their clothes, and their jewels. . . . On the wood sidewalks of Tia Juana one will rub shoulders one minute with a bronzed giant from Arizona and the next instant with a pale-faced sheik from Hollywood; with a stenographer from Long Beach and then a society girl from Santa Barbara. The crowd represents democracy at its densest . . . every type and class and disposition in the caldron of human society"; *New York Times*, January 19, 1930. Truth is, casinos are hardly democratic. Employees work in a rigid hierarchy, and wealthy patrons with more money to lose are favored over more ordinary customers.

7. Davis, "Three Hells," 262.

8. AGN, Presidenciales, Ortiz Rubio, Año 1930, 8/5598, Eleanor González of Los Angeles to Ortiz Rubio, April 22, 1930.

9. *Hollywood Reporter*, 28, no. 7 (July 9, 1935): 3.

10. Pileggi, *Casino*, 15.

11. Schwartz, *Suburban Xanadu*, 7.

12. For the "feel" and realities of casino management, see the excellent books of Schwartz and Pileggi. Schwartz sees casinos as corporate businesses complicated by their dependence on chance. Says Pileggi, "A casino is a mathematics palace set up to separate players from their money. Every bet made in a casino

has been calibrated within a fraction of its life to maximize profit while still giving players the illusion that they have a chance"; *Casino*, 14. I thank both Schwartz and Pileggi for their assistance on this project. Also pertinent to casinos are Chafetz, *Play the Devil*, and Skolnick, *House of Cards*.

13. Davis, "Three Hells," 263–64.
14. Gunning interview.
15. Pileggi, *Casino*, 15–17.
16. Morgenthau Collection, Report of Special Internal Revenue Agent F. S. Peabody to Elmer Irey, Chief of Bureau of Internal Revenue Intelligence Division, March 16, 1943, 6.
17. Ibid.
18. Ibid.
19. Ibid.
20. Ibid. Mobsters terrorized Zamansky and looted his home in 1934.
21. Ibid.
22. Details of Agent Peabody's investigation are on 5–12 of his report to Irey. A summary is provided on 12–14.
23. Carl Hayden's attempts to assist Bowman in his battles with the federal government are amply documented in the senator's personal papers archived in Special Collections in the library at Arizona State University, Tempe. Hereafter cited as "Hayden papers." See also Peabody's report to Irey, March 16, 1943, 8.
24. Calles Archive, Fondo Plutarco Elías Calles, Fondo 12, Serie, 011000, Exp. 82, Inv. 1284, Leg. 1, First National Bank, The; Bowman to Juan Platt, Feb. 20, 1936.
25. Morgenthau Collection, Peabody to Irey, March 16, 1943, 13.
26. Rodríguez papers, Caja 1 (1921–28), Exp. 1'2, "Wirt G. Bowman," James Crofton to Rodríguez, January 16 and 22, 1929. Calles Archive, Gav. 15, Exp. 154, Inv. 1010, Leg. 1; des. "Compañía Mexicana de Agua Caliente" [memorandum], Juan R. Platt to Presidente, November 19, 1930. AGN, Pascual Ortiz Rubio, Exp. 3/4/49, año 1930; [memorandum] Juan R. Platt to Presidente, November 19, 1930. Gómez Estrada, *Casinos y gobierno*, 180–81.
27. AGN, O-C, Exp. 168, 425-T-7, Subsecretario del Gobierno a Gov. Lugo, July 25, 1922; E. Ferreira [Mexican consul in San Diego] to Obregón, February 13 and March 14, 1923. For a good example of restrictions imposed and harassments that followed, see AGN, Dirección Gral del Gob, c.2.50.76, Caja 4, Exp. 24.
28. Calles Archive, Inv. 798, Gav. 84, Exp. 3, des.–fojas 14–15, Rodríguez to Col. José María Tapia, chief of presidential estado mayor, January 9, 1929. For Rodríguez protecting Agua Caliente against lawsuits see Rodríguez papers, Caja 1 (1921–1928), Exp. #12, "Wirt G. Bowman," Rodríguez to Bowman, June 1, 1929; and against tax increase, Rodríguez to Bowman, January 15, 1929. See also Ready, *Open Range and Hidden Silver*, 130–31.

29. Calles Archive, Gav. 66, Exp. 189, Inv. 5010, Leg. 7/11, Rodríguez, Abelardo L. (Gral), Calles to Rodríguez, March 2, 1929; and Rodríguez to Calles, January 10 and 12, 1929. Also, Gav. 10, Exp. 156, Inv. 909, des. "Wirt G. Bowman," Bowman to Calles, January 27, 1931. Gómez Estrada, *Casinos y gobierno*, 155, 158–59. Also see citations in following endnote.

30. Calles Archive, Gav. 15, Exp. 154, Inv. 1010, Leg. 1; des. "Compañía Mexicana de Agua Caliente," memorandum of Juan R. Platt to Presidente, November 19, 1930. AGN, Pascual Ortiz Rubio, Exp. 3/4/49, año 1930, Memorandum of Juan R. Platt to Presidente, November 19, 1930. Also Gómez Estrada, *Casinos y gobierno*, 180–81.

21. A DEAD COCK IN THE PIT

1. The literature on Cárdenas is vast and mushrooming. For an overview see Hernández Chávez, *La Mecánica cardenista*. Also, Knight, "The Rise and Fall of Cardenismo, c1930–c1940," and Knight's "Cardenismo: Juggernaut or Jalopy?"

2. Orcutt, "Too Much Money," 8.

3. *San Diego Evening Tribune*, July 20, 1935. *San Diego Union* and *San Diego Sun*, July 20 and 22, 1935. *Los Angeles Times*, July 21 and 22, 1935.

4. Gunning and Daniels interviews. The phrase "a dead cock in the pit" comes from testimony given at the Schenck tax trial in 1941. A lawyer asked Enrique S. Neidhart, secretary general of Agua Caliente from 1929 to 1932, if it was fair to say that the $4,051,000 operation was "dead as a cock in the pit." Neidhart declined to answer, because, he explained, litigation on the expropriation continued in Mexican courts.

5. *San Diego Union* and *New York Times*, July 14–15, 1932. *Los Angeles Times*, July 15 and 17, 1932. *Los Angeles Examiner*, July 15, 1932. Orcutt, "Too Much Money," 8–9.

6. *San Diego Union*, July 22–24, August 6, 1935. *San Diego Sun*, July 22, 1935. *Los Angeles Examiner*, July 27, 1935. *Los Angeles Times*, August 20, September 16, 1935. *El Hispano Americano*, August 8 and 14, 1935.

7. *San Diego Sun*, July 22, August 2, 1935. *San Diego Union*, July 22, 1935.

8. *San Diego Sun*, August 2, 1935.

9. Lears, *Something for Nothing*, 249. My assertions here lean heavily upon Lear's fine, provocative study.

10. *San Diego Sun*, July 22, 1935.

11. *San Diego Union*, July 23, 1935.

12. *San Diego Evening Tribune, San Diego Sun, Los Angeles Times*, July 23, 1935.

13. *San Diego Sun*, July 24–25, 1935.

14. U.S. National Archives, RG 59, Records of the Department of State Relating to the Internal Affairs of Mexico, 1930–1944, Consular Reports, Lower Califor-

nia, no. 213 Bowman [unrelated to Wirt], Mexicali, "Voluntary Report, Prevail-ing Political and Economic Situation in Mexicali consular district," October 21, 1935. Consular reports hereafter titled "Consular report," author, and date. Also, *San Diego Union*, September 11 and 15, December 3, 1935. *San Diego Sun*, September 11, 1935. *San Diego Evening Tribune*, October 11, 1935. *El Hispano Americano*, August 8, 1935.

15. Consular Report, William Smale, Ensenada, no. 244, "Political Review of Janu-ary, 1936," February 29, 1936. *San Diego Union*, February 21, March 22, August 4, 1936. AGN, Ramo Cárdenas, Exp. 437/67, "Varios [letters], Treviño to Cár-denas, April 20, 1936.

16. Consular report, Smale, Ensenada, no. 252, "Political Review of January, 1937," January 30, 1937. *San Diego Union*, February 24, 1937.

17. Ortiz Figueroa and Piñera Ramírez, *Historia de Tijuana*, vol. 1, 134–36.

18. *San Diego Union* and *San Diego Tribune*, October 16, 1935.

19. *San Diego Sun*, October 22, 1935. *San Diego Evening Tribune*, August 5–6, 1937. *New York Times*, June 28, July 5, 1937. Schenck appeal, 566–70, 621, 651. Vanderwood, *Juan Soldado*, 164–65.

20. *San Diego Sun*, January 3, 1938.

21. *San Diego Sun*, January 4, 1938.

22. *San Diego Sun*, January 5, 6, 14, and 25, 1938.

23. *San Diego Union*, January 28, 1938.

24. *San Diego Union*, January 28. *San Diego Sun*, January 27, February 13, 1938. Ortiz Figueroa and Piñera Ramírez, *Historia de Tijuana*, vol. 1, 159–60.

25. Vanderwood, *Juan Soldado*, part 1. The book examines Juan Soldado in the context of popular canonizations.

22. WHAT EVER HAPPENED TO?

1. Ortiz Figueroa and Piñera Ramírez, *Historia de Tijuana*, vol. 1, 137. Zavala, *Panorama histórico de la educación técnica en Tijuana, B.C.*, 12.

2. Schenck appeal, 568–70, 611.

3. *Nogales Herald*, June 7, 1934. *El Hispano Americano*, June 22, 1934. Interview with Ms. Jean Arbuckle, an acquaintance of the Bowmans, who now lives on their former Palm City property; December 28, 2003.

4. Hayden papers, "Wirt G. Bowman" file, Rodríguez to Bowman, December 21, 1932, and Calles to Bowman, December 28, 1932; Bowman to Hayden, Janu-ary 30, February 23, 1933; Hayden to Col. Dale Bumstead, March 7, 1933. Mor-genthau collection, statement of Bowman to John Edgar Hoover, March 7, 1932.

5. Hayden papers, "Wirt G. Bowman" file, Bowman to Hayden, December 9, 1940.

6. Hayden papers, "Wirt G. Bowman" file, Hayden to Bowman, March 7; Farley to

Bowman, May 21, 1941. The recommendations on Bowman's behalf are in the Hayden papers, "Wirt G. Bowman" file, dated February 1941.

7. Hayden papers, "Wirt G. Bowman" file, Hayden to Bowman, March 12, 1941, April 21, 1941.

8. Morgenthau collection, Peabody to Irey, March 16, 1943.

9. Ibid.

10. *San Diego Union*, *New York Times*, and *Nogales International*, April 22, 1949.

11. *San Diego Union*, July 14–15, 1932. *Los Angeles Times*, July 15, 1932. Daniels interviews.

12. Barras, *Long Road to Tehachapi*, 78. *San Diego Union*, October 29, 1933, January 12, 1934. *San Diego Sun*, February 24, 1934.

13. Daniels and Gunning interviews. Also, telephone interviews with Nick Sarilo, longtime resident of Tehachapi, February 2 and 5, 2005. "He paid us $1 a day," said Sarilo, "and gave us three meals and a bunk. In those days meals and the bunk were more important than pay. I didn't like him [Crofton], because his money was no good. His checks bounced."

14. Daniels interviews. "Bunker" Daniels was Crofton's nephew and in his teens milked cows and did other chores for $3 a day on Crofton's ranch. "I asked him for a raise," said Daniels, "and he put me down, saying he did not want me to end up spoiled like the other boys." Crofton spent lavishly on women, parties, and horses, but skimped on workers' pay and ranch equipment costs.

15. Phone interviews with J. D. "Dave" Logan, who has ranched around Tehachapi for many years; January 29 and 31, 2005. "Crofton was noted for having nothing that worked," according to Logan. "Equipment broke down, cars broke down, everything mechanical broke down." Interview with Kyle Morgan, former mayor of National City, Calif., at his National City home; March 20, 2005. As a teenager, Morgan tilled soil and moved hay from 1937 to 1939 on the Crofton ranch. "Crofton liked beautiful women," Morgan remembered, "and brought plenty of them to the ranch. He was not interested in us; we were just farm help."

16. Gunning interview. "I had a body guard," she said. "He [Crofton] was so wealthy, he feared that I would be kidnapped."

17. Daniels interviews.

18. Daniels interviews. A copy of Crofton's will is on microfilm in Kern County's Hall of Records, Bakersfield, Calif. See Book 4845, 2158–2211, June 14, 1974: Crofton, James N., deceased: Estate declaration of distribution. Filed in Los Angeles, File no. P536857, by Stephen Jones, La Fever & Smith, 600 Wilshire Blvd. Los Angeles, 90017. At Crofton's death, no obituaries appeared in the press. His death certificate states he died of heart disease, and he is buried in Forest Lawn Memorial Park, Los Angeles.

19. *Los Angeles Examiner*, December 30, 1933. *Los Angeles Times*, December 31, 1933, January 4, 1934. *San Diego Union*, February 25, 1962.

20. *Los Angeles Times*, February 9, March 29, April 5–6, 1934.

21. *Los Angeles Examiner*, January 5, 1934.

22. *Los Angeles Times* and *San Diego Union*, February 19, 1962.

23. *San Diego Evening Tribune* and *San Diego Union*, February 19, 1962. *Los Angeles Examiner*, February 28, 1962. *Los Angeles Times*, February 19 and 28, 1962.

24. *San Diego Union*, February 14, 1967.

25. *San Diego Union*, October 13, 1941. Martínez Assad, Pozas Horcasitas, Ramírez Rancaño, *Revolucionarios fueron todos*, 299–323. Rodríguez, *Autobiografía*, 162–70. Gómez Estrada, *Gobierno y casinos*, 118–19.

26. *San Diego Union*, February 15, 1962.

27. Schenck tax case, file C-107/440, 8–25. Also, Schenck appeal case, "Brief for Appellee," case no. 17851, vol. 1, 3.

28. Schenck tax case, file C-107/439, 781. Schenck appeal case, vol. 1, 8, 11–24.

29. Schenck tax case file, C-107/439, 161–79, 928. Schenck appeal case, vol. 1, 9, 24–41; the quotation is on 35.

30. Schenck tax case, [v. 3,] file, C-170/440, 1878–9. Schenck appeal case, vol. 1, 5–7.

31. Gerald Horne nicely develops the Schenck bribery case in context with its era in *Class Struggle in Hollywood, 1930–1950*, 45–48, 110–11, 121.

32. *San Diego Union*, April 4, 1949.

33. Linn's quotation is in *San Diego Union*, July 19, 1950. Also see *San Diego Union*, January 13, July 14, 1950; and Jack Kipp, "The Lloyd Sampsell Story" typescript. Kipp, a former mayor of Folsom wrote occasional pieces on Folsom prison for the local press; my gratitude to him for a copy of his piece on Sampsell. Sampsell not only wrote elegant and erudite legal briefs but poetry, which was published as pamphlets by the prison print shop. An excerpt from one example printed as "Folsom Reprieves" and dated "Christmas, 1939" (Folsom Historical Society, Folsom vertical file) says,

> When you read these verses in ms. you asked if they were apologia for the weak or eulogy of the strong. You will see that they are neither, but only repeat that the mighty have their weaknesses and the weak have the strength to continue. And that all men are all things—if not to others, at least to themselves. The point of it all is in the last line, which Winston Churchill enlarged into lines that might well be the prayer of all mankind, thus:
>
>> We shall not fail nor falter; we shall not weaken nor tire; neither the sudden shock of battle, nor the long-drawn trials of vigilance and exertion will wear us down. Give us the tools and we will finish the job.

> Time goes on. Man goes on. There is always a "job" to be finished and "tools" are not always material things—nor even always apparent. [Signed: L. S.]

34. *San Diego Union*, April 26, 1952.

35. California State Archives (Sacramento), Governor's Office, "Ralph Sheldon," Judge Charles S. Burnell to Advisory Pardon Board, July 17, 1940. Examples of Sheldon's legal prowess, as well as details of the Caress kidnapping which did not appear in the press, are contained in this substantial file and others, hereafter cited as "Governor's Office," plus file name. See also *Los Angeles Times*, June 1 and 30, 1933, and February 3, 1935.

36. Governor's Office, "Ralph Sheldon," M. Stanley Mosk, executive secretary, to Ralph Sheldon, August 26, 1940.

37. *Los Angeles Times*, May 22, 1941, June 28, 1942, and July 5, 1944.

38. Governor's Office, "Cochran, Robert Lee," and applicant's questionnaire to Adult Authority, February 16, 1973, and *passim*.

39. For Cochran's visit with Mason, see *San Diego Union*, April 17, 1949. Otherwise, Governor's Office, "Cochran, Robert Lee," Report of Community and Public Service Division, January 2, 1973.

40. Governor's Office, "Cochran, Robert Lee," Summary Statement, Health and Welfare Agency, Adult Authority, February 16, 1973.

41. Governor's Office, "Cochran, Robert Lee," Report of Parole and Community Service Division, to Adult Authority, January 2, 1973.

42. Governor's Office, "Cochran, Robert Lee," B. K. Johnson, manager, United Towing Company [to Health and Welfare], February 15, 1973; William H. Kenney, assistant district attorney, San Diego, to D. W. Moore, California Health and Welfare Agency, May 23, 1973; Gloria Bonadonna to D. W. Moore, March 8, 1973.

43. Governor's Office, "Cochran, Robert Lee," Joseph A. Spangler, administrative officer, Adult Authority, to Honorable Ronald Reagan, July 17, 1973.

44. Governor's Office, "Cochran, Robert Lee," James D. Garbolino, assistant legal affairs secretary, to Robert L. Cochran, November 2, 1973.

45. Governor's Office, "Cochran, Robert Lee," memorandum from Herb to Garbolino [undated].

23. GHOSTS

1. Alcarez, "La Farona o la bailarina de Agua Caliente." My gratitude to the author's son, José, who lives in one of the resort's original bungalows, for furnishing me a copy of this manuscript.

2. Vanderwood, *Juan Soldado*, 195–97.

3. Arbuckle interview.

Sources

ARCHIVES

Academy of Motion Picture Arts and Sciences, Library and Archives (Los Angeles).

American Film Institute, Library and Archives (Los Angeles).

Archivo General de la Nación (Mexico City).

Archivo Histórico, Instituto Municipal de Arte y Cultura (IMAC; Tijuana).

Archivo Histórico del Instituto de Investigacions Históricas, Archivo, Universidad Autónoma de Baja California (Tijuana).

Arizona Historical Society Library and Archives (Tucson).

Arizona State University Library, Special Collections (Tempe).

California Historical Society, Archives (San Francisco).

California State Archive (Sacramento).

California State Library, Special Collections (Sacramento).

Fideicomiso Archivos Putarco Elias Calles y Fernando Torreblanca (Mexico City).

Folsom Historical Society, Archives (Folsom, Calif.).

Franklin Delano Roosevelt Presidential Library and Museum, Archives (Hyde Park, N.Y.).

Instituto de Estudios Históricos, Universidad Autónoma de Baja California (Tijuana).

Kern County Hall of Records (Bakersfield, Calif.).

National City (California) Public Library, Special Collections.

Oregon Historical Society, Archives (Portland).

Pimería Alta Historical Society, Archives (Nogales, Ariz.).

Sacramento Archives and Museum Collection Center, History and Science Division.

San Diego County Courthouse, Superior Court Records, Old Records
Division.
San Diego Historical Society, Archives.
San Diego Public Library, California Room, Archives.
San Diego State University, Library, Special Collections.
San Francisco Public Library, History Center.
San Ysidro (Calif.) Public Library, Local History Collection.
The Dalles (Ore.) Public Library, Archives.
United States National Archives (Washington, D.C.).
University of Arizona, Library, Special Collections (Tucson).
University of California, Los Angeles, Charles E. Young Research Library, Special Collections.
University of Nevada, Las Vegas, Library, Special Collections.
University of Southern California, Doheny Library, Special Collections.

PERSONAL PAPERS

Georgia B. Allen (Folsom, Calif.)
Alvin "Bunker" Daniels Jr. (Grass Valley, Calif.)
Barbara Gunning (Oceanside, Calif.)
Axel Holm (Nogales, Ariz.)
Donald McAllister (Apple Valley, Calif.)
Luis Tamés León (Tijuana)
Andre Williams (Tijuana)

NEWSPAPERS

Border Vignette (Nogales, Ariz.)
Calexico (Calif.) *Chronicle*
Daily Transcript (San Diego)
El Hispano Americano (Tijuana)
Hollywood Reporter
Los Angeles Evening Express
Los Angeles Examiner
Los Angeles Times
Mexican Herald (Mexico City)
Nogales (Ariz.) *Herald*
Nogales (Ariz.) *International*
The Oregonian (Portland)
The Reader (San Diego)
The Rounder (Tijuana)

Sacramento Bee
Sacramento Union
San Diego Call
San Diego Evening Tribune
San Diego Herald
San Diego Sun
San Diego Union
San Francisco Bulletin
San Francisco Call
San Francisco Chronicle
The Dalles (Ore.) *Optimal*
The Dalles (Ore.) *Weekly Chronicle*

BOOKS, ARTICLES, DISSERTATIONS, TYPESCRIPTS

"Adobe . . . Gingerbread . . . and Glass: The Evolution of Architectural Design in San Diego." *Union Title-Trust Topics* 7, no. 4 (May 1967): 2–8.

Aguilar Camín, Hector. *La Frontera nomada: Sonora y la revolución Mexicana*. Mexico City, 1977.

Aguirre Bernal, Celso. *Tijuana, su historia, sus hombres*. Mexicali, 1975.

Aikman, Duncan. "Hell Along the Border." *Mercury* 5 (May 1925): 17–23.

Albertanti, Francis. "Saga of Sunny Jim Coffroth, California's Great Sportsman, Paved the Way for Tex Richard and Mike Jacobs—Staged Many of the World's Most Celebrated Contests—Fitz, McGovern, Gans, Attell and Ketchel His Idols." *The Ring*, May 1943, 8–10+.

Alcarez, Ramón G. "La Faraona o bailarina de Agua Caliente." n.d., typescript, Tijuana, held by author's family.

Armstrong, Geoff, and Peter Thompson. *Phar Lap*. Crows Nest, New South Wales, 2000.

Asbury, Herbert. *The Barbary Coast*. New York, 1989.

——. *The Great Illusion: An Informal History of Prohibition*. New York, 1968.

——. *Sucker's Progress: An Informal History of Gambling in America from the Colonies to Canfield*. New York, 1938.

Atwell, Jim. *Early History of Klickitat County*. Skamania, Wash., 1977.

Baca, Vincent Z. C. de. "Moral Renovation of the Californias: Tijuana's Political and Economic Role in Mexican Relations, 1920–1935." Ph.D. diss., University of California, San Diego, 1991.

Bailey, Richard C. *Heart of the Golden Empire: An Illustrated History of Bakersfield*. Woodland Hills, Calif., 1984.

Baritz, Loren. *The Culture of the Twenties*. New York, 1970.

Barras, Judy. *The Long Road to Tehachapi*. Tehachapi, Calif., 1976.

Beltrán, David Jiménez. *The Agua Caliente Story: Remembering Mexico's Legendary Racetrack*. Lexington, Ky., 2004.

Berumen, Humberto Félix. *Tijuana la horrible: Entre la historia y el mito*. Tijuana, 2003.

Bokovoy, Matthew F. *The San Diego World's Fairs and Southwestern Memory, 1880–1940*. Albuquerque, 2005.

Bottoms Up! Y Como! To Drink—How, What, When, Where. [El Catecismo in Old Mexico, Where Drinking Never Ceased.] Tijuana, 1929.

Bransburg, Pablo. "Remembering Agua Caliente." *San Diego Union-Tribune*, October 9, 1994.

Buffington, Robert. "Prohibition in the Borderlands: National Government– Border Community Relations." *Pacific Historical Review* 43, no. 1 (February 1994): 19–38.

Cabeza de Baca, Vincent, and Juan Cabeza de Baca. "The 'Shame Suicides' and Tijuana." *Journal of the Southwest* 43, no. 4 (Winter 2001): 630–35.

California of the South: A History, Biographical, III, Illustrated. Chicago, 1933.

Calvillo Velasco, Max. *Gobiernos civiles del Distrito Norte de la Baja California, 1920–1923*. Mexico, 1994.

Carpenter, Frank G. *Mexico*. New York, 1927.

Carr, Harry. *Los Angeles: City of Dreams*. New York, 1935.

Cashman, Sean Dennis. *Prohibition*. New York, 1981.

Castanian, Pliny. *To Protect and Serve: A History of the San Diego Police Department and Its Chiefs, 1889–1989*. San Diego, 1993.

Castillo Udiarte, Roberto, Alfonso Garcia Cortez, and Ricardo Morales Lira, compilers. *La Revolución también es una calle . . . Vida cotidiana y prácticas culturas en Tijuana*. Tijuana, 1996.

Cayce, William G. "The Case against 'Silent' Colson." *True Detective Magazine*, n.d. In the Arthur Hill Folder, Castanian Collection, San Diego Historical Society.

Celiceo, Selia, comp. "Happy 90th Anniversary, San Ysidro, A Special Community: 1908–1998." 1998, typescript, San Ysidro Public Library.

Chafetz, Henry. *Play the Devil: A History of Gambling in the United States from 1492 to 1955*. New York, 1960.

Cochran, Kent. "The Baron Long Story." *The Thoroughbred of California*. June 1962: 852–58.

Crawford, Richard W. "Gambling Ships of San Diego." *Stranger than Fiction: Vignettes of San Diego History*. San Diego, 1995.

Davis, Elmer. "The Extinct Wickedness of Tia Juana." *New York Times*, September 19, 1920.

Davis, H. L. "Three Hells: A Comparative Study." *The American Mercury* 20, no. 79 (July 1930): 257–67.

Davis, Mike, Kelly Mayhew, and Jim Miller. *Under the Perfect Sun: The San Diego Tourists Never See.* New York, 2003.

Denton, Sally, and Roger Morris. *The Money and the Power: The Making of Las Vegas and Its Hold on America, 1947–2000.* New York, 2001.

Díaz Castro, Olga Vicenta. *Narraciones y leyendas de Tijuana.* Mexico City, 1981.

Domanick, Joe. *To Protect and Serve: The LAPD's Century of War in the City of Dreams.* New York, 1994.

Elmer, Jeffrey. *An Illustrated History of Klickitat, Yakima, and Kittitas Counties.* Chicago, 1904.

Engstrand, Iris, and Kathleen Crawford. *Reflections: A History of the San Diego Gas and Electric Company.* San Diego, 1991.

Erie, Stephen P. *Globalizing L.A.: Trade Infrastructure and Regional Development.* Stanford, 2004.

Exner, M. J. "Prostitution in Relation to the Army on the Mexican Border." *Social Hygiene* 3 (April 1917): 205–19.

Findlay, John. *People of Chance: Gambling in American Society from Jamestown to Las Vegas.* New York, 1986.

Fitzgerald, F. Scott. *The Jazz Age.* New York, 1996.

Fleischer, Nat. "Coffroth Was Tops: As Promoter, Sportsman, Grand Character, 'Sunny' Jim Was in a Class by Himself." *The Ring* (April 1943): 25+.

Fletcher, Ed. *Memoirs of Ed Fletcher.* San Diego, 1952.

Franks, Kenny A., and Paul F. Lambert. *Early California Oil: A Photographic History, 1865–1940.* College Station, Texas, 1985.

Fraser, Miles. *Slow Boat on Rum Row.* Madeira Park, B.C., 1992.

French, Philip. *The Movie Moguls: An Informal History of the Hollywood Tycoons.* Chicago, 1969.

Gabler, Neil. *An Empire of Their Own: How the Jews Invented Hollywood.* New York, 1988.

The Gamblers. Alexandria, Va., 1978.

Gebhard, David. "The Spanish Colonial Revival in Southern California." *Journal of the Society of Architectural Historians* 26 (May 1967): 131–47.

Gia, Gilbert. "Death of the Tenderloin." *The Blackboard* (Bakersfield) 2, no. 10 (October 2002).

———. "If Christ Came to Bakersfield: Part I in a Two-Part Series on Bakersfield's Public Prostitution." *The Blackboard* (Bakersfield) 2, no. 7 (July 2002).

Gómez Estrada, José Alfredo. *Gobierno y casinos: el origin de la riqueza de Abelardo L. Rodríguez.* Mexico, 2002.

González, Adolfo. "Historical Case Study: San Diego and Tijuana Border Region Relationship with the San Diego Police Department, 1957–1964." Ph.D. diss., University of San Diego, 1995.

Hall, Chapin. "Where Gambling Flourishes along the Mexican Border." *New York Times*, September 28, 1930.

Hall, Linda. *Oil, Banks, and Politics. The United States and Post-Revolutionary Mexico, 1917–1934*. Austin, Texas, 1995.

Haller, Mark H. "The Changing Structure of American Gambling in the Twentieth Century." *Journal of Social Issues* 35, no. 3 (1979): 87–114.

Harmon, Wendell E. "The Bootlegger Era in Southern California." *Southern California Quarterly* 37 (1955): 335–46.

Harris, Bruce. *The Wasco County History Book*. The Dalles, Ore., 1983.

Heimann, Jim. *Out with the Stars: Hollywood Nightlife in the Golden Era*. New York, 1985.

Helmer, William J. *The Gun That Made the Twenties Roar*. New York, 1969.

Herman, Robert D. *Gambling*. New York, 1967.

Hernández Chávez, Alicia. *La Mecánica cardenista*. Vol. 16 of *Historia de la revolución mexicana, 1934–1040*. Mexico City, 1979.

Higgins, Shelly, as told to Richard Mansfield. "Hatfield's Flood." *This Fantastic City: San Diego*, 175–85. San Diego, 1956.

Hill, Joseph. "Dry Rivers, Dammed Rivers, and Floods: An Early History of the Struggle between Droughts and Floods in San Diego." *Journal of San Diego History* 48, no. 1 (Winter 2002): 44–65.

Hillenbrand, Laura. *Seabiscuit: An American Legend*. New York, 2002.

Historia de Tijuana: Semblanza general. Tijuana, 1985.

Historia viva de Tijuana. Tijuana, 1996.

Horne, Gerald. *Class Struggle in Hollywood, 1930–1950: Moguls, Mobsters, Stars, Reds and Trade Unionists*. Austin, Texas, 2001.

Irey, Elmer Lincoln. *The Tax Dodgers: The Inside Story of the T-Men's War with America's Political and Underworld Hoodlums as told to William J. Slocum*. New York, 1948.

James, Eleanor Minturn. "Agua Caliente: Heaven of the West." *Vogue* December 8, 1930, 64+.

Kenamore, Claire. "What Is Germany Doing in Mexico?" *The Bookman* 44 (June 1917): 342–46.

King, Frank Marion. *Pioneer Western Empire Builders: A True Story of the Men and Women of Pioneer Days*. Pasadena, 1946.

Kirk, Anthony. *A Flier in Oil: Adolph B. Spreckels and the Rise of the California Petroleum Industry*. San Francisco, 2000.

Knight, Alan. "Cardenismo: Juggernaut or Jalopy?" *Journal of Latin American Studies* 26, part 1 (February 1994): 73–107.

———. "The Rise and Fall of Cardenismo, c1930-c1940." *Mexico since Independence*, ed. by Leslie Bethell, 241–320. Oxford, 1990.

Kurtz, Gary F. "Agua Caliente: A Gambler's Paradise in Old Mexico, 1928–1935." *California State Library Foundation Bulletin* 61 (Fall 1997): 9–19.

Lears, T. J. Jackson. *Something for Nothing: Luck in America.* New York, 2003.

Leuchtenburg, William E. *The Perils of Prosperity: 1914–1932.* Chicago, 1993.

Levitt, Arthur, Lynn E. Turner, and Troy A. Dahlberg. *The Kroll Report.* San Diego, 2006.

Macchio, Melanie. "John Nolen and San Diego's Early Residential Planning in the Mission Hills Area." *Journal of San Diego History* 52, nos. 3 and 4 (Summer–Fall 2006): 131–50.

Martin, R. L. "Mexican Prospects." *Yale Review* 25 (March 1936): 511–36.

Martín del Campo Rothenhausler, Carlos. *Historia de los cuatro hipódromos de Tijuana.* Tijuana, 2007.

Martínez Assad, Carlos, Ricardo Pozas Horcasitas, and Mario Ramírez Rancaño. *Revolucionarios fueron todos.* Mexico City, 1982.

May, Pete. "A Kid's Eye View of Centerville." *History of Klickitat County*, ed. by Pete May. Goldendale, Wash., 1982.

McKanna, Clare V., Jr. "Prostitutes, Progressives, and Police: The Viability of Vice in San Diego, 1900–1930." *Journal of San Diego History* 35, no. 1 (Winter 1989): 48–71.

McWilliams, Carey. *Southern California: An Island on the Land.* New York, 1946.

Merz, Charles. *The Dry Decade.* Garden City, N.Y., 1930.

———. *The Great American Band-Wagon.* New York, 1928.

Messick, Hank, and Burt Goldblatt. *The Only Game in Town: An Illustrated History of Gambling.* New York, 1976.

Meyer, Jean. *The Cristero Rebellion: The Mexican People between Church and State.* New York, 1976.

Montague, Walter Powhatan. "Baron Long: Find His Equal and Take the Purse." *Turf and Sport Digest*, September 1931, 898+.

Morgan, Neil. *Westward Tilt: The American West Today.* New York, 1963.

Morgan, Neil, and Tom Blair. *Yesterday's San Diego.* Miami, 1976.

Morgan, Wallace M. *History of Kern County, California.* Los Angles, 1914.

Moring, John. *Arthur Hill: Western Actor, Miner, and Law Officer.* Manhattan, Kans., 1994.

Nichols, Chris. *The Leisure Architecture of Wayne McAllister.* Layton, Utah, 2007.

Orcutt, Edward. "Too Much Money." *Saturday Evening Post*, February 27, 1937, 8–9+.

Ortiz Figueroa, Jesús, and David Piñera Ramírez, coordinators. *Historia de Tijuana, 1889–1989. Edición commemorativa del centenario de su fundación.* 2 vols. Tijuana, 1989.

Padilla Corona, Antonio. *Agua Caliente: Oasis en el tiempo. Entrevista a Wayne D. McAllister diseñador del centro turístico de Agua Caliente.* Tijuana, 2006.

——. "Entrevista a Wayne y Corine McAllister . . . el día 17 de septiembre de 1983." 1983, typescript, Tijuana.

——. "Predio el Monumento en Tijuana, Baja California: Una historia de ambiciones extranjeras." *Meyibó* 1, no. 1 (July–December 1998): 83–97.

Pasley, Fred D. *Al Capone: Biography of a Self-Made Man.* Freeport, N.Y., 1930.

Patterson, Thomas W. "Hatfield the Rainmaker." *Journal of San Diego History* 16, no. 3 (Winter 1970): 2–27.

Perry, Ada. "Expo Buildings Keep Art, Beauty in Restoration." *San Diego Union*, July 29, 1934.

Pileggi, Nicholas. *Casino: Love and Honor in Las Vegas.* New York, 1995.

Piñera Ramírez, David. *Panorámico histórico de Baja California.* Tijuana, 1983.

Piñera Ramírez, David, and Anthony Padilla Corona. "Impacto de la Ley Seca en las fronteras canadienses y mexicanas." *Meyibó* 1, no. 2 (January–June 1991): 5–11.

"Playas Ensenada y hoteles y lugares de recreo afiliados en Baja California poseídos y operados por la Compañía Mexicana de Rosario." 1929, typescript, Ensenada.

Ports, Uldis. "Geraniums vs. Smokestacks: San Diego's Mayoralty Campaign of 1917." *Journal of San Diego History* 21, no. 3 (Summer 1975): 50–56.

Pourade, Richard. *The Rising Tide, 1920–1941.* San Diego, 1967.

Proffitt, T. D. *Tijuana: The History of a Mexican Metropolis.* San Diego, 1994.

Quinn, John Philip. *Gambling and Gambling Devices.* Canton, Ohio, 1912.

Rappleye, Charles, and Ed Becker. *All-American Mafioso: The Johnny Rosselli Story.* New York, 1991.

Rathburn, Morris M. "Facts about Lower California." *The Mexican Review* 1 (1917): 9+.

Ready, Alma. *Open Range and Hidden Silver: Arizona's Santa Cruz County.* Nogales, Ariz., 1973.

Reppetto, Thomas. *American Mafia: A History of Its Rise to Power.* New York, 2004.

Ridgely, Roberta. "Inside Tijuana." *San Diego and Point Magazine* 20, no. 8 (June 1968).

———. "The Man Who Built Tijuana, Part 1: 'Sunny Jim' Coffroth and the Free-wheeling Days of the High Rollers." *San Diego and Point Magazine* 18, no. 3 (January 1966): 58+.

———. "The Man Who Built Tijuana, Part 2." *San Diego and Point Magazine* 18, no. 5 (March 1966): 52+.

———. "The Man Who Built Tijuana, Part 3." *San Diego and Point Magazine* 19, no. 2 (December 1966): 68+.

———. "The Man Who Built Tijuana, Part 4: Tijuana, 1920, Prohibition Pops the Cork." *San Diego and Point Magazine* 19, no. 7 (May 1967): 70+.

———. "The Man Who Built Tijuana, Part 5: Sunny Jim Coffroth and the Border Barons, Joined by Baron Long, Cash in on T-Town's Whoopee Era." *San Diego and Point Magazine* 19, no. 11 (September 1967): 52+.

———. "The Man Who Built Tijuana, Part 6: U.S. Reformers and Mexican Courts Attack Sunny Jim; Tom Mix, Fatty Arbuckle, Buster Keaton, Norma Talmadge and All Hollywood to the Rescue." *San Diego and Point Magazine* 20, no. 4 (February 1968): 44+.

———. "The Man Who Built Tijuana, Part 7: Tod Sloan's Twenty-Trunk Wardrobe and Sunny Jim's Eight Red Horse-Palace Railway Car Barreled into a Loony, Liquid Tijuana." *San Diego and Point Magazine* 20, no. 9 (July 1968): 86+.

———. "The Man Who Built Tijuana, Part 8: A Track Goes Up in Flames, Million Dollar Thoroughbreds Escape to the Hills, an Old Wyoming Cowboy Saves the Day." *San Diego and Point Magazine* 20, no. 11 (September 1968): 98+.

Robinson, David. *Hollywood in the Twenties*. New York, 1968.

Robinson, W. W. "The Southern California Real Estate Boom of the Twenties." *Southern California Quarterly* 24 (1942): 25–30.

Rodríguez, Abelardo L. *Autobiografía*. Mexico City, 1962.

———. *Memoria administrativa del Gobierno del Distrito Norte de Baja California, 1924–1927*. Mexicali, 1993.

Rodríguez González, Raúl. "La Figura y época de Esteban Cantú (1914–1924) en el Archivo Nacional de los Estados Unidos: Un informe preliminar." *Meybó* 3, nos. 7–8 (1988): 163–70.

Rogers, Will. *Will Rogers' Weekly Articles: The Coolidge Years, 1925–1927*, 2 vols., ed. by James M. Smallwood. Stillwater, Okla., 1980.

Rolland, Modesto C. *Informe sobre el Distrito Norte de la Baja California*. Mexicali, 1993.

Rose, Judge Leon J. "The Tijuana Track." *Turf and Sport Digest*, June 1935.

Rosten, Leo C. *Hollywood: The Movie Colony, the Movie Makers.* New York, 1941.

Ruiz, Ramón Eduardo. *On the Rim of Mexico: Encounters of the Rich and Poor.* Boulder, 1998.

Ruíz González, Wulfrano. *Por fin habla Buchito sobre la zona libre.* Tijuana, 1988.

Runyon, Damon. *All Horse Players Die Broke.* New York, 1946.

———. *Short Takes.* New York, 1946.

Russo, Gus. *The Outfit: The Role of Chicago's Underworld in the Shaping of Modern America.* New York, 2001.

Ryan, Frederick L. "The Labor Movement in San Diego: Problems and Development from 1887 to 1957." 1959, typescript, San Diego State College.

Samaniego Lopez, Marco Antonio. "Formación y consolidación de las organizaciones obreras en Baja California, 1920–1930." *Mexican Studies / Estudios Mexicanos* 14, no. 2 (Summer 1998): 329–62.

———. *Los Gobiernos civiles en Baja California, 1920–1923.* Mexicali, 1998.

San Diego Federal Writers Project. *San Diego: A California City.* Works Progress Administration American Guide Series. San Diego, 1937.

Sandos, James A. "Northern Separatism during the Mexican Revolution: An Inquiry into the Role of Drug Trafficking, 1919–1920." *The Americas* 41, no. 2 (October 1984): 191–214.

Sasuly, Richard. *Bookies and Bettors: Two Hundred Years of Gambling.* New York, 1982.

Schantz, Eric Michael. "All Night at the Owl: The Social and Political Relations of Mexicali's Red Light District, 1913–1925." *Journal of the Southwest* 43, no. 4 (Winter 2001): 549–602.

———. "From the 'Mexicali Rose' to the 'Tijuana Brass': Vice Tours of the United States–Mexico Border, 1910–1965." Ph.D. diss., University of California, Los Angeles, 2001.

Schwartz, David G. *Suburban Xanadu: The Casino Resort on the Las Vegas Strip and Beyond.* New York, 2003.

Shaffer, George K. "Aunt Jane—the Old Lady from Hell: The Story of Tia Juana: 'Where There Aren't No Ten Commandments, and a Man Can Raise a Thirst.'" *Liberty* June 19, 1926, 7–9+.

Shragge, Abraham J. "Boosters and Bluejackets: The Civic Culture of Militarism in San Diego, California, 1900–1945." Ph.D. diss., University of California, San Diego, 1998.

———. "'I Like the Cut of Your Jib': Cultures of Accommodation between the U.S. Navy and Citizens of San Diego, California, 1900–1951." *Journal of San Diego History* 48, no. 3 (Summer 2002): 230–55.

Sifakis, Carl. *The Mafia Encyclopedia*. New York, 1999.

Sklar, Robert. *Movie-Made America: A Cultural History of American Movies*. New York, 1975.

Skolnick, J. H. *House of Cards: The Legalization and Control of Casino Gambling*. Boston, 1978.

Soule, George Henry. *Prosperity Decade: From War to Depression, 1917–1929*. New York, 1947.

Starr, Kevin. *Americans and the California Dream, 1850–1915*. New York, 1973.

——. *Endangered Dreams: The Great Depression in California*. New York, 1996.

Stone, Horace A., Don K. Price, and Kathryn H. Stone. *City Manager Government in San Diego*. Chicago, 1939.

Summers, June Nay. *Buenos Días, Tijuana*. Ramona, Calif., 1974.

Taylor, Lawrence D. "The Wild Frontier Moves South: U.S. Entrepreneurs and the Growth of Tijuana's Vice Industry, 1908–1935." *Journal of San Diego History* 48, no. 3 (Summer 2002): 204–29.

Tello Villalobos, Arturo. *Tijuana: El Principio, su nombre y semblanzas monográficas en 1930 y gráfica de 1887–1945*. Tijuana, 1999.

U.S. Congress. *Investigation of Organized Crime in Interstate Commence: Hearings before the Special Committee to Investigate Organized Crime in Interstate Commerce*. United States Senate, Eighty-First Congress, Second Session, and Eighty-Second Congress, First Session, part 5 (Illinois). Washington, D.C., 1951.

"Unwritten Wonder: Baja California, Territory Mexicana." Tijuana, 1929.

Vanderwood, Paul. *Juan Soldado: Rapist, Murderer, Martyr, Saint*. Durham, N.C., 2004.

Walker, Clifford James. *One Eye Closed, the Other Red: The California Bootlegging Years*. Barstow, Calif., 1999.

Wellman, William. *A Short Time for Insanity*. New York, 1974.

Werne, Joseph Richard. "Esteban Cantú y la soberanía mexicana en Baja California." *Historia mexicana* 30, no. 1 (July–September 1930): 1–30.

——. "Vice Revenue and the Rise of Esteban Cantú in Baja California Norte, 1911–1920." 2000, typescript, Stillwater, Okla., personal copy of the author.

Wilkerson, W. R., III. *The Man Who Invented Las Vegas*. Bellingham, Wash., 2000.

Wilkinson, Michael. *The Phar Lap Story*. Melbourne, 1980.

Woodiwiss, Michael. *Crime, Crusades and Corruption: Prohibitions in the United States, 1900–1987*. London, 1988.

Woods, Gerald. "A Penchant for Probity: California Progressives and Disreputable Pleasures." *California Progressivism Revisited*, ed. by William F. Deverell and Tom J. Sitton. Berkeley, 1994.

——. *The Police in Los Angeles*. New York, 1993.

Zavala, Ramiro León. *Panorama histórico de la educación técnica en Tijuana, B.C., 1939–1986*. Tijuana, 1986.

Index

Page numbers in italics indicate illustrations.

PAUL VANDERWOOD is professor emeritus of Mexican history at
San Diego State University. He is the author of *Juan Soldado:
Rapist, Murderer, Martyr, Saint* (Duke, 2004); *The Power of God against
the Guns of Government: Religious Upheaval in Mexico at the
Turn of the Nineteenth Century* (1998); *Disorder and Progress: Bandits,
Police, and Mexican Development* (1981; rev. and enlarged ed., 1992);
and *Border Fury: A Picture Postcard Record of Mexico's Revolution and
U.S. War Preparedness, 1910–1917* (1988); and, with Frank N. Samponaro,
is the author of *War Scare on the Rio Grande: Robert Runyon's
Photographs of the Border Conflict, 1913–1916* (1992).

Library of Congress Cataloging-in-Publication Data

Vanderwood, Paul J.

Satan's playground : mobsters and movie stars at America's greatest gaming resort /
Paul J. Vanderwood.

p. cm. — (American encounters/global interactions)

Includes bibliographical references and index.

ISBN 978-0-8223-4691-3 (cloth : alk. paper)

ISBN 978-0-8223-4702-6 (pbk. : alk. paper)

1. Gambling industry—Mexico—Tijuana (Baja California)—History—20th
century. 2. Gambling industry—Mexican-American Border Region—History—
20th century. 3. Gambling industry—Social aspects—Mexico—Tijuana
(Baja California) 4. Gambling industry—Social aspects—Mexican-American
Border Region. I. Title. II. Series: American encounters/global interactions.

HV6722.M6V36 2010

364.1'06097223—dc22   2009043917